CHRISTIAN CLASSICS

BROADMAN PRESS
NASHVILLE, TENNESSEE

Nineteenth Century Evangelical Theology

Fisher Humphreys

Editor

BROADMAN

Nashville, Tennessee

© Copyright 1983 • Broadman Press

4265-79

ISBN: 0-8054-6579-0

Dewey Decimal Classification: 230

Subject heading: THEOLOGY

Library of Congress Catalog Card Number: 83-071439

Printed in the United States of America

Library of Congress Cataloging in Publication Data
Main entry under title:

Nineteenth century evangelical theology.

  (Christian classics)
  1. Theology, Doctrinal—Addresses, essays, lectures.
2. Evangelicalism—Addresses, essays, lectures.
I. Humphreys, Fisher. II. Series.
BT80.N55 1984   230'.044   83-71439
ISBN 0-8054-6579-0 (pbk.)

To the memory of my parents

Hilda Sharkey Humphreys
and
Fisher Hugo Humphreys

CONTENTS

Introduction

Background

No one has ever found it easy to have authentic faith in God and to be a true disciple of Jesus Christ, for Christian faith and discipleship require a continuous personal commitment that demands all a person can give. Nevertheless, certain institutions and assumptions of society have served in the past to help the individual to practice Christian faith and discipleship. In the nineteenth century, much of that social assistance was withdrawn.

The nineteenth century was an age of revolution. It began with a political revolution in France and ended with one in Russia, and it saw the increasing power of the first nation to have been deliberately created by a revolution, the United States. The United States was also the first Western nation which did not have an established church and which therefore lacked the cement of religion to bind its people together. Yet it survived, a monument to the concept of separation of church and state which had been dreamed of by radical Christians since the Reformation. In the United States, people were not born into a national community of faith. They personally had to choose to accept faith for themselves. This also meant that the United States was officially secular, and the church would need decades to grasp the implications of this for Christian theology.

A second revolution established its hegemony during the nineteenth century, the industrial revolution, that collection of political and social upheavals which accompanied the replacement of hand tools with power-driven tools. This revolution led to the growth of cities and of the middle classes. It also led to a faster pace of life as communication and transportation were improved. Christian theology found that it needed to speak to new groupings of people, with new problems, at a new pace.

A third great revolution in the nineteenth century was intellectual. From the Enlightenment throughout the nineteenth century and into our own time, the sciences have grown at a vertiginous rate, each one putting its particular questions to the Christian faith. At first the most dramatic questions came from biology. Should man any longer be considered a creature of God in God's image, in view of his putative descent from lower forms of life? Is man's aesthetic, moral, and religious understanding valid in view of his biological evolution?

The social sciences added questions which were as serious as those of natural science. The critical study of history led to doubts concerning Christian affirmations about the past. The Bible should be read, urged Benjamin Jowett, as we read any other historical document, critically. When it is read thus, questions proliferate. Did Moses write the Pentateuch? Were the Gospels biographies of Jesus written by eyewitnesses?

Nor was the Bible itself the only subject of the historians' queries. So conservative a scholar as John Henry Newman acknowledged that Christian doctrine had not always been uniform, accepted always, everywhere, by everyone, as many in the church had believed. But if theology has developed over the centuries, how may one distinguish false from true development? History led to other doubts also. A human being was understood to be a part of the historical process, the product of forces far greater than himself. Could the religious judgments of such a being be dependable? Religious beliefs and practices were seen as productions of men in history. Was there any reason to suppose that they had been revealed by God, or that they in any sense transcended the relativities of history?

If history relativized man's religious self-understanding, psychology took things a step further and explained why men had developed and continued to hold religious beliefs. They did so, Freud said, out of an unconscious need left over from childhood, the need for an all-wise, all-powerful, all-loving father. Religion is a projection of human needs onto the cosmos. Even William James, who offered a far more sympathetic and better-informed view of religious psychology, defended faith not as an apprehension of the truth but as a decision which it is the right of a man—in a democracy, one might add—to make if he chooses to do so.

To the challenges from Darwin, from critical history, and from Freud, should be added the challenge from Karl Marx. Marx repudiated religion in the name of value. He argued that religion was not good enough to deserve men's loyalty, for it had acquiesced all too quickly to the miserable plight of the poor and powerless people in society and had served as a narcotic to prevent them from throwing off oppressive political arrangements. As early as the mid-nineteenth century, some Christians took socialistic teachings seriously enough to adopt forms of Christian socialism.

The Christian church did more than survive all these upheavals. It grew and flourished during them. In 1800, only 10 percent of the United States' population were church members. By 1910, 40 percent were church members. Much of this church growth in America should be attributed to active evangelization efforts using the techniques of revivalism. These were practiced in the frontiers and, before the century closed, in the cities as well. The Sunday Schools had originated late in the eighteenth century, and they grew and became the major medium for Christian education in the nineteenth. In the United States, many Christian colleges were founded. In England, Christians took the lead in outlawing the trade in slaves. The initiation of Protestant missionary efforts on a scale such as the world had never before seen was perhaps the most impressive achievement of all. The nineteenth century could be called the success story of Protestant Christianity.

Nor did the church spend all its energy on institutional goals, for the nineteenth century was a productive one for Christian theology. The Christian church has always had theologians, men and women who give their lives trying to understand the character, activities, and purposes of God and to communicate these to their world. The first century was the normative period for Christian theology, and it gave the church the New Testament. It was followed by the patristic age (c. AD 100-500) during which, as one historian noted, the Christian church not only outlived the pagan world and outdied the pagan world, but outthought the pagan world. The third period, the medieval, was the longest (c. AD 500-1500), and it is not an exaggeration to say that during this millennium theology reigned as queen of the sciences. The fourth great period began with the Reformation and continued with the domestication of the thought of the first reformers by their successors (c. AD 1500-1800).

Modern theology began in the nineteenth century, and two kinds of theology were done. One was largely apologetic. It was addressed to the world and to the academy, which were experiencing the radical doubts which accompanied the revolutions described above. The initiator of this theology was Friedrich Schleiermacher, a professor of theology at Berlin. Other influential participants were G. W. F. Hegel, Albrecht Ritschl, and Ernst Troeltsch. These men, all German, all Protestant, were the creators of a new Christian theology called liberal Protestantism. To the radical doubts of the century, each made a response in the name of Christ: Schleiermacher on the authority of religious feelings; Hegel on the authority of reason; Ritschl on the authority of values; and Troeltsch on the authority of scientific history. An apologist is always tempted to give away too much to the opposition. The debate continues today about whether each of these men did this. Perhaps the greatest products of liberalism were its many lives of Jesus and, in the United States, the social gospel. Representative of liberalism's apologetic theology are two books which appeared exactly a century apart: Schleiermacher's *Speeches on Religion to Its Cultured Despisers* (1799); and lectures given by the preeminent church historian, Adolf von Harnack, entitled *The Essence of Christianity* (delivered 1899, published 1900). Most historians would accept the verdict of B. M. G. Reardon that liberalism was the characteristic Christian theology of the nineteenth century. Certainly its story has been told repeatedly on that assumption. The story and texts of liberalism are accessible to readers today. They are not the primary concern of the present volume.

In addition to the theologians who addressed the world and the academy and their doubts, other theologians did their work for the community of faith, the church. It is from the books of these men that the readings in this volume have been taken. These theologians were not insulated from the world's doubts, and they often provided the church with responses to doubt. Nor were they unaware of liberal Protestant apologetic theology, and they sometimes mediated its results to the church. But their distinctive work was to speak "from faith to faith." Therefore, they attempted to preserve the traditions of the church, believing that those traditions would speak to their own time.

The word *evangelical* in the title of this book requires explanation, for over the centuries the word has been used in a number of different senses. All Christian theology may be said to be evangelical, in the sense that it bears witness to the evangel, the good news of the saving work of God in Jesus Christ. Protestantism has been said to be evangelical in contrast to Roman Catholicism because the former has proclaimed the gospel more vigorously than the latter. Lutheran theology has been called "evangelical," in contrast to Calvinistic theology which is known as "reformed." The warmhearted religion of Wesley and of revivalism has been called evangelical, in contrast to the more formal, established church life in England and America, because the former urged men to accept the gospel for themselves in a deliberate and life-changing way. In the twentieth century, the word *evangelical* has come to be used of more traditional, conservative theologies in contrast to more liberal, avant-garde theologies.

The editor has borne in mind all of these distinctions. He has not restricted his choice of readings to any single usage of the word *evangelical*. The reader will find that no rejection of the gospel, or of its clear proclamation, or of its warmhearted reception, or of its preservation of its heritage, appears in these pages. Still, the reader should be aware that evangelicalism has never been monolithic. It has always included a variety of views on a variety of subjects, and no one could be sensitive and agree with all of them, for they are not all compatible. This book does not attempt to conceal the differences within evangelicalism. The reader today will have to decide, just as the nineteenth century reader did, on many issues for himself.

Selection and Arrangement of the Book

This is a book by an amateur for amateurs. The editor is not a historian, and he has not attempted to produce a book for researchers. Books of that sort on nineteenth century theology are available and are known to scholars in the field.

The editor has attempted to produce a book of interest to evangelical Christians today. He has chosen topics which he believes to be present concerns of evangelicals; authors who speak, at least on the topics with which they deal in the present volume, as evangelicals; and texts which contain affirmations, expositions, and apologies of interest to contemporary evangelicals. Relevance has been a criterion in the selection of these fifty-six readings.

A second criterion has been authority. Each writer in the book was well informed about the issues concerning which he wrote. No writer has written out of ignorance.

A third criterion has been readability. The editor has omitted texts which seemed to him indefensibly obscure. Since most of the texts included are more than a century old, the reader will not expect to find the terse, fast, contemporary style of, for example, *Time* magazine. Nevertheless, the editor believes that each reading is sufficiently lucid that a reasonably interested reader will find it accessible.

The editor selected some of the readings because the writers were representative of a large group of thinkers, and others because the writers seemed to offer distinctive ideas. Neither originality nor widespread fame or influence was a sole criterion in any case.

The principal question which the editor asked himself as he made choices concerning the readings was: "Will reading this text enrich the theology and enhance the ministry of an evangelical Christian today?" Only those texts for which the answer might be yes were included.

Some readers will want to know how the texts were edited. Several have been drastically abridged. Reading 8 is an example. Further, the editor omitted footnotes except those which could be conveniently incorporated into the text. Other omissions were made in the interests of space or of contemporary relevance. No additions have been made to the texts themselves, though in a few cases the editor has added headings for clarity. Reading 20 is an example. Virtually no changes were made in spelling, punctuation, grammar, or syntax, though a number of passages which were italicized in the original have been set in roman typeface.

Readings have been arranged in the sequence in which they might appear in a systematic theology. The general groupings are prolegomena (readings 1–11); God (12–18); man (19–20); Christ (21–38); Holy Spirit and salvation (39–45); church (46–50); eschatology (51–53); and Trinity (54–55). The final reading (56) is an autobiographical essay by a beloved American Baptist theologian. Titles for virtually all of the readings are the work of the editor.

The editor has followed the common practice of including within the nineteenth century materials which were written through the period of World War I.

The Authors

The fifty-six readings included in the present book were written by thirty-two men. All of the authors were Christians, and all wrote as evangelicals on the topics selected for the present volume. Twelve were American, ten English, seven Scottish, two German, and one Danish. Eight writers were Anglicans, seven from Scottish churches, six Baptists, four Congregationalists, three Presbyterians, two Lutherans, and one each Reformed and Roman Catholic.

The brief comments which are given below about each of the writers are intended to provide the reader with basic but obviously limited information in order to enhance the value of each author's text or texts. The bibliographical information is provided for the guidance of readers who wish to identify or locate the original texts.

James Petigru Boyce (1827-1888) was a Baptist theologian and founder of The Southern Baptist Theological Seminary.

He was from a wealthy home and was educated at Princeton Seminary under Charles Hodge. Traces of Hodge's influence may be detected in the two brief readings. Boyce's writing is biblical and homiletical, though a little formal.

Bibliography. "The Image of God in Man" (reading 19) is from James Petigru Boyce, *Abstract of Systematic Theology* (Philadelphia: American Baptist Publication Society, 1887), pp. 213-215, and "Sanctification" (44) is from the same volume, pp. 412-421.

Alexander Balmain Bruce (1831-1899) was a minister of the Free Church of Scotland and Professor of Apologetics and New Testament Exegesis at Glasgow. As his title indicates, his two major concerns were New Testament studies and apologetics, and both subjects are represented in the present volume.

Bibliography. "The Limitations of Proofs for God's Existence" (11) is from Alexander Balmain Bruce, *Apologetics* (Edinburgh: T. & T. Clark, 1892), pp. 149-162, and "The Gospel Portraits of Jesus" (21) is from the same volume, pp. 46-55.

Horace Bushnell (1802-1876) was an American Congregational pastor and theologian. He was irenic in spirit and his writings were often heuristic, which sometimes, but by no means always, led him away from traditional ideas. Though he lived in a period of intense theological debate, his writing gives evidence of personal serenity. This is apparent in the four readings included in this book.

Bibliography. "Religious Language" (8) is from Horace Bushnell, *God in Christ* (New York: Scribner, Armstrong & Company, 1877), pp. 12-97, much abridged. "The Gentleness of God" (15) is from Horace Bushnell, *Sermons on Christ and His Salvation* (New York: Scribner, Armstrong and Company, 1877), pp. 28-37. "Christian Prayer" (45) is from Horace Bushnell, *The Spirit in Man* (New York: Charles Scribner's Sons, 1907), pp. 271-276. "The Church and the Divine Purpose" (46) is from Horace Bushnell, *Sermons on*

Living Subjects (New York: Charles Scribner's Sons, 1887), pp. 285-298.

Gilbert Keith Chesterton (1874-1936) was a layman in the Church of England when he wrote the essay included in the present book, but he joined the Roman Catholic Church in 1922. He was a poet, novelist, and essayist, and a lay apologist for the Christian faith. Though his theology was traditional, his writing style was not. Perhaps his best-known books were the Father Brown mystery stories.

Bibliography. "Defending Orthodoxy" (4) is from Gilbert K. Chesterton, *Orthodoxy* (London: John Lane, The Bodley Head, 1908), pp. 263-284.

William Newton Clarke (1841-1912) was a Baptist pastor and professor whose most productive years were spent at Colgate Theological Seminary. His *Outline of Christian Theology* (1898) was the first liberal Protestant survey of Christian theology. He was very concerned about the nature of God, whom he firmly believed to be personal, and about the essence of Christian faith, which he believed to be personal trust in God. Concerning these matters his views are shared by all evangelical Christians.

Bibliography. "God as Personal" (13) is from William Newton Clarke, *The Christian Doctrine of God* (Edinburgh: T. & T. Clark, 1909), pp. 59-69, and "Christian Faith" (42) is from the same volume, pp. 462-471.

John Leadley Dagg (1794-1884) was a self-educated Southern Baptist pastor, university president, and theologian whose long and influential ministry was all the more remarkable because of his near-blindness. His theological books were written and published following his retirement from a highly successful presidency at Mercer University in Georgia. He wrote with wonderful clarity and with loyal adherence to traditional Baptist beliefs.

Bibliography. "The Inspiration of the Bible" (5) is from J. L. Dagg, *The Evidences of Christianity* (Macon, Georgia: J. W.

Burke & Co., 1869), pp. 212-230. "The Value of Proofs for God's Existence" (10) is from J. L. Dagg, *Manual of Theology* (Philadelphia: American Baptist Publication Society, 1871), pp. 50-55, and "The Christian Hope for Heaven" (52) is from the same volume, pp. 357-364.

Robert William Dale (1829-1895) was an English Congregational pastor in Birmingham, where he exercised enormous influence upon the political and educational life of the city. In theology he is best remembered for his defense of the penal substitutionary view of atonement, which he expressed in ethical and moral terms as well as in legal ones. His writing style is direct and manly, and his books are eminently readable a century after he wrote.

Bibliography. "A Theory of Atonement" (37) is from R. W. Dale, *The Atonement* (London: Congregation Union of England and Wales, 1902), pp. 313-394, much abridged. "The Holy Spirit" (39) is from R. W. Dale, *Christian Doctrine* (London: Hodder and Stoughton, 1894), pp. 128-141, and "The Revelation of the Holy Trinity" (54) is from the same volume, pp. 148-169.

Andrew Bruce Davidson (1821-1902) was a member of the Free Church of Scotland and a teacher of Hebrew and Old Testament at the University of Edinburgh. Though his own theology was traditionalist, he introduced his students to the historical method for interpreting the Old Testament. He wrote in a style which possessed great dignity.

Bibliography. "Old Testament Teaching About God" (12) is from A. B. Davidson, *The Theology of the Old Testament* (Edinburgh: T. & T. Clark, 1904), pp. 30-38.

James Denney (1856-1917) was a theologian of the Free Church of Scotland and taught at Glasgow. In his early years, his theology was liberal, but he became more evangelical in his later years. One of his major concerns was for the atonement, and this is evident in the reading included herein.

Bibliography. "Preaching the Atonement" (38) is from James Denney, *The Death of Christ* (London: Hodder and Stoughton, 1909), pp. 282-294.

Isaac August Dorner (1809-1884) was a German Lutheran theologian who taught at several universities, the last of which was Berlin. He is best known for an immensely scholarly, detailed history of Christology in four volumes, and his interest in the doctrine of the person of Christ is evident in the reading included in the present book.

Bibliography. "Jesus: Prophet, Priest, King" (33) is from I. A. Dorner, *A System of Christian Doctrine*, translated by Alfred Cave and J. S. Banks (Edinburgh: T. & T. Clark, 1883), III, 381-411, much abridged.

Andrew Martin Fairbairn (1838-1912) was an English Congregational theologian. Among other responsibilities, he served as the first principal of Mansfield College, Oxford, for twenty-three years. He had a lifelong interest in philosophy of religion as well as in theology, and he exercised a great influence in his own denomination and in English church life generally.

Bibliography. "The City of God" (53) is from A. M. Fairbairn, *The City of God* (London: Hodder and Stoughton, 1883), pp. 349-370.

Charles Grandison Finney (1792-1875) was an American Presbyterian revival preacher. After his conversion experience, he repudiated the traditional Calvinistic view that a person should wait passively to be converted, and he taught that sinners should actively seek for salvation. He never attended seminary but worked out his own theology over years of revival preaching. In 1835, he became a professor of theology at Oberlin College. His independence of traditional Calvinism is evident in the reading included in the present volume.

Bibliography. "Election" (40) is from Charles Grandison Finney, *Lectures on Systematic Theology* (New York: George

H. Doran Company, 1878), pp. 481-489, abridged.

Peter Taylor Forsyth (1848-1921) was an English Congregational pastor and educator. In his early years, he was liberal in his theology, but he changed radically to a more traditionalist view out of a deep conviction that the Christian understanding of atonement alone provides an adequate reason for faith and hope in view of the moral realities of life. His major theological concerns were for the person and work of Christ, and both are represented in this volume.

Bibliography. "Analogies for the Incarnation" (29) is from P. T. Forsyth, *The Person and Place of Jesus Christ* (London: Independent Press, Ltd., 1909; fifth edition, 1946), pp. 293-300. "Atonement and the Gospel" (34) is from P. T. Forsyth, *The Cruciality of the Cross* (London: Independent Press Ltd, 1909; reprinted 1957), pp. 11-18.

Charles Gore (1853-1932) was probably the most influential theologian in the Church of England in his generation. He served the church in several positions, the last of which was Bishop of Oxford. His ecclesiology was Anglo-Catholic, and he referred to his theology as liberal Catholicism, meaning that he maintained the great traditions of the Catholic church while claiming the liberty to study them critically. The Catholic tradition is evident in the two readings in the present volume, on the nature of Christianity and the virgin birth of Christ. Gore wrote with grace and with immense self-assurance.

Bibliography. "Christianity" (1) is from Charles Gore, *The Incarnation of the Son of God* (London: John Murray, 1891, reprinted 1922), pp. 1-18. "The Virgin Birth of Christ" (22) is from Charles Gore, *Dissertations on Subjects Connected with the Incarnation* (London: John Murray, 1895), pp. 3-68, much abridged.

Charles Hodge (1797-1878) taught at Princeton Seminary for more than half a century and was the most influential theologian in Presbyterian church life in America in the nineteenth century. His three-volume *Systematic Theology* was for decades probably the most widely-used textbook on the subject in Protestant seminaries in America, and his clear, orderly, forceful theology had an impact upon the thinking of Christians outside his own denomination as well as on the thinking of Presbyterians.

Bibliography. "Natural Theology" (9) is from Charles Hodge, *Systematic Theology* (Grand Rapids: Wm. B. Eerdmans Publishing Company, no date given), I, 21-26. "The Coming of Christ" (51) is from the same work, III, 790-793.

Fenton John Anthony Hort (1828-1892) was a New Testament scholar in the Church of England. He, B. F. Westcott, and J. B. Lightfoot were together at Cambridge University and were known as the Cambridge trio. Hort was a modest person, and much of his energy was given to the study of the Greek text of the New Testament, an important, critical edition of which he produced with Westcott in 1881. His writing style is slightly opaque, particularly in the somewhat philosophical essay included in the present volume.

Bibliography. "Jesus the Lord" (31) is from Fenton John Anthony Hort, *The Way, the Truth, the Life* (London: Macmillan and Co., Limited, 1908), pp. 150-160.

Henry Parry Liddon (1829-1890) was a Church of England minister and canon of St. Paul's Cathedral in London. His major theological contribution was given in his Bampton Lectures for 1866, *The Divinity of Our Lord and Saviour Jesus Christ*, which was a lengthy biblical and historical defense of traditional Christology. The reading in the present book, though on the same topic, is from a collection of Liddon's sermons.

Bibliography. "The Incarnation of the Son of God" (27) is from H. P. Liddon, *Christmastide in St. Paul's* (London: Rivingtons, 1889), pp. 123-129.

Joseph Barber Lightfoot (1828-1889) was a patristics and New Testament scholar in the Church of England. He was Lady Margaret Professor of Divinity at Cambridge and later served as Bishop of Durham. He was careful historian, but he wrote in a lucid and nontechnical style, and his commentaries on several of Paul's epistles are still widely read today. The reading in the present volume is from a sermon which he preached in 1886.

Bibliography. "The Resurrection of Christ" (25) is from Joseph Barber Lightfoot, *Sermons Preached on Special Occasions* (London: Macmillan and Co., 1891), pp. 233-239.

George MacDonald (1824-1905) was a Scottish novelist and poet. He began his career as a Congregational minister, but he left the ministry to devote himself to writing. He was unconventional in his writing style, but he was a firm apologist for traditional Christianity. C. S. Lewis and others have recorded their indebtedness to his writings.

Bibliography. "Miracles" (18) is from George MacDonald, *On the Miracles of Our Lord* (Philadelphia: J. B. Lippincott Company, no date given), pp. 9-13.

Hugh Ross Mackintosh (1870-1936) was professor of systematic theology at New College, Edinburgh, and a minister of the Church of Scotland. He provided one of the shrewdest appraisals of nineteenth century theology ever written in his *Types of Modern Theology*. The reading given herein is from his early, massive, biblical and historical study of Christology.

Bibliography. "A Kenotic Christology" (28) is from H. R. Mackintosh, *The Doctrine of the Person of Jesus Christ* (Edinburgh: T. & T. Clark, 1912, reprinted 1962), pp. 466-482.

Hans Lassen Martensen (1808-1884) was a Danish Lutheran theologian and Bishop of Seeland. He is best known to many people today as one of the theologians attacked by Søren Kierkegaard. He believed that God speaks to men through reason as well as through the Christian revelation, and his own theology shows traces of nontraditional influences. However, on the topics dealt with in the present volume, namely, God's attributes, the church, and the Lord's Supper, he represented the Christian tradition well.

Bibliography. All three readings are from H. Martensen, *Christian Dogmatics*, translated by William Urwick (Edinburgh: T. & T. Clark, 1866). "The Attributes of God" (14) is from pp. 91-101; "The Marks of the Church" (47) is from pp. 344-353; and "The Lord's Supper" (50) is from pp. 432-436.

Frederick Denison Maurice (1805-1872) was a minister of the Church of England. He served in various positions, including a professorship in theology at King's College in London, from which he resigned because his view of heaven was considered unacceptable. He was one of the first scholars to recognize the variety and complexity of early man's view of sacrifice, and he attempted to reinterpret Christ's sacrifice with a view to these new understandings. The reading included herein was one of a series of sermons preached to a Young Men's Christian Association.

Bibliography. "The Sacrifice of Christ" (35) is from Frederick Denison Maurice, *The Doctrine of Sacrifice* (London: Macmillan and Co., 1879), pp. 118-125.

Robert Campbell Moberly (1845-1903) was a theologian of the Church of England and Regius Professor of Moral and Pastoral Theology at Oxford. Though not a prolific writer, two of his books received wide acclaim, namely, *Ministerial Priesthood* and *Atonement and Personality*.

Bibliography. "Punishment and Forgiveness" (36) is from R. C. Moberly, *Atonement and Personality* (London: John Murray, 1901, reprinted 1907), pp. 48-53.

James Orr (1844-1913) was Professor of Apologetics and Systematic Theology in the United Free Church College of Glasgow. He was a prolific and forceful writer. Because of his readable style, and also because he directly addressed so many of the concerns of evangelical Christians at the turn of the century, five selections from his writings are included in the present volume, more than from any other writer. Though he hesitated to affirm biblical inerrancy, he remained a close friend and co-worker with B. B. Warfield on the influential *International Standard Bible Encyclopedia*, and he continued to hold an extremely high view of Scripture and to attack what he saw as humanistic presuppositions in some biblical criticism.

Bibliography. "Christianity and Science" (3) is from James Orr, *The Faith of a Modern Christian* (New York: Hodder and Stoughton, no date given), pp. 203-217. "Biblical Criticism" (7) is from the same volume, pp. 39-57. "The Infallibility of the Bible" (6) is from James Orr, *Revelation and Inspiration* (Grand Rapids: Wm. B. Eerdmans Publishing Company, 1952), pp. 212-217. "The Doctrine of Creation" (16) is from James Orr, *Sidelights on Christian Doctrine* (New York: A. C. Armstrong & Son, 1909), pp. 55-66. "The Christian View of the World" (17) is from James Orr, *The Christian View of God and the World* (New York: Charles Scribner's Sons, 1897), pp. 32-35.

James Madison Pendleton (1811-1891) was a Southern Baptist pastor, professor, and journalist. He was a close friend of J. R. Graves and was the chief theologian of Landmark Baptist thinking. He taught at Union University in Tennessee and helped to found Crozer Theological Seminary in Pennsylvania. He wrote rapidly, and his writing is characterized by a beautiful simplicity and by confidence in his Baptist heritage.

Bibliography. "Regeneration" (41) is from J. M. Pendleton, *Christian Doctrines* (Philadelphia: American Baptist Publication Society, 1878; reprinted 1907), pp. 256-273. "The Importance of Local Congregations" (48) is from the same volume, pp. 329-341, and "Christian Baptism" (49) is from the same work, pp. 342-357.

Walter Rauschenbusch (1861-1918) was an American Baptist pastor and teacher and the chief theologian of the social gospel. He believed that Christian concern for the poor implied a kind of socialism, but he resisted the idea that Jesus was a mere social reformer and argued for the priority of religion over social change. He had an enormous influence in the church and was heard by politicians such as Theodore Roosevelt and Woodrow Wilson.

Bibliography. "Jesus' Social Teachings" (24) is from Walter Rauschenbusch, *Christianity and the Social Crisis* (New York: The Macmillan Company, 1907; reprinted 1912), pp. 44-49.

William Sanday (1843-1920) was a minister of the Church of England and Lady Margaret Professor of Divinity at Oxford. He had a special interest in New Testament studies, but he also worked to bring the theological and biblical studies of continental scholars to the attention of the English churches. Though he was a very cautious scholar, one of the readings included herein shows his willingness to venture into unexplored waters. Reading 30 contains a fascinating suggestion which never found very wide acceptance.

Bibliography. "Jesus and Eschatology" (23) is from William Sanday, *The Life of Christ in Recent Research* (New York: Oxford University Press, 1907), pp. 119-122. "Incarnation and Psychology" (30) is from William Sanday, *Christologies Ancient and Modern* (Oxford: The Clarendon Press, 1910), pp. 161-168.

Adolf Schlatter (1852-1939) was a Swiss New Testament scholar and theologian who taught in the German universities of Berlin and Tübingen. He argued that biblical theology is the only appropriate foundation for systematic theology, and some scholars today believe that Schlatter was ahead of his time in delineating the interface between biblical and systematic theology. None of his books was translated into English until after his death.

Bibliography. "Jesus the Word of God" (32) is from Adolf Schlatter, *The Church in the New Testament Period*, translated by Paul P. Levertoff (London: SPCK, 1955), pp. 299-306.

George Adam Smith (1856-1942) was born in India of Scottish parents. He became professor of Old Testament at Glasgow and later president of the University of Aberdeen.

He is known to many Old Testament students today through his commentaries on Old Testament books, particularly a two-volume work on the Minor Prophets. The reading included herein is from a sermon he preached in Aberdeen.

Bibliography. "Forgiveness and New Life" (43) is from George Adam Smith, *The Forgiveness of Sins and Other Sermons* (London: Hodder and Stoughton, 1909), pp. 7-25.

Augustus Hopkins Strong (1836-1921) was the preeminent American Baptist theologian at the end of the nineteenth century. He was president and professor of biblical theology at Rochester Theological Seminary. Though he accepted an evolutionary understanding of the world, in general his theology remained firmly traditional. His great three-volume work, *Systematic Theology*, has been one of the most widely-used textbooks in Baptist seminaries. It was written in a tedious style, but he was capable of a more engaging style, as may be seen in the last reading in this book.

Bibliography. "The Sin of Man" (20) is from A. H. Strong, *Systematic Theology* (Old Tappan, New Jersey: Fleming H. Revell Company, 1907, reprinted 1954), II, 559-640, much abridged. "A Theological Pilgrimage" (56) is from A. H. Strong, *One Hundred Chapel-Talks to Theological Students together with Two Autobiographical Addresses* (Philadelphia: The Griffith and Rowland Press, 1913), pp. 3-33.

Benjamin Breckinridge Warfield (1851-1921) was an American Presbyterian theologian. He succeeded A. A. Hodge as professor of theology at Princeton Seminary and there carried on the theological tradition of Archibald Alexander and of Charles Hodge and A. A. Hodge. Warfield was a prolific writer, but he never wrote a systematic theology, and his essays are expositions and defenses of a theology which he seems to have regarded as having been completed by his predecessors. His style is ponderous but always learned.

Bibliography. "Paul's Proclamation of Christ" (26) is from

Benjamin Breckinridge Warfield, *The Person and Work of Christ* (Philadelphia: The Presbyterian and Reformed Publishing Company, 1950), pp. 76-86.

Brooke Foss Westcott (1825-1901) was a New Testament scholar in the Church of England. He was Regius Professor of Divinity at Cambridge and later Bishop of Durham. He and F. J. A. Hort published a critical Greek text of the New Testament in 1881, and his commentaries on John's Gospel and Epistles and on Hebrews are widely studied today. He had a profound concern for social problems, and his theology emphasized the incarnation and the resurrection and their implications.

Bibliography. "Christianity and History" (2) is from Brooke Foss Westcott, *The Gospel of Life* (London: Macmillan and Co., 1895), pp. 254-257. "The Glory of the Holy Trinity" (55) is from Brooke Foss Westcott, *The Revelation of the Father* (London: Macmillan and Co., Limited, 1904), pp. 180-188.

1

Christianity

Charles Gore

Christianity exists in the world as a distinctive religion; and if we are asked, 'What is the distinguishing characteristic of this religion?' we can hardly hesitate for an answer. Christianity is faith in a certain person Jesus Christ, and by faith in Him is meant such unreserved self-committal as is only possible, because faith in Jesus is understood to be faith in God, and union with Jesus union with God. 'We know him that is true, and we are in him that is true, even in his Son Jesus Christ. This is the true God, and eternal life.'

I

That true Christianity is thus a personal relationship—the conscious deliberate adhesion of men who know their weakness, their sin, their fallibility, to a redeemer whom they know to be supreme, sinless, infallible—is shewn by the fact that it produces its characteristic fruit only in proportion as it is thus realized. We can make this apparently obvious proposition more emphatic if we recall to our mind some of the many ways in which the true character of our religion has been, and is, distorted or obscured.

1. For, first, Christianity has brought with it a visible society or church, with dogmatic propositions and sacramental ordi-

28

nances and a ministerial priesthood, and it has been easy so to misuse these elements of the ecclesiastical system, as to make Christianity no longer devotion to a living person, but the acceptance on authority of a system of theological propositions and ecclesiastical duties. When churchmanship assumes this degenerate form, Christianity is not indeed destroyed, nor does it cease to bring forth moral and spiritual fruit; but the fruit is of an inferior and less characteristic quality, it is not the spirit and temper of sonship. At the lowest it even tends to approximate to what any religious organization is capable of producing, merely on account of the discipline which it enforces, and the sense of security which its fellowship imparts. To the true and typical churchman, on the other hand, all the ecclesiastical fabric only represents an unseen but present Lord. The eyes of an Ignatius, or an Athanasius, or a Leo, or a Bernard, or a Pusey, however much history may rightly identify these men with zeal on behalf of the organization and dogmas of the church, were in fact, as their writings sufficiently testify, never off their Lord for whom alone and in whom alone all external things had their value.

2. Again, the constant outlook of the soul of the Christian upon the person of Jesus Christ may be intercepted by the undue exaltation of saintly intercessors. Thus there are districts of the church in which devotion to our Lord's mother has usurped such prominence in Christian worship as in fact to interfere with His unique prerogative, so that in some real sense there has been a division of territory effected between Him and her as objects of devotion. This statement may be justified by quoting from a writer who is specially representative of the attitude encouraged in the Roman communion towards the blessed Virgin—St. Alfonso de' Liguori. 'When she conceived the Son of God in her womb,' he writes, 'and afterwards gave Him birth, she obtained the half of the kingdom of God, so that she should be queen of mercy, as Christ is king of justice.' Thus, while the king must have regard to the interests of justice, the queen can be appealed to as unmixed compassion. Once again, then, when Mary is thus exalted to a pedestal, which no one would ever have refused so utterly as she herself, the wine of Christianity is mixed with water. For the human character of

Jesus, the historical character, combining the strength of manhood and the tenderness of womanhood in perfect alliance, is always strengthening to contemplate and to adore. In Him mercy and truth are met together, righteousness and peace have kissed each other; but the purely ideal figure of Mary, as it finds expression in all the weakly conceived images of the 'mater misericordiae' which meet our eyes so constantly in the churches of the Continent, appeals to a sentiment, a craving for a compassion unalloyed with severity, which it was part of the proper function of Christianity even to extirpate.

3. Once again, it is possible for our religion to lose its true centre by becoming what we may call unduly 'subjective.' Great stress may be laid on personal feeling, on the assurance of personal salvation. Questions may be freely asked and answers expected as to whether this or that religious emotion has been experienced, as to whether a person has 'found peace,' or 'gained assurance,' or 'is saved.' Now 'peace with God,' and 'joy in believing,' even assurance of a present state of salvation, are endowments of the Christian life, which God habitually bestows—which may be both asked for and thankfully welcomed. But they are not meant either to be the tests of reality in religion, or generally subjects of self-examination.

What our Lord claims of us is, first, service, the service of ready wills, then developing faith, and lives gradually sanctified by correspondence with Him. On these points we must rigorously examine ourselves, but the sense of the service of Another, of co-operation with Another, is meant to become so absorbing a consciousness as to swallow up in us the consideration of personal feeling, and at least to overshadow even the anxiety for our own separate salvation. By losing our lives in Christ and His cause, we are meant to save them; to serve Christ, not to feel Christ, is the mark of His true servants; they become Christians in proportion as they cease to be interested in themselves, and become absorbed in their Lord.

4. Once again; the enthusiasm of humanity may send men out using the name of Him who is the true liberator of man, but depreciating doctrine in the supposed interests of philanthropy. This inevitably results in the substitution of zeal for work for zeal

for Christ. Where Christ is really contemplated and meditated upon, it is impossible to be indifferent as to the explanation to be given of His person and work; in the knowledge of this lies the inspiration of labour and the ground of perennial hopefulness. When in fact this is ignored, the work becomes more and more the execution of the worker's own schemes, or the schemes of some one under whom he works, with less and less regard to what can truly and historically be called the purpose and method of Jesus. It becomes external or intellectual, it ceases to touch the springs of character; in a word, it becomes less and less a characteristic expression of the energy of Christian faith.

5. Once again and for the last time: the interests of a student may convert Christianity into a philosophical system, coloured intensely by the method and terminology of a particular phase of thought and very exceptional conditions of life. This was the case, more or less, with the Christianity of Clement of Alexandria; it has been the case not infrequently, since his day, in academic circles. Where it is the case, a system becomes the object of interest rather than a person, and the real appeal of Jesus of Nazareth, whether to the heart of the student himself, or of those whom he may be required to teach by word or by writing, is proportionately weakened. Nothing, I suppose, can keep the Christianity of a theoretical student from deterioration, save the constant exercise of prayer, which is the address of person to person, and the constant and regular contemplation of the character in the Gospels, even as the apostolic writer bids us 'consider the Apostle and High Priest of our confession, even Jesus' (Heb. iii. 1).

I have specified these various ways in which Christians of different tendencies may obscure, and have in fact obscured, the true glory of the Christian life, because it is important to throw into high relief, what is the simple verdict of Christian history, that the characteristic fruitfulness of our religion—its fruitfulness in the temper and spirit of sonship—varies with the extent to which Jesus, the historical person, the ever-living person, is recognised as the object of our devotion and the lord of our life. This is true equally of personal religion and official ministry, for it is converse with the perfect personality of Jesus, which gives the pastor his power to deal with the various personalities of his flock, and the preacher his power to move the wills and consciences of his hearers. It is devotion to Jesus which has been the source of the enduring forms of Christian heroism. It is the same reality of personal relationship which touches the Christian's private life with the brightness of sonship. 'To me,' says Paul the prisoner, summarizing his religion, 'to live is Christ and to die is gain,' for that too is 'to depart and to be with Christ,' which 'is very far better' (Phil. i. 21-23). 'Eighty and six years,' says the aged Polycarp, again summarizing his religion in response to the demand that he should revile the Christ,—'eighty and six years have I been His servant, and He never did me an injury; how then can I blaspheme my king who is my saviour?'

II

To recognise this truth is to be struck by the contrast which in this respect Christianity presents to other religions. For example, the place which Mohammed holds in Islam is not the place which Jesus Christ holds in Christianity, but that which Moses holds in Judaism. The Arabian prophet made for himself no claim other than that which Jewish prophets made, other than that which all prophets, true or false, or partly true and partly false, have always made,—to speak the word of the Lord. The substance of Mohammedanism, considered as a religion, lies simply in the message which the Koran contains. It is, as no other religion is, founded upon a book. The person of the Prophet has its significance only so far as he is supposed to have certificated the reality of the revelations which the book records.

Gautama, again, the founder of Buddhism, one, I suppose, of the noblest and greatest of mankind, is only the discoverer or rediscoverer of a method or way, the way of salvation, by which is meant the way to win final emancipation from the weary chain of existence, and to attain Nirvana, or Parinirvana, the final blessed extinction. Having found this way, after many years of weary searching, he can teach it to others, but he is, all the time, only a pre-eminent example of the success of his own method, one of a series of Buddhas or enlightened ones, who shed on other men the light of their superior knowledge. Thus, in *The Book of the Great Decease* he is represented, in conversation with his disciple Ânanda, as expressly repudiating the idea of the dependence of the Buddhist order on himself. 'The Perfect,' that is, the Buddha, he says, 'thinks not that it is he who should lead the brotherhood, or that the order is dependent upon him. Why then should he leave instructions in any matter concerning the order? . . . Therefore, O Ânanda, be ye lamps unto yourselves. Be ye a refuge to yourselves. Betake yourselves to no external refuge . . . And whosoever, Ânanda, either now or after I am dead, shall be a lamp unto themselves, and a refuge unto themselves, shall betake themselves to no external refuge, but holding fast to the truth as their lamp, shall look not for refuge to any one besides themselves . . . it is they, Ânanda, who shall reach the very topmost height.'

It was plainly the method of Buddha, not the person, which was to save his brethren. As for the person, he passed away, as the writer of the Buddhist scripture repeatedly declares, 'with that utter passing away in which nothing whatever is left behind,' living on only metaphorically in the method and teaching which he bequeathed to his followers. We are touching on no disputed point when we assert that according to the Buddhist scriptures, the personal, conscious life of the founder of that religion was extinguished in death. But this single fact points the contrast with Christianity. The teaching of Jesus differs in fact from the teaching of the Buddha not more in the ideal of salvation which he propounded than in the place held by the person who propounded the ideal. For Jesus Christ taught no method by which men might attain the end of their being, whether He Himself, personally, existed or was annihilated: but as He offered Himself to men on earth as the satisfaction of their being—their master, their example, their redeemer—so when He left the earth He promised to sustain them from the unseen world by His continued personal presence and to communicate to them His own life, and He assured them that at the last they would find themselves face to face with Him as their judge. The personal relation to Himself is from first to last of the essence of the religion which He inaugurated.

III

If we wish to account for the unique position which Jesus Christ has held in religion it is only necessary to examine the claim which He is represented to have made for Himself in the earliest records which we possess. History in fact gives a very distinct account of the positions relatively to the faith of their disciples, claimed by the three founders of religion whom we have just been considering. For however busy legend has been with the Buddha, there appears to be little difficulty in obtaining a clear picture of what he claimed to be, how he claimed to have become what he was, and how he wished his disciples to follow his example. Legend has not materially distorted the picture of his own estimate of himself. No more than Mohammed does he, on his own showing, enter into rivalry with the Jesus of the Christian tradition. Whether history has or has not left us the true image of the personal claim of Jesus of Nazareth will be matter for consideration afterwards. Here I am only concerned to make good the position that the teaching and the claim of Jesus as it is represented generally in the Gospels, or (let me say) more especially in the Synoptists, accounts for and justifies the place assigned to Him in historical Christendom.

This will be most apparent if we confine our attention chiefly to the education which He is represented as giving to that little company who united themselves to Him under various circumstances, and whom He bound together into the body of Apostles. For, diverting attention from others, He concentrated it more and more on these. We are admitted in the Gospels to observe how He trained these few men to understand His person and commit themselves body and soul to Him. . . .

I have endeavoured briefly to traverse very familiar ground in thus recalling to your minds how the Christ of the Gospels does make a claim for Himself which warrants (to speak generally) the belief about Him to which we are accustomed in the Christian Church. That this is familiar ground, upon which it is not necessary long to dwell, is due in great measure to one, the tones of whose memorable voice the majority of us must have heard from this pulpit last Whitsunday, and heard for the last time.

Among all Dr. Liddon's titles to our gratitude, none is more conspicuous than the service which he rendered when in his Bampton Lectures he put his faultless powers of analysis and expression at the disposal of his passionate faith in order to exhibit the nature and the significance of our Lord's assertion of Himself. He is identified, as with hardly anything else, with the re-statement of the great dilemma based on the claim of Jesus Christ, that either He was what alone could morally justify that claim, the very Son of God, or He was indeed guilty of the supreme arrogance of putting Himself in the place of God,—'aut Deus aut homo non bonus.'

Thoughtful men generally view with distrust the dilemma as a form of argument. We in Oxford may remember how a very brilliant contemporary of Dr. Liddon gave expression to this distrust by saying that he had made it a rule when anyone presented him with a dilemma to turn his back and refuse to have anything to say to it. But, after all, there are dilemmas, though they may not be many, the force of which grows upon us the more we consider them; the dilemma based upon the claim of Jesus Christ is one of these; and it may be asserted here at the beginning of our discussion, that to represent our Lord only as a good man conscious of a message from God, like one of the Prophets or John the Baptist, is to do violence not to one Gospel only or to single passages in various Gospels, but to the general tenor of the Gospels as a whole.

IV

Among those who cannot accept cordially the propositions of the Christian creed, but at the same time are anxious to maintain religion in society and in their own lives, there is an unmistakeable unwillingness to consider fairly what, historically and in experience, Christianity has been, wherein its great strength lies and has lain. They wish, for safety's sake, to fuse the distinctive outlines of our religion in a vague atmosphere. But it is never wise to refuse to look steadily at facts.

Whether Christianity can or can not be rationally maintained is another question. But there is not much doubt, so far, what

Christianity is. I do not think it can be reasonably gainsayed (1) that Christianity has meant historically, faith in the person of Jesus Christ, considered as very God incarnate, so much so that if this faith were gone, Christianity in its characteristic features would be gone also; (2) that, thus considered, Christianity is differentiated from other religions by the attitude of its members towards its Founder; (3) that this attitude of Christianity towards its Founder is (speaking generally) explained and justified by the witness of the earliest records to His personality and claim.

2

Christianity and History

Brooke Foss Westcott

We have seen that Christianity claims to be absolute, to extend without limit to all men, to the whole of man, to all being, to all time, or rather to eternity. At the same time since revelation comes through life and stands in a vital connexion with the whole life of humanity it must be progressive or apprehended progressively. Christianity therefore claims also to be historical; and by this claim it is distinguished from all other religions. Its teaching, its life, its essence is a history. It was prepared by a long national development, into which the typical elements of the ancient world entered as contributory forces. It is summed up in the facts of a divine-human life. It has been, and still is being, wrought out in the slow and unreturning growth of a society.

In this sense Christianity is the only historical religion. There is a sense in which Christianity and Mohammedanism, for example, may be classed together as historical religions, so far as the facts connected with the personality and life of their Founders, their origin and progress and development, can be traced in documents which are adequate to assure belief. But it is not in this sense primarily that Christianity is historical. Christianity is historical not simply or characteristically because Christ standing out before the world at a definite time and place proclaimed certain truths and laid down certain rules for the constitution and conduct of a society. It is historical because He offered Himself in His own Person, and He was shewn to be in the events of His Life, the revelation which He came to give. It is historical in itself, in its essence, and, this being so, it is, in a secondary and yet in a unique sense, historical in its antecedents and in its realisation.

Christianity is historical in its antecedents. It is the fulfilment of Judaism, which was in its very idea definitely prospective, and only really intelligible through the end to which it led. The Covenant with Abraham included the promise of which the later religious history of 'the people,' working throughout for and in 'the nations,' was the gradual accomplishment. The call of Abraham was the beginning of the universal life of Faith. For as Christianity was the goal of the revelations of the Old Testament, so it was also the answer to the questions of the whole pre-Christian world, the satisfaction of the aspirations of the 'many nations' with whom in the order of Providence the 'people' was brought into contact.

Christianity is historical in itself. It is not a code of laws: it is not a structure of institutions: it is not a system of opinions. It is a life in fellowship with a living Lord. The Work and the Person of Christ, this is the Gospel, both as it was proclaimed by the Lord Himself, and as it was proclaimed by His Apostles: the revelation, the gift, the power, of a perfect human life offered to GOD and received by GOD, in and with which every single human life finds its accomplishment. The laws, the institutions, the opinions, of Christendom are the expression of the life which works through them. In Christianity the thoughts by which other religions live are seen as facts.

Christianity is also historical in its realisation. All human experience must be a commentary on the perfect human Life. The new life which was communicated to men requires for its complete embodiment the services of all men. The fuller meaning of the Faith in Him Who is the Way and the Truth and the Life is slowly mastered through the ages by the ministry of nations and by the ministry of saints and heroes through which the thoughts of the nations are interpreted. Such a process must go on unhastingly, unrestingly, irreversibly to the end of time; and if anything can make us feel the nobility of life, it must be that in Christ we are enabled to recognise in the whole course of history a majestic spectacle of the action of Divine love in which no failures and no wilfulness of men can obliterate the signs and the promises of a Presence of God.

3

Christianity and Science

James Orr

The idea prevails in many quarters that the immense advances in the natural sciences since inductive inquiry began have led to an altered view of the world and man, which takes the foundations from Christian beliefs on these subjects, and renders the whole Christian scheme of things untenable.

I

Certainly nothing could be more amazing than the progress made during the last few centuries in man's knowledge of nature, and mastery of its laws and forces. The effect has been a revolution in the conception of the universe which leaves nothing untouched. The idea of our globe as the centre round which the heavens move has vanished. In extension in space, as in duration in time, the universe is seen to be practically illimitable. The earth was not created six thousand years ago, but has a geological history going back perhaps fifty or a hundred millions of years. Man, too, is older by millenniums—some would say by tens or hundreds of millenniums—than we had been accustomed to believe. The excavations in Babylonia and Egypt reveal an immensely remote antiquity of civilisation. Then there is the rise and universal extension of the idea of "evolution." Does not this overthrow the Bible account of the origin of man? A yet more fatal effect of the progress of science is thought to be the establishment of the idea of the reign of universal law. With this, do not miracles disappear?

Admittedly the change is great, but we are a long way still from the conclusion that the foundations of Christianity are overturned, or that there is any necessary conflict between science and the facts and doctrines of revelation. The question of miracle was dealt with in a previous paper, and it was there shown that no view of the universe which grants its origin from, and dependence on, a living Personal God, can ever legitimately deny the possibility of an economy of revelation, connected with supernatural interpositions, for higher ends than those which nature can attain. The relation of Christianity to the truths of science may now be looked at more precisely.

II

It is desirable, first, to set the consideration of the subject in its proper light by removal of misconceptions. These exist, both on the side of defenders of the Bible, and on the side of science.

The day is happily almost past when men looked on the Bible as a sort of anticipative text-book of natural science. When Copernicus affirmed that the earth was not the centre of the universe; that it was the earth that moved round the sun, and not the sun that moved round the earth, it was thought sufficient in order to confute him to quote texts like Psalm xix. 5, 6, where the sun is described as performing his circuit in the heavens. When geology was proving that the earth had a long and interesting history, the stages of which were embodied in the rocks, Genesis i. was relied on to show that everything was made in six ordinary days about six thousand years ago. The mistakes were perhaps natural; they none the less rested on an erroneous view of the relation of Scripture to science, and did harm to Christianity by seeking to bind it up with positions that could not be maintained. This teaches a lesson of caution in opposing the Bible to science. It is now getting to be well understood, what the wiser interpreters of Scripture have always maintained, that the Bible was not given to anticipate modern physical discoveries, but uses plain, popular language in speaking of natural phenomena, describing things by their appearances—not from a scientific standpoint—as we still do in our almanacs when we speak of the sun and moon "rising" and "setting." Calvin, in the sixteenth century, put this very clearly in his commentary on Genesis. "He who would learn astronomy and other recondite arts," he wrote, "let him go elsewhere. . . . Moses wrote in a popular style things which, without instruction, all ordinary persons endued with common sense are able to understand. . . . He does not call us up to heaven, he only proposes things that lie open before our eyes." The purpose of the Bible was different—to set things in their right relation to God, the first Cause of all; to show what God is, and what are His purposes and will for man. In this, its proper sphere, there is no conflict with science.

But science, too, has its lesson of caution and humility to learn. Everything is not science which chooses to call itself science. Rash theories have often been propounded which further inquiry has discredited; extravagant claims have often been made which have had afterwards to be retracted. The progress of knowledge itself is continually modifying or enlarging scientific conceptions, so that the knowledge of to-day is by no means the measure of the science of to-morrow. A quarter of a century ago science was decidedly materialistic in its bent.

Even Prof. Huxley, who was not, philosophically, a materialist, insisted on interpreting mental facts in terms of matter. He declared: "As surely as every future grows out of past and present, so will the physiology of the future extend the realm of matter and law till it is coextensive with knowledge, with feeling, and with action." It can safely be said that this phase is passing away, and is being replaced by a more spiritual view of the universe. Haeckel acknowledges in his *Riddle* that most of his former stalwarts . . . subsequently deserted him. Darwinism at first thought to get rid of "teleology"—of design—in nature, but it will be found that this is precisely one of the points where the newer evolution breaks with the old. Enormous periods have been postulated for man's duration on the earth, but these are being retrenched by more accurate observations of the time since the close of the Glacial Age. If Oriental discovery has led to surprising modification in older views of the age of ancient civilisation, its service has been not less conspicuous in the light it has thrown on the high character of early civilisations, and in the corroborations it has furnished of statements in the early pages of the Bible which had been long disputed.

III

In its older phases the controversy between the Bible and science had chiefly to do with astronomy and geology.

There was the astronomical objection to Christianity which Dr. Chalmers and others ably combated. The extension of view involved in the Copernican theory of the heavens was thought by many to render impossible the belief that the world—a mere speck in infinity—should be the special object of God's love and care; the scene of an Incarnation and work of redeeming grace such as the Christian religion affirms. Few Christians to-day feel much force in this objection. God's love is not on the scale of quantitative bigness. God is present in the atom and the animacule as truly as in suns and stars. He cares for the sparrow in its fall, as well as presides over the fates of empires. Man is not less the object of God's love because he may not be the only object.

God had always in Christian belief been held to be infinite, with a universe of intelligent spirits adoring and serving Him. His love to man in redemption is not contradicted, but is infinitely enhanced by every fresh demonstration of His majesty and power. A further question, however, is, Does science show that man's place in the universe is less unique than the Bible represents it to be? The thought of the universe in space is inconceivably enlarged; but are we brought any nearer to the proof of hosts of inhabited worlds and planets? It is very doubtful. So far as scientific knowledge goes, our earth remains the only spot in the material creation in which intelligent and moral life has emerged.

It is not otherwise with the difficulties in regard to the geological revelations of the age of the earth. However Genesis i. is to be interpreted—whether, as seems probable, its days are "æonic," great divisions in the creative work (the first three "days" precede the sun's measurement), or belong simply to the representation of the creation under the form of a divine "week" of work—one cannot but see the sublimity of its description of the origin of all things in comparison with heathen cosmogonies; must recognise, too, under divergencies of aim and form, the substantial accord of the ideas embodied in it with what reason and science unite to affirm. How grand and important are these ideas!—the creation of all things by the one true God, the gradual progress from lower to higher, the order of the stages—the settling of the earth, plant and water creations, birds, appointment of sun and moon, mammals, the culmination of the whole process in man! Science gives precision to these conceptions, but does not alter their essential truth.

IV

The scientific theory which, in recent times, presents most appearance of conflict with Christianity is Darwinian evolution. Darwin's great achievement was in winning for the theory of organic descent a general scientific acceptance which it did not before possess. Not only were the facts in support of evolution more skilfully marshalled, but a theory—that of "natural selection"—was propounded, which seemed to explain the process. (Darwin rested his special claim on his supposed discovery of the "how" of the development.) The consequences were far-reaching. Through the operation of a few simple laws, selecting and preserving variations favourable to individuals and species, the adaptations of which nature is full were thought to be accounted for without the interposition of mind or purpose. Man came under the general rule, and was held to be a slow development from simian ancestors. It is not necessary to break with the general doctrine of descent to recognise the defects of the Darwinian presentation of it. Darwinism and evolution are not synonymous. A considerable revolt has taken place in evolutionist circles from the idea of "natural selection," slowly operating, as the main factor in evolution. Confession is frankly made that the main factors are yet to seek, and must lie within the organism, not in external causes. The idea of fortuity is being abandoned, and in one form or another there is recognition of the fact that nature works towards an end. The process, too, is not always slow and gradual, but is often rapid, the result of sudden change ("mutation").

With such modifications, most of the aspects of conflict of evolution with Theism, and even with Christianity, are removed. The one thing evolution cannot do is to explain origins. The first origin of things; the origin of life and sentiency; the origin of rational intelligence—these remain for it insoluble problems. It may be claimed that, with our present knowledge, there is nothing to hinder that man, whatever the part of evolution in his origin, may have appeared on earth as a new type of being, pure in nature, made in God's image, destined for sonship to God, immortal in destiny. This is what Christianity affirms, and no science which knows its own limits will contradict it. With the change from infinitesimally gradual evolution to "mutation" theories, there is no need, even for carrying man's origin back many millenniums beyond the usual computation.

In brief, it may be confidently claimed that science does not in any serious way collide with the presuppositions of the Christian faith. In many ways it may and does enlarge our notions; it does not destroy a single postulate of our religion.

4

Defending Orthodoxy

Gilbert K. Chesterton

"Why cannot you simply take what is good in Christianity, what you can define as valuable, what you can comprehend, and leave all the rest, all the absolute dogmas that are in their nature incomprehensible?" This is the real question; . . . and it is a pleasure to try to answer it.

The first answer is simply to say that I am a rationalist. I like to have some intellectual justification for my intuitions. If I am treating man as a fallen being it is an intellectual convenience to me to believe that he fell; and I find, for some odd psychological reason, that I can deal better with a man's exercise of freewill if I believe that he has got it. But I am in this matter yet more definitely a rationalist. I do not propose to turn this book into one of ordinary Christian apologetics; I should be glad to meet at any other time the enemies of Christianity in that more obvious arena. Here I am only giving an account of my own growth in spiritual certainty. But I may pause to remark that the more I saw of the merely abstract arguments against the Christian cosmology the less I thought of them. I mean that having found the moral atmosphere of the Incarnation to be common sense, I then looked at the established intellectual arguments against the Incarnation and found them to be common nonsense. In case the argument should be thought to suffer from the absence of the ordinary apologetic I will here very briefly summarise my own arguments and conclusions on the purely objective or scientific truth of the matter.

If I am asked, as a purely intellectual question, why I believe in Christianity, I can only answer, "For the same reason that an intelligent agnostic disbelieves in Christianity." I believe in it quite rationally upon the evidence. But the evidence in my case, as in that of the intelligent agnostic, is not really in this or that alleged demonstration; it is in an enormous accumulation of small but unanimous facts. The secularist is not to be blamed because his objections to Christianity are miscellaneous and even scrappy; it is precisely such scrappy evidence that does convince the mind. I mean that a man may well be less convinced of a philosophy from four books, than from one book, one battle, one landscape, and one old friend. The very fact that the things are of different kinds increases the importance of the fact that they all point to one conclusion. Now, the non-Christianity of the average educated man to-day is almost always, to do him justice, made up of these loose but living experiences. I can only say that my evidences for Christianity are of the same vivid but varied kind as his evidences against it. For when I look at these various anti-Christian truths, I simply discover that none of them are true. I discover that the true tide and force of all the facts flows the other way. Let us take cases. Many a sensible modern man must have abandoned Christianity under the pressure of three such converging convictions as these: first, that men, with their shape, structure, and sexuality, are, after all, very much like beasts, a mere variety of the animal kingdom; second, that primeval religion arose in ignorance and fear; third, that priests have blighted societies with bitterness and gloom. Those three anti-Christian arguments are very different; but they are all quite logical and legitimate; and they all converge. The only objection to them (I discover) is that they are all untrue. If you leave off looking at books about beasts and men, if you begin to look at beasts and men then (if you have any humour or imagination, any sense of the frantic or the farcical) you will observe that the startling thing is not how like man is to the brutes, but how unlike he is. It is the monstrous scale of his divergence that requires an explanation. That man and brute are like is, in a sense, a truism; but that being so like they should then be so insanely unlike, that is the shock and the enigma. That an ape has hands is far less interesting to the philosopher than the fact that having hands he does next to nothing with them; does not play knuckle-bones or the violin; does not carve marble or carve mutton. People talk of barbaric architecture and debased art. But elephants do not build colossal temples of ivory even in a roccoco style; camels do not paint even bad pictures, though equipped with the material of many camel's-hair brushes. Certain modern dreamers say that ants and bees have a society superior to ours. They have, indeed, a civilization; but that very truth only reminds us that it is an inferior civilization. Who ever found an ant-hill decorated with the statues of celebrated ants? Who has seen a bee-hive carved with the images of gorgeous queens of old? No; the chasm between man and other creatures may have a natural explanation, but it is a chasm. We talk of wild animals; but man is the only wild animal. It is man that has broken out. All other animals are tame animals; following the rugged respectability of the tribe or type. All other animals are domestic animals; man alone is ever undomestic, either as a profligate or a monk. So that this first superficial reason for materialism is, if anything, a reason for its opposite; it is exactly where biology leaves off that all religion begins.

It would be the same if I examined the second of the three chance rationalist arguments; the argument that all that we call divine began in some darkness and terror. When I did attempt to examine the foundations of this modern idea I simply found that there were none. Science knows nothing whatever about pre-historic man; for the excellent reason that he is pre-historic. A few professors choose to conjecture that such things as human sacrifice were once innocent and general and that they gradually dwindled; but there is no direct evidence of it, and the small amount of indirect evidence is very much the other way. In the earliest legends we have, such as the tales of Isaac and of Iphigenia, human sacrifice is not introduced as something old, but rather as something new; as a strange and frightful exception darkly demanded by the gods. History says nothing; and legends all say that the earth was kinder in its earliest time.

There is no tradition of progress; but the whole human race has a tradition of the Fall. Amusingly enough, indeed, the very dissemination of this idea is used against its authenticity. Learned men literally say that this pre-historic calamity cannot be true because every race of mankind remembers it. I cannot keep pace with these paradoxes.

And if we took the third chance instance, it would be the same; the view that priests darken and embitter the world. I look at the world and simply discover that they don't. Those countries in Europe which are still influenced by priests, are exactly the countries where there is still singing and dancing and coloured dresses and art in the open-air. Catholic doctrine and discipline may be walls; but they are the walls of a playground. Christianity is the only frame which has preserved the pleasure of Paganism. We might fancy some children playing on the flat grassy top of some tall island in the sea. So long as there was a wall round the cliff's edge they could fling themselves into every frantic game and make the place the noisiest of nurseries. But the walls were knocked down, leaving the naked peril of the precipice. They did not fall over; but when their friends returned to them they were all huddled in terror in the centre of the island; and their song had ceased.

Thus these three facts of experience, such facts as go to make an agnostic, are, in this view, turned totally round. I am left saying, "Give me an explanation, first, of the towering eccentricity of man among the brutes; second, of the vast human tradition of some ancient happiness; third, of the partial perpetuation of such pagan joy in the countries of the Catholic Church." One explanation, at any rate, covers all three: the theory that twice was the natural order interrupted by some explosion or revelation. . . .

I have given an imaginary triad of such ordinary anti-Christian arguments; if that be too narrow a basis I will give on the spur of the moment another. These are the kind of thoughts which in combination create the impression that Christianity is something weak and diseased. First, for instance, that Jesus was a gentle creature, sheepish and unworldly, a mere ineffectual appeal to the world; second, that Christianity arose and flourished in the dark ages of ignorance, and that to these the Church would drag us back; third, that the people still strongly religious or (if you will) superstitious—such people as the Irish—are weak, unpractical, and behind the times. I only mention these ideas to affirm the same thing: that when I looked into them independently I found, not that the conclusions were unphilosophical, but simply that the facts were not facts. Instead of looking at books and pictures about the New Testament I looked at the New Testament. There I found an account, not in the least of a person with his hair parted in the middle or his hands clasped in appeal, but of an extraordinary being with lips of thunder and acts of lurid decision, flinging down tables, casting out devils, passing with the wild secrecy of the wind from mountain isolation to a sort of dreadful demagogy; a being who often acted like an angry god—and always like a god. Christ had even a literary style of his own, not to be found, I think, elsewhere; it consists of an almost furious use of the *a fortiori*. His "how much more" is piled one upon another like castle upon castle in the clouds. The diction used about Christ has been, and perhaps wisely, sweet and submissive. But the diction used by Christ is quite curiously gigantesque; it is full of camels leaping through needles and mountains hurled into the sea. Morally it is equally terrific; he called himself a sword of slaughter, and told men to buy swords if they sold their coats for them. That he used other even wilder words on the side of non-resistance greatly increases the mystery; but it also, if anything, rather increases the violence. We cannot even explain it by calling such a being insane; for insanity is usually along one consistent channel. The maniac is generally a monomaniac. Here we must remember the difficult definition of Christianity already given; Christianity is a superhuman paradox whereby two opposite passions may blaze beside each other. The one explanation of the Gospel language that does explain it, is that it is the survey of one who from some supernatural height beholds some more startling synthesis.

I take in order the next instance offered: the idea that Christianity belongs to the Dark Ages. Here I did not satisfy myself with reading modern generalisations; I read a little history. And in history I found that Christianity, so far from belonging to the Dark Ages, was the one path across the Dark Ages that was not dark. It was a shining bridge connecting two shining civilizations. If any one says that the faith arose in ignorance and savagery the answer is simple: it didn't. It arose in the Mediterranean civilization in the full summer of the Roman Empire. The world was swarming with sceptics, and pantheism was as plain as the sun, when Constantine nailed the cross to the mast. It is perfectly true that afterwards the ship sank; but it is far more extraordinary that the ship came up again: repainted and glittering, with the cross still at the top. . . .

I added in this second trinity of objections an idle instance taken from those who feel such people as the Irish to be weakened or made stagnant by superstition. I only added it because this is a peculiar case of a statement of fact that turns out to be a statement of falsehood. It is constantly said of the Irish that they are impractical. But if we refrain for a moment from looking at what is said about them and look at what is done about them, we shall see that the Irish are not only practical, but quite painfully successful. The poverty of their country, the minority of their members are simply the conditions under which they were asked to work; but no other group in the British Empire has done so much with such conditions. The Nationalists were the only minority that ever succeeded in twisting the whole British Parliament sharply out of its path. The Irish peasants are the only poor men in these islands who have forced their masters to disgorge. These people, whom we call priest-ridden, are the only Britons who will not be squire-ridden. And when I came to look at the actual Irish character, the case was the same. Irishmen are best at the specially hard professions—the trades, of iron, the lawyer, and the soldier. In all these cases, therefore, I came back to the same conclusion: the sceptic was quite right to go by the facts, only he had not looked at the facts. The sceptic is too credulous; he believes in newspapers or even in encyclopædias. Again the three questions left me with three very antagonistic questions. The average sceptic wanted to know how I explained the namby-pamby note in the Gospel, the connection of the creed with mediæval darkness and the political impracticability of the Celtic Christians. But I wanted to ask, and to ask with an earnestness amounting to urgency, "What is this incomparable energy which appears first in one walking the earth like a living judgment and this energy which can die with a dying civilization and yet force it to a resurrection from the dead; this energy which last of all can inflame a bankrupt peasantry with so fixed a faith in justice that they get what they ask, while others go empty away; so that the most helpless island of the Empire can actually help itself?"

There is an answer: it is an answer to say that the energy is truly from outside the world; that it is psychic, or at least one of the results of a real psychical disturbance. The highest gratitude and respect are due to the great human civilizations such as the old Egyptian or the existing Chinese. Nevertheless it is no injustice for them to say that only modern Europe has exhibited incessantly a power of self-renewal recurring often at the shortest intervals and descending to the smallest facts of building or costume. All other societies die finally and with dignity. We die daily. We are always being born again with almost indecent obstetrics. It is hardly an exaggeration to say that there is in historic Christendom a sort of unnatural life: it could be explained as a supernatural life. It could be explained as an awful galvanic life working in what would have been a corpse. For our civilization ought to have died, by all parallels, by all sociological probability, in the Ragnorak of the end of Rome. That is the weird inspiration of our estate: you and I have no business to be here at all. We are all revenants; all living Christians are dead pagans walking about. Just as Europe was about to be gathered in silence to Assyria and Babylon, something entered into its body. And Europe has had a strange life—it is not too much to say that it has had the jumps—ever since.

I have dealt at length with such typical triads of doubt in order to convey the main contention—that my own case for Christianity is rational; but it is not simple. It is an accumulation of varied facts, like the attitude of the ordinary agnostic. But the ordinary agnostic has got his facts all wrong. He is a nonbeliever for a multitude of reasons; but they are untrue reasons. He doubts because the Middle Ages were barbaric, but they weren't; because Darwinism is demonstrated,but it isn't; because miracles do not happen, but they do; because monks were lazy, but they were very industrious; because nuns are unhappy, but they are particularly cheerful; because Christian art was sad and pale, but it was picked out in peculiarly bright colours and gay with gold; because modern science is moving away from the supernatural, but it isn't, it is moving towards the supernatural with the rapidity of a railway train.

But among these million facts all flowing one way there is, of course, one question sufficiently solid and separate to be treated briefly, but by itself; I mean the objective occurrence of the supernatural. . . . My belief that miracles have happened in human history is not a mystical belief at all; I believe in them upon human evidences as I do in the discovery of America. Upon this point there is a simple logical fact that only requires to be stated and cleared up. Somehow or other an extraordinary idea has arisen that the disbelievers in miracles consider them coldly and fairly, while believers in miracles accept them only in connection with some dogma. The fact is quite the other way. The believers in miracles accept them (rightly or wrongly) because they have evidence for them. The disbelievers in miracles deny them (rightly or wrongly) because they have a doctrine against them. The open, obvious, democratic thing is to believe an old apple-woman when she bears testimony to a miracle, just as you believe an old apple-woman when she bears testimony to a murder. The plain, popular course is to trust the peasant's word about the ghost exactly as far as you trust the peasant's word about the landlord. Being a peasant he will probably have a great deal of healthy agnosticism about both. Still you could fill the British Museum with evidence uttered by the peasant, and given in favour of the ghost. If it comes to human testimony there is a choking cataract of human testimony in favour of the supernatural. If you reject it, you can only mean one of two things. You reject the peasant's story about the ghost either because the man is a peasant or because the story is a ghost story. That is, you either deny the main principle of democracy, or you affirm the main principle of materialism—the abstract impossibility of miracle. You have a perfect right to do so; but in that case you are the dogmatist. It is we Christians who accept all actual evidence—it is you rationalists who refuse actual evidence being constrained to do so by your creed. . . .

. . . It is only fair to add that there is another argument that the unbeliever may rationally use against miracles, though he himself generally forgets to use it. He may say that there has been in many miraculous stories a notion of spiritual preparation and acceptance: in short, that the miracle could only come to him who believed in it. It may be so, and if it is so how are we to test it? If we are inquiring whether certain results follow faith, it is useless to repeat wearily that (if they happen) they do follow faith. If faith is one of the conditions, those without faith have a most healthy right to laugh. But they have no right to judge. Being a believer may be, if you like, as bad as being drunk; still if we were extracting psychological facts from drunkards, it would be absurd to be always taunting them with having been drunk. Suppose we were investigating whether angry men really saw a red mist before their eyes. Suppose sixty excellent householders swore that when angry they had seen this crimson cloud: surely it would be absurd to answer "Oh, but you admit you were angry at the time." They might reasonably rejoin (in a stentorian chorus), "How the blazes could we discover, without being angry, whether angry people see red?" So the saints and ascetics might rationally reply, "Suppose that the question is whether believers can see visions—even then, if you are interested in visions it is no point to object to believers." You are still arguing in a circle—in that old mad circle with which this book began.

The question of whether miracles ever occur is a question of common sense and of ordinary historical imagination: not of any final physical experiment. One may here surely dismiss that quite brainless piece of pedantry which talks about the need for "scientific conditions" in connection with alleged spiritual phenomena. If we are asking whether a dead soul can communicate with a living it is ludicrous to insist that it shall be under conditions in which no two living souls in their senses would seriously communicate with each other. The fact that ghosts prefer darkness no more disproves the existence of ghosts than the fact that lovers prefer darkness disproves the existence of love. . . . It is as if I said that I could not tell if there was a fog because the air was not clear enough; or as if I insisted on perfect sunlight in order to see a solar eclipse.

As a common-sense conclusion, such as those to which we come about sex or about midnight (well knowing that many details must in their own nature be concealed) I conclude that miracles do happen. I am forced to it by a conspiracy of facts. . . . These supernatural things are never denied except on the basis either of anti-democracy or of materialist dogmatism—I may say materialist mysticism. The sceptic always takes one of the two positions; either an ordinary man need not be believed, or an extraordinary event must not be believed. For I hope we may dismiss the argument against wonders attempted in the mere recapitulation of frauds, of swindling mediums or trick miracles. That is not an argument at all, good or bad. A false ghost disproves the reality of ghosts exactly as much as a forged banknote disproves the existence of the Bank of England—if anything, it proves its existence. . . .

. . . All the real argument about religion turns on the question of whether a man who was born upside down can tell when he comes right way up. The primary paradox of Christianity is that the ordinary condition of man is not his sane or sensible condition; that the normal itself is an abnormality. That is the inmost philosophy of the Fall. In Sir Oliver Lodge's interesting new Catechism, the first two questions were: "What are you?" and "What, then, is the meaning of the Fall of Man?" I remember amusing myself by writing my own answers to the questions; but I soon found that they were very broken and agnostic answers. To the question, "What are you?" I could only answer, "God knows." And to the question, "What is meant by the Fall?" I could answer with complete sincerity, "That whatever I am, I am not myself." This is the prime paradox of our religion; something that we have never in any full sense known, is not only better than ourselves, but even more natural to us than ourselves. And there is really no test of this except the merely experimental one with which these pages began, the test of the padded cell and the open door. It is only since I have known orthodoxy that I have known mental emancipation. But, in conclusion, it has one special application to the ultimate idea of joy. . . .

Joy, which was the small publicity of the pagan, is the gigantic secret of the Christian. And as I close this chaotic volume I open again the strange small book from which all Christianity came; and I am again haunted by a kind of confirmation. The tremendous figure which fills the Gospels towers in this respect, as in every other, above all the thinkers who ever thought themselves tall. His pathos was natural, almost casual. The Stoics, ancient and modern, were proud of concealing their tears. He never concealed His tears; He showed them plainly on His open face at any daily sight, such as the far sight of His native city. Yet He concealed something. Solemn supermen and imperial diplomatists are proud of restraining their anger. He never restrained His anger. He flung furniture down the front steps of the Temple, and asked men how they expected to escape the damnation of Hell. Yet He restrained something. I say it with reverence; there was in that shattering personality a thread that must be called shyness. There was something that He hid from all men when He went up a mountain to pray. There was something that He covered constantly by abrupt silence or impetuous isolation. There was some one thing that was too great for God to show us when He walked upon our earth; and I have sometimes fancied that it was His mirth.

5

The Inspiration of the Bible

J. L. Dagg

In the preceding chapters it has been proved that the books of the New Testament were written by truthful men, and contain a faithful account of Christ and the doctrines which he taught. In the present chapter we are to investigate the claim of these writings, and those of the Old Testament, to divine authority. Are these books to be received by us as if immediately written by the finger of God?

It has been fully established that Jesus Christ exhibited satisfactory credentials of a mission from God to institute a religion for the benefit of mankind. Of his character and ministry the New Testament gives us an account, written by men who had the most favorable opportunities for knowing his history and doctrines, and who have left us their written testimony honestly given to the best of their knowledge and belief. The excellence of Christianity, its adaptedness to the general wants of men, and the evidences of its divine origin, make it obligatory on us to treat any credible account of it with respect, and derive from it all possible advantage towards attaining a knowledge of the religion. The New Testament professes to give full and exact information on the subject; and it is not only the best source of information, but the only original source on which we can rely. The writers of this book had devoted their lives to the study, practice, and dissemination of the new religion. Their conduct, their principles, their passions, had all been subjected to its rule. No teacher of philosophy or science was ever so devoted to his favorite pursuit. Nor were they unsuccessful instructors: but they taught their religion to hundreds of thousands who became proficient in the knowledge of the system, and gave practical demonstration of their attainments, and of its excellence. Now a written account of the system, prepared by these well-informed and successful teachers, and transmitted to us in a form well adapted to our use, is entitled to our respect, and ought to be highly prized by us. We should thankfully receive it as a benefit which Providence has kindly thrown in our way; and in consideration of the proof that the religion had a divine origin, we should feel our conscience bound to profit by all the information respecting it which Providence brings within our reach. In this view the New Testament, if regarded merely as a human composition, ought to bind our conscience; but as everything merely human is necessarily imperfect, it will add much to the confidence with which we bring our consciences to the rule of Scripture, if we can ascertain that the sacred writers were divinely inspired, and that what they have written may be received by us as the word of God, and used as an infallible guide in faith and practice.

Having ascertained that the Scriptures of the New Testament are worthy of our respect and confidence, as giving in general a faithful and true account of the Christian doctrine, we may safely proceed to inquire what they teach on the question of plenary inspiration.

Old Testament

The books of the Old Testament extant in Hebrew in the time of Christ, constituted the sacred canon of the Jews, publicly read in the synagogues. To it Christ and his apostles often appealed, as a rule of divine authority. Christ commanded to search the Scriptures (John, v. 39) with a view to learn and receive their testimony as indisputable truth. He charged the Jews with error, "not knowing the Scriptures" (Matt. xxii. 29). He taught that what the Scriptures had said must be accomplished (Matt. v. 18; Luke, xxi. 22; xxiv. 44), and, that "the Scriptures cannot be broken" (John, x. 35). And he accounted words recorded by Moses in the Pentateuch to be standing declarations of God to the people (Matt. xxii. 31, 32). The apostles in like manner ascribe to the Holy Spirit words which were written by David (Heb. iv. 7; Heb. iii. 7; Acts, ii. 30, 31; xiii. 32-37), and Isaiah (Acts, xxviii. 25). Though they preached the gospel under the influence of the Holy Spirit, they never claimed higher respect for their words than was due to the Scriptures of the Old Testament, but commended the Jews of Berea for testing their teaching by that infallible rule (Acts, xvii. 11). The prophecies committed to writing, as well as those orally delivered, are declared by the apostle Peter to have proceeded from the Holy Ghost (2 Peter, i. 20, 21). Paul, in writing to the Hebrews, after saying that God had spoken to the fathers by the prophets, refers to the instructions which they gave as contained in the Scriptures, and so complete does he regard the written rule, that he institutes an argument on its silence, "to which of the angels said he at any time, &c." (Heb. i. 13). In another epistle he declares, that the Scriptures in which Timothy had been instructed from his youth, are able to make wise unto salvation (2 Tim. iii. 15), and expressly affirms that they had been given by inspiration from God (2 Tim. iii. 16).

It is not necessary to assume the inspiration of the New Testament in order to render the above-cited passages decisive proof that Christ and his apostles accounted the Old Testament divinely inspired. As honest men merely, the apostles could not express other opinions on this subject than those which they really entertained; and on this point the supposition is inadmissible that they could have misunderstood or forgotten the doctrine of their master.

New Testament

The following arguments prove the plenary inspiration of the New Testament.

I. The revelation of the present dispensation is not less clear and certain than that of the former.

The Old Testament predicted that the new dispensation would be one of superior light, in which the knowledge of the Lord would cover the earth, (Isaiah, xi. 9). Messiah was to be a prophet, like unto Moses, to whom the people were to hearken (Deut. xviii. 15), and he was to be a light unto the Gentiles (Isaiah, xlii. 6; xlix. 6). It was foretold that extraordinary influences of the Spirit should be poured out, causing sons and daughters to prophesy (Joel, ii. 28, 29). John the Baptist exceeded all the prophets who preceded him; but so superior is the revelation of the new dispensation, that the least of those who enjoy it is superior in spiritual knowledge to John (Luke, vii. 28). But whatever may have been the superiority of the New Testament revelation at its outset, it could not have equalled that of the Old Testament in permanent advantage, if it had not been committed to writing without human error. If the New Testament is not a work of plenary inspiration, we have now less ground for confidence in what we have learned through Christ than in what we have learned through Moses.

II. The authority given by Christ to his apostles rendered plenary inspiration necessary to their office.

It was made the duty of the apostles to preach the gospel, and teach the observance of all things that Christ had commanded them; and the salvation of every creature who should hear them, was made dependent on his belief of their word. They were to determine whose sins should be remitted and retained, and what things should be binding on the consciences of men. Such was the authority with which their ministry was invested; and it therefore became the duty of all men to receive their word as the word of God. The promise which accompanied the commission, "Lo, I am with you always, even unto the end of the world" (Matt. xxviii 20), implies the perpetual force of the commission, and the obligation of men in all generations to receive the word of the apostles; and this obligation must now have respect to their written word, since their oral ministrations have forever ceased.

III. The apostles were under an extraordinary influence of the Holy Spirit guiding them into all truth.

Christ promised to his apostles that he would send the Holy Spirit to abide with them (John, xiv. 16), guide them into all truth (John, xvi. 13), and bring to their remembrance all things that he had taught (John, xiv. 26). This was precisely what they needed to qualify them to teach his doctrines and precepts with infallible certainty. And from the day of Pentecost, when the miraculous endowments came upon them, they became truly changed men. The cowardice which induced them to flee when their master was apprehended is now gone; and they boldly preach his gospel, fearless of danger. With new tongues they address the astonished multitudes; and with new skill quote and apply the Scriptures. They proclaim authoritatively on what terms sins shall be remitted, and they authoritatively direct the converts in their course of duty. These walked in the doctrines of the apostles with a full conviction that in so doing they were obeying God.

Less regard cannot now be due from us to the doctrine which we have received from the apostles in writing. The spirit which was given to abide with them did not desert them when they sat down to write, but a perfect remembrance of their master's teaching was not less needed or useful when they committed his doctrines and precepts to writing for the use of distant unborn generations, than when they were engaged in preaching his word.

IV. The apostles claimed that their preaching and writings were with plenary inspiration and divine authority.

In the first writing which the apostles sent forth, they said, "It seemed good to the Holy Ghost and to us" (Acts, xv. 28); and they sent forth the decree with divine authority for the observance of all Christians. Paul affirmed that the preaching of himself and other ministers was in demonstration of the spirit (1 Cor. ii. 4), "not in the words which man's wisdom teacheth, but which the Holy Ghost teacheth" (1 Cor. ii. 13), and that what he preached was the testimony of God (1 Cor. ii. 1). He pronounced an anathema on any who should preach any other gospel than that which he had preached (Gal. i. 8), and he commended those who had received it, not as the word of man, but, as it is, in truth, the word of God (1 Thes. ii. 13). His epistles did not teach a different gospel, but were sent to confirm the faith, correct the errors, and enlarge the spiritual knowledge of those to whom they were addressed; and he claimed as much respect for the gospel which he committed to writing as for that which he delivered orally. He expected what he wrote to be acknowledged by those who were endowed with spiritual discernment as "the commandments of the Lord" (1 Cor. xiv. 37).

At the close of the Epistle to the Romans a remarkable passage is introduced, affirming the inspiration and divine authority of the New Testament books; but its meaning is obscured by a faulty translation of the phrase, "the Scriptures of the prophets." In this phrase, as thus translated, the definite article occurs twice, though it is not found at all in the Greek original. The proper sense would be correctly expressed by the simple rendering, inspired writings. The entire passage teaches the following particulars: 1. At the age in which Paul lived, a new and greatly enlarged revelation was made to mankind. "According to the revelation of the mystery which was kept secret since the world began, but is now made manifest." 2. This revelation was in part made orally. "According to my gospel, and the preaching of Jesus Christ." 3. It was in part made in writing. "And by inspired writings made known to all nations for the obedience of faith." The scope of the passage shows that the writings here referred to are not the books left in the charge of the Hebrew nation by the ancient prophets; but writings which formed a part of the revelation made in the time of Paul, and published to all nations. 4. This revelation was made by divine authority, and was designed to be a rule of faith; "But now is made manifest, and by inspired writings, according to the commandment of the everlasting God, made known to all nations for the obedience of faith.". . .

V. The writings of the New Testament are quoted and referred to by the apostles as possessing equal authority with those of the Old Testament.

Paul quotes (1 Tim. v. 18) two passages as Scripture, one from Deuteronomy (Deut. xxv. 4), and the other from the Gospel of Luke (Luke, x. 7). Peter reckons the epistles of Paul as a part of the Scriptures which men abuse to their own destruction (2 Pet. iii. 15, 16). Peter, when he wrote his second epistle, and Paul, when he wrote his second to Timothy, had their decease in near prospect (2 Tim. iv. 6; 2 Pet. i. 15). They evinced much solicitude for those whom they were about to leave behind them, and earnestly recommended the Scriptures as a divinely inspired rule (2 Tim. iii. 16), an unerring light to guide (2 Pet. i. 19). These commendations of the Scriptures doubtless apply to those of the Old Testament, but there is reason to believe that they were designed to apply equally to those of the New Testament. Paul had quoted to Timothy the Gospel of Luke as Scripture, and he speaks of faith in Christ Jesus (2 Tim. iii. 15), in connection with the Scriptures, which he says are "able to make wise unto salvation, and are profitable to make the man of God perfect, thoroughly furnished unto every good work." Since Peter, in the same epistle in which he recommends the prophetic revelation of Scripture as a guide, has associated the epistles of Paul with the other Scriptures, we have reason to conclude that he esteemed these also as an unerring guide. When these two apostles wrote these passages, almost the whole of the New

Testament was written, and these passages may be taken as apostolic confirmation of the inspiration and authority of all the parts of it which were then in use. . . .

VI. The fulfilment of prophecy demonstrates the plenary inspiration of the Bible.

This argument applies to the Old Testament as well as to the New. In both, prophecies are recorded which have been fulfilled, and therefore the predictions were divinely inspired. Many of these predictions were not understood by the prophets who delivered or recorded them; and therefore they must have proceeded wholly from the Spirit which dictated them.

Mode of Inspiration

How the Holy Spirit operated on the minds of the sacred writers we are unable to explain. It is enough for us that God acknowledges what they have written to be his word. When he employed the tongues of the apostles to preach, they spoke in human language, and each with the voice peculiar to himself. Even the gift of tongues did not destroy the peculiarity of voice belonging to each, or set aside as useless the muscular power by which the tongue was moved. So the mental powers of the sacred writers were not set aside, but the divine wisdom has used them, and all the pecularities of style, and modes of thoughts, that distinguished the several writers, and has by means of them prepared just such a book as it was his pleasure to give to mankind.

Objections to Plenary Inspiration

It is objected that the word inspiration does not necessarily imply the communication of infallibility. We admit the objection, but we maintain that whatever God gives by inspiration is what he intended that it should be. Life was given to man by inspiration, for it is said, "God breathed into his nostrils the breath of life, and man became a living soul" (Gen. ii. 7). Understanding is given by inspiration, for it is said, "There is a spirit in man, and the inspiration of the Almighty giveth them understanding" (Job, xxxii. 8). Life and understanding are what God intended that they should be. Both these were possessed by the apostles, before Jesus breathed on them, and said, "Receive ye the Holy Ghost," and before he said to them, "Tarry ye in Jerusalem until ye be endued with power from on high." They were commissioned to preach the gospel to the world, and to teach the observance of all things that Christ had commanded; and the new and peculiar inspiration given to them, was designed to qualify them for this work. We may, therefore, conclude that the Scriptures which they have, in pursuance of their commission, left for the instruction of mankind, and which were given by divine inspiration for "instruction in righteousness," are what God intended that they should be.

It is objected that there is a human as well as a divine element in inspiration, and that, as the divine element must be perfect, so the human element must be imperfect. Our reply to this is, that inspiration is not in the proper sense a compound consisting of two distinct elements. God and man were both concerned in making revelation to the world; but their relation to each other was not that of partners. The design was God's, and the contrivance of the method was God's; and man had no partnership in either. When man was introduced into the work, it was not as a partner, but as an instrument; and the whole work was done with human instrumentality. If all with which man was concerned, is man's part, there is no other part left for God. We cannot say of a manuscript, that this portion is the author's part, and that portion the pen's; and, though the instrumentality of man in the work of revelation is different from that of an unconscious pen, it is nevertheless instrumentality. The whole of revelation is the work of God as the author; the whole is the work of man as the instrument; and the whole has this perfection, that it exactly fulfils the design of him who designed it.

It is objected that inspiration is positive, not negative, imparting truth to the minds of the inspired, without banishing their errors; and that, in this particular, it is like the ordinary influences of the Spirit, which have a sanctifying effect on the believer without annihilating his depravity. It is a fundamental error in this objection, that it contemplates inspiration as designed merely for the benefit of the inspired: whereas it is clear that God gave his word to be spoken and written by prophets and apostles for the instruction and benefit of other men, who were required to receive it, not as the word of man, but as in truth the word of God, attested by miracles. Positively, it is divine truth; negatively, it is not human error.

Infidels allege that the Bible contains mistakes in history and science, and that some parts of it are inconsistent with others; and on these allegations they found their most successful arguments against the credibility of the book. The chief of these alleged mistakes and inconsistencies are examined in other parts of this volume. . . . The result of the investigation will be found to be a great abatement, if not a complete removal of the difficulties; and it will be seen that the remaining difficulties, whatever may be their magnitude, do not reach the vital question concerning the divine origin of Christianity, but lie merely as objections against the plenary inspiration of the Scriptures. If there are imperfections in the Bible, it has in spite of them conferred such blessings on mankind as must have had their source in divine benevolence. If it contains mistakes and inconsistencies, it also contains systems of morality, doctrines, and prophecy, which must have proceeded from superhuman wisdom. And if there is in it an element of human weakness, it contains also a truthful record of miracles which must have been wrought by the power of God, and which were wrought in attestation of the religion that the book teaches. Hence the proper evidences of Christianity are not affected by the alleged imperfection of the sacred record.

Regarding the difficulties from this class of infidel objections, as relating properly to the doctrine of plenary inspiration, the present becomes the proper place for considering them; and it will be proper to inquire how are these difficulties to be disposed of, and what is our duty respecting them. On this subject the following observations are offered:

1. The investigation which has been made of the alleged facts, not only lessens very greatly the difficulties with which they were thought to embarrass the doctrine of plenary inspiration, but in some cases it furnishes proof of the minute accuracy and truthfulness of the inspired record. It is our duty to prosecute such investigations as we have opportunity, and we have reason to expect that these investigations will continue to lessen the

difficulties of the subject, and present the divine authority of the entire Bible in a clear light.

2. The difficulties which past investigations have not already removed, have very little weight when compared with the amount of evidence on which our belief of plenary inspiration rests. A well-balanced mind will yield its judgment to preponderating evidence, and will not give up to universal scepticism, because of the difficulties which everywhere attend belief even of demonstrated truth. Our senses sometimes deceive us; and even consciousness sometimes permits men to think themselves different from what they really are; but we must not, therefore, wholly reject the testimony of consciousness and the senses, and doubt our own existence and the existence of the world around us. We rightly confide in the testimony of consciousness and the senses, though we may be unable to explain away their possible illusions, and establish their universal credibility; and we ought to receive with unwavering faith the demonstrated truth that the Bible is the word of God, notwithstanding some difficulties respecting it that may remain unexplained.

3. The perfection which the doctrine of plenary inspiration attributes to the Bible, consists in its being what God intended that it should be. Men may sit in judgment on the works of God in creation and providence, and pronounce them in many particulars different from what might rationally be expected to proceed from infinite wisdom, power, and goodness; and, in like manner, they may judge that the Bible contains things that reason decides to be unsuitable to a divine revelation. But, in both these cases, it is our wisdom and duty to let God judge for himself. The evidence that God made the world and the Bible vastly preponderates over all the difficulties of our folly and scepticism. If we cannot account for some things which we meet with in the world and in the Bible, we should be willing to leave them unexplained until we have further light.

4. The perfection of the Bible does not imply that its language is perfect. The language is human, and human language is not a perfect vehicle of thought; but God has chosen to employ this vehicle; and, even if we could assign no reason for his choice, we may rest assured that it was wise, and that his design has not thereby been frustrated. Our duty is to accept the revelation as

he has given it to us, and to apply to it the proper rules for the interpretation of human language, that we may learn from it the divine truth which it conveys.

5. The perfection which our doctrine attributes to the Scriptures, belongs properly to the autographs of the prophets and apostles. God has not judged it necessary to work a continual miracle of inspiration, to preserve all the written and printed copies of his word from every possible error. As he has judged thus, so ought we; and we ought, therefore, thankfully to receive the copies and versions of his holy word, as they have come to us under his overruling providence, notwithstanding any imperfections which may have arisen from the uninspired agency of those who have copied, printed, or translated it. But it is also our duty to employ whatever means may be in our power for approaching as nearly as possible to the precise language and meaning of the inspired originals.

It is our duty thankfully to acknowledge the goodness of God in that the evidences of his religion, and the great truths of his gospel, may be clearly seen, and confidently received, unaffected by the difficulties respecting the comparatively unimportant matters on which the objections now under consideration are founded.

6

The Infallibility of the Bible

James Orr

While, by most of the older writers, the inspiration of the entire record in the Bible is strenuously affirmed, great diversity of view prevails as to the mode of the action of the divine influence by which this result is secured. Theories of dictation of historical matter, or of communication of facts that could be ascertained by ordinary methods, are now universally surrendered; the distinction of 'revelation' and 'inspiration' is better recognised; but whereas some would lay chief stress on the exaltation of the human faculties, and conscious direction and 'suggestion,' others are content to resolve inspiration into a divine 'superintendence,' often unconscious, leaving everything else—and this the greater part—in the production of an 'errorless' record to 'providence.' The question which here arises is—Does the Bible itself claim, or inspiration necessitate, such an 'errorless' record, in matters of minor detail? The discussion may close with a few words on this subject of 'inerrancy.'

1. Very commonly it is argued by upholders of this doctrine that 'inerrancy' in every minute particular is involved in the very idea of a book given by inspiration of God. This might be held to be true on a theory of verbal dictation, but it can scarcely be maintained on a just view of the actual historical genesis of the Bible. One may plead, indeed, for 'a supernatural providential guidance' which has for its aim to exclude all, even the least, error or discrepancy in statement, even such as may inhere in the sources from which the information is obtained, or may arise from corruption of anterior documents. But this is a violent assumption which there is nothing in the Bible really to support. It is perilous, therefore, to seek to pin down faith to it as a matter of vital moment. Inspiration, in sanctioning the incorporation of an old genealogy, or of an historic document in some respects defective, no more makes itself responsible for these defects than it does for the speeches of Job's friends in the Book of Job, or for the sentiments of many parts of the Book of Ecclesiastes, or for the imperfect translation of Old Testament passages in quotations from the Septuagint.

2. Even on the assumption of a 'verbal' inspiration, it has been seen in how wide a sense literal accuracy in the Biblical records has to be interpreted. The theory may be stretched, moreover, by qualifications, admissions, and explanations, till there is practically little difference between the opposite views.

Thus, writing on the New Testament quotations, with reference to the objection of Dr. S. Davidson that, on the theory of verbal inspiration, the New Testament writers should have adhered to the *ipsissima verba* of the Holy Spirit in the Old Testament, seeing these were best, the able defenders of an 'errorless' record already repeatedly cited remark: 'Here, however, a false view of inspiration is presupposed, and also a false view of the nature and laws of quotation. Inspiration does not suppose that the words and phrases written under its influence are the best possible to express the truth, but only that they are an adequate expression of the truth. Other words and phrases might be equally adequate:—might furnish a clearer, more exact, and therefore better expression, especially of those truths which were subordinate or incidental for the original purpose of the writings.' It would be difficult, however, to show that this superiority always belongs to the LXX. renderings adopted. More generally, we have such wide acknowledgments as the following: 'It is not claimed that the Scriptures any more than their authors are omniscient. The information they convey is in the forms of human thought, and limited on all sides. They were not designed to teach philosophy, science, or human history as such. They were not designed to furnish an infallible system of speculative theology. They are written in human languages, whose words, inflections, constructions, and idioms bear everywhere indelible traces of human error. The record itself furnishes evidence that the writers were in large measure dependent for their knowledge upon sources and methods in themselves fallible, and that their personal knowledge and judgments were in many matters hesitating and defective, or even wrong.' So much being admitted, it hardly seems worth while to deny the compatibility of inspiration with the possibility of minor errors also in the matter of the record. Yet 'the *ipsissima verba* of the original autographs' are held to be free from the slightest taint of such error.

3. These things have in justice to be said on the one side. On the other side, one finds himself in substantial harmony with the defenders of this view in affirming that the sweeping assertions

of error and discrepancy in the Bible often made cannot be substantiated. Ascribe it to 'providence,' to 'superintendence,' to 'suggestion,' or what one will,—and inspiration is probably more subtle and all-pervading than any of these things,—it remains the fact that the Bible, impartially interpreted and judged, is free from demonstrable error in its statements, and harmonious in its teachings, to a degree that of itself creates an irresistible impression of a supernatural factor in its origin. It is of little profit to discuss such a subject as 'inerrancy' in the abstract. When the objector descends from generalities to details, one knows where to find him; and here, in cases without number, it has been shown by the progress of knowledge that it is he, not the Bible, that is wrong. Many of the alleged discrepancies are such only in appearance, or are readily explained by difference in point of view or aim, or from technicalities of structure, as in genealogies, or from methods of grouping and generalising, where precise detail is not aimed at. Some are due to corruption in the texts—this frequently in names and numbers—either in the existing texts, or possibly in the MSS. sources used by the sacred writer himself. Archæology has brought confirmation to the statements of the Bible, even in its oldest parts, in a multitude of particulars in which its accuracy had been confidently challenged. Illustration of these assertions has been furnished in abundance elsewhere. When, in smaller matters, discrepancy is urged, as, e.g., in the various reports of the titles of the Cross, it is time for the discussion to stop.

4. On this broad, general ground the advocates of 'inerrancy' may always feel that they have a strong position, whatever assaults may be made on them in matters of lesser detail. They stand undeniably, in their main contention, in the line of apostolic belief, and of the general faith of the Church, regarding Holy Scripture. The most searching inquiry still leaves them with a Scripture, supernaturally inspired to be an infallible guide in the great matters for which it was given—the knowledge of the will of God for their salvation in Christ Jesus, instruction in the way of holiness, and the 'hope of eternal life, which God, who cannot lie, promised before times eternal' (Titus 1:2).

7

Biblical Criticism

James Orr

Criticism at every period inevitably reverts to the Gospels, for it is in them that the kernel of the whole Bible is to be sought. If God has spoken anywhere to man, it is in the person of His Son. In Christ's life, Christ's words, Christ's character, Christ's witness to the Father, we have the essence and acme of the whole Divine self-revelation. If, then, it is desired to do away with this revelation—to challenge its foundations or world-wide significance—it is the Gospels which must always bear the final brunt of the assault. For it is through the Gospels alone that we know Christ. If they can be trusted, they leave us in no doubt as to who He is, what He claimed, how He lived, what He said, how He acted, and the sequel of His life in death and resurrection. The picture is no ambiguous one. Its main features are patent to every reader. The figure of Jesus in the Gospels is the cornerstone of the Christian religion. What must first be done, if the revelation is to be got rid of, is to dislodge this stone. . . .

It is not overlooked that there is a genuine criticism of the Gospels, reverent in spirit, and following proper methods, from which immense gains are surely reaped for the better understanding of the Gospels. Interesting problems arise with regard to the relation of the first three Gospels to each other (the Synoptical problems, as they are called), to the sources from which these Gospels drew their materials (oral or written; dependence of one on another), and to the relation of all three to the Fourth Gospel, so different in structure and style. Into these questions, which lie within the sphere of faith in the Gospels, it is not proposed here to enter. The more weighty matter is: How far do the Gospels—the first three (Synoptics) and the Fourth Gospel—justify the claim made on their behalf to be genuine apostolic productions, and trustworthy records of the sayings and doings of Him whom we call Master and Lord? On this, the central and essential issue, for the help of faith, a few words may be said.

What is to be said on the historical question can be briefly summarised. Prejudice apart, it would be difficult to conceive a stronger case, on the ground of historical tradition, than that for the genuine and apostolic character of our four Gospels—Matthew, Mark, Luke, and John. These Gospels are at the head of the writings which, as the historian Eusebius tells, were never "controverted" in the Church. They are undoubtedly the Gospels which, in Justin Martyr's time, were, along with the prophets, read Sunday by Sunday in the assemblies of the Christians. A disciple of Justin's, Tatian, made a "Harmony" of the four, which has been recovered. The Fathers in the end of the second century used the Gospels as inspired productions, the authority of which was beyond all question. They knew no other Gospels to be put in the same rank as they. They are found in all lists of the canonical writings. They appear in all versions into other languages—Latin, Syriac, Egyptian, etc. Moreover, there is a firm tradition connecting the Gospels with their respective authors. Reasonable doubt cannot rest on the ascription of the Second Gospel to John Mark of Jerusalem, companion of both Paul and Peter. Luke's authorship of the Third Gospel and of the Acts has recently received a splendid vindication from Professor Harnack, of Berlin, at the cost of severance from the school of criticism with which he was before associated. That Matthew stands behind the First Gospel seems a fair result of criticism, though there is yet dispute as to whether his relation to it, in its present Greek form, is mediate or immediate. This, at least, is certain, that the Greek Gospel was from the first, and always, accepted in the Church as representing the genuine Gospel of Matthew. In the words of Westcott: "All early writers agree that Matthew wrote in Hebrew [Aramaic]. . . . At the same time, all equally agree in accepting the Gospel of Matthew without noticing the existence of any doubt as to its authenticity."

It is not different with the apostolic authorship of the Gospel of John, keenly as that has been controverted. External and internal evidence alike point decisively to the Gospel as the genuine work of the beloved disciple. Dr. James Drummond (Unitarian) does not exaggerate when he says: "The external evidence is all on one side." The trustworthiness of the Gospel is touched on below.

The conclusion to which this leads is that, in accordance with the testimony of tradition, the Gospels are genuine apostolic documents. They fall within the apostolic age, and are of apostolic origin. While not themselves Apostles, the writers (Mark and Luke) still convey the apostolic testimony given to the Church. Mark is described as the "interpreter" of Peter. Luke records that which has been delivered by those "who from the beginning were eye-witnesses and ministers of the word" (i. 2). The basis of the Gospel is rock, not sand.

It is not desired to argue from authorities; but in view of frequent assertions as to the trend of criticism, two leading names may be mentioned. Professor Harnack, of Berlin, will be admitted to be the highest living authority on Early Church history and literature. But Harnack declares that the whole tendency of recent research has been to re-establish the authority of tradition as respects the New Testament books, and to show that "the earliest literature of the Church is in its principal points and in most of its details, historically regarded, veracious and reliable." In regard to Luke's authorship of the Gospel and Acts he claims to prove "that criticism has gone wrong, and that tradition is right." Who, again, is, out of sight, the most learned scholar in New Testament criticism? Without doubt, Professor Zahn, of Erlangen. But in his *magnum opus* on this subject, a translation of which has just appeared, Zahn confirms what has above been affirmed of the age and apostolic character of the Four Gospels.

The trustworthiness of the Gospels, which is the main thing, is already largely established when one has made good their substantial apostolic origin. For years the Apostles wrought and taught together in Jerusalem. There, it may be assumed, their testimony took a relatively fixed form for catechetical purposes. In this form, orally, or in written shape, it was communicated to the various Churches, and finally found embodiment in the written Gospels (Luke i. 1-4). Resting, as the corroborative testimony of the first three evangelists shows, on first-hand apostolic witness, it has the highest guarantee of truth. There was no time for the extensive growth of legend, and the presence of elements contradicting the recognised tradition would at once have been detected and condemned.

To rest the trustworthiness of the Gospel narratives merely on historical evidence, however, is to put it on all too low a ground. There is an evidence internal to the matter itself which is even more potent in producing conviction of its truthfulness. Had no external evidence existed—had the Gospels come into our hands for the first time without any knowledge of the circumstances of their origin—we should still have been entitled, nay, constrained, to receive them as authentic. Who could have invented the sayings ascribed to Jesus—His parables, the Sermon on the Mount, the words of inimitable freshness, beauty, originality, and spiritual power which form the substance of the record? Mr. J. S. Mill was not a man of deep spiritual insight, but he wrote with truth: "It is no use to say that Christ as exhibited in the Gospels is not historical, and that we know not how much of what is admirable has been superadded by the traditions of His followers. . . . Who among His disciples or among their proselytes was capable of inventing the sayings ascribed to Jesus, or of imagining the life and character revealed in the Gospels?" Not one.

This last sentence of Mr. Mill's touches the supreme guarantee for the historicity of the Gospels—the image of Jesus Himself which they enshrine. If that image—so unique, perfect, original, divine—is not historically real, how did it originate? Who conceived it, and reduced it to this perfect historical form in word and act? Is Christ a creation of His own Church, a Church gathered out promiscuously from Jews and Gentiles, with no historical tradition to work on—a Church which even yet, after nineteen centuries, is only dimly rising to the adequate apprehension of the Master's thoughts and ideals! The supposition is absurd. But that image is constructed from the materials in the Gospels. If they vanish, it vanishes also. The Christ-figure in the Gospels is the sun-clear demonstration of the truth of the narratives. How simple, yet how sublime it all is! How reticent in detail, yet throwing into grandest relief the central Personality! How free from ostentation, yet producing the overwhelming impression of holiness and greatness! Not only is the record true; it could only be there as the product of God-inspired minds!

A marked contrast exists in scope and style between the first three Gospels and the Gospel of John. On this ground the historicity of the Fourth Gospel is often denied. Criticism here is becoming more sober, and is recognising more freely the essential oneness of the picture in the Synoptics and in John (e.g., Bousset). The contrasts, though real, may easily be exaggerated, and admit of explanation on simpler grounds. John's is the latest of the Gospels, and presupposes the others as well known. It does not, therefore, go over the ground they had already covered. It confines itself largely to matters drawn from John's personal recollections, chiefly the Judæan ministry, the visits of Christ to Jerusalem, and His last private discourses to His disciples. These are reproduced as they had passed through the crucible of much thought and reflection in the evangelist's own mind, and an interpretative element is blended with them, which it is sometimes difficult to disengage from Christ's bare words. It aims, too, at a doctrinal result—the confirming of faith in Jesus as the Divine Son of God (xx. 31). Withal there need not be the slightest hesitation in accepting the Gospel as a veracious record of the thoughts, words, and deeds of the Master, as John knew and loved Him. It is, as saints in all ages have felt, the truly "spiritual" Gospel, the unveiling of the eternal Christ in the historical Jesus. Nothing is wanting to the humanity. The Jesus of John's Gospel is born, suffers, dies; thirsts and is weary; sorrows, sympathises, weeps; experiences all true human emotions. But He is none the less everywhere manifest as the Word made flesh (i. 14), the ultimate revelation of the Father (i. 18; xiv. 9, 10), the God-sent Saviour of the world (iv. 42). In John the message of the whole Gospel culminates.

8

Religious Language

Horace Bushnell

I do not propose, in the dissertation that follows, to undertake a full investigation of language. I freely acknowledge my incompetence to any such undertaking. What I design is, principally, to speak of language as regards its significancy, or the power and capacity of its words, taken as vehicles of thought and of spiritual truth. What I may offer concerning other topics involved in the general subject, such as the origin of language; the phonology of words, or the reason why certain things are named by certain sounds, and not by others; letters and the written forms of words; laws of grammar; questions of ethnology, and the like; will be advanced in a purely incidental way, and with no other design than to make my theory of the significance of words more intelligible and clear. I cannot promise that I shall fall into no mistakes which the learned philologists and grammarians will detect, though I have little fear that they will discover any important error in what I advance, in regard to the philosophy of words, taken as instruments of thought, which is the particular subject under discussion. . . .

There are, as we discover, two languages, in fact, in every language. Or perhaps I shall be understood more exactly, if I say that there are, in every human tongue, two distinct departments. First, there is a literal department, in which sounds are provided as names for physical objects and appearances. Secondly, there is a department of analogy or figure, where physical objects and appearances are named as images of thought or spirit, and the words get their power, as words of thought, through the physical images received into them. Thus, if I speak of my pen, I use a word in the first department of language, uttering a sound which stands for the instrument with which I write. But if I speak of the spirit of a man, or the sincerity of a Christian, I use words that belong to the second department of language, where the sounds do not stand for the mental ideas as being names directly applied to them, but represent, rather, certain images in the physical state, which are the natural figures or analogies of those mental ideas. How it was necessary, in the genesis of language, that it should fall into this twofold distribution, has been shown already. The man who knows his tongue only by vernacular usage, is aware of no such distribution. Many, who are considered to be educated persons, and are truly so, are but half aware of it. At least, they notice only now and then, when speaking of matters pertaining to thought and spirit, that a word brought into use has a physical image in it. For example, when speaking of a good man's heart, they observe that the word has a physical image connected with it, or that it names also a vital organ of the body. Then they either say, that the word has two meanings, a physical and a spiritual, not observing any law of order or connection by which the physical becomes the basis or type of the spiritual; or, they raise a distinction between what they call the literal and figurative uses of the word. But this distinction of literal and figurative, it does not appear to be noticed, even by philologists, runs through the very body of the language itself, making two departments; one that comprises the terms of sensation, and the other the terms of thought. They notice, in the historical investigation of words, that they are turning up all the while, a subsoil of physical bases; and, though they cannot find in every particular case, the physical term on which the word is built, they attain to a conviction that every word has a physical root, if only it could be found; and yet the natural necessity, that all words relating to thought and spirit should be figures, and as such, get their significance, they do not state. They still retain the impression that some of the terms of thought are literal, and some figurative.

This is the manner of the theologians. They assume that there is a literal terminology in religion as well as a figurative, (as doubtless there is, in reference to matters of outward fact and history, but nowhere else,) and then it is only a part of the same mistake to accept words, not as signs or images, but as absolute measures and equivalents of truth; and so to run themselves, by their argumentations, with a perfectly unsuspecting confidence, into whatever conclusions the logical forms of the words will carry them. Hence, in great part, the distractions, the infinite multiplications of opinion, the errors and sects and strifes of the Christian world. We can never come into a settled consent in the truth, until we better understand the nature, capacities and incapacities of language, as a vehicle of truth.

In order, now, that I may excite our younger theologians especially to a new investigation of this subject, as being fundamental, in fact, to the right understanding of religious truth, I will dismiss the free form of dissertation, and set forth, under numerical indications, a series of points or positions inviting each their attention, and likely, though with some modifications, perhaps, to be finally verified.

1. Words of thought and spirit are possible in language only in virtue of the fact that there are forms provided in the world of sense, which are cognate to the mind, and fitted, by reason of some hidden analogy, to represent or express its interior sentiments and thoughts.

2. Words of thought and spirit are, in fact, names of such forms or images existing in the outward or physical state.

3. When we investigate the relation of the form, or etymological base, in any word of thought or spirit, to the idea expressed, we are able to say (negatively) that the idea or thought has no such form, or shape, or sensible quality, as the word has. If I speak of *right (straight, rectus,)* it is not because the internal law of the conscience, named by this word, has any straightness or lineal quality whatever. Or if I speak of *sin, peccatum,* ἁμαρτία, where, in so many languages, as I might also show in a great variety of others, the image at the root of the word is one of lineal divarication, (as when an arrow is shot at the mark, and misses or turns aside,) it is not because sin, as a moral state of being, or a moral act, has any lineal form in the mind. Thoughts, ideas, mental states, we cannot suppose have any geometric form, any color, dimensions, or sensible qualities whatever.

4. We can also say, (positively) in reference to the same subject, that there is always some reason in every form or image made use of, why it should be used; some analogic property or

quality which we feel instinctively, but which wholly transcends speculative inquiry. If there is no lineal straightness in rectitude, no linear crookedness or divarication in sin, taken as an internal state, still it is the instinct of our nature to feel some sense of correspondence between these images and the states they represent. . . .

5. There are no words, in the physical department of language, that are exact representatives of particular physical things. For whether we take the theory of the Nominalists or the Realists, the words are, in fact, and practically, names only of genera, not of individuals or species. To be even still more exact, they represent only certain sensations of sight, touch, taste, smell, hearing—one or all. Hence the opportunity in language, for endless mistakes and false reasonings, in reference to matters purely physical.

6. It follows, that as physical terms are never exact, being only names of genera, much less have we any terms in the spiritual department of language that are exact representatives of thought. For, first, the word here used will be the name only of a genus of physical images. Then, secondly, it will have been applied over to signify a genus of thoughts or sentiments. And now, thirdly, in a particular case, it is drawn out to signify a specific thought or sentiment which, of course, will have qualities or incidents peculiar to itself. What, now, can steer a word through so many ambiguities and complications, and give it an exact and determinate meaning in the particular use it is applied to serve? . . .

What, then, it may be asked, is the real and legitimate use of words, when applied to moral subjects? for we cannot dispense with them, and it is uncomfortable to hold them in universal scepticism, as being only instruments of error. Words, then, I answer, are legitimately used as the signs of thoughts to be expressed. They do not literally convey, or pass over a thought out of one mind into another, as we commonly speak of doing. They are only hints, or images, held up before the mind of another, to put him on generating or reproducing the same thought; which he can do only as he has the same personal contents, or the generative power out of which to bring the thought required. Hence, there will be different measures of understanding or misunderstanding, according to the capacity or incapacity, the ingenuousness or moral obliquity of the receiving party—even if the communicating party offers only truth, in the best and freshest forms of expression the language provides.

There is only a single class of intellectual words that can be said to have a perfectly determinate significance, viz., those which relate to what are called necessary ideas. They are such as time, space, cause, truth, right, arithmetical numbers, and geometrical figures. Here the names applied, are settled into a perfectly determinate meaning, not by any peculiar virtue in them, but by reason of the absolute exactness of the ideas themselves. Time cannot be anything more or less than time; truth cannot, in its idea, be anything different from truth; the numerals suffer no ambiguity of count or measure; a circle must be a circle; a square, a square. As far as language, therefore, has to do with these, it is a perfectly exact algebra of thought, but no farther. . . .

7. Words of thought or spirit are not only inexact in their significance, never measuring the truth or giving its precise equivalent, but they always affirm something which is false, or contrary to the truth intended. They impute form to that which really is out of form. They are related to the truth, only as form to spirit—earthen vessels in which the truth is borne, yet always offering their mere pottery as being the truth itself. Bunyan beautifully represents their insufficiency and earthiness when he says—

> "My dark and cloudy words, they do but hold
> The truth, as cabinets inclose the gold."

—only it needs to be added, that they palm off upon us, too often, their "dark and cloudy" qualities as belonging inherently to the golden truths they are used to express. Therefore, we need always to have it in mind, or in present recollection, that they are but signs, in fact, or images of that which has no shape or sensible quality whatever; a kind of painting, in which the speaker, or the writer, leads on through a gallery of pictures or forms, while we attend him, catching at the thoughts suggested by his forms. In one view, they are all false; for there are no shapes in the truths they represent, and therefore we are to separate continually, and by a most delicate process of art, between the husks of the forms and the pure truths of thought presented in them. We do this insensibly, to a certain extent, and yet we do it imperfectly, often. A very great share of our theological questions, or disputes, originate in the incapacity of the parties to separate truths from their forms, or to see how the same essential truth may clothe itself under forms that are repugnant. There wants to be a large digestion, so to speak, of form in the teacher of theology or mental philosophy, that he may always be aware how the mind and truth, obliged to clothe themselves under the laws of space and sensation, are taking, continually, new shapes or dresses—coming forth poetically, mystically, allegorically, dialectically, fluxing through definitions, symbols, changes of subject and object, yet remaining still the same; for if he is wanting in this, if he is a mere logician, fastening on a word as the sole expression and exact equivalent of a truth, to go on spinning his deductions out of the form of the word, (which yet have nothing to do with the idea,) then he becomes an opinionist only, quarreling, as for truth itself, with all who chance to go out of his word; and, since words are given, not to imprison souls, but to express them, the variations continually indulged by others are sure to render him as miserable in his anxieties, as he is meagre in his contents, and busy in his quarrels. . . .

8. But if we are liable thus to be carried away by the forms contained in our words, into conclusions or impressions that do not belong to the truths they are used to signify, we are also to peruse their forms with great industry, as being, at the same time, a very important key to their meaning. The original type or etymology of words is a most fruitful study. . . .

9. Since all words, but such as relate to necessary truths, are inexact representations of thought, mere types or analogies, or, where the types are lost beyond recovery, only proximate expressions of the thoughts named; it follows that language will be

ever trying to mend its own deficiencies, by multiplying its forms of representation. As, too, the words made use of generally carry something false with them, as well as something true, associating form with the truths represented, when really there is no form; it will also be necessary, on this account, to multiply words or figures, and thus to present the subject on opposite sides or many sides. Thus, as form battles form, and one form neutralizes another, all the insufficiencies of words are filled out, the contrarieties liquidated, and the mind settles into a full and just apprehension of the pure spiritual truth. Accordingly we never come so near to a truly well rounded view of any truth, as when it is offered paradoxically; that is, under contradictions; that is, under two or more dictions, which, taken as dictions, are contrary one to the other.

Hence the marvelous vivacity and power of that famous representation of Pascal: "What a chimera, then, is man! What a novelty! What a chaos! What a subject of contradiction! A judge of every thing, and yet a feeble worm of the earth; the depositary of truth, and yet a mere heap of uncertainty; the glory and the outcast of the universe. If he boasts, I humble him; if he humbles himself, I boast of him; and always contradict him, till he is brought to comprehend that he is an incomprehensible monster."

Scarcely inferior in vivacity and power is the familiar passage of Paul;—"as deceivers, and yet true; as unknown, and yet well known; as dying, and behold, we live; as chastened, and not killed; as sorrowful, yet always rejoicing; as poor, yet making many rich; as having nothing, yet possessing all things."

So, also, it will be found, that the poets often express their most inexpressible, or evanescent thoughts, by means of repugnant or somewhat paradoxical epithets; as, for example, Coleridge, when he says,—

> "The stilly murmur of the distant sea
> Tells us of silence."

Precisely here, too, I suppose, we come upon what is really the true conception of the Incarnation and the Trinity. These great Christian mysteries or paradoxes, come to pass under the same conditions or laws which pertain to language. All words are, in fact, only incarnations, or insensings of thought. If we investigate the relations of their forms to the truths signified, we have the same mystery before us; if we set the different, but related forms in comparison, we have the same aspect of repugnance or inconsistency. And then we have only to use the repugnant forms as vehicles of pure thought, dismissing the contradictory matter of the forms, and both words and the Word are understood without distraction,—all by the same process. . . .

10. It is part of the same view, that logic itself is a defective, and often deceitful instrument. I speak not here of logic as a science, but of that deductive, proving, spinning method of practical investigation, commonly denoted by the term logical. It is very obvious, that no turn of logical deduction can prove anything, by itself, not previously known by inspection or insight. And yet, there is always a busy-minded class of sophists or speculators, who, having neither a large observation, nor a power of poetic insight, occupy themselves as workers in words and propositions, managing to persuade themselves and others that they are great investigators, and even discoverers of truth. . . .

It seems to be supposed, or rather assumed, by the class of investigators commonly called logical, that after the subject matter of truth has been gotten into propositions, and cleared, perhaps, by definitions, the faculty of intuition, or insight, may be suspended, and we may go on safely, to reason upon the forms of the words themselves, or the "analogy the words bear to each other." And so, by the mere handling of words and propositions, they undertake to evolve, or, as they commonly speak, to prove important truths. They reason, not by or through formulas, but upon them. After the formulas are got ready, they shut their eyes to all interior inspection of their terms, as in algebra, and commit themselves to the mere grammatic laws or predications of their words—expecting, under these, by inversion, evolution, equation, *reductio ad absurdum*, and the like, to work out important results. And this is popularly called reasoning. They do not seem to be aware that this grammatic, or constructive method, while it is natural as language itself, having its forms in what I have called the grammar of the soul and of the creation, is yet analogical only to truth and spirit—a warp that is furnished out of form and sense, for the connecting into speech of symbols or types that lie in form and sense; on which account, propositions are called formulas, or little forms. Or we may represent the constructive method of logic and grammar as the iron track of speech, along which the separate cars of words, connected by iron copulas, are drawn out into regular trains, and determinate courses of motion; which iron track and copulas, however, we are not to fancy, are at all more intellectual, closer to the truth of reason, or less analogical than the separate cars themselves. And, therefore, whatever is wrought out by the combination of formulas, (of course I do not question the syllogism which really works out nothing,) having only a certain analogical or tropical force, must be received by insight, as all symbols are, not as any absolute conclusion, or sentence of reason. . . .

11. In the reading or interpretation of an author, writing on intellectual and moral subjects, we are to observe, first of all, whether he takes up some given word or figure, and makes it a law to his thinking. If some symbol that he uses to-day stands by him also to-morrow, rules his doctrine, shapes his argument, drawing every thing into formal consistency with it, then we are to take up the presumption that he is out of the truth, and set ourselves to find where his mistake is. . . .

12. If we find the writer, in hand, moving with a free motion, and tied to no one symbol, unless in some popular effort, or for some single occasion; if we find him multiplying antagonisms, offering cross views, and bringing us round the field to show us how it looks from different points, then we are to presume that he has some truth in hand which it becomes us to know. We are to pass round accordingly with him, take up all his symbols, catch a view of him here, and another there, use one thing to qualify and interpret another, and the other to shed light upon that, and, by a process of this kind, endeavor to comprehend his antagonisms, and settle into a complete view of his meaning.

13. The views of language and interpretation I have here

offered, suggest the very great difficulty, if not impossibility of mental science and religious dogmatism. In all such uses or attempted uses, the effort is to make language answer a purpose that is against its nature. . . .

. . . Poets, then, are the true metaphysicians, and if there be any complete science of man to come, they must bring it.

Is it to be otherwise in religion? Can there be produced, in human language, a complete and proper Christian theology; can the Christian truth be offered in the molds of any dogmatic statement? What is the Christian truth? Pre-eminently and principally, it is the expression of God—God coming into expression, through histories and rites, through an incarnation, and through language—in one syllable, by the WORD. The endeavor is, by means of expression, and under the laws of expression, to set forth God—His providence, and His government, and, what is more and higher than all, God's own feeling, His truth, love, justice, compassion. Well, if it be something for a poet to express man, it is doubtless somewhat more for a book to be constructed that will express God, and open His eternity to man. And if it would be somewhat difficult to put the poet of humanity into a few short formulas, that will communicate all he expresses, with his manifold, wondrous art, will it probably be easier to transfer the grand poem of salvation, that which expresses God, even the feeling of God, into a few dull propositions; which, when they are produced, we may call the sum total of the Christian truth? Let me freely confess that, when I see the human teacher elaborating a phrase of speech, or mere dialectic proposition, that is going to tell what God could only show me by the history of ages, and the mystic life and death of Jesus our Lord, I should be deeply shocked by his irreverence, if I were not rather occupied with pity for his infirmity.

It ought not to be necessary to remind any reader of the Bible, that religion has a natural and profound alliance with poetry. Hence, a very large share of the Bible is composed of poetic contributions. Another share, equally large, is that which comes to us in a form of history and fact; that is, of actual life, which is equally remote from all abstractions, and, in one view, equally poetic; for history is nothing but an evolution or expression of God and man in their own nature and character. The teachings of Christ are mere utterances of truth, not argumentations over it. He gives it forth in living symbols, without definition, without proving it, ever, as the logicians speak, well understanding that truth is that which shines in its own evidence, that which finds us, to use an admirable expression of Coleridge, and thus enters into us. . . .

14. It is important to notice, as connected with the subject of language, that dogmatical propositions, such as are commonly woven into creeds and catechisms of doctrine, have not the certainty they are commonly supposed to have. They only give us the seeing of the authors, at the precise stand-point occupied by them, at the time, and they are true only as seen from that point,—not even there, save in a proximate sense. . . .

On these accounts, the best creed is that which stays by the concrete most faithfully, and carries its doctrine, as far as possible, in a vehicle of fact and of real life. This is the peculiar excellence and beauty of what is called the "Apostle's Creed." If, however, creeds of theory, or systematic dogma, must be retained, the next best arrangement would be to allow assent to a great number of such creeds at once; letting them qualify, assist, and mitigate each other. . . .

15. I have said nothing of the manner in which the user of language imparts himself to it. Undoubtedly every human language has, in its words and forms, indelible marks of the personal character and habit of the men by whom it was originally produced. . . .

And just here, it is, that we come upon a matter, which, if it be too mysterious to be investigated, is yet too important to be overlooked. In every writer, distinguished by mental life, words have a significance and power breathed into them, which is wholly peculiar—whether it be in the rhythm, the collocations, the cadences, or the internal ideas, it may be impossible to guess. But his language is his own, and there is some chemistry of life in it that belongs only to him, as does the vital chemistry of his body. . . .

Accordingly, it is the right of every author, who deserves attention at all, to claim a certain liberty, and even to have it for a merit that he cannot be judged exactly by old uses and formulas.

Life is organic; and if there be life in his work, it will be found not in some noun or verb that he uses, but in the organic whole of his creations. Hence, it is clear that he must be apprehended in some sense, as a whole, before his full import can be received in paragraphs and sentences. Until then, he will, of necessity, appear to be obscure, enigmatical, extravagant, or even absurd. He cannot be tested by the jingle of his words, or by auscultation applied to the breathing of his sentences. No decree of condemnation must be passed upon him, because he does not make himself understood, sentence by sentence; for, if he infuses into words a life-power of his own, or does more than simply to recombine old impressions, he cannot make himself intelligible, fully, save through a kind of general acquaintance. It may, even, be to his praise, that he is not too easily understood. . . .

16. That I may not seem to be offering to the public, doctrines, the real import of which I have not considered myself, something must be said of the consequences likely to result to religion, from the admission of views such as I have here presented. Only, be it observed, that their truth depends, in no degree, on any expectations of good, or any vaticinations of evil, which the faith of one, or the panic of another may raise.

Unquestionably, the view of language here presented must produce, if received, a decided mitigation of our dogmatic tendencies in religion. It throws a heavy shade of discouragement on our efforts in this direction. It shows that language is, probably, incapable of any such definite and determinate use as we have supposed it to be in our theological speculations; that, for this reason, dogma has failed hitherto, and about as certainly will hereafter. Taking away, thus, the confidence of the speculative theologer, it will limit, proportionally, his eagerness. It will, also, reduce the very excessive eminence he has, at present, in the public estimation, requiring a re-adjustment of the scale that now pertains between this and the historical, literary, and practical departments of Christian study. Or, better still, showing that the advancement and the real amount of true theology depends, not on logical deductions and systematic solutions, but principally on the more cultivated and nicer apprehension of symbol, it may turn the industry of our teachers more in this direction, giving a more esthetic character to their studies and theories, and drawing them as much closer to the practical life of religion. . . .

The two principal results, then, which I suppose may follow, should these views of language be allowed to have their effect in our theology, are a more comprehensive, friendly, and fraternal state, than now exists between different families of Christians; and, as the confidence of dogma is mitigated, a more present, powerful, and universal conviction entering into the Christian body, that truth, in its highest and freest forms, is not of the natural understanding, but is, rather, as Christ himself declared—spirit and life. We shall have more of union, therefore, and more of true piety enlightened by the spirit of God—neither of which involves any harm or danger.

9

Natural Theology

Charles Hodge

We have, therefore, to restrict theology to its true sphere, as the science of the facts of divine revelation so far as those facts concern the nature of God and our relation to him, as his creatures, as sinners, and as the subjects of redemption. All these facts, as just remarked, are in the Bible. But as some of them are revealed by the works of God, and by the nature of man, there is so far a distinction between natural theology, and theology considered distinctively as a Christian science.

With regard to natural theology, there are two extreme opinions. The one is that the works of nature make no trustworthy revelation of the being and perfections of God; the other, that such revelation is so clear and comprehensive as to preclude the necessity of any supernatural revelation.

Scriptural Argument for Natural Theology

The Scriptures clearly recognize the fact that the works of God reveal his being and attributes. This they do not only by frequent reference to the works of nature as manifestations of the perfections of God, but by direct assertions. "The heavens declare the glory of God; and the firmament sheweth his handy-work. Day unto day uttereth speech, and night unto night sheweth knowledge. There is no speech nor language, where their voice is not heard. Their line is gone out through all the earth, and their words to the end of the world." (Ps. xix. 1-4.) . . .

The sacred writers in contending with the heathen appeal to the evidence which the works of God bear to his perfections: "Understand, ye brutish among the people: and ye fools, when will ye be wise? He that planted the ear, shall he not hear? He that formed the eye, shall he not see? He that chastiseth the heathen, shall not he correct? He that teacheth man knowledge, shall not he know?" (Ps. xciv. 8-10.) Paul said to the men of Lystra, "Sirs, why do ye these things? We also are men of like passions with you, and preach unto you that ye should turn from these vanities unto the living God, which made heaven and earth, and the sea, and all things that are therein: Who in times past suffered all nations to walk in their own ways. Nevertheless he left not himself without witness, in that he did good, and gave us rain from heaven, and fruitful seasons, filling our hearts with food and gladness." (Acts xiv. 15-17.) To the men of Athens he said: "God that made the world and all things therein, seeing that he is Lord of heaven and earth, dwelleth not in temples made with hands; neither is worshipped with men's hands, as though he needed anything, seeing he giveth to all life and breath, and all things; and hath made of one blood all nations of men for to dwell on all the face of the earth, and hath determined the times before appointed, and the bounds of their habitation; that they should seek the Lord, if haply they might feel after him, and find him, though he be not far from every one of us: for in him we live, and move, and have our being; as certain also of your own poets have said, 'For we are also his offspring.' Forasmuch then as we are the offspring of God, we ought not to think that the Godhead is like unto gold, or silver, or stone, graven by art and man's device." (Acts xvii. 24-29.)

Not only the fact of this revelation, but its clearness is distinctly asserted by the Apostle: "That which may be known of God is manifest in them; for God hath shewed it unto them. For the invisible things of him from the creation of the world are clearly seen, being understood by the things that are made, even his eternal power and Godhead; so that they are without excuse: because that when they knew God, they glorified him not as God, neither were thankful." (Rom. i. 19-21.)

It cannot, therefore, be reasonably doubted that not only the being of God, but also his eternal power and Godhead, are so revealed in his works, as to lay a stable foundation for natural theology.

Insufficiency of Natural Theology

The second extreme opinion respecting Natural Theology is, that it precludes the necessity of a supernatural revelation. The question whether the knowledge of God derived from his works, be sufficient to lead fallen men to salvation, is answered affirmatively by Rationalists, but negatively by every historical branch of the Christian Church. On this point the Greek, the Latin, the Lutheran, and the Reformed Churches are unanimous. . . .

The question as to the sufficiency of natural theology, or of the truths of reason, is to be answered on the authority of the Scriptures. No man can tell *à priori* what is necessary to salvation. Indeed, it is only by supernatural revelation that we know that any sinner can be saved. It is from the same source alone, we can know what are the conditions of salvation, or who are to be its subjects.

10

The Value of Proofs for God's Existence

J. L. Dagg

There is a God (Gen. i. 1; Ps. xiv. 1; Mark xii. 32; 1 Cor. viii. 6; Heb. iii. 4).

The doctrine that God exists, is not now to be demonstrated as a new truth. It has been supposed in all the preceding pages; and the proofs of it have been brought to view, in various ways. But, for the sake of systematic arrangement, it will be proper to collect these proofs under one head; and a clearer statement of them will tend to the confirmation of our faith.

1. Our moral nature demonstrates the existence of God.

Our moral nature is adapted to moral government. We find this government within us administered by conscience, and it meets us from without in the influence which we experience from the moral judgments and feelings of others. It restrains our appetites and passions; and, however unwelcome this restraint may be to our vicious propensities, every one knows that it is conducive to his well-being.

We are social as well as moral beings. The circumstances in which we enter the world, and the propensities which we bring with us, unite to render the establishment of society necessary. The birds congregate in flocks, and the bees in swarms, and their instincts are adapted to the social relations which they form. To man in society, moral principles are indispensable. Banish from every member of human society the restraints which his conscience and the moral sense of the community impose on him, and you will desolate the earth, or convert it into a hell. Brute-force, and diabolical cunning, under the dominion of lawless passions, will take the mastery of the world, and fill it with wretchedness.

From the combined influence of our moral and social principles, civil governments have originated, and their existence has been found by experience indispensable to the well-being of society. These governments have differed very widely in their degrees of excellence; and some of them have been most unrighteously and cruelly administered; yet the very worst of them has been considered preferable to wild anarchy.

The notion of moral government, and the feeling of its necessity, spring up naturally in the human mind; but no earthly form of it satisfies our desires, or meets our necessities. Conscience restrains us; and, when we have disregarded its monitions, stings us with remorse; but men are still wicked. Public sentiment stamps vice with infamy; but, in spite of public sentiment, men are vicious. Civil government holds out its penalties, and the ruler brandishes his sword; but men persevere in wickedness, and often with impunity. The voice of nature within us calls for a government free from these imperfections. If, from the idea of a petty ruler over a single tribe or nation, we ascend to that of a moral governor over all intelligent creatures; if, instead of the imperfect moral judgments and feelings which we find in men, we attribute to this universal ruler, all possible moral perfections, if we invest him with knowledge sufficient to detect every crime, and power sufficient to manifest his disapprobation of it in the most suitable and effectual way; and if this exalted sovereign, instead of being far from us, is brought into such a relation to us, that in him we live, move, and have our being; we shall have the most sublime conception of moral government, of which our minds are capable. This conception is presented in the proposition, THERE IS A GOD. The idea of God's existence, as the moral ruler of the universe, accords precisely with the tendencies and demands of our moral nature; and, without admitting it, our moral faculties and the phenomena which they exhibit, are totally inexplicable.

The moral principles of our nature find occasion for development and exercise, in the relations which we sustain to our fellow-creatures. But, for their full development and exercise nothing furnishes opportunity, but the relation which we bear to God, and his universal dominion. This exercise of them constitutes religion. Religion is, therefore, the perfection of morality; and the fundamental doctrine of religion is the existence of God.

2. The existence of the world and the contrivances which it contains, demonstrate the existence of God.

While our moral nature leads us to the conception of God, as the moral governor of the universe, and to the belief of his existence, our intellectual nature approaches him, as the Great First Cause. Reason traces the chain of cause and effect throughout its links. It finds every link dependent on that which precedes it; and it asks on what does the entire chain depend? It obtains no satisfactory answer to this question, until it has admitted the existence of an eternal, self-existent, and independent being, as the first cause of all things. Here, and here only, the mind finds repose.

The argument which has been most relied on in natural religion, to prove the existence of God, is derived from the indications of contrivance, with which Nature abounds. The adaptation of means to ends, and the accomplishment of purposes by contrivances of consummate skill, are everywhere visible. Contrivance implies a contriver. The intelligence displayed is often found in creatures that have no intelligence; and in other cases, when found in intelligent creatures, it is manifestly not from themselves; because it exists without their knowledge, and operates without their control. The contrivance must be referred to an intelligent First Cause. This argument for the existence of God, is of great practical value, because it is presented to our minds daily, and hourly, in all the works of Nature. We meet it in the sun-beams, which impart to plants and animals, the warmth necessary to life; and, to every eye, the light without which, eyes would be useless. It presents itself in the eyes of every man, beast, bird, fish, insect, and reptile, and is most convincingly exhibited in the arrangements for receiving and refracting the light, and employing it for the purposes of vision; a contrivance as truly mechanical, and conformed to the laws of optics, as that which is seen in the structure of the telescope. We behold it in the descending shower which fertilizes the earth, and causes the grass to grow; and in the bursting germ, the spreading blade, the rising stalk, and the ripening grain, in all which a skilful contrivance is displayed, that infinitely transcends all human art. We discover it in the instincts by which the parent hen hatches her eggs, and takes care of her young; and in the adaptation of every species of animals on land, in air, or in water, to their mode and condition of life. It is seen in the return of day and night, the revolution of the seasons, the wind that sweeps the sky, and the vapor that rises from the ocean, and floats through the atmosphere. We find it in the bones of the body, fitted for their respective motions, and in the muscles which move them; in the throbbing heart, the circulating blood, the digesting stomach, and the heaving lungs. In every thing which the eye beholds, or the mind contemplates, we discover the manifestations of the Creator's wisdom and power. The devotional heart is struck with the evidence of God's existence, so abundantly displayed in all his handiworks, and is incited to admire and adore. The whole universe becomes a grand temple, pervaded with the presence and glory of the deity; and every place becomes an altar, on which may be offered to him the sacrifice of praise and thanksgiving.

3. The doctrine that there is a God, is confirmed by the common consent of mankind.

There have been tribes of men without literature, and, to a great extent, without science and arts; but the notion of an invisible, overruling power, with some form of religious worship, has been nearly, or quite universal. In this particular, man is distinguished from all other animals that inhabit the globe; and if there has been any portion of our race in whom no idea of God and religion has appeared, it may be said of them, that they have so far brutalized themselves, as to hide from view the characteristic distinctions of human nature. Now, however it may be accounted for, that a belief in the existence of God has prevailed so generally among mankind; the fact of its prevalence is an argument for the truth of the opinion. If it is an ancient revelation handed down by tradition, that revelation proceeded from God, and therefore proves his existence; and if it springs up naturally in the human mind, in the circumstances in which we are placed, what Nature universally teaches, may be received as true.

4. Divine revelation dispels all doubt as to the existence of God.

In the Bible, the existence of God is from the very first

assumed. "In the beginning, God created the heavens and the earth" (Gen. i. 1). The doctrine, though formally declared in scarcely a single passage, is represented as fundamental in religion. "He that cometh to God, must believe that he is" (Heb. xi. 6); and the denial of it is attributed to folly; "the fool hath said in his heart, there is no God" (Ps. xiv. 1). The volume of revelation is a light emanating from the Father of lights, and is, of itself, an independent proof of his existence. As we study its pages, in his light we shall see light; and a more realizing and abiding conviction that he, the great Source of light, exists, will occupy our minds.

The perfect harmony between natural and revealed religion, with respect to this doctrine, confirms the teaching of both. "The heavens declare the glory of God, and the firmament showeth his handiwork. Day unto day uttereth speech, and night unto night showeth knowledge" (Ps. xix. 1, 2). While heaven and earth, day and night, speak for God, he speaks for himself in his inspired word, confirming the testimony which they give, and completing the instruction which they convey. Revelation never contradicts or sets aside the teachings of natural religion. God affirms, that "the invisible things of him are from the creation of the world clearly seen, being understood by the things that are made; even his eternal power and Godhead" (Rom. i. 20). It is no derogation from the authority or perfection of the Scriptures, that we study natural religion. The Scriptures themselves direct us to this study. "Ask the beasts, and they shall teach thee, and the fowls of the air, and they shall tell thee" (Job xii. 7). The same God who speaks to us in his word, speaks to us also in his works; and in whatever manner he speaks, we should hear, and receive instruction.

It is a lamentable proof of human depravity, that men should deny or disregard the existence of God. We read of the fool, who says in his heart, there is no God; of nations that forget God; and of individuals who have not God in all their thoughts. Such persons do not delight in God; and therefore they say, "Depart from us; we desire not the knowledge of thy ways." Of such atheism, the only effectual cure is a new heart. For the occasional suggestion of atheistic doubts, with which a pious man may be harassed, the remedy is, a diligent study of God's word and works, a careful marking of his hand in Providence, and a prayerful and confiding acknowledgment of him in all our ways. If we habitually walk with God, we shall not doubt his existence.

The invisibility of God is one of the obstacles to the exercise of a lively faith in his existence. It may assist in removing this obstacle, to reflect that the human mind is also invisible; and yet we never doubt that it exists. We hear the words, and see the actions of a fellow-man, and these indicate to us the character and state of his mind, so as to excite in us admiration or contempt, love or hatred. If, while we listen to his words, and observe his actions, we clearly perceive the intelligence from which these words and actions proceed, why can we not, with equal clearness, perceive the intelligence from which the movements of nature proceed? If we can know, admire, and love, an unseen human mind, it is equally possible to know, admire, and love an unseen God.

11

The Limitations of Proofs for God's Existence

Alexander Balmain Bruce

Among the theistic proofs which have commanded wide acceptance, the foremost place is due to the three entitled respectively the cosmological, the teleological, and the ontological, which may be called the standard arguments for the existence of a great First Cause, almighty, wise, good, and perfect. The first argues from the mere existence of a world to an absolutely necessary Being from whom it took its origin. The world as a whole it regards as an effect whose cause is God. The argument implies that the world as we know it is contingent, that is, does not necessarily exist, and that it is an event, or had a commencement. The principle on which it proceeds is that for all contingent being the ultimate source must be a cause necessarily and eternally existing. Its force may be evaded either by denying that the world had a beginning; or by denying that any contingent system of things needs any cause other than an antecedent system also contingent, explicable in turn by a third, and so on *ad infinitum* in an eternal succession of causes and effects; or yet again, more boldly, by maintaining that the category of causality is inapplicable to God as the Supersensible and the Infinite.

The teleological argument is based on the manifold instances of adaptation discernible in the world, as of the parts of an organism to its function, or of an organ to its environment. These adaptations wear the aspect of design, and suggest the thought that a world full of them must be the work of an infinitely wise Mind. "He that planted the ear, shall He not hear? He that formed the eye, shall He not see?" To the religious spirit the reasoning quaintly conveyed in these questions of the Psalmist will never cease to appeal. Science and philosophy may criticise, but science itself only supplies new materials for an argument, which, suggested by a single instance of adaptation, acquires through the indefinite multiplication of examples a cumulative force which many feel to be irresistible. Living in a cosmos everywhere pervaded by order, the man of unsophisticated mind finds it impossible to acquiesce in the dictum of Strauss: "This world was not planned by a highest reason, though it has the highest reason for its goal." He rather endorses with emphasis the verdict of Mr. J. S. Mill, no prejudiced witness, that "It must be allowed that in the present state of our knowledge the adaptations in nature afford a large balance of probability in favour of creation by intelligence."

Yet since the days of Kant this ancient, popular, and still impressive argument has been regarded with more or less disfavour by many philosophers and theologians. Kant himself, while treating it with respect, strove to minimise its value, partly in order to read a lesson of moderation to the men of the *Aufklärung*, who did their best to make it ridiculous. He held that it yields at most a World-Architect, not a creator, Author of the form not of the matter of the universe, and only a very wise Architect, not an absolutely wise, and doubted if in strict logic it can give us so much. He robbed it of all support in the internal adaptations of an organism such as the eye, by his conception of an organism as a structure in which all the parts mutually condition and produce each other, are mutually to each other at once cause and effect, and all alike are possible only through their relation to the whole and owe their existence to their relation. In this bearing of all the parts on the whole he recognised a teleology of nature, yet not such as implies a cause outside of them who has an idea of their design. He admitted that it comes very natural to us to think of such an outside designing cause, but held nevertheless that the conception comes from our own spirit, and has no objective value. In this view he was followed by Hegel, who, in his lectures on the proofs of the existence of God, remarks: "The inner construction of the bodily organism, the functions of the nerve and blood system, of the lungs, liver, stomach, and their mutual harmony, are certainly very surprising. Does not this harmony demand Another besides the organic subject as its cause? This question we may leave on one side, as if one grasps the notion of an organism, this development of teleological adaptation is a necessary consequence of the vitality of the subject."

The Darwinian theory has largely restricted the material available for the teleological argument, by inverting the mode of conceiving the relation between an organ and its environment. Whereas of old the fitness between the two was regarded as the result of intentional adaptation of organ to environment, according to the new scientific point of view the fitness is the result of the slow, unconscious action of environment on organ, producing in the course of ages development from a crude condition to a very high state of perfection. While thus accounting for all cases of useful adaptation, the theory claims to have this advantage over the old teleological view of the world, that it can explain such phenomena as are presented in rudimentary and useless organs, which it is difficult to imagine being made by design.

Some scientific writers have sought to bring discredit on the teleological view of the world by pointing out defects in organs which, on that view, would have to be regarded as instances of blundering on the part of the Creator. The eye, formerly a favourite theme for the teleologist, has been carefully studied in this controversial interest. Generally the tendency of physical inquiry has been to enlarge the sphere of the unintentional in nature. Thus a well-known writer, himself a theist, and very competent to speak on the topic, remarks: "It is not in accordance with the facts of experience that all parts of nature point to ideal significance and definite aims. Along with a thousand appearances which give this impression go a thousand others which look like aimless by-products of an accidental self-formed combination of atoms, which by no means ought to arise under a preconceived plan, and which have arisen and maintained themselves in being because they did not contradict the mechanical conditions of continued existence."

The ontological argument infers the existence of God from the idea of Him necessarily entertained by the human mind. The idea we cannot help forming of God is that of a Being than which a higher cannot be conceived, absolutely perfect in all respects. Into this conception existence necessarily enters as an element, for a supposed highest, most perfect Being not conceived as existing would not be the highest conceivable. Therefore a most perfect Being exists. Such is the gist of the argument as first formulated by Anselm. It wears a subtle scholastic air, which puzzles the mind and makes it difficult to decide whether to regard it as a very profound and conclusive piece of reasoning, or as a sample of ratiocinative trifling. On the whole, one inclines to the view of Kant, who, in his criticism of this argument, while conceding that the idea of existence entered into the idea of the most perfect Being, argued that the idea no more involves the reality of existence than the notion of a hundred dollars in my mind proves that I have them in my purse.

Through lengthened and continuous criticism of these famous arguments, it has come to pass that in their old forms they are no longer available, and that they must therefore either be abandoned or transformed. Some pursue the one course, some the other. It was not to be expected that so valuable a line of proof as that supplied in the second of the three would be lightly given up by theists, and accordingly efforts have been made recently to restate the "design argument" so as to fit it to the present condition of scientific knowledge and thought. Those who have laboured in this sphere have striven to show that accepting the modern doctrine of evolution and the account which it gives of the order and method of creation, there is still ample scope for an argument which aims at proving that the world has been made, and its upward development guided, by an almighty, wise, and beneficent Creator. Others have sought a foundation for their theistic convictions in entirely different directions. Abandoning the region of teleology to the tender mercies of sceptical scientists, they have justified belief in God either by an appeal to the facts of the moral world, or by an analysis of self-consciousness; in the one case following Kant, in the other Hegel. Kant, failing to find any sure trace of God in the region within which the theoretic reason bears sway, turned to the domain of practical reason, and found there as an actual existence the Being who had hitherto been only a regulative idea. Virtue and happiness ought to correspond, but happiness depends largely on external conditions over which we have no control; therefore we must postulate a moral Governor who is able to bring the order of nature into harmony with the moral world—such was the gist of the argument which certified for him the reality of Deity. To some it has appeared not less weak than the arguments it superseded, as, e.g., to Strauss, who criticises it in these terms: "The agreement of virtue and happiness from which the argument starts is in one respect, in the inner man, already present; that the two should be harmonised in outward conditions is our natural wish and rightful endeavour; but the ever incomplete realisation of the wish is to be found not in the postulate of a *Deus ex machina*, but in a correct view of the world and of fortune." Nevertheless for many the "moral argument" of the great critical philosopher in one form or another remains the sheet-anchor of faith. . . .

When one considers the facts connected with the history of

theistic evidence: how few arguments command the general assent even of theists, how much the line of proof adopted depends on the advocate's philosophic viewpoint, and how little respect the rival schools of philosophy pay to all methods of establishing the common faith but their own, he is tempted to think that that faith is without sure foundation, and that the agnostic is right when he asserts that knowledge of God is unattainable. But there is another way of looking at the matter which deserves serious attention. While differing as to what proofs are valid and valuable, all theists are agreed as to the thing to be proved: that God is, and to a certain extent what God is. This harmony in belief ought to weigh more in our judgment than the variation in evidence. It suggests the thought that the belief in God is antecedent to evidence, and that in our theistic reasonings we formulate proof of a foregone conclusion innate and inevitable. How otherwise can it be explained that men who have demolished what have passed for the strongest arguments for the theistic creed are not content to be done with it, but hold on to the conviction that God is, on grounds which to all others but themselves appear weak and whimsical? Thus a recent writer, after searching in vain the whole universe of matter and of mind for traces of Deity, finds rest at last for his weary spirit in this train of thought: There is such a thing as error, but error is inconceivable unless there be such a thing as truth, and truth is inconceivable unless there be a seat of truth, an infinite all-including Thought or Mind, therefore such a Mind exists. That Mind is God, the "infinite Seer," whose nature it is to think, not to act. "No power it is to be resisted, no plan-maker to be foiled by fallen angels, nothing finite, nothing striving, seeking, losing, altering, growing weary; the All-Enfolder it is, and we know its name. Not Heart, nor Love, though these also are in it and of it; Thought it is, and all things are for Thought, and in it we live and move." How weak the proof here, but how strong the conviction! So it is, more or less, with us all. In our formal argumentation we feebly and blunderingly try to assign reasons for a belief that is rooted in our being. In perusing works by others devoted to the advocacy of theism, we are conscious of disappointment, and possibly even of doubt suggested rather than of faith established, only to recover serene and strong conviction when the book is forgotten. It would seem as if the way of wisdom were to abstain from all attempts at proving the divine existence, and, assuming as a datum that God is, to restrict our inquiries to what He is. Without pronouncing dogmatically as to the incompetency of any other method of procedure, I shall here adopt this policy, and confine myself in the remainder of this chapter to a few hints in answer to the question, How far is the Christian idea of God "a hypothesis which all we know tends to verify"?

Christ taught that God is a Father and that man is His son, and that it is a leading purpose of God to establish between Himself and men a kingdom of filial relations and loving fellowship. This doctrine implies that there is a close affinity of nature between God and man, that, indeed, the most direct and certain way to the knowledge of God is through human nature. Now the view thus suggested of the man-like nature of God is in accordance with the teaching of the most recent science. Man, according to science not less than Scripture, stands at the head of creation as we know it. He is the crown and consummation of the evolutionary process, by the frank admission of one of the most brilliant expounders of the modern theory. "So far from degrading humanity," writes Mr. Fiske, "or putting it on a level with the animal world in general, the doctrine of evolution shows us distinctly for the first time how the creation and the perfecting of man is the goal towards which Nature's work has been tending from the first. We can now see clearly that our new knowledge enlarges tenfold the significance of human life, and makes it seem more than ever the chief object of divine care, the consummate fruition of that creative energy which is manifested throughout the knowable universe." It is a reasonable inference that from the creature who occupies this distinguished place something may be learned concerning the nature of the Creator. The author just quoted, indeed, protests against this inference, and maintains, as we have seen, that God's nature cannot be known from one part of the creation more than from another.

But this view is compatible only with such a conception of the universe as that of Spinoza—a mere monotonous wilderness of being in which all things are equally significant or insignificant, not to be distinguished as lower and higher. This is not the conception of the evolution theory, which teaches us to regard the universe as the result of a process which, beginning with a fiery cloud, passed through many successive stages in an ever-ascending scale, from star-vapour to stars, from dead planets to life, from plants to animals, from apes to men. It is in keeping with this grand conception to see in the final stage of the process a key to the meaning of the whole, and in man a revelation of God as a Being possessing mind and guided by purpose.

If the Creator be not only like man in nature, but had man in view from the first as the end of creation, we may expect to find traces of a purposeful guidance of the evolutionary process so as to insure that it should reach its end. There is reason to believe that such traces are not wanting, and recent theistic writers have done good service in pointing them out, and in so doing have furnished the restatement of the teleological argument rendered necessary by the dislodgment of it from its old ground through the influence of the Darwinian theory as to the origin of species. The details cannot be gone into here. Suffice it to say that the end has been reached: man is here, and it has been reached through a steadily upward process, not as a matter of course, but through manifold risks of miscarriage, which have not been escaped by happy accident, but by creative control. There is no known law of necessary advancement, no reason in the nature of the case why variation should proceed in an upward direction. "Apart from the internal constitution of an organism having been so planned, and its external circumstances so arranged as to favour the one rather than the other, its variations could not have been more towards self-perfection than self-destruction."

The Christian doctrine of God, as in nature like man, is in accordance with the latest teaching of science regarding the nature of force. According to that teaching, all physical forces are convertible into each other, and are all but diverse manifestations of one ultimate force. Thus the question arises, What is the nature of that ultimate force? The agnostic replies, It is inscrutable. But reason suggests, What if the Power that is at work in the universe be like that form of power with which we are most familiar, the power exercised by the being who stands at the head of creation, and reveals the mind of the Creator—Willpower?

Once more, if God, as Christ teaches, be like man, He possesses not only Intellect, Purpose, and Will, but moral character. Many have seen in the moral nature of man, the conscience, a powerful witness to the existence of God. Without calling in question the validity of the argument, my present purpose is to point to the human sense of right and wrong as showing not that God is, but what He is. Man's place in the universe, as assigned to him by science, makes it legitimate and reasonable to do so. And history confirms the inference to morality in God suggested by an inspection of man's moral nature. Men of all schools, pessimists excepted, are agreed that a moral order is revealed in the story of the human race. Carlyle and Arnold interpret its lesson in much the same way as the Hebrew prophets. Whether the Power that makes for righteousness be conscious and personal or otherwise may be a subject of dispute or doubt. The main point is that the Power exists—imperfectly manifested, it may be, a tendency rather than a completely realised fact, yet indubitably there. As revealed in human affairs, it possesses some noticeable characteristics. It is slow in action, especially on the punitive side, and it seems, not now and then, as if by accident, but with all the regularity of a law, to treat the best of men as if they were the worst, making the good suffer as the bad ought. Prophetically interpreted, and expressed in religious language, these facts mean: that God is patient, slow to anger, prone to pardon, giving evil men ample space to repent; and that in the moral world the good are called to the heroic function of redeemers, propagators of righteousness, and as such have to suffer, the just by and for the unjust. In other words, the moral order of the world is not only a reign of retributive justice, but a reign of grace, under which love is the supreme law, with full scope for the display of its nature as a spirit of self-sacrifice, and the stream of tendency is steadily towards the grand consummation, the bringing in of the kingdom of God.

In the foregoing observations, man, his nature and position in the universe, is made the basis of the theistic argument. And this is as it ought to be. Science aims at explaining man from the world, but religion explains the world, in its first Cause and last End, from man. The two attitudes are not incompatible, but their tendencies are as diverse as their points of view. The one tends to minimise, the other to magnify, the peculiarity of man. The patrons of the two methods are apt to be unjust to each other, either undervaluing the aim of the other, and remaining comparatively unimpressed by his lines of proof. In the case of the scientific man this defect may appear specially excusable. For the demonstrations offered by the representatives of the religious view of the world are not of that strict order to which the scientist is accustomed. The results arrived at are not logically inevitable conclusions from absolutely certain premises. They are value-judgments resting on moral grounds, and involving an exercise of freedom, or, to speak more correctly, a bias due to the esteem in which we hold man as a moral personality, and to the habit of regarding his moral nature and destiny as the key to the riddle of the universe. A man can be an agnostic if he pleases. Faith in God is an affair of personal conviction. No offence is meant by this statement. It is not intended to insinuate that unbelief is the effect of an unsatisfactory moral condition. It may be frankly acknowledged that many worthy men are agnostics, as many worthless men are theists. Nevertheless it remains true that it is with the heart man believeth. God is the postulate of a soul that finds the world without God utterly dark and unintelligible. And those who believe in God most firmly best know what it is to doubt. Faith is the result of a successful struggle against all that tends to produce religious atrophy, including too exclusive devotion to scientific habits of thought, which may turn the mind into "a machine for grinding out general laws out of large collections of facts," and prove fatal not only to religious faith, but even to all taste for poetry, music, and pictures.

12

Old Testament Teaching About God

A. B. Davidson

On the subject of God the ideas of the ancient world are in many respects different from our own. And the ideas of the Old Testament have, in these points of difference, naturally greater affinity with those of the ancient world in general than with ours. One such point of difference is this, that it never occurred to any prophet or writer of the Old Testament to prove the existence of God. To do so might well have seemed an absurdity. For all Old Testament prophets and writers move among ideas that presuppose God's existence. Prophecy itself is the direct product of His influence. The people of Israel in their character and relation are His creation. It is not according to the spirit of the ancient world in general either to deny the existence of God or to use arguments to prove it. The belief was one natural to the human mind and common to all men. Scripture does indeed speak of men who say in their heart there is no God, but these are the fools, that is, the practically ungodly; and their denial is not a theoretical or speculative one, but merely what may be held to be the expression of their manner of life. Even the phrase "there is no God" hardly means that God is not, but rather that He is not present, does not interfere in life; and counting on this absence of God from the affairs of the world, and consequently on impunity, men become corrupt and do abominable deeds (Ps. xiv.). And for their wickedness they shall be cast into hell, the region of separation from God, along with all the nations that forget God (Ps. ix. 17). Yet even this forgetfulness of God by the nations is regarded as something temporary. It is a forgetting only; it is no obliteration of the knowledge of God from the human mind. That is impossible, and these nations shall yet remember and turn unto the Lord. Scripture regards men as carrying with them, as part of their very thought, the conception of God.

This being the case, the Old Testament naturally has no occasion to speculate on how this knowledge that God is arises in the mind. Its position is far in front of this. It teaches how God who is, is known, and is known to be what He is. But it seems nowhere to contemplate men as ignorant of the existence of God, and therefore it nowhere depicts the rise or dawn of the idea of God's existence on men's minds. In the historical period the idea of God's existence is one of the primary thoughts of man. He comes possessed of this thought to face and observe the world. His conception of God already possessed explains the world to him; the world does not suggest to him an idea hitherto strange, that of the existence of God. And, of course, the bare idea of the existence of God is not the primary thought which Scripture supposes all men to possess. This abstract idea gathers body about it, namely, a certain circle of ideas as to what God is.

And with these ideas the Hebrew took up his position over against the world. To him God and the world were always distinct. God was not involved in the processes of nature. These processes were caused by God, but were quite distinct from God.

The Hebrew thinker, however, came down from his thought of God upon the world; he did not rise from the world up to his thought of God. His primary thought of God explained to him the world, both its existence and the course of events upon it; these did not suggest to him either the existence or the character of God, these being unknown to him. The thought of the Hebrew, and his contemplation of providence and life, were never of the nature of a search after God whom he did not know, but always of the nature of a recognition and observation of the operation of God whom he already knew. There seems no passage in the Old Testament which represents men as reaching the knowledge of the existence of God through nature or the events of providence, although there are some passages which imply that false ideas of what God is may be corrected by the observation of nature and life. When the singer in the xixth Psalm says that "the heavens declare the glory of God," all that he means is that the glory of God, who is, and is known, and is Creator, may be seen reflected on the heavens. But the Psalmist only recognised on the heavens what he already carried in his heart. When, however, in Isa. xl. 25, 26, Jehovah, asks "To whom then will ye liken Me? . . . Lift up your eyes on high, and see who hath created these things, that bringeth out their host by number," it is implied that false views of what God is may be corrected, or at least that they may be brought home to men's consciousness. There is an approximation to the arguments of Natural Theology in some of these passages. And even more in a passage in one of the Psalms (xciv. 5-11), when, speaking probably of the excuses of the heathen rulers of Israel, the writer says: "They break in pieces Thy people, O Lord, and afflict Thine heritage. They slay the widow and the stranger, and murder the fatherless. And they say, The Lord doth not see, neither doth the God of Jacob observe. Consider, ye brutish among the people: and ye fools, when will ye be wise? He that planted the ear, shall He not hear? He that formed the eye, shall He not see? He that instructeth the nations, shall not He correct? Even He that teacheth men knowledge? The Lord knoweth the thoughts of men."

The Revelation of God

The Old Testament as little thinks of arguing or proving that God may be known as it thinks of arguing that He exists. Its position here again is far in front of such an argument. How should men think of arguing that God could be known, when they were persuaded they knew Him, when they knew they were in fellowship with Him, when their consciousness and whole mind were filled and aglow with the thought of Him, and when through His Spirit He moved them and enlightened them, and guided their whole history? There is nothing strictly peculiar, however, here.

The peculiarity of the Old Testament conception rather comes out when the question is raised, how God is known. Here we touch a fundamental idea of the Old Testament—the idea of Revelation. If men know God, it is because He has made Himself known to them. This knowledge is due to what He does, not to what men themselves achieve. As God is the source of all life, and as the knowledge of Him is the highest life, this knowledge cannot be reached by any mere effort of man. If man has anything of God, he has received it from God, who communicates Himself in love and grace. The idea of man reaching to a knowledge or fellowship of God through his own efforts is wholly foreign to the Old Testament. God speaks, He appears; man listens and beholds. God brings Himself nigh to men; He enters into a covenant or personal relation with them; He lays commands on them. They receive Him when He approaches; they accept His will and obey His behests. Moses and the prophets are nowhere represented as thoughtful minds reflecting on the Unseen, and forming conclusions regarding it, or ascending to elevated conceptions of Godhead. The Unseen manifests itself before them, and they know it.

Such a revelation of God is everywhere supposed in the Old Testament. God is not a God that hides Himself in the sense that He is self-engrossed or self-absorbed. His Spirit streams through the world, producing all life and maintaining it, and begetting in men a fellowship with the life of God. His word goes forth to the world that it shall be, and shall be upholden, and to men that they may know Him and live in Him. He appears and manifests Himself to the patriarchs in angelic forms, to the prophets in the inspiration of their minds, in visions and dreams or spiritual intuitions, and to Moses speaking face to face. The form of His manifestation of Himself may change, but the reality of it remains the same. The conviction in the mind of the prophet that God revealed Himself and His word to him when the truth broke upon his mind, was not less vivid than that of the patriarch who was visited by angelic forms when sitting in the door of his tent. The prophet speaks the word of God, has his ear awakened by God, is the messenger and interpreter of God, as much as Moses who saw the God of Israel on the mount. And this is not because the prophet rose to the conception of God, or attained to know His will by reflection. It was because God called him and put His words in his mouth.

But, however much the Old Testament reposes on the ground

that all knowledge of God comes from His revealing Himself, and that there is such a true and real revelation, it is far from implying that this revelation of God is a full display of Him as He really is. An exhaustive communication of God cannot be made, because the creature cannot take it in. Neither, perhaps, can God communicate Himself as He is. Hence Moses saw only a form, saw only His back parts. His face could not be beheld. Thus to the patriarchs He appeared in the human form. So in the tabernacle His presence was manifested in the smoke that hung over the Ark. So, too, in Eden He was known to be present in the cherubim, who were the divine chariot on which He rode. All these things signified His presence, while at the same time intimating that in Himself He could not be seen. Yet this may refer only to a bodily vision of Him. There is no trace of the idea in the Old Testament that God, as revealed to men, is not really God as He is in Himself. There is no such idea as that His revelation of Himself is meant merely to be regulative of human life, while what He is in truth remains far away in a transcendental background, out of which it is impossible for it to advance, or unto which it is impossible for men to approach. The revelation God gives of Himself is a revelation of Himself as He is in truth. Yet it may be impossible to reveal Himself fully to men, and it is impossible for any form appreciable to the senses either to contain Him or do much more than indicate His presence. The Hebrew idea of God, however, is not physical; it nowhere speculates on His essence; its idea of Him is ethical.

This conception of revelation is just the characteristic conception of the Old Testament. It reposes on such ideas as that Jehovah is a living God, and that He rules by His activity all the life of men. And it reposes on the idea that the religious life of men is mainly their practical conduct. And revelation is His ruling practically the whole life of the people by making known His will. This must be done to individual persons, not to the whole people directly. Hence all revelation is oral, because it is continuous—the constant impression by Himself of the living God. Even the priests' decisions on questions of right between man and man—their *torah*—were oral, and always caused by occasions. Now, on man's side this revelation was an operation of Jehovah in the mind. Revelation was the arising in the mind of man of thoughts or impulses accompanied by the conviction that the thoughts and impulses were from God. In such thoughts the mind of man and God coalesced, and the man was conscious of meeting God.

The Idea of the Divine Name

In so far as God reveals Himself He acquires a name. Men call that which they know by a name. God, in revealing Himself, proclaimed His own name—Jehovah, Jehovah merciful and gracious. Among the Hebrews the name was never a mere sign whereby one person could be distinguished from another. It always remained descriptive; it expressed the meaning of the person or thing designated. The name bore the same relation to the significance of the thing or person as a word does to a thought. It was always the expression of it. Hence when a person acquired a new significance, when he began to play a new role, or entered into new relations, or was in some sense a new man, he received a new name. Therefore Abram became Abraham; Jacob, Israel; Solomon, Jedidjah—'beloved of God' (2 Sam. xii. 25). So even to God men have a name. Thus He calls Moses and Cyrus by their name. That is, He conceives to Himself what their significance is, what meaning they have in His redemptive providence; and He recognises this, and enters into relations with them as men having this meaning. And the same is true of God's own names. Such a name expresses that which is known to men of the nature of God. When a new or higher side of the Being of God is revealed to men there arises a new name of God. Any name of God expresses some revelation of His Being or character. When the word *name* is used absolutely as God's name, it describes His nature as revealed, as finding outward expression. So when the Psalmist in Ps. viii. exclaims, "How excellent is Thy name in all the earth!" he means how glorious is God's revelation of Himself, or God as revealed on the earth,— that is, among the family of men, whom He has so dignified as to put them over the work of His hands, with all things under their feet. His grace to men is His name here, His revelation of

Himself. So when Israel is warned to give heed to the Angel of the Lord that leads them, for His name is in him (Ex. xxiii. 21), the sense is that the significance of God is present there; what God is, His majesty and authority, is there embodied. So His name is holy and reverend; He, as being what He is known to be, is *reverendus*. . . .

13

God as Personal

William Newton Clarke

Before proceeding to unfold the doctrine of the character of God, it is necessary to dwell for a little upon that element of Personality which the Christian experience and doctrine so evidently imply.

The idea of divine personality is as old as religion. In the early days of unsophisticated activity, prayer came into practice because there was no doubt that there was some one there to be spoken to and to respond. Some one was believed in who could hear the confession of sins and forgive them, who could receive thanksgiving and grant new gifts, and who could keep that which was committed to his care. Man has always regarded the divine as similar to the human, and pictured the gods as personal like himself. What was true in early ages has been true in general ever since. Where divine personality has been ignored in theory through pantheistic thought, it has been restored in practice by the incursion of polytheism. The conviction of divine personality is no part of the childishness of mankind. Man has often been scoffed at for thinking that God is like himself, but instead of folly this is a beginning of wisdom. Anthropomorphism has taken many false and misleading forms, but the truth that man bears the likeness of God and God the likeness of man lies at the foundation of all strong religion.

The Christian doctrine implies personality in God in the same manner with all the religions. It deals with the common experiences of dependence, trust and communion with God, and assumes that they are not false and delusive experiences. If they are not, God must be able to meet the praying soul with an intelligent and active response. But the Christian doctrine lays an emphasis of its own upon the divine personality, for it insists beyond all others upon the divine character, and character inheres in personality, and in nothing else. All doctrine of an ethical God is doctrine of a personal God; and one may almost say that the whole of Christianity consists in the unfolding of God's character. Since character is the vital point in the Christian conception of God, God is necessarily conceived as capable of possessing character; and the capacity for character is identical with what we know as personality.

When we turn to our Christian documents, their testimony to the personality of God is perfectly informal and overwhelmingly abundant. In the Old Testament, as we have seen, God speaks as I, is addressed as Thou, and is referred to as He. His personality is taken for granted, after the manner of the ages in which it was unquestioned. Jesus does not proclaim the personality of God, but he assumes it always, for he is always ascribing to God qualities that could not possibly inhere in anything but personal being. The Christian doctrine has always followed the Master in attributing to God not only the name but the powers and actions of a personal Spirit. In the times of the Bible the question of divine personality did not arise, for the metaphysical definition of personality did not yet exist, though the fact was acted upon as consistently as in any age; but if it had arisen we can see how prophets and apostles would have answered it. That God is holy, or that God is love, would have been sufficient evidence that God may be spoken of as He and addressed as Thou. The reasoning is sound. Character implies personality: no personality, no character. Morality inheres in nothing else: right and wrong are possible only to persons. So common knowledge testifies. In forming our Christian doctrine of God we do not so much attribute character to a Person—though we might do this—as we affirm personality as the only possible basis for character.

Now and then some one rises to assert the existence of a moral order without a personal God. Righteousness is affirmed to be characteristic of the natural order and movement of the world, though no mind made it so. Somehow universal nature brings forth justice, and men may expect right to be done and wrong to be punished by the unconscious order of the world. Sometimes benevolence is attributed to the same mindless movement, and sometimes malevolence and cruelty are said to be its traits. But it is unsatisfactory to attribute genuine moral qualities, whether good or bad, to a mindless order. The only soil in which they can grow has no existence there. Our acquaintance with the habits and habitat of right and wrong is too much for such a doctrine, and we are not surprised that it does not attain to a position of lasting power. The only tenable interpretation of character is that which grounds it in the nature and relations of a personal being. If character be attributed to God, he must be a being who is capable of having it, and such a being has the powers that make up personality. The thought has its difficulties, but the necessity of personality as the substratum of character is inexorable, and the difficulties must be met in loyalty to this requirement.

What do we mean when we speak of God as personal? Our answer to this question must be incomplete, but need not be obscure or doubtful, and there is no reason why we should shrink from the definition that we can obtain. We know on what basis of knowledge personality must be defined. Personality is a human gift, known to us only in ourselves and other men. We know that there may be higher personalities than the human, but we are not acquainted with them. We see suggestions of personality in animals below us, but they are not so clear and full as to provide us with personal companionship in that region. We human beings are persons, and from ourselves alone can we define what we indicate by that name. If we say that God is personal, we must mean that in certain respects God is like ourselves. We may own that in these very respects there may be important differences between God and us, and yet we must mean that the likeness in constitution is genuine, and consists in something that is essential in the nature of both. From this assertion we need not shrink, and should not be repelled by any charges of folly. The doctrine that God is like man is the most ancient of all doctrines of God, and is destined to survive, in some form, as long as a doctrine of God is held. It has not to be accounted for: the only question is, in what sense is it true? What likeness between God and men is affirmed when it is said that God is personal? What facts justify us in speaking thus of God? . . . It is quite superfluous to show that the God and Father of Jesus Christ is thus a self-conscious being who directs his own action, that he knows, loves and acts, that he exercises the powers of a rational mind and does the work of a reasonable will, in relations with other existence. What this modern language expresses is all implied in what Jesus says more simply of God. All Christian thought accepts him as such a Being, and all Christian life proceeds as if such he were. "Pray to thy Father," said Jesus. The Christian faith is faith of one personal being in another. With a conscious mind the worshipper stands face to face.

Thus reaching the idea of personality in God from that of personality in men, we must observe what changes come to the idea in this transference. Of course we drop all such anthropomorphisms as relate to bodily form and aspect, locality and local environment. No longer do we picture or locate God. If we quote the ancient pictorial language, we understand that it is figurative. What is more important, we drop all idea of incompleteness and limitation. We cannot imagine the perfect, but we can to some degree imagine the annihilation of imperfections of which we are aware in ourselves. We have an incomplete self-consciousness, but in God we think of it as complete, or consciousness of all that the self-knowing One contains. We know self-direction, applied to parts of our action, but in God we think of it as unhindered and perfect, governing all that he does. We know relations with other beings, which in our case are partly chosen and partly accepted, whether we will or not, but in God

we think of them as appointed by himself, entered and maintained in full independence. In God the elements of personality
are carried up to perfection. In tracing the process we have
transcended the range of humanity, but not the nature of personality. The God whom we discover is a personal being in the
same sense with us, notwithstanding that his personality rises
above ours by the height of perfection.

Sometimes we are led to fear that we must lose the fact of
personality when we rise to the height of God. We are compelled
to define personality in terms of our own because we know no
other, and in such conditions it is easy to assume that in us the
type or ideal of personality must reside. When we look at
ourselves, personality seems very closely surrounded by confining lines. Our theories have drawn them too closely, in fact, for
until of late we have never recognized the social aspect of personality as one of its elements. Yet we do find human personality a mysteriously bounded and exclusive thing. Each person
has his own field of life: if modern psychology suggests weird
possibilities of division and overlapping, still the normal experience thus far testifies that persons are ordinarily separate from
one another, and one personal consciousness does not take in
another's contents. These restrictions are so real to us that we
may think they are of the nature of the case, and judge finitude
to be of the very essence of personality. So personality in God
may seem inconceivable: infinite personality is often said to be a
contradiction in terms, since one element in the conception is
limited and the other unlimited. . . .

If we could not . . . expand and fill out our conception of
personality, the doctrine of a personal God would be a restriction upon the range of our thought and the upreach of our faith.
Such a restriction it is often alleged to be, but it is not. On the
contrary we find liberty and rest in the thought that perfect
personality requires the largeness of infinity, and can exist in
God alone. In affirming perfect personality in God, the present
Christian doctrine reaffirms a thought that has been among its
vital elements from the beginning, namely, "God is a Spirit" (Jn.
iv. 24). The text is sometimes translated, "God is spirit," as if it

were intended for a statement of God's metaphysical nature. But the context gives the words a simpler and stronger meaning, for it adds that because God is a Spirit, "they that worship him must worship him in spirit and in truth." The declaration is that God and man correspond each to the other: man is a spirit, and so is God: "spirit with Spirit can meet," and only in such meeting is there genuine worship. So wherever the human spirit seeks the divine, the divine may be found, whether in a so-called sacred place or not; for the divine is indeed a Spirit, that knows and loves and acts without such limits of time and space as confine the human. It would not have been quite the same to say, "God is a Person, and they that worship him must bring him genuine personal worship," and yet this poor paraphrase is not so very far from the meaning of the words.

In this consideration of divine personality it has been assumed that a spiritual anthropomorphism is a true key to right knowledge of God. Man is like God, and may learn of him by knowledge of himself. This claim is sometimes condemned as presumptuous, even by men of faith, and many deny that we have the right to project our own likeness up to the region where we are looking for our God. Such action, we are told, vitiates our whole endeavour: what but childishness would be so rash? But the condemnation is not valid. Personality is the highest fact that we know in all the realm of being. As to what there really is above us, we are far more likely to find the truth by seeking from the height of the human spirit than by searching in regions that are farther away from the supreme reality. Surely the Highest is to be discovered in the light of the highest that we know. God is to be discovered in the light of man, rather than of nature and the world non-human, and from finite personality we may best ascend, if we wish to think upward to the reality that surpasses all our thoughts. Starting from this human personality of ours, we are able to perceive that the like of it, carried above the human and expanded to infinity, would be a God, adequate to the universe. Without fear, therefore, the Christian faith holds the doctrine of the personal God as true doctrine, to be completed, not superseded, by knowledge yet to come.

14

The Attributes of God

H. Martensen

The nature of God reveals itself in His attributes. If God were the simply One . . . the mystic abyss, in which every form of determination is extinguished, there would be nothing to be known in the unity. But the living God reveals the unity of His nature by a variety of determinations of His essence, or attributes. His attributes express the different aspects of the same essence; they are different fundamental utterances of one and the same nature. They are therefore not separate from each other, but in each other, penetrate each other, and have their common centre of unity in the same divine Ego. Although, therefore, they are distinctions which in the act of acknowledging we are compelled again to deny, they are by no means to be taken for human modes of looking at the nature of God; they are not man's modes of apprehending God, but God's modes of revealing Himself. We are unable, therefore, to agree with Nominalism when it represents ideas and general conceptions as merely ours, and consequently treats the conceptions which we form of the divine essence as nothing but forms in which we express our religious need of the world, lacking anything objective corresponding thereto in God himself. Distinctly as we must allow that the idea of God ought to be purged of everything merely human, of all untrue anthropomorphisms, we cannot but raise our voice against Nominalism as incompatible with the idea of revelation. To say that we are bound to conceive of God as the Holy and Just One, whilst He in Himself is not holy and just, to call upon God by this name, whilst He does not thus make Himself known to us, is to brand the inmost of truth, of faith, a lie. We teach, accordingly, with Realism, that the attributes of God are objective determinations in His revelation, and as such are rooted in His inmost essence. . . .

In treating of the subject of the divine attributes, our older theologians adopted the division into *"attributa absoluta,"* and *"attributa relativa"*; that is, into attributes which express the relation of God to Himself, and such as express His relation to the world. This division, however, is attended with the difficulty that there are no divine attributes, which, if conceived as living attributes, are not transitive, that is, do not express a relation of God to the world;—nor are there any which are not reflexive, that is, which do not go back on God himself. We gain a more determinate principle of division when we consider the twofold relation which God holds to the world. The relation of God to the world, namely, is on the one hand a relation of unity, on the other hand, a relation of diversity or antithesis. Indeed, our religious life, with all its morals and states, moves between these two poles—that of unity and that of diversity, that of freedom and that of dependence, that of reconciliation and that of separation. In our treatment of this subject, therefore, we shall have to give prominence now to the one and then to the other of the *momenta* of unity and diversity.

As the Being who has life in Himself (John v. 26), in whom is contained all fulness, God is THE ETERNAL. In the eternal God are all the possibilities of existence, all the sources of the entire creation. The eternal is the one who is, the I AM, who is *a se,* the unalterable and unchangeable. But His unchangeableness is not a dead unchangeableness; for it is to produce Himself with infinite fruitfulness out of Himself. His eternity, therefore, is not an eternity like that of the "eternal Hills;" it is not a crystal eternity, like that of the "eternal stars;" but a living eternity, blooming with never-withering youth. But His self-production, His Becoming . . . is not the fragmentary growth or production we witness in time. Created life has time outside of itself, because it has its fulness outside of itself. The Eternal lives in the inner, true time, in a present of undivided powers and fulness, in the rhythmic cycle of perfection. The life He lives is unchangeably the same, and yet He never ceases to live His life as something new, because He has in Himself an inexhaustible fountain of renovation and of youth. For this reason the Church magnifies the "Ancient of Days," as the "incorruptible" and eternal

King, who alone hath immortality (1 Timothy i. 17; vi. 16; Psalm xc. 2.)

The eternal God is OMNIPRESENT in His creation. Creation as a mere possibility without reality lies in the depths of the Eternal Being; as an actuality, possessing any existence different and separate from that of God, it "lives and moves" in the omnipresent One. Everything is filled by God; but that which is filled is different from that by which it is filled. The omnipresent God is the inmost fundamental being of everything that exists; He is the life of all that lives, the Spirit of all spirits. And as He is all in all, so is all in Him. As the bird in the air, as the fish in the sea, so do all creatures live and move and have their being in God. The world of time and space, of nature and history, is contained in Him. . . . But although creation is contained in God, God is not contained in His creation (Psalm cxxxix. 7). Although the omnipresent One is essentially present in every leaf and every grain of wheat . . . He dwells and moves freely in Himself, in virtue of His eternity. He is above and outside of all His creatures, and governs all the possibilities of their existence. . . . Omnipresence, therefore, must be conceived as the free, self-determining presence of God with His creatures, to each of whom He wills to stand in a different relation. The fundamental error of pantheism is the notion that God is omnipresent of necessity. God is present in one way in nature, in another way in history; in one way in the Church, in another way in the world; He is not, in the same sense, present alike in the hearts of His saints, and in those of the ungodly; in Heaven and in Hell (James iv. 8). That we live and move and have our being in God,—an idea which pantheism sets forth as the profoundest and loftiest wisdom,—is one of the most elementary truths of Christianity, and was comprised in the first instruction given to its Catechumens (Acts xvii. 28). But they were also taught by no means to stop there; for that which chiefly concerns us is the special presence of God in His church, and not merely that universal presence by which all creatures alike are embraced, and in which there is nothing to bless the soul.

The eternity and omnipresence of God are one in His absolute KNOWLEDGE. None but a God who knows is able to live at once in Himself and in His creatures.

The OMNISCIENT God is the self-manifest God, whose own essence is clear to Himself and to whom all other beings are naked and open. His eternal being is transfigured into eternal thought; in Him the life is light. The life of the creature is never completely laid open to its intelligence; there always remains a mystery which it has not fathomed; God on the contrary knows the entire fulness of His being; He is completely transparent to Himself. Hence the custom from of old of representing God under the figure of an eye; not that He has an eye, but that He is eye; His essence is knowledge. Relatively to the creature omniscience is an omnipresent, all-searching, all-penetrating vision (Heb. iv. 13; Matt. x. 30). In that he knows all things in their eternal unity, He knows them also in their inner diversities and distinctions. It was God who divided between light and darkness; He knows substance as substance and appearance as appearance; He knows the possible as possible and the actual as actual (Matt. xi. 23; 1 Sam. xxiii. 11); He knows the necessary as necessary, and the free under the conditions which He has Himself imposed on freedom.

The omniscient God is . . . OMNIPOTENT. . . . The omniscient God has complete dominion over Himself, and in affirming His own being He acts with the most complete freedom and with thorough will. But omnipotence can only reveal itself as omnipotence by revealing itself as power over beings other than itself, by realizing its eternal thoughts in a world, different from God. If God is to have power over all and in all, He cannot Himself be all. Omnipotence as thinking, reveals itself in the rational order of existences, in the laws which pervade and regulate history and nature; but it is by no means confined and shut in by this course of laws. Pantheism recognizes only an omnipotence which, as it were, is encompassed by the laws of the world; theism, on the contrary, recognizes a God who had the beginning of the world in His power, and who is able to commence a new work of creation in the midst of the already existing order of nature. We discern, therefore, the Divine omnipotence with special clearness, when we look to the super- natural commencement of the world. By faith we know that the visible world was produced, not by a mere force of nature but by the Word of God; and in the economy of redemption we recognize the God of marvels who is able to create a new thing on earth (Ps. lxxvii. 15; Jer. xxxi. 22). The declaration, "With God nothing is impossible," (Luke i. 37, Matt. xix. 26), is in this respect the great canon of faith, in revelation; and has no limitation save the internal one, that it refers to the God of revelation, who cannot deny Himself, but must necessarily act in harmony with His own eternal thoughts. With this exception, however, it teaches that the divine omnipotence is absolutely unlimited; it sets before us the idea of the wonder-working God who has not expended His creative power in the laws and forces of nature, but still contains within Himself, in the depths of His being, an inexhaustible fountain of possibilities of new beginnings, new revelations, new signs. To profess that the Divine omnipotence expended all the possibilities open to it when it created the present order of nature, is to represent Him either as not a creator at all, after the manner of pantheism, or as having exhausted His power as creator in producing the world, after the manner of deism.

Omniscience and omnipotence are combined in the Divine WISDOM, in the practical, teleological knowledge of God.

The only WISE God is not merely a God of knowledge, but also a God of action—a God of decrees, of providence, of foresight,—who directs His efforts to the realisation of the infinite design of His will. The subject of the divine wisdom was the eternal image of the world, which was to be realized in time. In the Holy Scriptures, accordingly, wisdom is regarded not merely as a divine attribute, but also as the divine thought, which the Only Wise God "possessed in the beginning of His ways." What speculation calls the idea, the world-forming thought, is called in the Holy Scripture wisdom, which was with the Lord, and "daily His delight, rejoicing always before Him" (Prov. viii. 30). It is described not merely as the inner reflection of the divine mind, but also as operative, all-moulding thought. For wisdom (the idea, the divine *sophia*, the heavenly maiden, as theosophists have styled her,) is the "worker of all things" (Wisdom vii. 22). This artist was with the Most High when He prepared the heavens, when He set bounds to the depths, when He established the clouds above and laid the foundation of the earth. But in man alone can it complete its work. It sought rest in all things: it received an heritage amongst all peoples and Gentiles, but in Israel alone (Ecclus. xxiv.), in the Church of God, did it receive an abiding place, where "she entereth in all ages into holy souls, making them friends of God, and prophets." (Wisdom vii. 27). Under the Old Covenant, the Church learned the wisdom of God from the law and the prophets, and from its works in the visible creation. But the riddle of wisdom is first solved in the New Covenant, where prophecy finds its fulfilment, where the topstone is put to the manifestations of wisdom in creation, and the wisdom that is in Christ is all in all. The glorious descriptions of nature, which throughout the Old Testament proclaim the glory of the Creator, are in the New Testament thrown into the shade by the wisdom displayed in the work of redemption. (Eph. iii. 10: "To the intent that now unto the principalities and powers in heavenly places might be known by the church, the manifold wisdom of God." Rom. xi. 33: "O the depth of the riches both of the wisdom and knowledge of God!") Solomon in his wisdom "spake of trees, from the cedar-tree that is in Lebanon, even unto the hyssop that springeth out of the wall" (1 Kings iv. 33); but his wise discourse is cast into the shade by the words of Him in whom "all things are to be gathered together in one" (Eph. i. 10); and the Pauline wisdom was 'to know nothing among men save Christ alone' (1 Cor. ii. 2).

The power of wisdom is RIGHTEOUSNESS. What omnipotence is in relation to omniscience, that righteousness is in relation to wisdom. In saying that God is a righteous God, we expressly postulate omnipotence as moral power. A complete revelation of righteousness is therefore possible only in the world of Freedom. That of which we find the type in nature, where a power may be discerned reducing to order its wild and irregular forces, and setting bounds and limits—which says, "hitherto shalt thou come, and no further; here shall thy proud waves be stayed," (Job xxxviii. 11)—shows itself in its full significance in the domain of the Will. Righteousness is the organizing power in wisdom—it is that distributive energy which assigns to each creature in the divine state its ordained place. But this distributive power is also discriminative; it maintains intact the distinctions it has established; it brings to light the difference between good and evil, and reveals itself in judgment and retribution. (Gal. vi. 7; "Be not deceived; God is not mocked: for whatsoever a man soweth that shall he also reap." See also Romans ii. 6-8.) In righteousness, wisdom has an eternal guarantee against all human arbitrariness: for the just and righteous power of God is present wherever man works unrighteousness, and causes that it hastens with unavoidable necessity onwards to its crisis. There is nothing hid that shall not one day be brought to light, sifted and judged, and in this sense we can say that the world's history is a continuous self-judgment. It is due to righteousness that wisdom continues to be wisdom, notwithstanding the folly of the world; that the wisdom of this world is shown to be folly in the light of the Gospel; that the might of the world is brought to nought by the Word of God. Whether righteousness be considered as distributive or judicative, we must hold fast the canon that, inasmuch as its manifestations are manifestations of the eternal wisdom, every such revelation has a teleological bearing on the highest good. Separated from wisdom, the idea of divine righteousness or justice is a blind levelling power, nothing more nor less than the heathen Nemesis or Fate. . . .

The wisdom and righteousness of God are combined in His GOODNESS. So far from righteousness standing in irreversible antagonism to goodness, it forms in point of fact a constituent element of goodness. (1 John i. 9; "If we confess our sins He is faithful and just to forgive us our sins, and to cleanse us from all unrighteousness." Romans iii. 26; "To declare his righteousness, that he might be just, and the justifier of him which believeth in Jesus.") Goodness which does not do justice, which does not uphold laws, is not goodness; for precisely in executing justice, nay, even in executing punitive justice, does goodness reveal itself; for in that way it seeks to conduct creation to, and educate it for itself. We may characterize the goodness of God in a general way by saying that He has constituted the great end of creation His own end ($\tau\acute{\epsilon}\lambda o\varsigma$), that in constituting creation a means of revealing Himself, He makes His own revelation of Himself a means for the furtherance of the good of creation. It is the nature of goodness to possess its own fulness only in communication, to have only as it gives. But no one is good save the one God (Mark x. 18). As every good and perfect gift comes down from the Father of lights, so also do we derive our susceptibility for these gifts from the same source. . . . He has created the need and the yearning, in order that He might be able to be its fulness and satisfaction. Susceptibility to the communication of the Divine life we find at all stages of creation, but in man alone does it exist in a perfect form—to wit, as susceptibility for God Himself. On this very ground man is the most perfect creature, because he is created to stand in absolute need of God. It is in man that the goodness of God first reveals itself as love.

Considered in relation to the universe the communication of the Divine life is goodness; considered in relation to personality, it is LOVE. All creatures participate in the goodness of God; but personal creatures alone can be constituted partakers of His love. God is love (1 John iv. 16): He neither can nor will be without His kingdom—the kingdom which is constituted by "I and Thou," in which not merely Divine powers and gifts, but the Divine personality itself dwells in the soul and the soul in it. All the Divine attributes are combined in love, as in their centre and vital principle. Wisdom is its intelligence; might its productivity; the entire nature creation and the entire revelation of righteousness in history are means by which it attains its teleological aims. When the fulness of the time came love revealed its true nature to the object beloved, and prepared itself in Christ a Church for eternity. And as Christ in His gospel made known to our race the inmost thoughts of His wisdom—"if He had had a better gospel, He would have given it us"—so does He make those who believe partakers of His own divine nature (2 Peter i. 4). This unity is more than a moral union; it is one of essence; it is more than the mystical unity of pantheism, for it is one of holiness. Viewed in relation to sin eternal love is compassionate grace; viewed in relation to the education of sinful man, it is longsuffering; viewed in relation to its promises and the hope which it awakens in the hearts of men, it is faithfulness (1 Peter iv. 19: "As unto a faithful Creator.")

The kingdom of love is established on the foundation of

HOLINESS. Holiness is the principle that guards the eternal distinction between Creator and creature, between God and man, in the union effected between them; it preserves the Divine dignity and majesty from being infringed by the Divine love; it eternally excludes everything evil and impure from the Divine nature (Isaiah vi. 3: "Holy, holy, holy, is the Lord of Hosts." See also Deut. vii. 21; James i. 13; Heb. x. 27; xii. 29). The Christian mind knows nothing of a love without holiness. Error has been fallen into relatively to this subject, both in a speculative and practical direction. The speculative error we find embodied in pantheistic mysticism, which converts the free moral necessity which moved love to create man, into a mere metaphysical, natural necessity. For example, Angelus Silesius says:—

> "God has as much need of me, as I of Him;
> His nature I help Him to guard and He guards mine.
>
> I know that without me God cannot live a moment,
> If I should perish, He too must needs give up the Ghost.
>
> Nothing there is save I and Thou; if we two cease to be,
> God then is no more God, and heaven falls to ruin."

These mystical paradoxes are true indeed, so far as they give expression to the element of necessity in the divine love—the necessity under which it lies of willing to reveal itself by an infinite communication of itself. But the position that God needs man as much as man needs God, is true only so far as it is accompanied by the recognition of the majesty of God as revealed in His holiness; so far as reverence is guarded in the midst of love. The holy God testifies to us in our consciences, that He has no need of man, in order that He may be able to say to Himself "I." The holy God testifies to us in conscience, that love is not an indefinite flowing over of the nature of man into that of God, but a community of persons, the purity of which depends on strict regard being paid to the limits separating the one from the other. The practical error is antinomism, which consists in rending asunder gospel and law, and in pouring contempt on the law and God of the Old Testament,—a contempt which we find expressed by several Gnostic writers, who, supposing that love gave something of the license commonly awarded to genius, set at naught the idea of duty as something appropriate solely to subordinate beings. We acknowledge, indeed, that holiness without love, as embodied in the Pharisees, is no true holiness; that mere duty, the mere categorical imperative "thou shalt," apart from the promises of the Gospel, is not the spiritual law of Christ; but we must at the same time maintain with equal distinctness, that a gospel of love without law, is a false and impure gospel. The true Gospel confirms and is itself the fulfilment of the law.

The reflection of the rays of love back on God, after passing through His kingdom, is BLESSEDNESS. Blessedness is a term expressive of a life which is complete in itself. It is the eternal peace of love, which is higher than all reason; it is the sabbath of love in its state of eternal perfection (Heb. iv. 3). But the sabbath of love must not be compared with the ευδαιμονία, with the idle enjoyment attributed to heathen gods; love's eternal rest is eternal activity. "My Father worketh hitherto" (John v. 17). In the more exact development of the idea of blessedness this difficulty arises, that on the one hand God must be conceived of as self-sufficient, and needing no one—"not having need of anything" (Acts xvii. 25)—and on the other hand that His blessedness must be conceived of as conditional upon the perfecting of His kingdom; because divine love can satisfy itself only as it is bliss-giving, only therefore as it becomes all in all. The only way to solve this contradiction, is to assume that God has a twofold life—a life in himself of unclouded peace and self-satisfaction, and a life in and with His creation, in which He not only submits to the conditions of finitude, but even allows His power to be limited by the sinful will of man. To this life of God with His creation, must be referred the Biblical ideas of divine grief, divine anger (Eph. iv. 30; Rom. i. 18), and others which plainly imply a limitation of the divine blessedness. This limitation, however, is again swallowed up in the inner life of perfection which God lives, in total independence of His creation, and in triumphant prospect of the fulfilment of His great designs. We may therefore say with the old theosophic writers, "in the outer chambers is sadness, but in the inner ones unmixed joy."

15

The Gentleness of God

Horace Bushnell

"Thy gentleness hath made me great."—Ps. xviii. 35.

Gentleness in a deity—what other religion ever took up such a thought? When the coarse mind of sin makes up gods and a religion by its own natural light, the gods, it will be seen, reveal both the coarseness and the sin together, as they properly should. They are made great as being great in force, and terrible in their resentments. They are mounted on tigers, hung about with snakes, cleave the sea with tridents, pound the sky with thunders, blow tempests out of their cheeks, send murrain upon the cattle, and pestilence on the cities and kingdoms of other gods—always raging in some lust or jealousy, or scaring the world by some vengeful portent.

Just opposite to all these, the great God and creator of the world, the God of revelation, the God and Father of our Lord Jesus Christ, contrives to be a gentle being; even hiding his power, and withholding the stress of his will, that he may put confidence and courage in the feeling of his children. Let us not shrink then from this epithet of scripture, as if it must imply some derogation from God's real greatness and majesty; for we are much more likely to reach the impression, before we have done, that precisely here do his greatness and majesty culminate.

What then, first of all, do we mean by gentleness? To call it sweetness of temper, kindness, patience, flexibility, indecisiveness, does not really distinguish it. We shall best come at the true idea, if we ask what it means when applied to a course of treatment. When you speak, for example, of dealing gently with an enemy, you mean that, instead of trying to force a point straight through with him, you will give him time, and ply him indirectly with such measures and modes of forbearance as will put him on different thoughts, and finally turn him to a better mind. Here then is the true conception of God's gentleness. It lies in his consenting to the use of indirection, as a way of gaining his adversaries. It means that he does not set himself, as a ruler, to drive his purpose straight through, but that, consciously wise and right, abiding in his purposes with majestic confidence, and expecting to reign with a finally established supremacy, he is only too great to fly at his adversary, and force him to the wall, if he does not instantly surrender; that, instead of coming down upon him thus, in a manner of direct onset, to carry his immediate submission by storm, he lays gentle siege to him, waiting for his willing assent and choice. He allows dissent for the present, defers to prejudice, watches for the cooling of passion, gives room and space for the weaknesses of our unreasonable and perverse habit to play themselves out, and so by leading us round, through long courses of kind but faithful exercise, he counts on bringing us out into the ways of obedience and duty freely chosen. Force and crude absolutism are thus put by; the irritations of a jealous littleness have no place; and the great God and Father, intent on making his children great, follows them and plies them with the gracious indirections of a faithful and patient love.

It is scarcely necessary to add that there are many kinds of indirection, which are wide, as possible, of any character of gentleness. All policy, in the bad sense of the term, is indirection. A simply wise expedient has often this character. But the indirections of God are those of a ruler, perfectly secure and sovereign, and their object is, not to turn a point of interest for himself, but simply to advance and make great the unworthy and disobedient subjects of his goodness.

This character of gentleness in God's treatment, you will thus perceive, is one of the greatest spiritual beauty and majesty, and one that ought to affect us most tenderly in all our sentiments and choices. And that we may have it in its true estimation, observe, first of all, how far off it is from the practice and even capacity generally of mankind. We can do almost any thing more easily than consent to use any sort of indirection, when we are resisted in the exercise of authority, or encounter another at some point of violated right.

There is a more frequent approach to gentleness, in the parental relation, than any where else among men. And yet even here, how common is the weak display of a violent, autocratic manner, in the name of authority and government. Seeing the child daring to resist his will, the parent is, how often, foolishly exasperated. With a flush of anger and a stern, hard voice, he raises the issue of peremptory obedience; and when, either by force or without, he has carried his way, he probably congratulates himself that he has been faithful enough to break his child's will. Whereas, raising an issue between his own passions and his child's mere fears, he is quite as likely to have broken down his conscience as his will, unnerving all the forces of character and capacities of great manhood in him for life. Alas, how many parents, misnamed fathers and mothers, fancy, in this manner, that when self-respect is completely demolished in their poor defenseless child, the family government is established. They fall into this barbarity, just because they have too little firmness to hold their ground in any way of indirection or gentleness. They are violent because they are weak, and then the conscious wrong of their violence weakens them still farther, turning them, after the occasion is past, to such a misgiving, half apologizing manner, as just completes their weakness.

It will also be observed, almost universally, among men, that where one comes to an issue of any kind with another, matters are pressed to a direct point-blank Yes or No. If it is a case of personal wrong, or a quarrel of any kind, the parties face each other, pride against pride, passion against passion, and the hot endeavor is to storm a way through to victory. There is no indirection used to soften the adversary, no waiting for time, nothing meets the feeling of the moment but to bring him down upon the issue, and floor him by a direct assault. To redress the injury by gentleness, to humble an adversary by his own reflections, and tame his will by the circuitous approach of forbearance and a siege of true suggestion—that is not the manner of men, but only of God.

True gentleness, we thus perceive, is a character too great for any but the greatest and most divinely tempered souls. And yet how ready are many to infer that, since God is omnipotent, he must needs have it as a way of majesty, to carry all his points through to their issue by force, just as they would do themselves. What, in their view, is it for God to be omnipotent, but to drive his chariot where he will. Even Christian theologians, knowing that he has force enough to carry his points at will, make out pictures of his sovereignty, not seldom, that stamp it as a remorseless absolutism. They do not remember that it is man, he that has no force, who wants to carry every thing by force, and that God is a being too great for this kind of infirmity; that, having all power, he glories in the hiding of his power; that holding the worlds in the hollow of his hand, and causing heaven's pillars to shake at his reproof, he still counts it the only true gentleness for him to bend, and wait, and reason with his adversary, and turn him round by his strong Providence, till he is gained to repentance and a volunteer obedience.

But God maintains a government of law, it will be remembered, and enforces his law by just penalties, and what room is there for gentleness in a government of law? All room, I answer; for how shall he gain us to his law as good and right, if he does not give us time to make the discovery of what it is? To receive law because we are crammed with it, is not to receive it as law, but only to receive it as force, and God would spurn that kind of obedience, even from the meanest of his subjects. He wants our intelligent, free choice of duty—that we should have it in love, nay have it even in liberty. Doubtless it is true that he will finally punish the incorrigible; but he need not therefore, like some weak, mortal despot, hurry up his force, and drive straight in upon his mark. If he were consciously a little faint-hearted he would, but he is great enough in his firmness to be gentle and wait. . . .

. . . It is the very genius of Christianity itself to prevail with man, or bring him back to obedience and life by a course of loving indirection. What we call the gospel is only a translation, so to speak, of the gentleness of God—a matter in the world of fact, answering to a higher matter, antecedent, in the magnanimity of God. I do not say that this gospel is a mere effusion of divine sentiment apart from all counsel and government. It comes by counsel older than the world's foundations. The salvation it brings is a governmental salvation. It is, at once, the crown of God's purposes and of his governmental order. And the gentleness of God must institute this second chapter of gracious indirection, because no scheme of rule could issue more directly in good without it. For it was impossible in the nature of things that mere law—precept driven home by the forces of penalty—should ever establish a really principled obedience in us. How shall we gladly obey and serve in love, which is the only obedience having any true character, till we have had time to make some experiments, try some deviations, sting ourselves in some bitter pains of trial, and so come round into the law freely chosen, because we have found how good it is; and, what is more than all, have seen how good God himself thinks it to be, from what is revealed in that wondrous indirection of grace, the incarnate life and cross of Jesus. Here the very plan is to carry the precept of law by motives higher than force; by feeling, and character, and sacrifice. We could not be driven out of sin by the direct thrust of omnipotence; for to be thus driven out is to be in it still. But we could be overcome by the argument of the cross, and by voices that derive a quality from suffering and sorrow. And thus it is that we forsake our sins, at the call of Jesus and his cross, freely, embracing thus in trust, what in willfulness and ignorance we rejected.

Nor does it vary at all our account of this gospel, that the Holy Spirit works concurrently in it, with Christ and his cross. For it is not true, as some Christian teachers imagine, that the Holy Spirit works conversion by a direct, soul-renewing fiat or silent thunderstroke of omnipotence. He too works by indirection, not by any short method of absolute will. Working efficiently and, in a certain sense, immediately in the man, or subject, he still circles round the will, doing it respect by laying no force upon it, and only raising appeals to it from what he puts in the mind, the conscience, the memory, the sense of want, the fears excited, the aspirations kindled. He moves upon it thus by a siege, and not by a fiat, carries it finally by a process of circumvallation, commonly much longer even than the ministry of Jesus. He begins with the child, opening his little nature to gleams of religious truth and feeling—at the family prayers, in his solitary hours and dreams, in the songs of praise that warble on the strings of his soul, and among the heavenly affinities of his religious nature. And thenceforward he goes with him, in all the future changes and unfoldings of his life, turning his thoughts, raising tender questions in him, working private bosom-scenes in his feeling, forcing nothing, but pleading and insinuating every thing good; a better presence keeping him company, and preparing, by all modes of skill and holy inducement, to make him great. So that, if we could follow a soul onward in its life-history, we should see a Spirit history running parallel with it. And when it is really born of God, it will be the result of what the Spirit has wrought, by a long, and various, and subtle, and beautiful process, too delicate for human thought to trace.

16

The Doctrine of Creation

James Orr

It was stated under last head that the transition from the doctrine of God to that of the world is given in the idea of the divine Purpose, and a little was said on what the purpose of God means, and of love as defining the end of God's purpose. The nature of the purpose of God, however, is best seen by observing it in its execution, and the two spheres in which that execution is to be traced are Creation and Providence.

I pass then to speak of Creation, as the first way in which the purpose of God is realised.

I do not need to delay long on what is meant by the word creation. By this term is simply signified that all things that are in heaven and in earth, "things visible and things invisible" (Col. i. 16), have been brought into being by a free act of God's wisdom and almighty power, and that they continue to subsist in Him (Acts xvii. 28; cf. Col. i. 17), and to be dependent on Him for their existence (cf. Heb. i. 2). This is a doctrine which runs through all Scripture; is, indeed, as will be shown immediately, peculiar to it. It is not the first chapter of Genesis only which affirms this doctrine. It is found from the first page of the Bible to its last. The first words of Scripture are: "In the beginning God created the heavens and the earth" (Gen. i. 1); among its last are: "Thou didst create all things, and because of Thy will they were, and were created" (Rev. iv. 11).

In strictness the above definition includes what theology would call "conservation," as well as creation; but in the large sense in which I use the term, "creation" is meant to cover both God's initial act in calling things into existence, and His preserving power in sustaining them in existence after they are created. The two ideas are inseparably connected. Things do not get out of God's hands after they have been created, or ever attain an independent existence. This is the error of Deism. God cannot get rid of His world in this way. The world is sustained and preserved by Him; and this, in a manner, also is, as it has been phrased, "a continual creation."

Here, however, the question may be raised: "After all, does it very much matter how the world has come into being, now that it is here? Has religion any real interest in such a doctrine as creation—in the Bible doctrine, or in any other theory of the origin of the world?" The answer must be "Yes"; religion has a very deep stake—one of the deepest stakes—in this doctrine of creation. It is always a safe thing to assume that there is no great doctrine of Scripture in which religion has not a deep and vital interest. Let no one be tempted to make light of any one of these doctrines, or to barter them away on the ground that they are of no great importance. What is the interest of religion in this doctrine of creation? It is that faith requires above all things the assurance that everything in the world—in the universe—is absolutely under the power and control of God; and you cannot have this assurance unless on the view which the Bible gives, that everything has been brought into being by God, and depends on Him for its continuance.

Suppose it were otherwise. Suppose there was something in this world which God did not create—some eternal matter, for instance, as theorists have imagined, which existed independently of God, and lay outside of His power. Then see what follows. Here is something which is uncreated, which has existed from eternity, which exists by a necessity of its own nature, which exists by as good a right as God Himself—something, therefore, over which God has no control. You have this resisting, refractory element in the world, and you have no guarantee that God's purpose will not be thwarted, defeated, or, at any rate, limited and broken, by it. Where the doctrine of creation comes in is to assure us that there is nothing of this kind in the whole universe. Everything that exists, seen and unseen, is there, because God has brought it into being; and God has the most absolute control of that which He has created. Human wills can resist God; but it is He who has endowed them with their freedom, and He prescribes the limits within which they are permitted to exercise it. Because of this faith can look confidently up and say: "My help cometh from the Lord, who made heaven and earth" (Ps. cxxi. 2).

Faith, therefore, it will be seen, has a vital stake in this doctrine of creation. It knows that all things are at God's disposal; that there is nothing outside the sphere of His agency; that everything is at His command, to be used for the execution of His will.

The New Testament carries this doctrine still further. You remember how much stress is laid in the New Testament on the fact that Jesus Christ, our Lord, had His part in the work of creation. "In Him were all things created . . . In Him all things consist," or hold together (Col. i. 16, 17): He is the beginning—

the origin and principle—of creation, and He is its end ("Through Him"—"Unto Him"; cf. John i. 2; Col. i. 15-17; Heb. i. 2, 10; Rev. iii. 14, &c.). Christ had to do therefore, with the creation; this means that the created world is in the hands of our Saviour as well as of our Father.

The next thing I wish to say about this doctrine is that the Bible doctrine of creation is an absolutely unique doctrine. It is a doctrine which belongs to the religion of the Bible, and to no other religion in the world. It is important to bring out this uniqueness of the doctrines of the Bible. I do not think it is commonly brought out with half the emphasis it ought to be. If it were brought out more, there would be far less difficulty and trouble in many people's minds; for they would see in every one of these doctrines the signature of God Himself, a uniqueness that points to a divine origin. This is true of the doctrine of creation as well as of every other. You take up books on other religions, and read a great deal in them about creation. You take up the old Babylonian epic of creation, and you read there of Merodach the Creator. You find the word "Creator" scattered over the Babylonian hymns. But in these it means something very different from what it does in the Bible story. In the Babylonian epic the poem begins, in fact, with an account of the origin of the gods, or of the oldest of them, from the chaotic deep. You see you are in a totally different region from what you are in the Bible.

It is the same with other systems of religion and with philosophic theories. In these systems and theories you have a great variety of speculations. The world is viewed either as eternal, which is the Atheistic view; or is made out of an eternally pre-existing matter which God works up into form, which is the Platonic view; or you find the idea of two principles—a good principle and an evil principle—contending together (Dualism), which is the old Zoroastrian or Parsic view. The Zoroastrian set down all that was bad and harmful in the world to the evil principle, and credited all the good in the world to the good principle; and this strife is ever going on. It was overlooked that good and evil in nature are but relative terms (e.g., fire burns and cooks our food; the sun fructifies, but also scorches), and that an eternal principle which is only evil is not an ethical principle in the proper sense at all: is hardly different from a baneful nature-force. Then, again, there are the many forms of theory already spoken of (Pantheistic) in which there is a confounding of the world with God. The world is simply a manifestation of God. God is the "world-soul," or the world is regarded as proceeding from God by a kind of evolutionary process or logical necessity—all things flowing from the nature of God, to use a figure of Spinoza's, with the same necessity as the properties of a triangle flow from the nature of the triangle.

Over against all these doctrines and theories you find in the world about the origin of things—many of them having their recrudescence in our own day—stands in its grand simplicity the doctrine of the Bible. Many are the crude speculations that crop up from time to time in regard to nature and creation. One of the most marvellous in recent years is that which bears the name of "Christian Science," though it is difficult for most people to see either Christianity or science in it. What one does discover, in regard to the doctrine I am dealing with, is that this world which the Bible speaks of as the creation of God is, on the new theory, an illusion of our "mortal mind," whatever precisely that may be. I think it is a very "mortal mind" indeed from which that idea came. It is very strange, is it not, that human beings should happen to be all affected by this illusion alike; and that, as science shows, the world should have been there for long ages before there was any "mortal mind" to think of it! But in regard to all these theories which have been named, it is unwise to think of them as now outside of practical range. They are just the kind of things that are being served up under new names, though in reality they are as old as the hills; only the old-time people did not know better, whereas we ought to know better with our Bibles in our hands.

The doctrine of the Bible, then, I repeat, stands out amidst all these doctrines as something quite different and absolutely unique. As against these theories the Bible declares:—

1. That the world is not eternal, but had a beginning in time. This truth is becoming continually the more evident the more we grow to understand what the world is. Science itself has intro-

duced a word to express the idea that the world is in the position of a clock running down—constantly working off its energy. It calls it "entropy." There will come an end to the world. Similarly, when you go backwards, you come to a beginning—a nebulous fire-mist, or something of the kind, the origin of which science cannot explain. Where does the fire-mist, or its atomic constituents, come from? Only creation can give the answer.

2. Then the world is distinct from God, not in the sense that the world is not from God, and that His presence and power are not everywhere manifested in it—that all the life and power in it are not derived from Him (immanence)—but in the sense that the world is still not God, but is the product of His free creative act, distinguished by God from Himself in the very act of creating it. This is the line which separates a true Theism from Pantheism. God is not simply the life, or soul, or inner law of the world, but has His own eternally-complete life above the world, and in independence of it (transcendence). He is "over all," as well as "through all, and in all" (Eph. iv. 6).

3. It follows that this world is not the product of necessity—of any necessary emanation or logical unfolding of God's Being—but is the result of a free act of His wisdom and power: something which exists because He chose for ends of holiness and love to call it into existence. It need not be added that the only power adequate to such a work is Almighty power—omnipotence.

4. Last of all, the doctrine teaches that the matter as well as the form of the world is the creation of God. There is nothing left outside of God's creative power. The first verse of Genesis gives the deepest philosophy of the whole subject: "In the beginning God created the heavens and the earth." This is what is meant when it is said that God made all things "out of nothing." The expression has sometimes been ridiculed, as if meant that "nothing" was a kind of stuff out of which God shaped the world. The youngest Sunday-school child is not so foolish as to be unaware that that this is not the meaning intended. What the expression means is simply that God brought this world into being where there was no world before; where nothing before existed. As the writer to the Hebrews says: "The worlds have

been framed by the word of God, so that what is seen hath not been made out of things which appear" (Heb. xi. 3; cf. Ps. xxxiii. 6).

It will not be expected that I should enter at length here into the disputed questions as to the relation of the Biblical accounts of creation to modern science, but I may at least indicate what I take to be the right point of view in these matters. There are those who profess to make light of the first chapter of Genesis. I do not. The man who makes light of the first chapter of Genesis does not very well know about what he speaks. I grant at once that it is no part of the function of Biblical revelation to anticipate the discoveries of the nineteenth and twentieth centuries—to tell us beforehand—e.g., what geology has brought to light regarding the age of the earth, or the precise order of its formations. When the Bible does speak of these things, or describes natural phenomena, it does so in plain, popular language, just as we ourselves do every day in speaking of the sun's rising and setting. What the Bible does is not to anticipate the discoveries of later ages, but to tell us about the relation of God to the world, and to convey those great truths of its origin and ordering which are necessary as the basis of a true religious view of the world, no matter to what stage knowledge or science may attain. When, accordingly, we look at the great ideas which the first chapter of Genesis is intended to teach—still more, when we compare them with the fantastic legends found in other religions—we can have little difficulty in seeing, I think, that they have their origin in that Spirit of revelation which was in Israel, and in no lower source.

What are these great ideas which stand in the forefront of this record in Genesis?

1. As already said, there is the great truth that there is One sole Creator of the world—God. Put that over against all forms of polytheistic religion, and remember that the world was full of polytheism when this chapter was written.

2. There is the truth that the world is not eternal, but that God in the beginning created it; "He spake and it was done; He commanded, and it stood fast" (Ps. xxxiii. 9.)

3. It tells us, and this is important, that the world originated,

not in a single creative act, but in a series of divine acts; a series ascending higher and higher, and culminating in the creation of man.

4. It tells us that man was made in God's image, and unites in himself both nature and spirit; that he is the crown of nature, but at the same time the link between nature and a higher spiritual world—between nature and God.

Now, take these ideas, and I think it will be granted that not one of them comes into conflict with science: that, on the contrary, where the two spheres touch, they perfectly coincide, and corroborate each other.

But I venture to go further. I have said that it is not the function of the Genesis chapter to anticipate the discoveries of modern science. But this is not to say that it contradicts them. I do not believe that it does. There is evidence rather of a singular and profound agreement. Take almost any book that has been written on the relation between the first chapter on Genesis and geology—such an old book, e.g., even as Hugh Miller's *Testimony of the Rocks*—and, without entering into details, the very fact, it seems to me, that it is possible to present the two series of things, the Biblical and the geological, alongside of each other as is done in these books, and to show so large and marvellous an amount of harmony between them, is of itself an evidence that we are in presence of something wholly unusual. Could the same be done with any other "cosmogony" or story of creation in existence? This writer in Genesis has clearly the right point of view, and so true is the insight yielded by the Spirit of revelation into the ascending order of nature, that there is marvellously little in this primitive picture of creation—I take it to be one of the oldest things in the Bible—that is not in harmony with what our own most advanced science teaches. To all time this Genesis picture will remain a wonder, not for its disagreement with science, but for its marvellous accuracy. With it in his hands, the simplest peasant is wiser than all his teachers on the great subjects of which it treats, if the teachers are those who ignore or despise its lessons.

There is one question more. Does not this doctrine of creation, it may be said, come at any rate into conflict with the great reigning theory of evolution, particularly in the denial by the latter of what are called "special creations"? I cannot discuss that subject fully here. But a suggestion or two may be offered. I freely admit that the Biblical doctrine of creation does come into conflict with such a theory of evolution as the late Dr. Darwin promulgated. But science has long come to see that "Darwinism" and "evolution" are not synonymous terms; and all down the line leading representatives have taken up a stand against the evolution of fortuity—the evolution that excludes design, and brings in chance in nature to do the work of mind. It was not long before his death that, at the close of a scientific lecture in London, the late Lord Kelvin, the most eminent scientific man of his time, made the declaration that science did not deny creative power, but affirmed the necessity of an organising and directive intelligence in nature.

So far, in truth, from the Biblical doctrine coming into conflict with the doctrine of evolution, it seems to me that it furnishes that doctrine with its necessary limits.

(1) There is the initial limit of origins. No theory of evolution can get over that. However far, as we have already seen, you carry back your process, you come to a point at which you must begin. If it is a fiery, gaseous cloud you start with, you have to explain your gaseous cloud. If it is atoms you start with, you have to explain your atoms. Atoms are not engendered by a process of natural selection. They are there in their countless multiplicity, stamped and fixed with their unchanging characteristics, bearing on them, as Clerk Maxwell said, all the marks of "manufactured articles." If you try to get behind atoms to "sub-atoms," and to electric strains in ether, it is the same thing. How came these wonderful "strains" to be there, the equivalents of the old atoms, only infinitely more complicated in their structure?

(2) Next, there are the limits imposed by the rise of new kingdoms. Evolution has never yet explained the transition from the inorganic to the organic (non-vital to vital), from the insentient to the sentient, from animal consciousness to human rationality. It is significant that it is just at such points as the original creation of matter, the introduction of animal life, and

the creation of man, that the old Hebrew narrator uses the word *bara*, which expresses the idea of true creation—the production of something new and higher by the direct act of God (Gen. i. 1, 21, 27).

(3) There is the limit set to evolution by the law of kinds. For evolution is not, after all, a ceaseless flux. Variation is not absolutely indefinite. Its limits are soon reached, and there is a constant tendency to revert to type. There are "terminal points" along the different lines beyond which evolution cannot go. The Bible affords the necessary check to error here by its insistence on the creation and propagation of "kinds" (Gen. i. 11, 12, 21, 24).

With due recognition of the determinative activity of God in the rise of new kingdoms, or orders of existence, and the production of new types or kinds, there is nothing in evolution that need conflict with a doctrine of "creation," provided the co-operation of secondary causes is not excluded.

17

The Christian View of the World

James Orr

It may conduce to clearness if, having indicated the general scope and purport of these Lectures, I now give a brief statement, in propositional form, of what I consider the Christian view of the world to be, and sketch on the basis of this the course to be pursued in the succeeding Lectures.

1. First, then, the Christian view affirms the existence of a Personal, Ethical, Self-Revealing God. It is thus at the outset a system of Theism, and as such is opposed to all systems of Atheism, Agnosticism, Pantheism, or mere Deism.

2. The Christian view affirms the creation of the world by God, His immanent presence in it, His transcendence over it, and His holy and wise government of it for moral ends.

3. The Christian view affirms the spiritual nature and dignity of man—his creation in the Divine image, and destination to bear the likeness of God in a perfected relation of sonship.

4. The Christian view affirms the fact of the sin and disorder of the world, not as something belonging to the Divine idea of it, and inhering in it by necessity, but as something which has entered it by the voluntary turning aside of man from his allegiance to his Creator, and from the path of his normal development. The Christian view of the world, in other words, involves a Fall as the presupposition of its doctrine of Redemption; whereas the "modern" view of the world affirms that the so-called Fall was in reality a rise, and denies by consequence the need of Redemption in the scriptural sense.

5. The Christian view affirms the historical Self-Revelation of God to the patriarchs and in the line of Israel, and, as brought to light by this, a gracious purpose of God for the salvation of the world, centring in Jesus Christ, His Son, and the new Head of humanity.

6. The Christian view affirms that Jesus Christ was not mere man, but the eternal Son of God—a truly Divine Person—who in the fulness of time took upon Him our humanity, and who, on the ground that in Him as man there dwells the fulness of the Godhead bodily, is to be honoured, worshipped, and trusted, even as God is. This is the transcendent "mystery of godliness" (1 Tim. iii. 16)—the central and amazing assertion of the Christian view—by reference to which our relation is determined to everything else which it contains.

Pausing for a moment on this truth of the Incarnation, we have to notice its central place in the Christian system, and how through its light every other doctrine is illuminated and transformed.

(1) The Incarnation sheds new light on the nature of God, and, in conjunction with the work of the Spirit, reveals Him as triune—Father, Son, and Spirit—one God.

(2) The Incarnation sheds new light on the doctrine of crea-

tion—all things being now seen to be created by Christ as well as for Him.

(3) The Incarnation sheds new light on the nature of man, alike as respects his capacity for union with the Divine, its possibilities of perfection, and the high destinies awaiting it in the future.

(4) The Incarnation sheds new light on the purpose of God in the creation and Redemption of men—that end being, in the words of Paul, "in the dispensation of the fulness of times to gather together in one all things in Christ, both which are in heaven, and which are on earth, even in Him" (Eph. i. 10).

(5) The Incarnation sheds new light on the permission of sin by showing the possibility of Redemption from it, and how, through the Revelation of the Divine purposes of mercy, a far grander discovery is made of the Divine character, and far higher prospects are opened up for humanity.

7. The Christian view affirms the Redemption of the world through a great act of Atonement—this Atonement to be appropriated by faith, and availing for all who do not wilfully withstand and reject its grace.

8. The Christian view affirms that the historical aim of Christ's work was the founding of a Kingdom of God on earth, which includes not only the spiritual salvation of individuals, but a new order of society, the result of the action of the spiritual forces set in motion through Christ.

9. Finally, the Christian view affirms that history has a goal, and that the present order of things will be terminated by the appearance of the Son of Man for judgment, the resurrection of the dead, and the final separation of righteous and wicked,—final, so far as the Scriptures afford any light, or entitle us to hold out any hope.

Beyond this are the eternal ages, on whose depths only stray lights fall, as in that remarkable passage—"Then cometh the end, when He shall have delivered up the kingdom to God, even the Father: . . . then shall the Son also Himself be subject unto Him that put all things under Him, that God may be all in all" (1 Cor. xv. 24-28)—and on the mysterious blessedness or sorrow of which, as the case may be, it is needless to speculate.

I have for clearness' sake exhibited this outline of the Christian view in a series of propositions, but I need hardly say that it is not my intention to attempt to exhaust this outline, or anything like it, in this brief course of Lectures. In the actual treatment of my subject I shall be guided very much by the way in which the main positions of the Christian view are related to current theories and negations.

1. It is plain that the Christian view of the world is Theistic, and as such is opposed, as already said, to all the views which deny a living personal God, and also to Deism, which denies Revelation.

2. The Christian views of nature and man come into conflict with many current theories. They involve, for example, the ideas of creation, and of the spirituality, freedom, and immortal destiny of man—all of which the thoroughgoing "modern" view of the world opposes.

3. The Christian view of sin is irreconcilable with modern theories, which represent sin as a necessity of development, and nullify its true conception by starting man off at a stage but little removed from that of the brutes. At least I take this to be the case, and shall endeavour to give reasons for my opinion.

The above denials, if logically carried out, involve the rejection of the Christian view as a whole. We reject the Christian view *in toto* if we deny the existence of God, the spiritual nature and immortality of man, or destroy the idea of sin. In what follows we are rather in the region of Christian heresy; at least the total rejection of the Christian view is not necessarily implied, though in its mutilation it is found that neither can that which is preserved be permanently maintained.

4. The assertion of the Incarnation may be met by a lower estimate of Christ's Person than the full Christian doctrine implies; or by the complete denial of the supernatural dignity of His Person.

5. The Christian view may be met by the denial of the need or the reality of Atonement, or by inadequate or unscriptural representations of that great doctrine.

6. There may be unscriptural denials, as well as unwarrantable dogmatisms, in the matter of eschatology.

18

Miracles

George MacDonald

I have been requested to write some papers on our Lord's miracles. I venture the attempt in the belief that, seeing they are one of the modes in which his unseen life found expression, we are bound through them to arrive at some knowledge of that life. For he has come, The Word of God, that we may know God. Every word of his, then, as needful to the knowing of himself, is needful to the knowing of God, and we must understand, as far as we may, every one of his words and every one of his actions, which, with him, were only another form of word. I believe this the immediate end of our creation. And I believe that this will at length result in the unravelling for us of what must now more or less appear to every man the knotted and twisted coil of the universe.

It seems to me that it needs no great power of faith to believe in the miracles, for true faith is a power, not a mere yielding. There are far harder things to believe than the miracles. For a man is not required to believe in them save as believing in Jesus. If a man can believe that there is a God, he may well believe that, having made creatures capable of hungering and thirsting for him, he must be capable of speaking a word to guide them in their feeling after him. And if he is a grand God, a God worthy of being God, yea (his metaphysics even may show the seeker), if he is a God capable of being God, he will speak the clearest, grandest word of guidance which he can utter intelligible to his creatures. For us that word must simply be the gathering of all the expressions of his visible works into an infinite human face, lighted up by an infinite human soul behind it—namely, that potential essence of man, if I may use a word of my own, which was in the beginning with God. If God should thus hear the cry of the noblest of his creatures—for such are all they who do cry after him—and in very deed show them his face, it is but natural to expect that the deeds of the great Messenger should be just the works of the Father done in little. If he came to reveal his Father in miniature, as it were (for in these unspeakable things we can but use figures, and the homeliest may be the holiest), to tone down his great voice—which, too loud for men to hear it aright, could but sound to them as an inarticulate thundering—into such a still small voice as might enter their human ears in welcome human speech, then the works that his Father does so widely, so grandly that they transcend the vision of men, the Son must do briefly and sharply before their very eyes.

This, I think, is the true nature of the miracles, an epitome of God's processes in nature beheld in immediate connection with their source—a source as yet lost to the eyes and too often to the hearts of men in the far-receding gradations of continuous law. That men might see the will of God at work, Jesus did the works of his Father thus.

Here I will suppose some honest, and therefore honourable, reader objecting: But do you not thus place the miracles in dignity below the ordinary processes of nature? I answer: The miracles are mightier far than any goings on of nature as beheld by common eyes, dissociating them from a living Will; but the miracles are surely less than those mighty goings on of nature with God beheld at their heart. In the name of him who delighted to say "My Father is greater than I," I will say that his miracles in bread and in wine were far less grand and less beautiful than the works of the Father they represented, in making the corn to grow in the valleys, and the grapes to drink the sunlight on the hill-sides of the world, with all their infinitudes of tender gradation and delicate mystery of birth. But the Son of the Father be praised, who, as it were, condensed these mysteries before us, and let us see the precious gifts coming at once from gracious hands—hands that love could kiss and nails could wound.

There are some, I think, who would perhaps find it more possible to accept the New Testament story if the miracles did not stand in the way. But perhaps, again, it would be easier for them to accept both if they could once look into the true heart of these miracles. So long as they regard only the surface of them, they will, most likely, see in them only a violation of the laws of nature: when they behold the heart of them, they will recognize there at least a possible fulfilment of her deepest laws. With such, however, is not my main business now, any more than with those who cannot believe in a God at all, and therefore to whom a miracle is an absurdity. I may, however, just make this one remark with respect to the latter—that perhaps it is better they should believe in no God than believe in such a God as they have yet been able to imagine. Perhaps thus they are nearer to a true faith—except indeed they prefer the notion of the Unconscious generating the Conscious, to that of a self-existent Love, creative in virtue of its being love. Such have never loved woman or child save after a fashion which has left them content that death should seize on the beloved and bear them back to the maternal dust. But I doubt if there can be any who thus would choose a sleep-walking Pan before a wakeful Father. At least, they cannot know the Father and choose the Pan.

Let us then recognize the works of the Father as epitomized in the miracles of the Son. What in the hands of the Father are the mighty motions and progresses and conquests of life, in the hands of the Son are miracles. I do not myself believe that he valued the working of these miracles as he valued the utterance of the truth in words; but all that he did had the one root, obedience, in which alone can any son be free. And what is the highest obedience? Simply a following of the Father—a doing of what the Father does. Every true father wills that his child should be as he is in his deepest love, in his highest hope. All that Jesus does is of his Father. What we see in the Son is of the Father. What his works mean concerning him, they mean concerning the Father.

19

The Image of God in Man

James Petigru Boyce

In the first account of creation God is represented as saying: "Let us make man in our image, after our likeness." Gen. 1:26. A natural question has arisen whether there is any difference between the words "image" and "likeness." It has been earnestly contended that there is some distinction to be made between them, and various conflicting opinions have been expressed as to what that distinction is. But it is not probable that any was meant or can be established. None is apparent between the original Hebrew words; and the Scriptural use of them elsewhere seems to imply that none exists. In Gen. 1:27, the first of these is used alone, and is twice used. In Gen. 9:6, we have the first word alone, while in Gen. 5:1, the second alone appears, although in Gen. 5:3, both are employed in stating the image and likeness of Adam in which Seth was begotten. The New Testament equally fails to make any distinction. In 1 Cor. 11:7 image (εἰκών) and glory (δόξα) are used; in Col. 3:10 image (εἰκών) alone and James 3:9 likeness (ὁμοίωσις). The assumption, therefore, that there is any distinction between the words is entirely gratuitous. The two are merely synonymous, and are used in accordance with a common Hebrew mode of speech.

A more important question is as to what is meant by that image or likeness.

1. There is certainly no reference to the bodily form of man. God, as pure spirit, has no body in the likeness or image of which man could be created. The body of man, although in many respects superior to that of the brutes, is in a great measure like theirs. The analogy between man and animals generally is very striking and especially that between him and those nearest to him in the stage of being. But there can be no analogy

147

between him and God in this respect. In no way even could special honour be put on man in his physical nature, except as that nature gives evidence of the existence with it of those spiritual powers which elevate man above the brutes. It is as the dwelling-place of that spirit, and because of its intimate association with the life existent in that body, that any sacredness can be attached to the bodily form. It is this, therefore, that is doubtless meant by Gen. 9:6, where the shedding of the blood of man is made punishable on the ground that "in the image of God made he man."

2. That image and likeness consists in the possession of a spiritual nature. It is in this respect that man is like God, who is called "the God of the spirits of all flesh" (Num. 16:22; 27:16); and the Father of spirits (Heb. 12:9). The spirits of men are also spoken of as peculiarly the works of his hands (Ecc. 12:7; Isa. 57:16; Zech. 12:1), and it was to him that our dying Lord commended his spirit. (Luke 23:46.)

As thus spiritual, man has all the peculiarities of a true spirit.

(1.) He is a personal being with individual conscious existence and action.

(2.) He has the intellectual powers by which he knows all things within the sphere of his being.

(3.) He has that power of contrary choice which constitutes him a free agent, although controlled in that choice by the prevailing motive,—by which is meant the motive which most pleases him, and which is, therefore, that to which his own nature gives prevalence.

(4.) He has a moral nature, or a nature with reference to which we can say "ought," and "ought not."

(5.) This moral nature as originally existent must have been (a.) not only without taint of sin, and (b.) without tendencies to sin, and (c.) not merely in a condition of such equipoise between sin and holiness as would make the soul indifferent to the one or the other, but (d.) must have been entirely inclined towards the right, with a holy taste for the holiness of God, having capacity to discern its beauty, and inclination to love him as its possessor, accompanied by readiness to obey the law of God, and perception of man's duty to serve him.

(6.) Perpetuity of existence also belongs to the nature of created spirit, and is another point of similarity between all spirits and God. This is commonly called immortality. But created spirits have not an immortal spiritual life. The soul may die. The death of the soul, however, is not the cessation of conscious personal existence. It is simply the destruction of its spiritual life by its contamination by sin and its separation from the favour of God. What the Scriptures teach of the death of the soul shows, therefore, that natural immortality should not be affirmed of man's spiritual nature. But perpetual existence has been given by God to the nature of created spirits. He might have made that nature otherwise. But he has chosen that it shall be ever existent. This perpetuity of existence is, however, merely in his purpose. He could have willed otherwise. No creation of God could have such a nature as of itself to be imperishable. It has been argued from the simplicity of the soul that it cannot be destroyed by God. But evidently he who created without compounding could also destroy without dividing. But he has chosen to give such a nature to spirit that to that nature belongs perpetuity of existence. It is, however, not self-existent, as is God, for it has not in itself the power of self-existence. Without God it could no longer be. It must be preserved, in the conferred nature, by that same power which created it. But God has given this nature to spirits, which he purposes ever to preserve, and, through that gift and that preservation, they have an endless existence.

3. When God purposed to make man, he also said, "And let them have dominion over the fish of the sea, and over the fowl of the air, and over the cattle, and over all the earth, and over every creeping thing that creepeth upon the earth." Gen. 1:26.

Because of this language some have supposed that this dominion was also a part of the image and likeness of God.

But, evidently, this was an office conferred upon the man made in God's image, and not a part of that image. The Scripture presents it as something that was to follow after the nature was conferred upon man. The resemblance between him and God, in this respect, is very striking. That becomes more so, when we recognize the fulfilment of this purpose in its highest sense in the mediatorial dominion of the Godman. But this position is one of office, and not of nature, and the image of God declared of man is manifestly an image of his nature.

20

The Sin of Man

Augustus Hopkins Strong

The Nature of Sin

The definition of sin as lack of conformity to the divine law does not exclude, but rather necessitates, an inquiry into the characterizing motive or impelling power which explains its existence and constitutes its guilt. Only three views require extended examination. Of these the first two constitute the most common excuses for sin, although not propounded for this purpose by their authors: Sin is due (1) to the human body, or (2) to finite weakness. The third, which we regard as the Scriptural view, considers sin as (3) the supreme choice of self, or selfishness.

In the preceding section on the Definition of Sin, we showed that sin is a state, and a state of the will. We now ask: What is the nature of this state: and we expect to show that it is essentially a selfish state of the will.

1. Sin as Sensuousness.

This view regards sin as the necessary product of man's sensuous nature—a result of the soul's connection with a physical organism. This is the view of Schleiermacher and of Rothe. More recent writers, with John Fiske, regard moral evil as man's inheritance from a brute ancestry.

In refutation of this view, it will be sufficient to urge the following considerations:

(a) It involves an assumption of the inherent evil of matter, at least so far as regards the substance of man's body. But this is either a form of dualism and may be met with the objections already brought against that system, or it implies that God, in being the author of man's physical organism, is also the responsible originator of human sin.

(b) In explaining sin as an inheritance from the brute, this theory ignores the fact that man, even though derived from a brute ancestry, is no longer brute, but man, with power to recognize and to realize moral ideals, and under no necessity to violate the law of his being.

(c) It rests upon an imcomplete induction of facts, taking account of sin solely in its aspect of self-degradation, but ignoring the worst aspect of it as self-exaltation. Avarice, envy, pride, ambition, malice, cruelty, revenge, self-righteousness, unbelief, enmity to God, are none of them fleshly sins, and upon this principle are incapable of explanation.

2. Sin as Finiteness.

This view explains sin as a necessary result of the limitations of man's finite being. As an incident of imperfect development, the fruit of ignorance and impotence, sin is not absolutely but only relatively evil—an element in human education and a means of progress. This is the view of Leibnitz and of Spinoza. Modern writers, as Royce, have maintained that moral evil is the necessary background and condition of moral good.

We object to this theory that

(a) It rests upon a pantheistic basis, as the sense-theory rests upon dualism. The moral is confounded with the physical; might is identified with right. Since sin is a necessary incident of finiteness, and creatures can never be infinite, it follows that sin must be everlasting, not only in the universe, but in each individual soul.

(b) So far as this theory regards moral evil as a necessary presupposition and condition of moral good, it commits the serious error of confounding the possible with the actual. What is necessary to goodness is not the actuality of evil, but only the possibility of evil.

(c) It is inconsistent with known facts,—as for example, the following: Not all sins are negative sins of ignorance and infirmity; there are acts of positive malignity, conscious transgressions, wilful and presumptous choices of evil. Increased knowledge of the nature of sin does not of itself give strength to overcome it; but, on the contrary, repeated acts of conscious transgression harden the heart in evil. Men of greatest mental powers are not of necessity the greatest saints, nor are the greatest sinners men of least strength of will and understanding.

(d) Like the sense-theory of sin, it contradicts both conscience and Scripture by denying human responsibility and by transferring the blame of sin from the creature to the Creator. This is to explain sin, again, by denying its existence.

3. Sin as Selfishness.

We hold the essential principle of sin to be selfishness. By selfishness we mean not simply the exaggerated self-love which constitutes the antithesis of benevolence, but that choice of self as the supreme end which constitutes the antithesis of supreme love to God. That selfishness is the essence of sin may be shown as follows:

A. Love to God is the essence of all virtue. The opposite to this, the choice of self as the supreme end, must therefore be the essence of sin.

We are to remember, however, that the love to God in which virtue consists is love for that which is most characteristic and fundamental in God, namely, his holiness. It is not to be confounded with supreme regard for God's interests or for the good of being in general. Not more benevolence, but love for God as holy, is the principle and source of holiness in man. Since the love of God required by the law is of this sort, it not only does not imply that love, in the sense of benevolence, is the essence of holiness in God—it implies rather that holiness, or self-loving and self-affirming purity, is fundamental in the divine nature. From this self-loving and self-affirming purity, love properly so-called, or the self-communicating attribute, is to be carefully distinguished.

B. All the different forms of sin can be shown to have their root in selfishness, while selfishness itself, considered as the choice of self as a supreme end, cannot be resolved into any simpler elements. . . .

C. This view accords best with Scripture. (a) The law requires love to God as its all-embracing requirement. (b) The holiness of

Christ consisted in this, that he sought not his own will or glory, but made God his supreme end. (c) The Christian is one who has ceased to live for self. (d) The tempter's promise is a promise of selfish independence. (e) The prodigal separates himself from his father, and seeks his own interest and pleasure. (f) The "man of sin" illustrates the nature of sin, in "opposing and exalting himself against all that is called God."

Sin, therefore is not merely a negative thing, or an absence of love to God. It is a fundamental and positive choice or preference of self instead of God, as the object of affection and the supreme end of being. Instead of making God the centre of his life, surrendering himself unconditionally to God and possessing himself only in subordination to God's will, the sinner makes self the centre of his life, sets himself directly against God, and constitutes his own interest the supreme motive and his own will the supreme rule.

We may follow Dr. E. G. Robinson in saying that, while sin as a state is unlikeness to God, as a principle is opposition to God, and as an act is transgression of God's law, the essence of it always and everywhere is selfishness. It is therefore not something external, or the result of compulsion from without; it is a depravity of the affections and a perversion of the will, which constitutes man's inmost character.

The Universality of Sin

We have shown that sin is a state, a state of the will, a selfish state of the will. We now proceed to show that this selfish state of the will is universal. We divide our proof into two parts. In the first, we regard sin in its aspect as conscious violation of law; in the second, in its aspect as a bias of the nature to evil, prior to or underlying consciousness.

I. Every Human Being Who Has Arrived at Moral Consciousness Has Committed Acts, or Cherished Dispositions, Contrary to the Divine Law.

II. Every Member of the Human Race, Without Exception, Possesses a Corrupted Nature, Which Is a Source of Actual Sin, and Is Itself Sin.

1. Proof from Scripture.

This corrupt nature (a) belongs to man from the first moment of his being; (b) underlies man's consciousness; (c) cannot be changed by man's own power; (d) first constitutes him a sinner before God; (e) is the common heritage of the race.

All men are declared to be by nature children of wrath (Eph. 2:3). Here 'nature' signifies something inborn and original, as distinguished from that which is subsequently acquired. The text implies that: (a) Sin is a nature, in the sense of a congenital depravity of the will. (b) This nature is guilty and condemnable,—since God's wrath rests only upon that which deserves it. (c) All men participate in this nature and in this consequent guilt and condemnation.

Death, the penalty of sin, is visited even upon those who have never exercised a personal and conscious choice (Rom. 5:12-14). This text implies that (a) Sin exists in the case of infants prior to moral consciousness, and therefore in the nature, as distinguished from the personal activity. (b) Since infants die, this visitation of the penalty of sin upon them marks the ill-desert of that nature which contains in itself, though undeveloped, the germs of actual transgression. (c) It is therefore certain that a sinful, guilty, and condemnable nature belongs to all mankind.
2. Proof from Reason.

Three facts demand explanation: (a) The universal existence of sinful dispositions in every mind, and of sinful acts in every life. (b) The preponderating tendencies to evil, which necessitate the constant education of good impulses while the bad grow of themselves. (c) The yielding of the will to temptation, and the actual violation of the divine law, in the case of every human being so soon as he reaches moral consciousness.

The fundamental selfishness of man is seen in childhood, which human nature acts itself out spontaneously. It is difficult to develop courtesy in children. There can be no true courtesy without regard for man as man and willingness to accord to each man his place and right as a son of God equal with ourselves. But children wish to please themselves without regard to others. . . . No other animal does things habitually that will injure and destroy it, and does them from the love of it. But man does this, and he is born to do it, he does it from birth.

Reason seeks an underlying principle which will reduce these multitudinous phenomena to unity. As we are compelled to refer these common moral phenomena to a common moral nature, and to find in it the cause of this universal, spontaneous, and all-controlling opposition to God and his law. The only possible solution of the problem is this, that the common nature of mankind is corrupt, or in other words, that the human will, prior to the single volitions of the individual, is turned away from God and supremely set upon self-gratification. This unconscious and fundamental direction of the will, as the source of actual sin, must itself be sin; and of this sin all mankind are partakers.

With regard to the origin of this sinful nature which is common to the race, and which is the occasion of all actual transgressions, reason affords no light. The Scriptures, however, refer the origin of this nature to that free act of our first parents by which they turned away from God, corrupted themselves, and brought themselves under the penalties of the law.

As the result of Adam's transgression, all his posterity are born in the same state into which he fell. But since law is the all-comprehending demand of harmony with God, all moral consequences flowing from transgression are to be regarded as sanctions of law, or expressions of the divine displeasure through the constitution of things which he has established. Certain of these consequences, however, are earlier recognized than others and are of minor scope; it will therefore be useful to consider them under the three aspects of depravity, guilt, and penalty.

By [depravity] we mean, on the one hand, the lack of original righteousness of holy affection toward God, and, on the other hand, the corruption of the moral nature, or bias toward evil, That such depravity exists has been abundantly shown, both from Scripture and from reason, in our consideration of the universality of sin.

Salvation is two fold: deliverance from the evil—the penalty and the power of sin; and accomplishment of the good—likeness to God and realization of the true idea of humanity. It includes all these for the race as well as for the individual;

removal of the barriers that keep men from each other; and the perfecting of society in communion with God; or, in other words, the kingdom of God on earth. It was the nature of man, when he first came from the hand of God, to fear, love, and trust God above all things. This tendency toward God has been lost; sin has altered and corrupted man's innermost nature. In place of this bent toward God there is a fearful bent toward evil. Depravity is both negative—absence of love and of moral likeness to God—and positive—presence of manifold tendencies to evil. Two questions only need detain us:

Depravity partial or total?

The Scriptures represent human nature as totally depraved. The phrase "total depravity," however, [is] liable to misinterpretation, and should not be used without explanation. By the total depravity of universal humanity we mean:

Negatively,—not that every sinner is: (a) Destitute of conscience,—for the existence of strong impulses to right, and of remorse for wrong-doing, show that conscience is often keen; (b) devoid of all qualities pleasing to men and useful when judged by a human standard,—for the existence of such qualities is recognized by Christ; (c) prone to every form of sin,—for certain forms of sin exclude certain others; (d) intense as he can be in his selfishness and opposition to God,—for he becomes worse every day.

Positively,—that every sinner is: (a) totally destitute of that love to God which constitutes the fundamental and all-inclusive demand of the law; (b) chargeable with elevating some lower affection or desire above regard for God and his law; (c) supremely determined, in his whole inward and outward life, by a preference of self to God; (d) possessed of an aversion to God which, though sometimes latent, becomes active enmity, so soon as God's will comes into manifest conflict with his own; (e) disordered and corrupted in every faculty, through this substitution of selfishness for supreme affection toward God; (f) credited with no thought, emotion, or act of which divine holiness can fully approve; (g) subject to a law of constant progress in depravity, which he has no recuperative energy to enable him successfully to resist. (a) John 5:42—"But I know you, that ye have not the love of God in yourselves." (b) 2 Tim. 3:4—"lovers of pleasure rather than lovers of God"; cf. Mal. 1:6—"A son honoreth his father, and a servant his master: if then I am a father, where is mine honor? and if I am a master, where is my fear?" (c) 2 Tim. 3:2—"lovers of self"; (d) Rom. 8:7—"the mind of the flesh is enmity against God." (e) Eph. 4:18—"darkened in their understanding . . . hardening their heart"; Tit. 1:15—"both their mind and their conscience are defiled"; 2 Cor. 7:1—"defilement of flesh and spirit"; Heb. 3:12—"an evil heart of unbelief"; (f) Rom. 3:9—"they are all under sin"; 7:13—"in me, that is, in my flesh, dwelleth no good thing." (g) Rom. 7:18—"to will is present with me, but to do that which is good is not"; 23—"law in my members, warring against the law of my mind, and bringing me into captivity under the law of sin which is in my members."

Ability or inability?

In opposition to the plenary ability taught by the Pelagians, the gracious ability of the Arminians, and the natural ability of the New School theologians, the Scriptures declare the total inability of the sinner to turn himself to God or to do that which is truly good in God's sight. A proper conception also of the law, as reflecting the holiness of God and as expressing the ideal of human nature, leads us to the conclusion that no man whose powers are weakened by either original or actual sin can of himself come up to that perfect standard. Yet there is a certain remnant of freedom left to man. The sinner can (a) avoid the sin against the Holy Ghost; (b) choose the less sin rather than the greater; (c) refuse altogether to yield to certain temptations; (d) do outwardly good acts, though with imperfect motives; (e) seek God from motives of self-interest.

But on the other hand the sinner cannot (a) by a single volition bring his character and life into complete conformity to God's law; (b) change his fundamental preference for self and sin to supreme love for God; nor (c) do any act, however insignificant, which shall meet with God's approval or answer fully to the demands of law. . . .

21

The Gospel Portraits of Jesus

Alexander Balmain Bruce

In making an attempt in the present chapter to state the Christian facts, it may be well, in order to prevent misunderstanding, to begin by explaining that by the expression is not meant all that a Christian man believes to be true concerning the person, life, and teaching of Jesus, but only the things related in the Synoptical Gospels on these topics which possess such a high degree of probability that they may be provisionally accepted as facts, even by those who scan the evangelic records with a critical eye. The task now on hand is beset with difficulty, arising from the circumstance that these records cannot, without proof, be assumed to contain only pure objective history, but may at least plausibly be regarded as history coloured more or less by the faith of the narrators. How much or how little solid fact any one finds in them depends partly on the philosophical bias which he brings to the examination, partly on the extent to which, on grounds of historical criticism, he thinks he can trace the colouring influence of faith. The estimates formed of the amount of historical matter in the Gospels are, accordingly, very diverse. Some reduce the kernel of hard fact to a meagre minimum: the beautiful moral teaching in the Sermon on the Mount, or a new method and secret for attaining the reward of righteousness—the method of inwardness, the secret of self-denial. Some even go the length of doubting whether anything whatever can be definitely ascertained concerning Jesus; whether "the Sermon on the Mount" was ever preached, and whether "the Lord's Prayer" was ever prayed by Him. Such style themselves, with reference to the history of Christ, agnostics, men who do not know, and who maintain that it is impossible to know. The imposing authority of great names that could be cited in support of such sceptical views might well scare one from attempting to determine the outlines of the Christianity of Christ. Nevertheless, in spite of discouragement we must try.

We may find a good clue, to begin with, as to what was central in the thought and religion of Jesus, in the apologetic elements contained among His recorded sayings. What was He above all things obliged to apologise for? It was, as we have already learned, His love to the outcast sinful, the "publicans and sinners" of Jewish society. That love, then, we may take to be the first and fundamental Christian fact. It is a very instructive fact. It shows us for one thing that Christ is not to be thought of primarily and principally as a teacher coming with some wonderful new doctrines, moral or religious, revealing to the initiated some unheard of method and secret for the attainment of felicity. This needs to be said and to be reiterated; for there is an inveterate tendency among believers and unbelievers alike to assume that revelation must consist in the communication of instruction, and that the founder of a religion must before all things be a great original teacher. And, beyond doubt, Jesus was such a teacher; but the thing to be insisted on is that, great though He was as a teacher, He was still greater in His love. His love was the great novelty, the primary revelation He had to make—a revelation made, as all God's greatest revelations have been made, by deeds rather than by words. But by words likewise. For no recorded word of Jesus is more characteristic, more credibly authentic, and more significant as an index of His own conception of His mission, than this: "The Son of man is come to save that which was lost," with which may be associated that other parabolic saying: "They that be whole need not a physician, but they that are sick." Thereby He intimated that His proper vocation was that of a Saviour or Healer of spiritual disease, and suggested the thought that Christianity is the religion of redemption, a religion which announces and applies a new divine power of love to cure moral evil. That power He splendidly exemplified in His own ministry, effecting marvellous spiritual recoveries among the depraved by a sympathy which no moral vileness could repel, drawing the sinful to Him in perfect confidence of welcome, and making credible the existence of similar love in the heart of God.

Jesus healed men's bodies as well as their souls. The same

sympathy which made Him pity them in their sin, caused Him also to bear on His heart the burden of their sicknesses. Some of the best authenticated narratives in the Gospels are accounts of cures wrought instantaneously on the bodies of sick persons. The stories are found in all the three first Gospels, and may be regarded as belonging to the original stock of apostolic tradition. They are all very marvellous; some, if not all, seem positively miraculous, not explicable otherwise than by the assumption that Jesus had at His command a supernatural divine power. That one so exceptionally humane should desire, if possible, to remove all evil, physical as well as moral, was perfectly natural; that He was able by a word to heal a leper seems to show that in some preternatural manner "God was with Him."

Apart from their miraculous aspect, these works of healing possess permanent significance as showing the comprehensiveness of Christ's conception of salvation. Nothing lay out of His way which in any respect concerned the wellbeing of man. In His healing ministry He was the pioneer of Christian philanthropy, and lent the sanction of His example to all movements which aim at social amelioration.

Though Jesus was not a philosopher or mere ethical teacher, yet He did teach, and in a most characteristic style. What a religious teacher has to say concerning God and man is always important and worth noting. Now Christ's doctrine of God was not elaborate. It was remarked of Him by shrewd observers among the common people of Judæa that He taught "not as the scribes," which was as if we should say now of any new religious teacher arising among us, "He teaches not as a professional theologian." Jesus taught His doctrine of God by a single word. He always called God "Father," and that in connections which gave His thought about God a very new and startling aspect, offensive to those who were reputedly holy and righteous called "Pharisees," very welcome to all others, that is to the great mass of the Jewish people. The name as He used it implied that God had paternal goodwill to the unthankful and evil, to the immoral and irreligious, to the outcasts; that He was the God and Father of the mob, of the publicans and sinners, of the lost sheep of the house of Israel, not merely of Pharisees, scribes, and priests. It was only an extension of Christ's thought about

God when Paul said that God was not the God of the Jews only, but also of the Gentiles; and we simply apply His grand inspiring doctrine to our modern circumstances when we say God is the God and Father of the churchless, of the proletariat, of the denizens of the lanes and slums of our great cities, of society's out-casts and non-elect. It was a new idea of God, whose import is not yet fully realised, a revelation full of hope for humanity.

Christ's idea of man was kindred to His idea of God. It was as remote as possible from that of Celsus, whose feeling towards mankind was one of cynical contempt. Jesus thought a man a being of infinite value, in view of his spiritual endowments and possibilities. He said with an emphasis previously unknown, a man is a man, yea a son of God. He said this not with reference to picked samples—holy, wise, learned men; on the contrary, of the holiness, wisdom, and learning in vogue He seemed to have a very poor opinion; still less with reference to men that were rich, for of mere material wealth He always spoke with a compassionate disdain. He affirmed the indefeasible worth of human nature with reference to the poor, the ignorant, the foolish, the immoral, the irreligious; to the amazement and disgust of those belonging to the upper select classes of society. He taught this revolutionary doctrine not as a Rabbi delivering theoretical lectures in the school to his disciples, but chiefly by the far harder and more testing method of action; freely associating with people low down in the social scale, whose worth to God and men, in spite of degradation, He persistently proclaimed. The reality and extent of the degradation He was well aware of, and often described by the pathetic term "lost." He knew that His outcast friends much needed saving, but He believed, in defiance of all appearances and assertions to the contrary, that they were capable of being saved and worth saving; that, though lost, they were still lost sons. This genial, hopeful, optimistic humanitarianism of Jesus was an astonishment and scandal to His contemporaries. It is not more than half sympathised with yet, even by Christendom. Were all that bear the Christian name earnestly of Christ's mind, how many degraded ones would be raised, and, what is more important, how many would be kept from ever sinking down! What countless possible victims of lust and greed would be rescued from wrong by the spirit of humanity expelling these evil demons from the heart! So, not otherwise, will God's kingdom come.

But it is not merely through care for the good of others that Christ's doctrine of man works for the establishment of the divine moral order. It tends thereto with equal power through the stimulus it brings to bear on the individual conscience to realise the ideal of sonship. For the doctrine that man is the son of God has two sides—the one the side of privilege, the other that of duty. It is a great privilege to be able to call God our Father. But the grace in which we stand imposes high obligations. God's sons must be God-like. They must realise in their character the Christian ethical ideal. It is a very high, exacting ideal as set forth, e.g., in the Beatitudes, implying a passion for the right, and a willingness even to suffer for righteousness' sake. That ideal, not less than God's gracious love to all, is a part of Christ's gospel for the million. And though it seems too high for all but the few elect ones, the aristocracy of the kingdom of heaven, it ought to be proclaimed in all its Alpine elevation in the hearing of all. For its elevation is its charm. Christ's moral ideal commands universal respect, and to lower its claims to adapt it to average capacity, a policy too often pursued, is only to expose Christianity to contempt.

The foregoing facts suggest the thought that Jesus was a very remarkable person, exceptional, unique in goodness and wisdom, a moral phenomenon difficult to account for in any age and country, and especially in such an arid spiritual wilderness as Judæa was at the beginning of our era. Men of all shades of opinion acquainted with His history are agreed in this. All subscribe to this creed at least, that Jesus was an extraordinary man, a religious genius. The Church believes Him to be God. If this solemn affirmation be true, then the story recorded in the Gospels presents to our view this great spectacle: God entering into the world in human form and under the limited conditions of humanity, as a redemptive force, to battle with the moral evil that afflicts mankind. If we form the highest idea possible of divine love and grace, the amazing thing will not appear utterly incredible. On the physical and metaphysical side the doctrine may seem to present a difficulty bordering on impossibility, but on the moral side it is worthy of all acceptation. The world has a religious interest in the faith that Jesus is divine; for what can be more welcome than the idea that God is like Him, loves men as He loved them—nay, is Himself personally present and active in that Good Friend of publicans and sinners?

There is good reason to believe that Jesus was conscious of being in some sense an exceptional person. He had a peculiar way of designating Himself. He called Himself sometimes the Son of God, but oftenest the Son of man. What the precise import of these names may be is a subject for careful inquiry. But they at once suggest thoughts of a notable personage, and provoke the question, Who can this be? The titles are in harmony with what He who wore them taught concerning God and man. "Son of man," to mention the more familiar and less mysterious title first, probably expresses sympathy and solidarity with mankind. It is the embodiment in a name of the faith, hope, and love of Jesus for the human race. The other title, Son of God, expresses the consciousness of intimate relations to God; not necessarily exclusive, possibly common to Jesus with other men, but certainly implying affinity of nature between God and man, and great possibilities of loving fellowship. It is in that view the correlate of the name "Father" employed by Jesus to express His conception of the Divine Being. If God be our Father, we are, of course, His sons. In one recorded saying Jesus seems to claim for Himself some special and exceptional privilege in the matter of Sonship: "No man knoweth the Son, but the Father; neither knoweth any man the Father save the Son." The use of the definite article before Son and Father instead of the pronoun "my," seems to express an absolute antithesis and suggest a unique relation. But this need not be insisted on here. It is enough to signalise in general Christ's manner of self-designation as expressing His consciousness of being in some sense an exceptional person, and as, in that view, one of the notable Christian facts.

Two other features in Christ's teaching claim attention here: His proclamation of the advent of the kingdom of God, and His allusions to the Messianic hope. These both imply something going before, and are suggestive of the historical presuppositions of Christianity, an elect race, a sacred literature, and the expectation ever cherished in Israel, amid present trouble, of brighter days to come. The utterances of Jesus on these topics were rooted in the past history of His people. It was perfectly natural that He as a Jew should speak about a kingdom of God and a Christ as coming, or possibly, if there were apparently good reasons for thinking so, as come. But did He think and call Himself the Christ? It is a momentous question, on which there is not, as yet, entire agreement of opinion. That Jesus might have His Messianic idea, and, in common with His countrymen, cherish the Messianic hope, and even believe in Messiah's speedy advent, no one denies; but that He actually identified Himself with the Messiah, or complacently allowed His disciples to make the identification, some are extremely unwilling to admit. The able and eloquent author of *The Seat of Authority in Religion* regards the ascription of Messiahship to Jesus as the earliest of several theories concerning His person formed by the Primitive Church, and finds in all gospel texts that impute to Jesus Himself Messianic pretensions the reflection of this later faith. Among his reasons for adopting this view is a regard to the modesty of Jesus, and to the unity and harmony of His spiritual nature. Now unquestionably these are to be respected and even jealously guarded; and if the Messianic consciousness ascribed to Jesus really involved an "inner breach of character," it would have to be discarded at all hazards. But let us see how the case actually stands. What does "Messiah" translated into our modern European dialect mean? It signifies the bringer-in of the *summum bonum*, the realiser of all religious ideals, the establisher of the loving fellowship between God and man, and between man and man, for which the Hebrew equivalent is the kingdom of heaven. Now is this not what Jesus actually did? He introduced the religion of the spirit, the final, ideal, absolute religion. He brought into the world supremely valuable and imperishable boons: a God who is a Father, a regenerated human brotherhood, a love that had in it purpose and power to redeem from sin, a love that could die, and that expected to die a "ransom" for the million. To say that Jesus thought of Himself as Messiah is to say that He was aware what He was doing, that He understood His endowments and the tasks they imposed on Him. The name is foreign to us, and if we do not like it we can translate it into our own tongue. The thing it denotes is good, and we owe it to Jesus. Why should we hesitate to say that He knew He was bringing to the world that good? It is not necessary to think of that knowledge as involving pretension and claim. We should think of it rather as involving simply recognition of a vocation arising out of endowment, above all out of the unparalleled wealth of human sympathy with which the heart of Jesus was filled. Recognition, or better still, submission; for the hardships and sorrows of the Messianic vocation were such as effectually excluded all vain ambitious thoughts, and insured that the Elect One in entering on His high career should be simply suffering Himself to be led into a path from which all egoistic feelings would instinctively shrink. But be this as it may, Jesus was the Christ, if He did not call Himself Christ. He did Messiah's work, and that is another of the essential Christian facts.

Jesus represented the kingdom of God, whose advent He announced, as the chief good and the chief end of man, for the acquisition of which one should be ready cheerfully to part with all other possessions, and to whose sovereign claims all other interests should be subordinated. He further taught that that kingdom is a chief end for God as well as for men. He strongly and repeatedly asserted the reality of a paternal providence continually working for the good of those who make the kingdom of God their chief end. "Seek ye" He said, "the kingdom of God, and all these things shall be added unto you" (Matt. vi. 33); "The very hairs of your head are all numbered" (Matt. x. 30); "Fear not, little flock; for it is your Father's good pleasure to give you the kingdom" (Luke xii. 32). His absolute faith in the fortunes of the kingdom, and in God's power and will to promote its interest in spite of all untoward influences, found emphatic expression in reference to His own personal concern therein in the words: "All things are delivered unto me of my Father" (Matt. xi. 27; Luke x. 22). These simple, pathetic utterances are profoundly significant. They implicitly enunciate Christ's doctrine of God's relation to the world, and teach in effect that the universe has a moral end, and that the creation is an instrument in God's hands for the advancement of that end—the establishment of His kingdom of love.

22

The Virgin Birth of Christ

Charles Gore

Among subjects of present controversy not the least important is the Virgin Birth of Jesus Christ. It is not only that natu-
ralistic writers frequently speak as if it were unmistakeably a
fable; but writers who do in some sense believe in the Incarnation are found at times to imply that, while the Resurrection
must be held to, the Virgin Birth had better be discarded from
the position of an historical fact. And even writers of a more
orthodox character are occasionally found to speak of it with
some considerable degree of doubt or disparagement. Such
rejection or doubt is in part based upon the silence, or presumed
silence, on the subject of two of the evangelists, St. Mark and St.
John, also of the apostolic epistles, especially those of St. Paul. In
part it is held to be justified by discrepancies between the
accounts of the birth in St. Matthew and St. Luke; and by
circumstances which are supposed to render those accounts
unworthy of the credit of serious critics. At the same time it is
often maintained that the belief in the Incarnation is not bound
up with the belief in the virginity of Mary: and that, even if this
latter point were rejected or held an open question, we could still
believe Jesus Christ to be not as other men, but the Son of God
incarnate. This latter belief in the person of Christ is, it is maintained, legitimate as warranted by His claims, His miracles, His
resurrection, His kingdom; but it does not therefore follow that
legend may not have gathered around the circumstances of His
birth. There is analogy, it is suggested, for such an accretion in
the birth-stories of innumerable heroes, both Jewish and Gen-

tile, from Buddha, Zoroaster, and Samson downwards to Augustus and John the Baptist.

In view of this tendency of thought, I will endeavour—

(1) to account for the silence of St. Mark, St. John, and St. Paul, so far as it is a fact, while at the same time indicating evidence which goes to show that these writers did in reality recognize the fact of the Virgin Birth;

(2) to justify the claim of Luke i-ii to contain serious history;

(3) to do the same for Matt. i-ii taken by itself;

(4) to indicate the relation of the two accounts;

(5) to show cause for believing that the Virgin Birth has in Christian tradition from the first been held inseparable from the truth of the Incarnation;

(6) to deal with the argument derived from the birth-legends of heroes;

(7) to show cause for believing that the doctrine of the person of Christ is in reality inseparable from the fact of His birth of a virgin.

First however it is necessary to make plain the point at which this argument begins, and the class of persons towards whom it is addressed. I am assuming the substantial historical truth of the evangelical narrative common to the three synoptists and supplemented by St. John: I am assuming the reality of the physical resurrection and, accordingly, the possibility of miracles and their credibility on evidence: I am assuming that Jesus Christ really was the Son of God incarnate. One who entertains doubts on these matters must satisfy himself by considerations preliminary to our present undertaking, just as in the beginning of Christianity the belief in Jesus as the Son of God was, as will be presently explained, prior to the knowledge of His Virgin Birth. The question now is,—granted the miraculous personality of Christ and His resurrection, granted the idea of the Incarnation to be the right interpretation of His person, is there still reason to doubt the historical character of the miracle of the birth, and is it reasonable to imagine that such doubt will be compatible with a prolonged hold on the belief in the Incarnation itself? . . .

The Connexion of Doctrine and Fact

What has been hitherto attempted is both to vindicate the historical character of the records of our Lord's miraculous birth at Bethlehem and also to show that in the earliest tradition of the Christian churches, as far as we can trace it, the belief in the Virgin Birth is found as a constant accompaniment of the confession of His Incarnation. What we have finally to do is to show cause why we should regard the belief in the Virgin Birth as, in fact, inseparable from belief in the Incarnation and, even more from belief in the sinless Second Adam.

For beyond a question, our opinion as to the inseparability of the supposed fact from the Christian idea will affect our estimate of the evidence. The historical evidence for our Lord's birth of a virgin is in itself strong and cogent. But it is not such as to compel belief. There are ways to dissolve its force. To produce belief there is needed—in this as in almost all other questions of historical fact—besides cogent evidence, also a perception of the meaning and naturalness, under the circumstances, of the event to which evidence is borne. To clinch the historical evidence for our Lord's virgin birth there is needed the sense, that being what He was, His human birth could hardly have been otherwise than is implied in the virginity of His mother.

The logic of the matter may be represented on the ground of the Incarnation. Granted that the eternal Son of God did at a certain moment of time take flesh by a real incarnation in the womb of Mary,—granted that He was born as man, without change of personality or addition of another personality, but simply by the assumption of a new nature and by an entrance into new conditions of life and experience—granted in this sense the incarnation of the Son of God in the womb of Mary, can we conceive it to have taken place by the ordinary process of generation? Do not we inevitably associate with the ordinary process of generation the production of a new personality? Must not the denial of the Virgin Birth involve the position that Jesus was simply a new human person in whatever specially intimate relations with God? This seems to the present writer to be very probably the case, but at the same time to be a question very difficult to argue. But the argument becomes almost irresistible when the question is removed from the idea of incarnation strictly considered, to the associated idea of the sinless humanity, the humanity of a 'Second Adam.'

Jesus Christ was a new departure in human life. Philosophers of different ages, from Plato to Carlyle, have been found scoffing at contemporary reformers, on the ground that their proposed reforms did not, could not, go deep enough to get at the root of the evils of human society. What is wanted to remedy these evils is a fresh departure—in some sense, a new birth, or regeneration of humanity. So moral philosophers have reasoned: but it has been a matter of words. Jesus Christ alone has, in any adequate sense, translated this logical demand into actual reality. In Him we really find a 'Second Adam,' a new manhood. He appears among men in all the fulness of human faculties, sympathies, capacities of action and suffering; He was in all points such as we are except sin. But what an exception! As Jesus moves among the men of His day, as His historical presentation renews His image for each generation, by how great a gulf is He separated in His sinlessness, His perfection, from other men. He is very man, but new man. And with this quality of His person coincides His method. He will not take other men as He finds them and make the best of them. He demands of them the acceptance of a new birth; the fundamental reconstruction of their moral being on a new basis, and that basis Himself. 'Except a man be born anew he cannot see the kingdom of God.' 'Except ye turn'—with a radical conversion of the moral tendency of your being—'except ye turn and become as little children, ye shall in no wise enter into the kingdom of heaven' (St. John iii. 3; St. Matt. xviii. 3). Christ demands, then, a fundamental moral reconstruction of humanity, and He makes it possible because He offers to men a new life. He offers to reproduce in each man who will believe in Him and yield himself to Him, the quality of His own life by the bestowal of His own Spirit. Himself the New Man, He can make all men new. But granted that in this fundamental sense Christ Jesus is a new moral creation, is it possible that this new moral creation can have involved anything short of a new physical creative act? Does not all we know of physical heredity, all we know of the relation of spirit and body, lead us to believe that the miracle of a new moral creation must mean the miracle of a new physical creation? If the moral character was new, must not the stuff of the humanity have been new too? Must not the physical generation of the Second Adam have been such as to involve at once His community with our nature and His exemption from it? I am not laying all the stress on this sort of logic. I would, here and elsewhere, keep *a priori* arguments in their place. But this logic seems to me at least strong enough to clinch the historical argument or even to condition the historical discussion by an antecedent expectation that the birth of the Second Adam must have been physically as well as morally miraculous. . . .

I have come to the end of the task which I set myself at the beginning of this discussion. Something I trust has been done to show on the one hand the weakness of the objections brought against the historical character of the narratives of the nativity and on the other hand the strength of the positive ground on which they stand. We cannot be accused of an uncritical, unhistorical disposition in accepting the Virgin Birth of Jesus Christ as a fact of history. Throughout this discussion I have, for obvious reasons, avoided resting anything on the question of authority. But considering the position which the Virgin Birth holds in the creeds, it cannot be denied that the authority of the Christian Church is committed to it as a fact, beyond recall. To admit that its historical position is really doubtful would be to strike a mortal blow at the authority of the Christian Church as a guide to religious truth in any real sense. Such a result is in itself an argument against the truth of any position which would tend to produce it; for it is very difficult to scrutinize narrowly those articles of the Christian faith which have really been believed and taught in the Church *semper, ubique, ab omnibus*, without being struck with the conviction that a divine providence has been guarding the Church in her production of such definitions or formal declarations of her faith as can really be called catholic—guarding her from asserting anything which can reasonably be called unwarranted or superstitious; and such a conviction does in itself create a presumption against any conclusion which would invalidate any single article of the original creed.

23

Jesus and Eschatology

William Sanday

In the three preceding lectures I have been trying to put before you what I may call the eschatological theory of the Life and Teaching of our Lord: first, to trace its history, and the steps by which it has come to the front: then to expound and, in expounding, also partly to criticize it.

Speaking very summarily, the theory—or so much of it as most demands our attention—is something of this kind.

Although our Lord, at least from the Baptism onwards, had the clear consciousness that He was Himself the promised Messiah, yet He did not at once press His claim, but deliberately sought rather to conceal than to assert it. Although He was the Messiah, the time for entering upon His full Messianic functions was not yet. The Kingdom of God, which the Messiah was to inaugurate, was not as yet present but future. The announcement with which our Lord began His ministry repeated exactly the announcement made by the Baptist: it was not 'The kingdom of God is here,' but 'The kingdom of God is at hand.' The petition in the Lord's Prayer is also future: 'Thy kingdom come.' The kingdom thus intended was not merely an increased activity of Divine working conducted through the ordinary natural channels, but a supernatural divine activity, such as the Jews expected at the close of the existing aeon or world-age. As being supernatural, it was necessarily not present, but future. This was the sense in which our Lord preached the Gospel of the Kingdom. His public ministry, as we look back upon it, was not the establishment of the kingdom, but a stage preliminary to its establishment. The real inauguration of the kingdom was to take place when the Messiah came to His own in declared supremacy. The precautions which our Lord took to prevent a premature disclosure of the Divine counsels were successful. Only His

171

most intimate disciples guessed the secret, and even they not until His ministry was far advanced, when St. Peter, acting as their spokesman, rose to the confession that his Master was the Christ. The people at large knew that Jesus of Nazareth was a prophet, and they had a sort of uneasy feeling that He might be more; but not until our Lord assented to the interrogation of the high priest did He Himself publicly and categorically affirm His own Messiahship.

Before He did this, He already knew and had already foretold that His present condition must come to an end, and a great change intervene before the consummation could come. The coming of the Messiah with the clouds of heaven was not to be confused with the earthly mission of Him who had not where to lay His head. Before He could come from heaven, He must first be transported thither. He must needs die; and He must needs rise again; it was through the grave and gate of death alone that He could enter upon His full Messianic inheritance.

I am free to confess that in the theory, thus broadly stated, there seems to me to be a large element of truth, and of what I suspect for most of us will be new truth. I doubt if we have realized—I am sure that I myself until lately had not adequately realized—how far the centre of gravity (so to speak) of our Lord's ministry and mission, even as they might have been seen and followed by a contemporary, lay beyond the grave. I doubt if we have realized to what an extent He conceived of the kingdom of heaven, that central term in His teaching, as essentially future and essentially supernatural. I doubt if we have quite understood the reticence and reserve with which our Lord put forward His own claim, though the claim was there, or rather the consciousness on which it was based, all the time. I doubt if we have appreciated the preliminary or preparatory character of His mission; the gradualness of the disclosures made in the course of it; in particular, the 'mysteries' or secrets which were an important part of His teaching—the mystery of the Messiah, the mystery of the Kingdom, the mystery of Suffering. I doubt if we have recognized the extent to which our Lord, while transcending the current Jewish notions of the time, yet in almost every instance starts from them.

One main argument for such a construction of the Gospel

History as I have been describing seems to me to be the way in which it fits in with the attitude of mind that we find prevailing in the Early Church, when the curtain rises and we get our first contemporary pictures of it.

And if I am asked further, as to the transition from an eschatological way of looking at things to a noneschatological, I would reply that we can nowhere see it better carried out than in the writings that have actually come down to us from the Apostolic age, and that I fully believe were in the main working out hints and intimations of our Lord Himself. I also think that we have evidence enough that our Lord's own teaching was deeply symbolical and that, if we did but know, the ultimate reality would be found to correspond more nearly to the actual historical course of events than we are apt to suppose. I am inclined to believe—though this is speculation, that I would not express otherwise than very tentatively—that the real coming of the Kingdom—the fact corresponding to it in the field of ultimate realities—is what we are in the habit of calling the work of the Holy Spirit, from the day of Pentecost onwards; the presence of a divine force, drawing and annexing (so far as the resistance of human wills allows it) the world to itself, but as yet still in mid process, and with possibilities in the future of which we perhaps hardly dream.

24

Jesus' Social Teachings

Walter Rauschenbusch

A man was walking through the woods in springtime. The air was thrilling and throbbing with the passion of little hearts, with the love-wooing, the parent pride, and the deadly fear of the birds. But the man never noticed that there was a bird in the woods. He was a botanist and was looking for plants.

A man was walking through the streets of a city, pondering the problems of wealth and national well-being. He saw a child sitting on the curbstone and crying. He met children at play. He saw a young mother with her child and an old man with his grandchild. But it never occurred to him that little children are the foundation of society, a chief motive power in economic effort, the most influential teachers, the source of the purest pleasures, the embodiment of form and color and grace. The man had never had a child and his eyes were not opened.

A man read through the New Testament. He felt no vibration of social hope in the preaching of John the Baptist and in the shouts of the crowd when Jesus entered Jerusalem. He caught no revolutionary note in the Book of Revelation. The social movement had not yet reached him. Jesus knew human nature when he reiterated: "He that hath ears to hear, let him hear."

We see in the Bible what we have been taught to see there. We drop out great sets of facts from our field of vision. We read other things into the Bible which are not there. During the Middle Ages men thought they saw their abstruse scholastic philosophy and theology amid the simplicity of the gospels. They found in the epistles the priests and bishops whom they knew, with robe and tonsure, living a celibate life and obeying the pope. When the Revival of Learning taught men to read all books with literary appreciation and historic insight, many things disappeared from the Bible for their eyes, and new things appeared. A new language was abroad and the Bible began to speak that language. If the Bible was not a living power before the Reformation, it was not because the Bible was chained up and forbidden, as we are told, but because their minds were chained by preconceived ideas, and when they read, they failed to read.

We are to-day in the midst of a revolutionary epoch fully as thorough as that of the Renaissance and Reformation. It is accompanied by a reinterpretation of nature and of history. The social movement has helped to create the modern study of history. Where we used to see a panorama of wars and strutting kings and court harlots, we now see the struggle of the people to wrest a living from nature and to shake off their oppressors. The new present has created a new past. The French Revolution was the birth of modern democracy, and also of the modern school of history.

The Bible shares in that new social reinterpretation. The stories of the patriarchs have a new lifelikeness when they are read in the setting of primitive social life. There are texts and allusions in the New Testament which had been passed by as of slight significance; now they are like windows through which we see miles of landscape. But it is a slow process. The men who write commentaries are usually of ripe age and their lines of interest were fixed before the social movement awoke men. They follow the traditions of their craft and deal with the same questions that engaged their predecessors. Eminent theologians, like other eminent thinkers, live in the social environment of wealth and to that extent are slow to see. The individualistic conception of religion is so strongly fortified in theological literature and ecclesiastical institutions that its monopoly cannot be broken in a hurry. It will take a generation or two for the new social comprehension of religion to become common property.

The first scientific life of Christ was written in 1829 by Karl Hase. Christians had always bowed in worship before their Master, but they had never undertaken to understand his life in its own historical environment and his teachings in the sense in which Jesus meant them to be understood by his hearers. He had stood like one of his pictures in Byzantine art, splendid against its background of gold, but unreal and unhuman. Slowly, and still with many uncertainties in detail, his figure is coming out of the past to meet us. He has begun to talk to us as he did to his Galilean friends, and the better we know Jesus, the more social do his thoughts and aims become.

Under the influence of this new historical study of Christ, and under the pressure of the intense new social interest in contemporary life, the pendulum is now swinging the other way. Men are seizing on Jesus as the exponent of their own social convictions. They all claim him. "He was the first socialist." "Nay, he was a Tolstoian anarchist." "Not at all; he was an upholder of law and order, a fundamental opponent of the closed shop." It is a great tribute to his power over men and to the many-sidedness of his thought that all seek shelter in his great shadow.

But in truth Jesus was not a social reformer of the modern type. Sociology and political economy were just as far outside of his range of thought as organic chemistry or the geography of America. He saw the evil in the life of men and their sufferings, but he approached these facts purely from the moral, and not from the economic or historical point of view. He wanted men to live a right life in common, and only in so far as the social questions are moral questions did he deal with them as they confronted him.

And he was more than a teacher of morality. Jesus had learned the greatest and deepest and rarest secret of all—how to live a religious life. When the question of economic wants is solved for the individual and all his outward adjustments are as comfortable as possible, he may still be haunted by the horrible emptiness of his life and feel that existence is a meaningless riddle and delusion. If the question of the distribution of wealth were solved for all society and all lived in average comfort and without urgent anxiety, the question would still be how many would be at peace with their own souls and have that enduring joy and contentment which alone can make the outward things fair and sweet and rise victorious over change. Universal prosperity would not be incompatible with universal *ennui* and *Welt-schmerz*. Beyond the question of economic distribution lies the question of moral relations; and beyond the moral relations to men lies the question of the religious communion with that spiritual reality in which we live and move and have our deepest being—with God, the Father of our spirits. Jesus had realized the life of God in the soul of man and the life of man in the love of God. That was the real secret of his life, the well-spring of his purity, his compassion, his unwearied courage, his unquenchable idealism: he knew the Father. But if he had that greatest of all possessions, the real key to the secret of life, it was his highest social duty to share it and help others to gain what he had. He had to teach men to live as children in the presence of their Father, and no longer as slaves cringing before a despot. He had to show them that the ordinary life of selfishness and hate and anxiety and chafing ambition and covetousness is no life at all, and that they must enter into a new world of love and solidarity and inward contentment. There was no service that he could render to men which would equal that. All other help lay in concentric circles about that redemption of the spirit and flowed out from it.

No comprehension of Jesus is even approximately true which fails to understand that the heart of his heart was religion. No man is a follower of Jesus in the full sense who has not through him entered into the same life with God. But on the other hand no man shares his life with God whose religion does not flow out, naturally and without effort, into all relations of his life and reconstructs everything that it touches. Whoever uncouples the religious and the social life has not understood Jesus. Whoever sets any bounds for the reconstructive power of the religious life over the social relations and institutions of men, to that extent denies the faith of the Master.

25

The Resurrection of Christ

Joseph Barber Lightfoot

Hath begotten us again unto a lively hope by the resurrection of Jesus Christ from the dead.

1 PETER i. 3.

The religion of Jesus Christ presented one great contrast to the heathen religions with which it found itself in conflict. It pointed steadily forward, while they looked wistfully backward. The religions of Greece and Rome placed their golden age in the irrevocable past. Poets and moralists cast back a mournful gaze on this bygone age of bliss, when toil and sorrow were unknown, when the earth brought forth her choicest flowers and fruits unsolicited, and when Justice was everywhere supreme. The glory had gone and could not be recalled. The present was only the darker by the contrast. On the other hand the golden era of the Gospel lay in the far-off hereafter. The eye of the prophet pierced into the future, and saw there a great restitution, the creation of a new heaven and a new earth—a bright and blissful eternity, when all the inequalities and wrongs of the present should be redressed, when sighing and sorrow should be no more, when the tears should be wiped from every eye— the ineffable glory of a city whose sunlight was the presence of God Himself. The religions of classical heathendom were religions of regret. The Gospel is a gospel of hope.

In this respect, as in most others, the temper of the Old Testament was an anticipation of the temper of the New. This forward gaze, of which I have spoken, was eminently characteristic of the Israelite people. Through all the stupendous trials and vicissitudes of the nation—the subjugations and defeats, the thraldoms and the captivities overwhelming them from without; the anarchies and dissensions and shameful apostasies rending them within—this beacon light of hope shone ever clear in the heavens. A great future lay before them. Israel was foreordained to be a light to the nations, and to give its laws to mankind. Israel's triumph might be postponed, but it could not be averted. This consciousness of God's purpose was the secret of their marvellous vitality—the recuperative force which sustained a national life unparalleled in the annals of the world.

Then came the Resurrection to justify and to interpret this confidence. It was the crowning victory of hope. It shed a glory over all creation and all history—a glory which irradiated even the darkest passages of human life. Death had been hitherto the one obstinate, impregnable barrier, which baffled hope itself; and death had yielded to the victor's might. All the voices of earth and sky were found now at length to speak of resurrection, of renewal, of life—to proclaim in one grand chorus the triumph of hope for humanity. To the heathen poet and moralist they had sung a wholly different strain. He had looked out upon nature, and his heart had been saddened by the sight. The lot of man seemed only the darker by contrast of the brightness without. If the day deepened into night, the night was not final. It was the prelude to a bright and rosy dawn. If the summer waned into autumn and the autumn darkened into winter, the winter was not the end. It was the harbinger of the freshness, the delight, the glory, of the opening springtide. For man alone there was no revival, no hope. No morrow ever dawned on the night of the grave; no springtide renewed the winter of decay and death. The very plants seemed to him to repeat the same mournful ditty. The flowers of the garden, he sung sadly, will revive with the reviving year, will put forth fresh leaves and bear bright blossoms again. Man only—man the mighty, the powerful, and the wise—once buried in the hollow earth sleeps the endless, hopeless, irrevocable sleep of death. Not so the Christian Apologist. Interpreted in the light of the Easter message, these very same voices, in which the heathen poet had heard only a funeral dirge over the littleness of man's greatness, rang out in his ears a jubilant peal of triumph. The passage from night to day, the succession from winter to summer, the decay and revival of plants, were so many analogies of nature, proclaiming the hopes of humanity and witnessing to the glories of the Resurrection.

We, who have lived all our lives in the sunshine of this hope, can hardly realize the difference it has made to mankind. Who shall deny that there were among the great nations of the civilised world anxious yearnings, eager foreshadowings, doubtful surmises, more or less faint, pointing to man's immortality? But to surmise is one thing and to know is another. When we read how the most devout philosopher of antiquity on the solemn eve of his departure discussed with his favoured pupils whether the soul was or was not immortal, when we remember that even among the Jews themselves, the two chief sects were divided on this point—the Pharisees maintaining and the Sadducees denying a resurrection—we see how much we owe to the unseen hand, which on that first Easter dawn rolled away the stone from the tomb and transformed a vague hope into an assured fact. Can we wonder that the Apostles placed the Resurrection in the forefront as the central doctrine, because the central fact of the Gospel; or that S. Peter in the words which I took as my text, speaks of the believer as 'begotten again into a living hope,' born, as it were, into a new world, endowed with a fresh and perennial spring of life—by reason of Christ's Resurrection from the Dead?

Two great ideas are involved in the fact of the Resurrection—ideas influencing human thought and action at every turn—ideas coextensive in their application with human life itself.

First: By opening out the vista of an endless future, it has wholly changed the proportions of things. The capacity of looking forward is the measure of progress in the individual and in the race. Providence is God's attribute. In proportion as a man appropriates this attribute of God, in proportion as his faculty of foresight is educated, in the same degree is he raised in the moral scale. The civilised man is distinguished from the barbarian by the development of this faculty. The barbarian lives only for the day; if he has food and shelter for the moment, he thinks of nothing more. The civilised man forecasts the needs of the future; lays up stores for the future; makes plans for the future. The Christian again is an advance upon the civilised man, as the civilised man was an advance upon the barbarian. His vista of knowledge and interest is not terminated abruptly by the barrier of the grave. The Resurrection has stimulated the faculty and educated the habit of foresight indefinitely, by opening out to it an endless field of vision, over which its sympathies range.

But secondly; the Resurrection involves another principle, not less extensive or less potent in its influence on human life. The Resurrection does not merely proclaim immortality. There would have been no need of Christ's death for that. It declares likewise that death leads to life. It assures us that death is the portal to eternity. Thus it glorifies death; it crowns and consecrates the grave. What is the message of the Risen Christ—the Alpha and Omega—to His Churches? Not merely 'I am He that liveth.' This was a great fact, but this was not all. Read on. 'I am He that liveth, and I was dead.' Death issuing in life—death the seed, and life the plant and blossom and fruit—this is the great lesson of the Gospel. 'I was dead; and, behold, I am alive for evermore, Amen; and have the keys of hell and of death.'

See how far-reaching are the applications of this lesson to human life. Death had been hitherto the chief foe of humanity—

the one paramount, intolerable, ultimate evil, with which man must wrestle, though only with the absolute certainty of defeat. But now death himself was conquered. He was not only conquered, but he was turned into an ally. There was a beneficence, a joy, a glory, in death itself, when death meant entrance into an endless life. Moreover the principle which applied to death, applied *a fortiori* to all the other evils of life. Through darkness to light, through sorrow to joy, through suffering to bliss, through evil to good—this is the law of our Heavenly Father's government, whereby He would educate His family—His sons and His daughters—into the likeness of His own perfections. Accordingly we find this same principle extending throughout the Gospel teaching. Everywhere it speaks of renewal, of redemption, of restitution—yes, of resurrection.

26

Paul's Proclamation of Christ

Benjamin Breckinridge Warfield

Paul is writing the Address of his Epistle to the Romans, then, with his mind fixed on the divine dignity of Christ. It is this divine Christ who, he must be understood to be telling his readers, constitutes the substance of his Gospel-proclamation. He does not leave us, however, merely to infer this. He openly declares it. The Gospel he preaches, he says, concerns precisely "the Son of God . . . Jesus Christ our Lord." He expressly says, then, that he presents Christ in his preaching as "our Lord." It was the divine Christ that he preached, the Christ that the eye of faith could not distinguish from God, who was addressed in common with God in prayer, and was looked to in common with God as the source of all spiritual blessings. Paul does not speak of Christ here, however, merely as "our Lord." He gives Him the two designations: "the Son of God . . . Jesus Christ our Lord." The second designation obviously is explanatory of the first. Not as if it were the more current or the more intelligible designation. It may, or it may not, have been both the one and the other; but that is not the point here. The point here is that it is the more intimate, the more appealing designation. It is the designation which tells what Christ is to us. He is our Lord, He to whom we go in prayer, He to whom we look for blessings, He to whom all our religious emotions turn, on whom all our hopes are set—for this life and for that to come. Paul tells the Romans that this is the Christ that he preaches, their and his Lord whom both they and he reverence and worship and love and trust in. This is, of course, what he mainly wishes to say to them; and it is up to this that all else that he says of the Christ that he preaches leads.

The other designation—"the Son of God"—which Paul prefixes to this in his fundamental declaration concerning the Christ that he preached, supplies the basis for this. It does not tell us what Christ is to us, but what Christ is in Himself. In Himself He is the Son of God; and it is only because He is the Son of God in Himself, that He can be and is our Lord. The Lordship of Christ is rooted by Paul, in other words, not in any adventitious circumstances connected with His historical manifestation; not in any powers or dignities conferred on Him or acquired by Him; but fundamentally in His metaphysical nature. The designation "Son of God" is a metaphysical designation and tells us what He is in His being of being. And what it tells us that Christ is in His being of being is that He is just what God is. It is undeniable— and Bousset, for example, does not deny it,—that, from the earliest days of Christianity on, (in Bousset's words) "Son of God was equivalent simply to equal with God" (Mark xiv. 61-63; John x. 31-39).

That Paul meant scarcely so much as this, Bousset to be sure would fain have us believe. He does not dream, of course, of supposing Paul to mean nothing more than that Jesus had been elevated into the relation of Sonship to God because of His moral uniqueness, or of His community of will with God. He is compelled to allow that "the Son of God appears in Paul as a supramundane Being standing in close metaphysical relation with God." But he would have us understand that, however close He stands to God, He is not, in Paul's view, quite equal with God. Paul, he suggests, has seized on this term to help him through the frightful problem of conceiving of this second Divine Being consistently with his monotheism. Christ is not quite God to him, but only the Son of God. Of such refinements, however, Paul knows nothing. With him too the maxim rules that whatever the father is, that the son is also: every father begets his son in his own likeness. The Son of God is necessarily to him just God, and he does not scruple to declare this Son of God all that God is (Phil. ii. 6; Col. ii. 9) and even to give him the supreme name of "God over all" (Rom. ix. 5).

This is fundamentally, then, how Paul preached Christ—as the Son of God in this supereminent sense, and therefore our divine Lord on whom we absolutely depend and to whom we owe absolute obedience. But this was not all that he was accustomed to preach concerning Christ. Paul preached the historical Jesus as well as the eternal Son of God. And between these two designations—Son of God, our Lord Jesus Christ—he inserts two clauses which tell us how he preached the historical Jesus. All that he taught about Christ was thrown up against the background of His deity: He is the Son of God, our Lord. But who is this that is thus so fervently declared to be the Son of God and our Lord? It is in the two clauses which are now to occupy our attention that Paul tells us.

If we reduce what he tells us to its lowest terms it amounts just to this: Paul preached the historical Christ as the promised Messiah and as the very Son of God. But he declares Christ to be the promised Messiah and the very Son of God in language so pregnant, so packed with implications, as to carry us into the heart of the great problem of the two-natured person of Christ. The exact terms in which he describes Christ as the promised Messiah and the very Son of God are these: "Who became of the seed of David according to the flesh, who was marked out as the Son of God in power according to the Spirit of holiness by the resurrection of the dead." This in brief is the account which Paul gives of the historical Christ whom he preached. . . .

Paul does not, however, say of Christ merely that He became

of the seed of David and was marked out as the Son of God in power by the resurrection of the dead. He introduces a qualifying phrase into each clause. He says that He became of the seed of David "according to the flesh," and that He was marked out as the Son of God in power "according to the Spirit of holiness" by the resurrection of the dead. What is the nature of the qualifications made by these phrases?

It is obvious at once that they are not temporal qualifications. Paul does not mean to say, in effect, that our Lord was Messiah only during His earthly manifestation, and became the Son of God only on and by means of His resurrection. It has already appeared that Paul did not think of the Messiahship of our Lord only in connection with His earthly manifestation, or of His Sonship to God only in connection with His post-resurrection existence. And the qualifying phrases themselves are ill-adapted to express this temporal distinction. Even if we could twist the phrase "according to the flesh" into meaning "according to His human manifestation" and violently make that do duty as a temporal definition, the parallel phrase "according to the Spirit of holiness" utterly refuses to yield to any treatment which could make it mean, "according to His heavenly manifestation." And nothing could be more monstrous than to represent precisely the resurrection as in the case of Christ the producing cause of—the source out of which proceeds—a condition of existence which could be properly characterised as distinctively "spiritual." Exactly what the resurrection did was to bring it about that His subsequent mode of existence should continue to be, like the precedent, "fleshly"; to assimilate His post-resurrection to His pre-resurrection mode of existence in the matter of the constitution of His person. And if we fall back on the ethical contrast of the terms, that could only mean that Christ should be supposed to be represented as imperfectly holy in His earthly stage of existence, and as only on His resurrection attaining to complete holiness (cf. I Cor. xv. 44, 46). It is very certain that Paul did not mean that (II Cor. v. 21).

It is clear enough, then, that Paul cannot by any possibility have intended to represent Christ as in His pre-resurrection and His post-resurrection modes of being differing in any way which can be naturally expressed by the contrasting terms "flesh" and "spirit." Least of all can he be supposed to have intended this distinction in the sense of the ethical contrast between these terms. But a further word may be pardoned as to this. That it is precisely this ethical contrast that Paul intends has been insisted on under cover of the adjunct "of holiness" attached here to "spirit." The contrast, it is said, is not between "flesh" and "spirit," but between "flesh" and "spirit of holiness"; and what is intended is to represent Christ, who on earth was merely "Christ according to the flesh"—the "flesh of sin" of course, it is added, that is "the flesh which was in the grasp of sin"—to have been, "after and in consequence of the resurrection," "set free from 'the likeness of (weak and sinful) flesh.' " Through the resurrection, in other words, Christ has for the first time become the holy Son of God, free from entanglement with sin-cursed flesh; and, having thus saved Himself, is qualified, we suppose, now to save others, by bringing them through the same experience of resurrection to the same holiness. We have obviously wandered here sufficiently far from the declarations of the Apostle; and we have landed in a *reductio ad absurdum* of this whole system of interpretation. Paul is not here distinguishing times and contrasting two successive modes of our Lord's being. He is distinguishing elements in the constitution of our Lord's person, by virtue of which He is at one and the same time both the Messiah and the Son of God. He became of the seed of David with respect to the flesh, and by the resurrection of the dead was mightily proven to be also the Son of God with respect to the Spirit of holiness.

It ought to go without saying that by these two elements in the constitution of our Lord's person, the flesh and the spirit of holiness, by virtue of which He is at once of the seed of David and the Son of God, are not intended the two constituent elements, flesh and spirit, which go to make up common humanity. It is impossible that Paul should have represented our Lord as the Messiah only by virtue of His bodily nature; and it is absurd to suppose him to suggest that His Sonship to God was proved by His resurrection to reside in His mental nature or even in His ethical purity—to say nothing now of supposing him to assert that He was made by the resurrection into the Son of God, or into "the Son of God in power" with respect to His mental nature here described as holy. How the resurrection—which was in itself just the resumption of the body—of all things, could be thought of as constituting our Lord's mental nature the Son of God passes imagination; and if it be conceivable that it might at least prove that He was the Son of God, it remains hidden how it could be so emphatically asserted that it was only with reference to His mental nature, in sharp contrast with His bodily, thus recovered to Him, that this was proved concerning Him precisely by His resurrection. Is Paul's real purpose here to guard men from supposing that our Lord's bodily nature, though recovered to Him in this great act, the resurrection, entered into His Sonship to God? There is no reason discoverable in the context why this distinction between our Lord's bodily and mental natures should be so strongly stressed here. It is clearly an artificial distinction imposed on the passage.

When Paul tells us of the Christ which he preached that He was made of the seed of David "according to the flesh," he quite certainly has the whole of His humanity in mind. And in introducing this limitation, "according to the flesh," into his declaration that Christ was "made of the seed of David," he intimates not obscurely that there was another side—not aspect but element—of His being besides His humanity, in which He was not made of the seed of David, but was something other and higher. If he had said nothing more than just these words: "He was made of the seed of David according to the flesh," this intimation would still have been express; though we might have been left to speculation to determine what other element could have entered into His being, and what He must have been according to that element. He has not left us, however, to this speculation, but has plainly told us that the Christ he preached was not merely made of the seed of David according to the flesh, but was also marked out as the Son of God, in power, according to the Spirit of holiness by the resurrection of the dead. Since the "according to the flesh" includes all His humanity, the "according to the Spirit of holiness" which is set in contrast with it, and according to which He is declared to be the Son of God, must be sought outside of His humanity. What the nature of this element of His being in which He is superior to humanity is, is already clear from the fact that according to it He is the Son of God. "Son of God" is, as we have already seen, a metaphysical designation asserting equality with God. It is a divine name. To say that Christ is, according to the Spirit of holiness, the Son of God, is to say that the Spirit of holiness is a designation of His divine nature. Paul's whole assertion therefore amounts to saying that, in one element of His being, the Christ that he preached was man, in another God. Looked at from the point of view of His human nature He was the Messiah—"of the seed of David." Looked at from the point of view of His divine nature, He was the Son of God. Looked at in His composite personality, He was both the Messiah and the Son of God, because in Him were united both He that came of the seed of David according to the flesh and He who was marked out as the Son of God in power according to the Spirit of holiness by the resurrection of the dead.

27

The Incarnation of the Son of God

H. P. Liddon

And the Word was made flesh, and dwelt among us.

Christmas Day, we are all agreed, is the greatest birthday in the year. It is the birthday of the greatest Man, of the greatest Teacher of men, of the greatest Benefactor of the human race that ever lived. It is this; but it is also much more. For as on this day was born One Who, while He is truly man, is also and immeasurably more than man.

He Who was born, as on this day, did not begin to be when He was conceived by His human Mother; since He had already existed from before all worlds—from an eternity. His human nature, His human Body, and His human Soul were not, as in the case with us, the whole outfit of His Being; they were, in truth, the least important part of it. He had already lived for an eternity when He condescended to make a human body and a human soul in an entirely new sense His own, by uniting them to His Divine and Eternal Person; and then He wore them as a garment, and acted through them as through an instrument, during His Life on earth, as He does not in the courts of Heaven. Thus the Apostle says that He "took upon Him the form of a servant" (Phil. ii. 7), and that "He took not on Him the nature of angels, but He took on Him the seed of Abraham" (Heb. ii. 16); and so the Collect for to-day pleads that He "took our nature upon Him, and was as at this time born of a pure Virgin." And it was in this sense that He became or was made flesh: after having existed from eternity, He united to Himself for evermore a perfect and representative Sample of the bodily and immaterial nature of man, and thus clothed with It, as on this day, He entered into the world of sense and time. "The Word was made flesh, and tabernacled among us."

It is perhaps not surprising that from the early days of Christianity men should have misconceived or misstated what was meant by this central but mysterious truth of the Christian Creed, the Incarnation of the Eternal Son. In truth, the misconceptions about it have been and are many and great.

Sometimes Christians have been supposed to hold that two persons were united in Christ, instead of two natures in His single Person; sometimes that the Infinite Being was confined within the bounds of the finite Nature which He assumed; sometimes that God ceased to be really Himself when He thus took on Him man's nature; sometimes that the Human Nature which He took was absorbed into or annihilated by its union with the Deity. All the chief misconceptions of the true sense of the Apostles have been successively considered and rejected by the Christian Church; and "the right faith is, that we believe and confess that our Lord Jesus Christ, the Son of God, is God and Man. God of the substance of His Father, begotten before all worlds, and Man of the substance of His mother, born in the world; perfect God and perfect Man, of a reasonable soul and human flesh subsisting. Equal to the Father as touching His Godhead, and inferior to the Father as touching His manhood. Who although He be God and man, yet is He not two, but one Christ" (Athanasian Creed).

Thus did God the Son take the simple out of the dust and lift the poor out of the mire (Ps. cxiii. 6) when He raised our frail human nature to the incomparable prerogative of union with Himself. So real was and is this union, that all the acts, words, and sufferings of Christ's Human Body, all the thoughts, reasonings, resolves, emotions of His Human Soul, while being properly human, are yet also the acts, words, sufferings, the thoughts, reasonings, resolves, and emotions of the Eternal Son, Who controls all, and imparts to all the value and elevation which belong to the Infinite and the Supreme. Thus, although Christ suffered in His Human Soul in the garden, and in His Human Body on the Cross, His sufferings acquired an entirely superhuman worth and meaning from the Person of the Eternal Word to Whom His Manhood was joined; and St. Paul goes so far as to say that God purchased the Church with His own Blood (Acts xx. 28)—meaning that the Blood which was shed by the Crucified was that of a Human Body personally united to God the Son.

It was perhaps inevitable that the question should be asked how such a union of two natures, which differ as the Creator differs from the creature—as the Infinite differs from the finite—was possible. It might be enough to reply that "with God all things are possible" (St. Matt. xix. 26); all things, at least, which do not contradict His moral Perfections, that is to say, His essential Nature. And most assuredly no such contradiction can be detected in the Divine Incarnation. But, in truth, it ought not to be difficult for a being possessed of such a composite nature as is man to answer this question; perhaps such a being as man might have been reasonably expected never to have asked it. For what is the Incarnation but the union of two natures, the Divine and the human, in a single Person, Who governs both? And what is man, what are you and I, but samples, at an immeasurably lower level, of a union of two totally different substances; one material, the other immaterial, under the presidency and control of a single human personality? What can be more remote from each other in their properties than are matter and spirit? What would be more incredible, antecedently to experience, than the union of such substances as matter and spirit, of a human body and a human soul, in a single personality? Yet that they are so united is a matter of experience to every one of us. We only do not marvel at it because we are so intimately familiar with it. Day by day, hour by hour, minute by minute, we observe, each within himself, a central authority, directing and controlling, on the one hand, the movements and operations of an animal frame, and on the other the faculties and efforts of an intelligent spirit, both of which find in this central authority or person their point of unity. How this can be we know not. We know not how an immaterial essence can dictate its movements to an arm or a leg, but we see that it does this; and we can only escape from the admitted mystery into difficulties far greater than those which we leave behind, by frankly avowing ourselves materialists, and denying that man has anything that can properly be called a soul, or that he is anything more than an oddly agitated mass of bones and muscles. If we shrink from this, we must recognize, in the composite structure of our own mysterious being, the means of answering the question about the possibility of the Incarnation. "As the reasonable soul and flesh is one man, so God and man is one Christ" (Athanasian Creed). He Who could thus bring together matter and spirit, notwithstanding their utter contrariety of nature, and could constitute out of them a single human personality or being, might surely, if it pleased Him, raise both matter and spirit—a human body and a human soul—to union with His Divinity, under the control of His Eternal Person. Those who have taken even superficially the measure of the twofold nature of man, ought not to find it hard to understand that for sufficient reasons God and man might be united in a single person, or, as St. John says, that the Word might be made flesh, and might dwell among us.

But what, it may be asked, can be conceived of as moving God thus to join Himself to a created form? Is not such an innovation on the associations, if not on the conditions, of His Eternal Being too great to be accounted for by any cause or motive that we can possibly assign for it?

Here we enter a region in which, it need hardly be said, we dare not indulge our own conjectures as to the fitness of things. We do not know enough of the Eternal Mind to presume to account for Its resolves by any suppositions of human origin. If we are to take a single step forward, it must be under the guidance of Revelation. But when men speak of the Incarnation as an innovation on the Eternal Life of God so great as to be beyond accounting for or even conceiving, they forget a still older innovation—if the word may be permitted—about which there is, assuredly, no room for doubt. They forget that, after existing for an eternity in solitary blessedness, contemplating Himself and rejoicing in the contemplation, God willed to surround Himself with creatures who should derive their life from Him, and be sustained in it by Him, and should subsist within His all-encompassing Presence, while yet utterly distinct from Him. Creation, surely, was an astonishing innovation on the Life of God; and creation, as we know, involved possibilities which led to much else beyond. If God was to be served by moral creatures endowed with reflective reason, and conscience, and free will, that they might offer Him the noblest, because a perfectly voluntary service, this prerogative dignity necessarily carried with it the possibility of failure; and man, in fact, at the very beginning of his history, did fail. That God should have created at all is, indeed, a mystery; that He should have created a moral world of which He must have foreseen the history, is a still greater mystery; but that, having done this, He—the Eternal Justice, the Eternal Charity—should have left His handiwork to itself, would have been, had it been true or possible, a much greater, and I will add, a much darker mystery. As God must have created out of love (Jer. xxxi. 3), so out of love must He bring a remedy to the ruined creature of His Hands (St. John iii. 16); though the form of the remedy only He could prescribe. We do not know whether there were other ways of raising a fallen race; probably there were, since God is infinite in His resources as in all else. But we may be sure that the way adopted was the best. Of other remedies nothing has been told us. What we do know is the truth of that saying, "that Christ Jesus came into the world to save sinners" (1 Tim. i. 15); what we do confess before God and man is that, "being of one substance with the Father, by Whom all things were made, He for us men and for our salvation came down from Heaven, and was incarnate by the Holy Ghost of the Virgin Mary, and was made Man."

28

A Kenotic Christology

H. R. Mackintosh

Somehow—to describe the method exactly may of course be beyond us—somehow God in Christ has brought His greatness down to the narrow measures of our life, becoming poor for our sake. This must be taken as seriously in dogmatic as in Christian piety, and a place must be found for the real fact which it denotes in our construction of the Incarnate life. To surround or accompany it with neutralising qualifications is inept. The difficulties of a Kenotic view are no doubt extremely grave; yet they are such as no bold construction can avoid, and in these circumstances it is natural to prefer a view which both conserves the vital religious interest in the self-abnegating descent of God (*Deus humilis*) and adheres steadfastly to the concrete details of the historic record. Obviously these details constitute our sole medium of revelation; and orthodox writers are occasionally prone to forget that it is no merit in a Christological doctrine that it claims to deal successfully with remoter problems not forced on the mind by New Testament representations of Jesus, while at the same time it makes our one trustworthy source of information, the Gospel narrative, dubious or unintelligible. Our only use for a theory is to synthesise facts definitely before us, not to do something else.

Take the central thought of the Gospel, which has captured and subdued the Christian soul, and let us ask whether it has received full justice at the hands of eccelesiastical Christology. God in Christ, we believe, came down to the plane of suffering men that He might lift them up. Descending into poverty, shame, and weakness, the Lord was stripped of all credit, despoiled of every right, humbled to the very depths of social and historical ignominy, that in this self-abasement of God there might be found the redemption of man. So that the Gospel tells of Divine sacrifice, with the cross as its unspeakable consummation; the Saviour's lot was one of poverty, suffering, and humiliation, until the triumphant death and resurrection which wrought deliverance and called mankind from its grave. Hearts have thrilled to this message that Christ came from such a height and to such a depth! He took our human frailty to be His own. So dear were human souls to God, that He travelled far and stooped low that He might thus touch and raise the needy. Now this is an unheard-of truth, casting an amazing light on God, and revolutionising the world's faint notions of what it means for Him to be Father; but traditional Christology, on the whole, has found it too much to believe. Its persistent obscuration of Jesus' real manhood proves that after all it shrank from the thought of a true "kinsman Redeemer"—one of ourselves in flesh and spirit. Christ's point of departure was Godhead, no doubt, yet in His descent He stopped half-way. The quasi-manhood He wore is so filled with Divine powers as to cease to belong to the human order.

He became poor—there a new light falls on God, who for us became subject to pain; but one may well feel that the light is not enhanced but rather diminished if with tradition we have to add that nevertheless He all the time remained rich. For in so far as He remained rich—in the same sense of riches—and gave up nothing to be near us, our need of a Divine Helper to bear our load would be still unsatisfied. What we require is the never-failing sympathy which takes shape in action, "entering," as it has been put, "into conditions that are foreign to it in order to prove its quality." Jesus' life then becomes a study in the power, not the weakness, of limitations, while yet the higher Divine content transfigures the limits that confine it. And it is just this sympathy without reserve which appears when the fact of Christ becomes for us a transparent medium through which the very grace of God is shining. God, we now know, is love; but it was necessary that He should live beside us, in the form of one finite spirit, in order that His love and its sacrifice might be known to men and win back their love. So Browning thought of it:—

> "What lacks then of perfection fit for God,
> But just the instance which this tale supplies
> Of love without a limit! So is strength,
> So is intelligence; let love be so,
> Unlimited in its self-sacrifice,
> Then is the tale true and God shows complete."

There are obvious differences between the older Kenotic theories and the new. For the Christian thinker of today is more reserved and proportionally less vulnerable on points of speculation. A favourite charge against the older construction was the charge of mythology. Kenoticism, it was said, was like nothing so much as pagan stories of the gods. The reproach is natural on the lips of one who totally repudiates the idea of incarnation. If a man does not feel that in Christ we stand confronted with the outcome of a vast Divine sacrifice—with what is nothing less than an ineffable fact of Divine history—for him the problem which Thomasius and the rest were trying to solve (and, as a preliminary, to state) has of course no existence. He cannot see what the discussion is about. But the more recent Kenotic statements have the advantage that they aim rather at proceeding by way of interpretative postulate, *a parte post*, so reaching after the Kenotic conception as the key by which alone it is possible to unlock the problems of the historic Life, but not venturing, as some earlier hypotheses had ventured, to expatiate in the domain of speculation *a parte ante*, or to describe the steps in which the incarnation was actualised with theosophical minuteness. We have learnt from Lotze, many of us, that it is vain to ask "how being is made." It is vain to speak as if the view-point of Deity were our own, or to ignore the peripheral character of our judgments; and any construction of Christ's person in which the modern mind is to feel an interest must start from, and proceed through, the known facts of His human life. The known facts, we say advisedly; for discussion has made it clear that Kenoticism, be it right or wrong, does not in the least depend for its cogency on two or three isolated passages in St. Paul. We have only to place side by side the two words of Jesus: "Lo, I am with you alway, even unto the end of the world," and "Of that day and that hour knoweth no man, neither the Son but the Father," to have the entire problem before us. It is present in the unchallenged facts of the New Testament, whether or not we choose to theologise upon it.

Four positions may be taken, I think, as implicit in the completely Christian view of Jesus; and it is difficult to see how Kenoticism in some form is to be avoided by one who asserts them all, and at the same time believes that a reasoned Christology is possible. They may be put as follows:—

(1) Christ is now Divine, as being the object of faith and worship, with whom believing men have immediate, though not unmediated, fellowship.

(2) In some personal sense His Divinity is eternal, not the fruit of time, since by definition Godhead cannot have come to be *ex nihilo*; His pre-mundane being therefore is real, not ideal merely.

(3) His life on earth was unequivocally human. Jesus was a man, a Jew of the first century, with a life localised in and restricted by a body organic to His self-consciousness; of limited power, which could be, and was, thwarted by persistent unbelief; of limited knowledge, which, being gradually built up by experience, made Him liable to surprise and disappointment; of a moral nature susceptible of growth, and exposed to life-long temptation; of a piety and personal religion characterised at each point by dependence on God. In short, He moved always within

the lines of an experience humanly normal in constitution, even if abnormal in its sinless quality. The life Divine in Him found expression through human faculty, with a self-consciousness and activity mediated by His human milieu.

(4) We cannot predicate of Him two consciousnesses or two wills; the New Testament indicates nothing of the kind, nor indeed is it congruous with an intelligible psychology. The unity of His personal life is axiomatic.

Now it is impossible to think these four positions together save as we proceed to infer that a real surrender of the glory and prerogatives of deity, "a moral act in the heavenly sphere," must have preceded the advent of God in Christ. We are faced by a Divine self-reduction which entailed obedience, temptation, and death. So that religion has a vast stake in the *kenosis* as a fact, whatever the difficulties as to its method may be. No human life of God is possible without a prior self-adjustment of deity. The Son must empty Himself in order that from within mankind He may declare the Father's name, offer the great sacrifice, triumph over death; and the reality with which, to reach this end, He laid aside the form and privilege of deity is the measure of that love which had throbbed in the Divine heart from all eternity.

It is clear that the value of this discussion, if any, will lie not in the untrammelled nature of a speculation, but in the luminous explication of historic fact. We would know the limits within which must lie the truth we are seeking, but there is no suggestion that it is given to man to watch God as He becomes incarnate. Yet once it has been made clear that Christ is God—since redemption is as typically a Divine work as creation—the possible alternatives are few. It may be said that He acquired Godhead—which is pagan. Or that He carried eternal deity unmodified into the sphere of time—which is unhistoric. Exclude these options, and it only remains to say that in Christ we are face to face with God, who in one of the distinguishable constituents of His being came amongst us by a great act of self-abnegation. But there is no possibility of forming a precise scientific conception of what took place; for that, be it reverently said, we should have to become incarnate personally. We cannot know with final intimacy any experience through which we have not passed. Everywhere in life, in nature, in history, in personality, there are, for each of us, irreducible and enigmatic facts, which we can touch and recognise and register, but of which we never become masters intellectually. Nature itself is full of new beginnings, of real increase, of novel fact not deducible from the previous phases of the cosmos; and this we are bound simply to report, admitting its inscrutability. In short, there is an alogical element in things, not to be measured by the canons of discursive mind. Over and over again it meets us in theology. There is for example the relation of an eternal God to events of time. No mystery could be deeper than the fact—accepted by all types of Christianity—that the Eternal has revealed Himself notably in a human being who lived at the beginning of the Christian era, and that the meaning of Jesus is at once immersed in past historic fact and perpetually present to faith. But if this difficulty, so opaque for minds like ours, is an essential implicate of belief in revelation, may it not be that such mystery as is involved in the passage of the Son from His eternal being to a life of limitation and growth is inseparable from a reasoned conviction of Christ's higher nature? Have we the right to ask that Christology should be more transparent than Theology? Whether we are dealing with the surprises of nature, the free personal entanglements of history, the antinomies of grace and freedom, or the incarnation of the living God, plainly we must follow the same path. If the facts contain a wonderful and transcendent element, the theory by which we elucidate them will reproduce this wonderfulness and transcendence. In any case, being is too rich and manifold for us to lay down *à priori* regulations to the effect that this or that, even though worthy and morally credible, is impossible for God.

It is essential, however, that the categories we employ should be genuinely moralised. Our theological calculus must rise above the physical and partially mechanical conceptions which served the Ancient Church. There will always be metaphysic in Christology, but it ought to be a metaphysic of the conscience, in which not substance but Holy Love is supreme. Nothing in Dr. Forsyth's treatise is more wholesome or more inspiring than his sustained contention that we may help our age to conceive the incarnation by giving full scope to this ethicising vein. He shows that the habit of ethical construction must be carried over the whole field. A real *kenosis* is a moral as well as a theological necessity: the impulse from which it sprang was moral; it is the moral constitution of Godhead which made it possible; moral forces sustained the self-reduced Life on earth and gave it spiritual value. As it has been put, the conditions under which Christ lived "were the moral result of a moral pro-mundane act, an act in virtue of which, and of its moral quality continued through His life and culminating in His death, Christ redeems and saves." And yet in all this there is nothing of mere dull 'moralism," draining the red life-blood out of a great Gospel; instead, the incarnation comes home to us as an ethically appealing act of God, not overwhelming us by display, but subduing, because enlightening and persuading, the conscience and the will.

This is too often ignored when the discussion comes to circle round the idea of Divine immutability. For then the subject of *kenosis* may be canvassed quite irrespectively of holy love, the changelessness of the Absolute—with its implicit denial that prayer is answered, or that there can be such a thing as a Divine saving act—being used to put the very idea of Divine self-limitation out of court. Sheer unchangeableness is, of course, something against which no human pleading can bear up; but it is worth asking whether it ought to figure in a Christian argument. The immutability to which certain writers appeal would really involve—given a world of changing moral agents—the gravest ethical caprice. God would be arbitrary, inasmuch as in varying moral situations He would act with mere mechanical self-consistency. Now it is not at all excessive to say that what Christ reveals in God is rather the infinite mobility of absolute grace bent on the redemption of the lost, the willingness to do and bear whatever is compatible with a moral nature. What is immutable in God is the holy love which makes His essence. We must let Infinitude be genuinely infinite in its moral expedients; we must credit God with infinite sacrifice based on His self-consciousness of omnipotence. We must believe that the love of

God is "an almighty love in the sense that it is capable of limiting itself, and, while an end, becoming also a means, to an extent adequate to all love's infinite ends. This self-renouncing, self-retracting act of the Son's will, this reduction of Himself from the supreme end to be the supreme means for the soul, is no negation of His nature; it is the opposite, it is the last assertion of His nature as love" (Forsyth).

This may be put otherwise by saying that omnipotence—in this discussion a quite fundamental attribute—exists and operates in a moral universe and under moral conditions, and that if we think away this pervasive ethical quality from almightiness, it is not predicable of the God we Christians believe in. Now, while omnipotence is in one sense limited or conditioned by holy love, in another sense it is magnified. In virtue of that love, its range of possibility broadens out endlessly. God's moral freedom opens doors to Him which otherwise are shut. May it not be that only the perfectly Holy is free to transcend self and live in other lives, the sinful being so immured in self that for them it is impossible to overflow the estranging bounds, and pass into alien forms of experience? Love with resource like God's has a boundless capacity of self-determination. For us men and our salvation, it may well be, He committed Himself, in one aspect of His personal being, to a grade of experience qualified by change and development, thus stooping to conquer and permitting the conditions of manhood to prevail over His own freedom. If the alternatives are an unethical conception of immutability and a pure thought of moral omnipotence, which makes room for Divine sacrifice, the Christian mind need not hesitate. Every theory which accepts a real incarnation must deny that the lowliness of our life is incongruous with Godhead, and hold that, as it has been put, our Lord became "representative of mankind not only on the sacrificial side but also on the side of human weakness."

Can analogies be found which help us with the thought of Divine self-limitation? None certainly which take us the whole way. It is the very depth of nature in deity which makes the idea of self-confinement difficult; for we cannot see how infinitude could narrow its own circle. Yet it is noteworthy that always in the human world growth of moral nature brings with it a deepened power of self-abnegation. Elevation of life means more power to descend. From omnipotence let us now turn to omniscience. Here it is easy to make a commencement. We are constantly limiting our actually present knowledge without altering our personal identity. We do this when we voluntarily close our eyes, or fall asleep. . . .

This, however, brings up the question whether the Son Incarnate can ever have known Himself to be Divine. Was the *kenosis* such that it annulled even the consciousness of a higher relationship? Some writers have contended that to the end Christ remained unaware of His being God in flesh, urging that on no other terms can we assert the genuinely human character of His experience. In particular, it has been held that while sin was an impossibility for Jesus, we may conceive this impossibility as having been hidden from Himself, so that He faced each new conflict with that reality of effort, that refusal to count the issue a foregone conclusion which is vitally characteristic of moral life. And from this it might seem to follow that His primary descent into the sphere of finitude had veiled in nescience His eternal relationship to the Father. Yet we need not entangle the two positions with each other. It can only have been in mature manhood and perhaps intermittently that Christ became aware of His divinity—which must have remained for Him an object of faith to the very end. Now, if incarnation means Divine self-subjection to the conditions of our life, it does not appear that even such a discovery on Christ's part of His own essential Sonship must inevitably suggest to Him the total impossibility of moral failure. But while His assurance of victory can never have been mechanical, or such as to dispense Him from vigilance, or effort, or seasons of depression, it was none the less real and commanding. There is no reason why His consciousness of unique intimacy with the Father, and of the crucial importance of His mission, should not have imparted to Jesus, in each temptation, a firmly-based confidence of victory, though He knew not in advance how or how soon the final triumph would be vouchsafed.

In any case, it is only by degrees that the full meaning of His relationship to the Father, with its eternal implicates, can have broken on Jesus' mind. The self-sacrifice in which His earthly life originated drew a veil over these ultimate realities. But if He lives in glory now, and if an uninterrupted unity binds the present majesty to the mortal career, we are led to believe that the veil must gradually have worn thinner and more translucent, until, at least in high moments of visitation, He knew Himself the Son conditioned in and by humanity. In whatever ways the significance of His relationship to God betrayed itself, His unshared unity with the Father must at length have come to stand before His mind definitely as constitutive of His personality. Otherwise we should have to think of some moment of mysterious apocalypse—at the resurrection presumably—when in conditions to which we can attach no ethical significance the Risen Lord awoke to His own divinity. This has no relation to the data of the New Testament. The subject, however, of the gradual expansion of the Divine-human experience will come before us in the next chapter. I only note here in passing what will there be dwelt on.

It would seem that the self-imposition of limits by Divine love must be conceived of as a great supra-temporal act by which, in the almightiness of grace, the Son chose to pass into human life. An infinitely pregnant act; for in truth it involved all the conflict, renunciation, and achievement of the life to which it was the prelude. But it is not possible to conceive of this act as having been continuously repeated throughout the earthly life. We cannot think of the Incarnate One as confining Himself from moment to moment, by explicit volition, within the frontiers of manhood. That would simply lead back to the old untenable conception of a *krypsis* by which the Divine Self in Christ veils His loftier attributes, now less now more, and is actuated in each case by didactic motives. To return thus to a theoretic duality of mental life in our Lord against which all modern Christology has been a protest, is surely to sin against light. The acceptance of human relationships—to nature, to man, to God—belongs to the eternal or transcendent sphere, as a definitive settled act; it is not something consciously and continuously renewed in time. What is continuous with the decisive act of self-reduction is the moral quality of the life on earth, the permanent self-consecration of Jesus' will. But the self-limitation, transcendently achieved as a single, final deed, inaugurates a permanent condition or state of life, amid circumstances of change and suffering once for all accepted.

29

Analogies for the Incarnation

P. T. Forsyth

It is all but impossible to discuss a question like the Kenosis without entering a region which seems forbidding to the lay mind, and is certainly more or less technical. And yet some appeal may perhaps be made to the ministry, among those Churches where the education of the ministry has been taken seriously and theologically. It is only when the ministry despises theology and sacrifices it to a slight and individualist idea of religion, that the Church immolates intelligence and finally commits suicide. It parts with staying power in order to capture a hearing, and surrenders faith to gain sympathy. The minds that are trained enough to ask relevant questions on such a subject are also trained enough to know that they cannot be answered without considerable effort on both sides—effort both to present and to grasp. And such earnest minds are in possession of some at least of the postulates here involved, the ideas handled, or the methods used. The real difficulty is with those who will neither qualify to understand such questions nor let them alone.

If there was a personal pre-existence in the case of Christ it does not seem possible to adjust it to the historic Jesus without some doctrine of Kenosis. We face in Christ a Godhead self-reduced but real, whose infinite power took effect in self-humiliation, whose strength was perfected in weakness, who consented not to know with an ignorance divinely wise, and who emptied himself in virtue of his divine fulness. The alternative to a Kenosis used to be a Krypsis, or conscious concealment of the active divine glory for practical or strategic purposes. But that is now an impossible idea. While on the other hand an acquired Godhead would really be none. It would be but deification. And at bottom it is a contradiction. No creature could become God.

I am aware of the kind of objection raised to the kenotic theory. Many difficulties arise readily in one's own mind. It is a choice of difficulties. On the one hand living faith finds it difficult to believe that the Christ who created it was not God. And on the other thought finds it hard to realise how God should become Christ. But it is something gained to note that the chief difficulties arise on the latter head, in connexion with the way in which the fact came to pass rather than with the fact itself. That is, they are scientific and not religious. When we are not so much questioning the fact as discussing the manner of it—not the what but the how—it is a matter of theological science not of religious faith. And the science of it can wait, but the religion of it cannot.

We cannot form any scientific conception of the precise process by which a complete and eternal being could enter on a process of becoming, how Godhead could accept growth, how a divine consciousness could reduce its own consciousness by volition. If we knew and could follow that secret we should be God and not man. It is a difficulty partly ethical, partly psychological. Even if we admit psychologically that certain attributes could be laid aside—the less ethical attributes like omniscience, omnipotence, or ubiquity—could self-consciousness be thus impaired and a love still remain which was fully divine? And how can an infinite consciousness be thought of as reducing itself to a finite? God's infinite consciousness might indeed determine itself so as to pervade, sustain, and bind a variety of finite detail without losing consciousness. An immanent God, we believe, does so in creation. But if He parted with His self-consciousness as infinite would it not come as near to suicide as infinite could? . . .

But leaving the metaphysical psychology of the matter for a moment, have we any analogy in our experience that would make this intelligible or even credible?

I am not sure that we have not.

(1.) I will first allude to the familiar experience of reducing or obscuring the self-consciousness by a drug voluntarily taken. Here the really effective cause is not the drug but the will to use it. Let us put a case. Suppose an Oriental court, a foolish young Sultan, and a venerable vizier, wise, vigilant and devoted, amidst a ring of plotting pachas. As the vizier sits next to his master at a feast he observes a pinch of poison stealthily dropped into the imperial cup. He has heard some rumour of a conspiracy; and he knows that poison. It means slow paralysis and lingering death. In a moment he must decide; and he takes the resolve. There is no other way. He challenges the king to a pledge in exchanged cups. And in due course he feels the consequence in the impaired powers with which he drags through a year or two of life. He lives thus till the ruler at last learns of his devotion, is stung to his feet by the sacrifice, and show his gratitude by such a change of life and a growth in royal worth as rewards his saviour's love for all it had borne. Now what was it that really eclipsed the good statesman's powers? It was not the drug, but the love, the will, the decision to take it with open eyes, and to part with all that made his high place and peace, when no other course could save the youth he loved.

(2.) Again, are there no cases where, by an early act of choice and duty, a man commits himself to a line of life which entails an almost complete extinction of his native genius, tastes and delights. Could no story be made of a great musical genius, say in Russia, who, being as full of pity as of genius, was also a passionate sympathiser with the people; who deliberately committed himself, while young and in the flood of artistic success to certain democratic associations and enterprises, well knowing what would happen upon discovery; who was discovered, and deported to Siberia, to an exile both rigorous and remote, where the violin and all it stood for was denied to him and all his comrades for the rest of their life. He must spend his whole heart in loving fellowship with the commonest toils and needs, and in patient ministrations to a society which prison debased. After a lifetime of this the first brief years of artistic joy and fame might well seem to him at moments almost to belong to another life, and the æsthetic glory and power be felt to have turned entirely to social love and service. And all as the consequence neither of a spiritual process, nor of a mere indiscretion, nor of a martyrdom only forced on him, but of a resolve taken clearly and gravely at a point in his spiritual life.

(3.) Or again. A student at the University develops an unusual faculty and delight in philosophic study, and even shows clear metaphysical genius. He is not only at home in those great matters which live next door to the very greatest, but he offers promise of real, not to say striking, contribution to the historic development of that high discipline. Or his gift may be in poetic or plastic art, to the like high degree. But he is the only son in a large family; and, at a critical period in the family affairs, the father's death makes it his duty to leave study, learn an unpleasant business, pull things round, and devote himself to them for the rest of his life with the absorption demanded by modern industrial conditions. He has to resign his intellectual delights, call in his speculative powers, unlearn his native tastes and associations, and give himself up to active conflict with a vexatious world doubly galling to him. And in due course he comes to forget most of what it was once his joy to know. He becomes subdued (in no ignoble way, in a way of duty) to the element in which he has to work, and he is acclimatised to a world both alien and contemptuous towards his congenial treatment of the greatest realities. His contact with reality must now be by the way of faith and action, and not by the way of thought. He becomes at his best a practical mystic and amateur, who might have been a leading genius. Economic, social and ethical interests, even to drudgery and heart sickness, come to take the place of the more solemn and unearthly concerns at the divine call. And the old high joy of thinking, or art's old calm, must be postponed until another life; with many an hour of longing, and many a homesick retrospect to what is, after all, the native land of his suppressed powers. He loses a life but he finds his soul. Is this not a case where a moral and sympathetic volition leads to a certain contraction of the consciousness; not indeed by a single violent and direct act of will, but by a decision whose effect is the same when it is spread over a life? He has put himself (*sich gesetzt*) in a position where he is put upon (*gesetzt sein*). And, in applying the illustration to the theology of a kenosis in Eternity, where a thousand years are but as one day, the element of time between choice and result in the earthly case is negligible.

(4.) Speaking more generally, is there not often in our experience a connection between the resolutions and the limitations of our personality? By certain deliberate and early acts of freedom, love, and duty we so mortgage and limit ourselves that in due course, as we follow them up, the moral consciousness ripens. We come to a spirituality which is really ethical and not merely instinctive, a thing of moral discipline and not naïve nature, something which comes to itself by way of challenge and conflict, and is not mere legacy. We become men of faith and not mere religion, men of moral sagacity and not mere honest impulse. By voluntary discipline we may come to love truth for truth's sake and not for our own; we learn to hold by habit and not mere heredity to the "ought" of conscience; we lose self in the love and worship of God, or in the service of man. But for the most part these conscious heights are touched but in rare hours—though they may be the hours of decision and committal that fashion life. We may soon grow weary in the course we have taken up. The very physical, or psychical, nature which was the organ of our first free resolve, asserts itself, and makes us feel its clouding power as we pursue the path to which only our freedom, our supernatural self, committed us. By our will we have come where our will is itself often obscured and hampered; and our first estate, where the choice was made, is recalled but in a dream. So also Godhead, by the same free and creative will which gave His creation freedom, may pass into a state where He is not only acted on by that creation but even submerged in the human part of it; and where He is victimised, indeed, for a time by the perverse freedom He created, and is imprisoned in its death; by consenting to which death, however, He gives the supreme and saving expression to his divine will and life. He lives out a moral plerosis by the very completeness of his kenosis; and he achieves the plerosis in resurrection and ascension. And thus He freely subdues to Himself the freedom which in His creative freedom He made.

The more moral the original power is, so much the more strength there is to sacrifice glory to service, and enjoyment to benediction. So that were the moral power that of deity itself, the power of self-disglorification would be enhanced accordingly. Just because He was holy God, the Son would be morally capable of a self-dispowering more complete than anything that could be described by human analogy. As God, the Son in his freedom would have a kenotic power over Himself corresponding to the infinite power of self-determination which belongs to deity. His divine energy and mobility would have a power even to pass into a successive and developing state of being, wherein the consciousness of perfect fulness and changelessness should retire, and become but subliminal or rare. The world of souls was made by Him; and its power to grow must reflect some kindred mobile power in him whose image it is. The infinite mobility of the changeless God in becoming human growth only assumes a special phase of itself.

30

Incarnation and Psychology

William Sanday

In the last lecture we found ourselves led to the conclusion that the proper seat or *locus* of whatever there is of divine in man—by whatever name we call it, 'immanence,' 'indwelling,' 'mystical union,' or the like, and whatever the extent of the real experience corresponding to those names—is that part of the living organism of man which we are learning to call the subliminal consciousness. Perhaps we ought in this instance to use an even stronger term, and to speak of 'infraliminal' instead of 'subliminal'. But no; I am inclined to think that 'subliminal' is better. It is true that the proper seat of the really divine—as well as, I am afraid, the really diabolical—in man is that part of the living self which is most beyond his ken. And yet, as I shall have occasion presently to point out in greater detail, although this divine element lies so deep, and in its quiescent state is so far withdrawn from our contemplation, it is by no means always quiescent, but sends up impulses from time to time which—if they elude us still in their deeper roots themselves—nevertheless produce effects which come within the field of consciousness, so that they can be rightly called subconscious. That which comes to expression is for the most part not so much the divine itself (though this too appears sometimes, in the great mystics, to reach direct expression) as indications of the presence of the divine.

If we look into ourselves, this is what we shall see. There is an impulse to right action, and we act; there is an impulse to prayer, and we pray; there is an impulse towards thanksgiving, and we give thanks; there is above all that central impulse of faith, the impulse as it were to take hold of God in Christ and cling fast to Him, so that no outward deterrent, no other conflicting attraction, can loosen the hold. We feel that all these promptings come from a hidden source within us. We can say with St. Paul 'the Spirit also helpeth our infirmity: . . . the Spirit Himself maketh intercession for us with groanings which cannot be uttered' (Rom. viii. 26). We know enough of what goes on within us to be able to trace it to its source, but we cannot go beyond this; we cannot in any more explicit way describe or define the ultimate cause of these abysmal motions. Not only the ordinary life but the highest life of the saintliest of men is conducted upon the human plane; to all superficial appearance he leads just the same kind of life as his neighbours. He knows, and we know, that that is not a full account of the matter—that he really has 'meat to eat' that we others 'know not of'; but, however true that may be, however deep the source of this inward sustenance, his outward acts, so far as they are outward, are subject to precisely the same laws, and present the same generic appearance, as those of other men. It would take some time before we should discover that the saint or the mystic was what he was; and we should discover it, not by direct inspection, but by inference—or rather, by inference within inference, as by a cunning arrangement of mirrors the surgeon is able to see further into the interior of the body than is possible to direct observation. It is literal truth to say that the inner life of the spirit is 'hid with Christ in God'; but the medium through which that inner life is manifested—so far as it is ever manifested—is the common workday life of men.

Now it seems to me that the analogy of our human selves can at least to this extent be transferred to the Incarnate Christ. If whatever we have of divine must needs pass through a strictly human medium, the same law would hold good even for Him. A priori we should expect that it would be so; and a posteriori we find that as a matter of fact it was so. We have seen what difficulties are involved in the attempt to draw as it were a vertical line between the human nature and the divine nature of Christ, and to say that certain actions of His fall on one side of this line and certain other actions on the other. But these difficulties disappear if, instead of drawing a vertical line, we rather draw a horizontal line between the upper human medium, which is the proper and natural field of all active expression, and those lower deeps which are no less the proper and natural home of whatever is divine. This line is inevitably drawn in the region of the subconscious. That which was divine in Christ was not nakedly exposed to the public gaze; neither was it so entirely withdrawn from outward view as to be wholly sunk and submerged in the darkness of the unconscious; but there was a sort of Jacob's ladder by which the divine forces stored up below found an outlet, as it were, to the upper air and the common theatre in which the life of mankind is enacted.

The advantage of this way of conceiving of the Person of Christ is that it leaves us free to think of His life on earth as fully and frankly human, without at the same time fixing limits for it which confine it within the measures of the human; it leaves an opening, which in any case must be left, by which the Deity of the Incarnate preserves its continuity with the infinitude of Godhead.

The great gain from the recognition of the subliminal activities of consciousness lies in the fact that it reduces the conscious self to its proper proportions, and makes us realize in a way in which we hardly did realize before how much larger the Whole Self is than this limited part of it. And, in like manner, the application of this analogy to the Life of Christ enables us to realize it much more in its true proportions—in the proportions, that is, which the human life as lived on earth really bore to the whole transcendent manifestation of the Son of God.

On the one hand, we think of the human consciousness of the Lord as entirely human; we make no attempt to divide it up and fence off one part of it as human and another part as divine. Whatever there was of divine in Him, on its way to outward expression whether in speech or act, passed through, and could not but pass through, the restricting and restraining medium of human consciousness. This consciousness was, as it were, the narrow neck through which alone the divine could come to expression. This involves that only so much of the divine could be expressed as was capable of expression within the forms of humanity. We accept this conclusion unreservedly, and have no wish to tamper with it. The Life of our Lord, so far as it was visible, was a strictly human life; He was, as the Creeds teach, 'very Man'; there is nothing to prevent us from speaking of this human life of His just as we should speak of the life of one of ourselves. Over this we can shake hands with those continental theologians who insist on taking the humanity of our Lord in real earnest, and as no mere matter of form.

But, on the other hand, we no less emphatically refuse to rule out or ignore or explain away the evidence which the Gospels and the rest of the New Testament afford that this human life was, in its deepest roots, directly continuous with the life of God Himself. If St. Paul could quote and endorse the words of a pagan poet claiming for the children of men that they are also God's offspring; and if they are this notwithstanding the fact that they are confined in the body as creatures of perishable clay; if in spite of these limitations it may still be said of them that in God they 'live and move and have their being', might not the same be said in a yet more searching and essential sense of Him who was Son in a more transcendent and ineffable mode of being than they? Whatever the Homoousion means—and in the last resort it remains a symbol rather than a term of direct description, because it is a corporeal metaphor applied to Spirit—whatever it means, can it be doubted that on this view there is ample room for it? Indeed, whatever room there is in the universe is at our command, and we can fill it as we will. That which stays our hand in the freedom of theorizing is not any external condition but only the reverence which does not seek to be wise beyond that which is written. There may well have been a self-determination of the Godhead, such as issued in the Incarnation, as far back as thought can go. I add that as perhaps a tenable modern paraphrase of the primary element in the doctrine of the Trinity. This doctrine, in its essence as in its origin, turns upon the recognition of the Incarnation of the Son. But in these regions the modern thinker will desire to walk warily, and not to intrude further than he is compelled.

31

Jesus the Lord

Fenton John Anthony Hort

The earthly life and acts of the Lord, in Himself and in the Church of His disciples, are divided according to His own express teaching into two parts. Before the discourse of the Last Supper reaches its close, He opposes them to each other in sharp contrast. "I came out from the Father and am come into the world: again I leave the world and go unto the Father." When these two words of His are received in their distinctness and their mutual necessity, as setting forth at once historical fact and eternal truth, then the Gospel is embraced. To refuse both is to fall back into heathenism. To receive the first but let go the second, or to confuse the second with the first, is to retrace our steps and become once more believing Jews. To hold fast both together is to stand and move in the faith of Christ.

The first period is in its origin a coming forth, in its progress a descent. The Father or the Father's presence is the beginning. The Son is sent forth and Himself comes forth into the world which He is to redeem. The weight of the world's sin and misery lies on Him more and more. Each step in His ministry brings Him into deadlier conflict with the world; and as He goes steadily forward, the conflict ends in His death. The Death belongs to both periods. It is the lowest point of the descent, the testimony sealed in blood, the obedience perfected in sacrifice. But it is also the beginning of the ascent. The Cross is already a lifting up out of the earth, a prophecy of the lifting up into the heavens. God accepts the sacrifice, raises His Son from the dead as by a second birth, and exalts Him to sit at His own right hand till He has put all His enemies under His feet. By the descent is closed the long line of revelations by which God came down and visited His people Israel; by the ascent is announced and begun the gathering of men upward to God, accomplished once for all in the person of the Son of Man, and wrought out through the ages in the power of that first accomplishment.

In each of the two periods the presence of the disciples is an essential part of the Gospel. Throughout the first period they are almost wholly receivers. All elements of their discipleship are combined in attachment to their Lord's person. They are being prepared for a time when they will have to bear witness of what they have seen and heard and known of Him: and while this process is going on, He is acquiring a mastery over their whole nature, which is destined to disable them for a purely independent life hereafter.

After the Resurrection the passive discipleship continues in both respects under changed conditions. But the change is not

fully manifest till the day of Pentecost, when they finally enter
into that new stage of discipleship which is expounded throughout the discourse at the Last Supper on the eve of the Passion,
discipleship being now fulfilled in apostleship. From that time
forwards their work consists in the appropriation and distribution of His work. As the Father sent Him into the world, so He
sent them into the world. Their destiny and their office are
fashioned after His.

This double relation of the Lord's journey to the journey of the
disciples shapes both parts of His answer to St. Thomas. On the
one hand it is for the sake of mankind that He takes His journey,
and it is through men, learners from Him, that mankind are to be
blessed by it. On the other hand it is on His own journey that
both the possibility and the efficacy of the disciples' journey
depends. Thus He first by a threefold revelation of Himself lays
down the conditions of their journey; I am the Way, the Truth,
and the Life: and then He points to the conditions and the goal of
their journey as alike determined by His; No one cometh unto
the Father save through me.

These last words "through me" bind together the three heads
which have preceded. Christ is not merely the Way and also the
Truth and also the Life; but He is these all at once. Each office
involves the others. The coming to the Father by Him includes
all. His hallowing lordship over human life demands the full and
harmonious cooperation of its several functions. The prætermis-
sion of any one function is to that extent an abnegation of Him.
The limitation of His supremacy to any one function, while the
others are reserved for the control of self or of the world without,
is to that extent a rebellion against Him. His discipleship and His
apostolate can be duly executed in any one sphere only when He
is recognised and diligently served as Lord of all.

But the Lordship of Christ is more than an issuing of commands for His disciples to obey. His commandments are part of
His own action, and His own action is the foundation of His
disciples' action. His coming to the Father is the prophecy of
their coming to the Father, and the power by which they are
enabled to come. His coming to the Father followed the close of
His work in human flesh, even of that work which the Father

had given Him to do. We may have a natural shrinking from using language of this kind; but it is His own language, constantly repeated; and it is written for our instruction that we may know the meaning of our own work and our own sonship. It abounds in His last prayer: "I glorified Thee on the earth, finishing the work which Thou hast given me that I should do; and now glorify me thou Father with Thyself with the glory which I had, before the world was, with Thee." "I am no longer in the world, and they themselves are in the world, and I come unto Thee." "And now I come unto Thee, and these things I speak in the world that they may have the joy that is mine fulfilled in themselves." The coming to the Father therefore of which He speaks as set before them can in no sense be an escape from sharing His work. It is not a private felicity, to be bought by neglect of the wider fields of various activity in the midst of which the lot of all men is cast, and by concentration upon Himself in isolation from His kingdom. Its joy is that of the welcome given to the good and faithful servant bidden to enter into the joy of his Lord.

Except as denoting the crown of willing and intelligent discipleship, the words "coming to the Father" have in this connexion no meaning. They offer no promise except to those who have loved and honoured the Son. If the responsibility of sonship and the subjection to the Son are accepted grudgingly, still more if they are repudiated, 'coming to the Father' can be only an object of dread. Submission to the Son of God as the supreme Way, Truth, and Life is the test whether the sonship of men and the fatherhood of God are more than hazy metaphors to be whispered in moods of pathetic languor.

On the other hand it was necessary for Christ's first disciples in prospect of His departure, and it is necessary for all who in any measure succeed to their discipleship now, that coming to the Father should be distinctly pronounced to be the goal of the journey, the completion of discipleship to the Son. The danger of so cleaving to the Son as to forsake the Father was always close to the Eleven; as it is of perpetual recurrence. The whole of Christ's own teaching had been directed towards strengthening no less than widening the ancestral faith in the Lord God of

Israel. The stronger the affirmation of His own Divine nature, the clearer became His testimony to the Father who sent Him. When the Jews sought to kill Him because He not only loosened the sabbath but also called God His own Father, making Himself equal to God, His answer was, "Verily verily I say to you the Son can of Himself do nothing unless He see the Father doing it; for what things He doeth these the Son also doeth in like manner: for the Father loveth the Son and sheweth Him all things whatsoever He doeth Himself, and greater works than these shall He shew Him, that ye may marvel." When they murmured because He spoke of having come down out of the heaven, He answered, "No one can come unto me except the Father which sent me draw him:" and again, "It is written in the prophets, 'And they shall be all taught of God:' every one therefore who heareth from the Father and learneth cometh unto me." Yet the nature of the personal devotion to Himself which went on increasing, necessary as it was for the time and the purpose, might well, if it had continued longer in its original shape, have imperilled the faith in the invisible Father. The danger lay not in an increase of faith in Christ but in an adhesion to Him which was not faith, as walking with Him not by faith but by sight. The possibility of the danger lurks in St. Philip's request, "Lord, shew us the Father and it sufficeth us": his Lord, he felt, was manifest to him; the Father, he supposed, was not; he had no desire to let go the Father, but while the Lord on earth was known to him by flesh and blood, the God above was becoming to him a shadowy name in contrast. Christ's departure then came at the right season: it was time not only that the personal Guide should Himself become known as the Way, the Truth, and the Life, but that all progress in Him should be seen to conduct to the Father. This had been the original purpose for which the disciples had been drawn to the Son. Coming to Christ had a separate meaning only while Christ was gone out from the Father into the world. To choose it afterwards as a better and dearer privilege than coming to the Father would have been to return perversely to the unripe partial discipleship of the probationary period,— discipleship, that is, to a Christ after the flesh, a Christ not glorified, because either not slain, or else slain only but left hanging on the Cross,—not buried, and not raised from the dead.

Thus the Lord taught His disciples that the long and various journey which was henceforth to constitute the following of Him was not a random wandering but a perpetual progress towards a certain end. The end was nothing less than the Father's immediate presence. While Christ as the One Way, the One Truth, and the One Life took up into Himself the whole universe as related to man, even as it first came into being through Him the Eternal Word, yet He was not Himself the end. Those to whose goings and knowledge and affections He gave at once the master impulse and the ruling standard would be thereby conducted to His Father and their Father, His God and their God. Each step in discipleship to Him would be a step in the perfecting of sonship to God. Of the Word become flesh it was true as it was in the elder time, "As many as received Him, He gave them authority to become children of God."

These considerations may help us to understand how it was that the Lord was not content with saying "Through me shall ye come unto the Father," but shut out all vaguer possibilities by a peremptory negation, "No one cometh unto the Father save through me." Part of the undefined mistrust with which we all sometimes shrink from accepting the declaration in its full rigour arises from a proneness to paraphrase the words 'cometh unto the Father' by some loose notion of arriving ultimately at happiness. Yet they are fixed to their strict sense by the occasion on which they were used, and by the whole context. The human coming to the Father derives its character from the homeward return of Him in whom the Father was well pleased. Such a return implies of necessity the mind and spirit of sonship; and where these have yet to be formed, discipleship to the Eternal Son has yet to begin.

On another side the exclusiveness of Christ's affirmation is inseparable from the nature of the office which He has been claiming for Himself. Its effect is simply to fix with absolute certainty the definiteness and universality of the preceding revelation. It forbids us to understand Christ as saying no more than, "I am a way, I am truth, I am life." On the other hand it receives its own interpretation from the threefold revelation. "Through me" cannot mean only "by my favour" or "by my intercession": it cannot bear any sense limited by the conditions of a single human career: it is coextensive with the Way, the Truth, and the Life.

Since then these two parts of the Lord's answer to St. Thomas mutually explain each other, the exclusiveness of the second declaration becomes an assurance that the keys of all worlds with which we have to do are in the hands of Him who took our nature and died for our sake. His exclusive mediation means first the unity of all things in Him, and then the privilege bestowed on us as His brethren of finding that when we yield ourselves to Him all things whatsoever that we touch are bearing us onward to God. All things lead to Him; while through Him alone can any one come to the Father; and there is no way that can be walked in, no truth that can be known, no life that can be felt and lived, which is without access to the Supreme Way, the Supreme Truth, the Supreme Life. We are taught by the Apostles to believe that there is a Divine purpose in every outward and inward movement of man and of all creation. We are taught that the Eternal Word, He who is in the bosom of the Father, is the expression of that purpose and the accomplishment of it. We are taught that His Incarnation was the primary accomplishment of it for mankind, and the revelation of its full accomplishment hereafter. We are taught that men, being instructed out of the imperishable record of His revelation by the progressive enlightenment of His Spirit, are able in part to discern this purpose, and to yield willing service towards its fulfilment. But then if this teaching be true, to suppose that any one could come to the Father except through the Son, would involve the strangest contradiction.

The exclusiveness of Christ is in truth but another name for the absolute universality of His kingdom combined with its absolute unity.

32

Jesus the Word of God

Adolf Schlatter

The supreme achievement of St. John was the publication of his Gospel. We do not know the exact year in which this happened. He looks back on Peter's crucifixion and corrects the wide-spread expectation that he himself would remain alive until the coming of Christ in a way which suggests that when he wrote the Gospel he was an old man. Even if he had been considerably younger than Jesus when he first joined him, say about twenty years old, he would have been over seventy by A.D. 80. This then, must be the approximate date of the Gospel. The idea that he wrote it in extreme old age is ruled out by the vivacity of his narrative. True, he uses recollections and formulas which he had long since made his own. Yet even the shaping of these reminiscences in literary form betokens a creative ability of undiminished vigour.

The Apocalypse was an exposition of Christian hope, the epistles of Christian behaviour, but both were based on a single assumption, which was clearly implied but not yet explicitly formulated. This assumption was that Christians believed in Jesus. Everything the Church possessed—her hope that the "Lamb" and not the "Beast" would be Lord over humanity, her ethic which made falsehood and hatred impossible and fostered truth and love—was founded on the assumption that she was firmly united with Jesus. And why was she thus united? What was the cause and content of her faith, which kept her firmly attached to Jesus?

For St. John the foundation of faith lay solely in Jesus himself—not in a metaphysical Christology or a doctrine of the Trinity, not in speculation about the life of God before the creation or of the eternal glory of the Son, but in a particular history. By expanding the ground of faith, he also suggested the

218

true way of worship. This was to preserve the memory of Jesus—for instance, by reading the Gospels in liturgical worship. In Paul's time this liturgical reading of the Gospels had not yet begun. But by now the Gospels were treasured at Ephesus, not just for private use, but as the property of the Church, with a definite place in her worship. Like the other evangelists, St. John wrote his Gospel for liturgical use; it was to be read in the congregation. Here is another significant change in Church order, representing a considerable advance from the primitive conditions prevailing in the time of St. Paul. The New Testament canon was growing and the first step was the adoption of the Gospels.

St. John's intention was to reinforce the influence of the earlier accounts of Jesus, and it is evident that he succeeded in this purpose. That he had any wish to suppress the other Gospels is out of the question. His relationship to them is certainly different from that between Mark and Matthew or between Luke and Mark. When Luke reproduced a great part of Mark but enlarged his Gospel by new material, he assumed that his Gospel would replace the Marcan Gospel, not that both Gospels would be used together in the Church. The relation of St. John to the two older records is different in that he does not repeat these older accounts. True, there are a certain number of parallels between the Fourth Gospel and the Synoptists, but St. John presents the earlier narratives in an entirely different light by connecting them with his dominant themes, with the result that they become completely new narratives. The narrative of the cleansing of the Temple, for example, repeats the earlier account, but the added dialogue between Jesus and the priest gives the final, profoundest expression to his judgement on the Temple (John 2:19). The meal in the desert-place on the other side of the lake of Gennesaret leads to the discourse at Capernaum, revealing Jesus as the Bread of Life, who by his death will feed the world (John 6:51-8). The anointing of Jesus and his entry into Jerusalem have a new light thrown on them by their connection with the raising of Lazarus (John 12:1-19). All the material derived from the earlier accounts is made subservient to the dominant purpose of the Gospel, which is to enable us to apprehend in the history of Jesus his passion, and in his passion the revelation of his glory.

St. John reinforced the older tradition by preventing the Church from losing touch with Jesus and his history, which was the ground of her faith. His purpose was to lay bare the eternal significance of that history and to show how Jesus' ministry in Jerusalem and his crucifixion had a contemporary relevance for the Greek world. That is what gives the Gospel its dominant theme. It showed the Church the divine origin of Jesus. Since Jesus was sent by God and impelled by him because he was one with the Father and was the revelation of God, his presence among men meant the reception of God's grace. To cut adrift from Jesus was therefore to cut adrift from God.

Thus the evangelist diverted the minds of his contemporaries from their favourite preoccupations. No doubt they had a certain justification in exploiting the opportunities of their religious environment. Baptism was "enlightenment", the Eucharist a means of union with Christ, the Church's doctrine was a guarantee of participation in the truth; and in their bishop they heard one who proclaimed to them God's commandment and who had authority to punish the guilty. All this was true and important, but not decisive. John would not speak of the success which Jesus had attained in the world, nor of the Church as his creation, through which he had become the benefactor of the nations, nor of Christianity and its wealth of truth and power. All he wanted to emphasize was that Jesus was the Son of God and therefore the vehicle of God's presence. Thus he links hope, love, and faith in indissoluble unity. In the Apocalypse he ignored all the achievements and successes of the Christians on earth and beheld only the Christians in heaven celebrating God's victory and worshipping him. In his epistles he speaks only of the duty of preserving the Church's heritage, and passes over all natural and temporal necessities. Similarly in his Gospel he emphasizes that faith has its ground only in the relation of Jesus to the Father. We should, however, misinterpret the unity of the evangelist's spiritual experience if we regarded this merely as an intellectual achievement; it shows rather the reality of his faith which, being genuine, necessarily determined the whole character of his spiritual experience.

This led St. John to his doctrine of the "Word". Was there no formula to express the relationship of Jesus to God? Following Jesus himself, the Church had used the father-son relationship to describe the unity between Jesus and God, a metaphor which readily suggested the term "Spirit" to describe the work of the Father in the Son. For the Jews, however, this transference of the fellowship between father and son to Jesus' relationship to God had proved a great stumbling-block, as the apostle frequently discovered in the course of his work in Jerusalem and Ephesus. But he refused to regard it as a stumbling-block himself, and boldly described Jesus as the "Son of God" and the believers as men who were "born of God", making these points the centre of his Gospel. But in order to elucidate this analogy a biblical word had to be found, and St. John found it in a term which the Old Testament, the teaching of the Synagogue, and Greek religious thought had filled with such a rich content: "the Word". Various associations combined to give this term a strength and depth of meaning which made it appropriate for elucidating the unity of Jesus with God. Scripture begins with the "word" as the medium of God's creative acts. Thus it was natural for the Synagogue to answer the question how the world was sustained and ordered by God by saying that he created it through his word. Similar notions came in from the Greek side, which affected Jewish thought long before the Jewish theologians at Alexandria, contemporaries of St. John, began to develop their Logos philosophy. Men were discussing whether there was a divine element in the cosmic process; how Nature could be defined as the work of God, and what it was that united man in his innermost being with God. The answer given was: reason, which thinks and speaks "the Word". St. John took up this formula and said: "The Word—not one of the many words which express various thoughts and purposes of God, but the one will of God, his creative and redemptive will—became flesh." It was not only heard, as in prophetic inspiration, where it acted externally on the recipient's mind and will, but it actually became a concrete human life. This was John's answer to the gnostic denial of the historical reality of Jesus. Jesus remained in his context in history, which linked him with the past and the future. But at the same time it did full justice to the universal scope of his activity, and helped the Greeks to understand why the call to faith in Christ was addressed to them. God was speaking in Jesus, proclaiming his will, and granting his grace to all.

In all this there is not the slightest trace of gnosticism, such as St. John had for many years considered it his sacred duty to refute. There is scarcely a sentence in the New Testament which so resists the tendency to make religion a speculative abstraction as the prologue of St. John's Gospel. "In the beginning was . . ."—at the mention of the "beginning", every gnostic pricks up his ears. But he is not satisfied, like St. John, with two words taken from the Old Testament (John 1:1; cf. Gen. 1:1; Prov. 8:30). At this point the gnostic becomes a philosopher, a dreamer, a poet, who stirs up his imagination in order to see what was before the beginning and what produced it. St. John, on the other hand, sticks to tangible reality, to the concrete event, to the Man Jesus, and affirms that he is the Word. But this is just what the Greek needed: a standard by which to order his relation to Jesus; it gave him a basis for his faith.

In every attempt to commend the Gospel it was vital to present the Cross of Christ in its true light. To St. John, who saw in Jesus a perfect union with the Father, and who saw the basis of faith in him in his divine Sonship, the problem of the Cross was accentuated. But he had no difficulty in fitting the Cross into his general theme and thereby throwing new light upon it. To him the Cross was the glorifying of Christ, not his shame; not surrender, but exaltation. Such notions were not the outcome of a kind of docetism which attempted to lift Jesus above physical and mental pain. For what transfigures the Cross is the obedience of Jesus, which is one with perfect love. That is why the evangelist did not look for some isolated purpose to explain the necessity of the Cross. That necessity arose from what Jesus was in relation to God and to the world. As the Son, he lived in the love of the Father and imparted to his disciples both light and life. Thus he lived a life of perfect obedience to the Father, and united in perfect fellowship with his disciples. And this obedience and this fellowship were sealed by his death. So the Cross was no embarrassment to faith but the ground on which it stood.

Moreover the Johannine portrait of Christ gave a deeper meaning and a new purpose to Christian life. Here is another instance where St. John enhanced the effect of the earlier Gospels. There is truth in the contention that his Gospel opened the door to mysticism. In the earlier accounts of the life and teaching of Jesus, the call to repentance determined the whole bearing of the disciples. Jesus set before them the contrast between sin and the will of God, making it their chief aim to renounce sin and to become obedient to God. It was now time for the vineyard to bring forth fruit for him who had planted it. The religious experience of St. Paul introduced into the Gospel an element of what may be called mysticism. For Paul spoke of dying and rising with Christ, of union with him, of being so embraced by him that he was "in Christ". But for St. Paul as for the Synoptic Gospels the decisive question was whether sin or righteousness determined a man's relation to God. The Gospel is the revelation of the righteousness of God, which meant that the whole energy of religious aspiration must be engaged in good works, whilst the aim of evangelization was to make the Church able and willing to serve God. And when hopes were directed towards the *Parousia*, St. John also emphasized the same truth. Christ spoke to the Churches about their work: "I know thy works." And now the evangelist directs our attention to the history of Jesus, that we may see in him the Son of God and perceive in his life the service which the Son offered to the Father, and that the Cross may shine to us in the splendour of perfect obedience. But in so doing, he opens the door to a movement of religious thinking and volition which looks inward and upward. "Ye in me, and I in you." Love looks upward; it is assured of its union with Christ and possesses the peace and joy of communion with God. Thus the individual Christian is united with God, and his spiritual life acquires a depth and fullness which have an absolute value of their own.

If St. John had not, at the same time, fought so resolutely against gnosticism—which sees knowledge as the aim of religion—his mysticism might have become a danger for the Church. Mysticism is always dangerous: there is no telling whether it will continue in the path of Jesus or undermine the ethics of the Gospel. The mystic is in danger of neglecting the moral imperative of the Gospel when he confines his encounter with God to his subjective experience. Nature, history, and human society tend to fade from his view. When the mystic shuts his eyes to God's presence in the outside world he becomes a prey to self-interest. And once the world about him fades from his sight, duty and vocation also disappear, and so eventually he lives only for himself, caring only for his own transfiguration, illumination, and immortality. St. John, however, was immune, and made the Church immune from the worst consequences of mysticism, because his union with God was dependent on his allegiance to Jesus. History was to him the determining factor in the relation of man to God. The word came to him from the outside—the word which proclaimed the Invisible. The Word-made-flesh proclaimed it to him, made him a child of God, and imparted to him the life which is born of God. Though Christ was present and at work in man, this did not impair the historical content of the Gospel, nor could it do so, since faith, that trusting attachment to Jesus, was for John the hallmark of Christianity. By this, even the mystic was turned away from himself; the fetters binding the ego to himself were burst asunder. He opened his heart to a Lord who stood before him and spoke to him, and thus a Community was created. The individual was taken out of his solitariness, and brought into contact with others. He was admitted into a fellowship, and so acquired a duty, a vocation to service and to work. Thus the Church, in the Johannine presentation, was not dissolved into a crowd of mystics, each of whom was occupied exclusively with himself; rather, she became a fellowship, united in him who by his active Presence took possession of one and all.

St. John's description of the Spirit has a profound bearing on all these questions. The Church claimed that her distinctiveness from Judaism and the Greek world lay in "the fellowship of the Spirit", a claim which John vindicated by defining the gift of Jesus to the Church as her growth into unity with him. As a result, God sets to work in the soul of man and creates in him a new, supernatural life. Then he is "born anew". The evangelist knew that in attributing this to the work of Jesus he was leaving far behind even the highest degree of spirituality reached by Jewish piety (John 3:3). If he had wanted to reach agreement with the gnostics, he would have described the Spirit as the dispenser of knowledge, or as the source of ecstasy. But here again he drew a sharp line of demarcation against gnosticism by characterizing the Spirit as the disciples' "Advocate", who stands at their side to assist them in work which would otherwise be beyond their power. The activity of the Spirit had nothing to do with self-seeking and was entirely at one with the work of the Church, whose sole motive was to glorify Christ. The Spirit enables her to accomplish her work because he is "the Spirit of truth". St. John preferred truth to "knowledge". Of course, he admits that the Spirit is also the One who knows and dispenses knowledge, for he inspires prophecy, keeps alive the memory of Jesus and his words, brings his teaching to life, and makes it active in the hearer, whether it be to convince him or to establish the Faith. But for John the essential work of the Spirit is not to produce an abundance of knowledge in the Church, but to deliver her from falsehood in religion, from all illusion and make-believe, from all fantasy and unreality. The Spirit's work is to make the Church true. The disciple differs from the world because he is led by the Spirit into all truth, and thus he possesses the armour, the only armour, which can assure him of victory.

This teaching on the Spirit secured the Church's inner life (for which John had done so much) against the corruption of selfishness, and made her confident in his Gospel despite its individuality and novelty. And it drove home the main lesson of the Apocalypse by clearing up the perplexities to which it had given rise. The Church could no longer stand aside from the maelstrom of human thought and volition. She was forced to come out in opposition to the status quo and take up the battle with the world, as John saw it. Yet she remained unshaken and undefeated, because the Spirit is one with the truth and makes the Church invincible.

33

Jesus: Prophet, Priest, King

I. A. Dorner

The usual division of Christ's official activity into a threefold office, rightly understood, is justifiable both historically and in itself.

It has long been usual in the Evangelical Church to represent the work of salvation in the form of the diverse function or office of Christ, either twofold or, still more completely, threefold. The division into prophetic, high-priestly, kingly, in the Reformation age was especially worked out by Calvin. In the Lutheran Church, J. Gerhard was its first successful advocate. Still the mode of treatment varies very much, even where a triplicity is accepted, and not merely, as often happens, the priestly and kingly offices. . . .

. . . But as concerns the allegation that the three titles affirm nothing definite and distinctive, but the one is rather already involved in the correct idea of the other, this objection applies indeed to such a doctrine of the offices as is often met with in the history of Dogmatics, but not to the doctrine rightly treated. The demand underlying this objection is just; but we shall see presently that the offices may be definitely distinguished in idea notwithstanding their interconnection. Further, it must indeed be conceded that these three offices had a different signification in the theocracy of the O. T., a signification transcended in Christianity. In the old covenant the priest slew the sacrificial victims, and watched over the purity and holiness of the ceremonial law in behalf of himself and others; the king stood at the head of a particular commonwealth, and by means of power and authority had to watch over the outward existence of the political community; the most usual work of the prophets was to guard the welfare and progress of the community by means of the Word. All this is transcended in the new covenant, where the ends and means of the three offices are partially different. But despite these differences, which indeed are conceded beforehand in the typical application of the O. T., a common element is left, which is pre-eminently adapted for use in the language of the N. T. And that definite ideas may be attached to the expressions without prejudice to their figurativeness, is suggested by the fact that in the O. T. kingship and priesthood were kept separate by law. Prophecy again rose in opposition to both, according to need. From this it follows that what characterizes the essence of each of the offices constitutes something well capable of distinction from the rest, and that they do not merge into each other, although a prophet like Moses had also the kingly, or a king like David the prophetic character, nay, although prophecy sees the consummation of the theocracy in the union of the three offices in One. . . .

In point of fact, the excellency of the doctrine of Offices is not merely the plastic character of the expression, easily yielding a clear sense, but also its historic and intrinsic worth. The former lies in this, that the beginnings of this division are found already in the ancient Church, and that the word Χριστός, Anointed, is early referred to the fact of His being King, Prophet, Priest. Just so the division has New Testament support (Acts ii. 22; Rev. i. 5, iii. 14; John xviii. 36; cf. Eph. i. 7, 20; Col. i. 12-20; Phil. ii. 5-11; cf. Heb. vii.-ix). This triple division is of special value, because it sets in vivid light the continuity between the O. T. theocracy and Christianity; for it is these three offices through which the former was founded and preserved. The fact of the consummation of the O. T. being given in Christ may be made specially clear by this, that in Him is demonstrably given the consummation of the offices, through which the O. T. became what it was. Now the three offices of the old covenant had the following meaning. The office of the kings and judges had to control the relation of the citizens to the theocracy, to keep them together as a community, and guard them against foes external and internal. The priests presided over the relation of the Church to God as mediators of reciprocal intercourse; for as they presented prayers and sacrifices as from the Church, so again they distributed blessing as from God. They were the nation's mouth to God in prayer and sacrifice, and God's mouth to the nation in dispensing blessing and theocratic forgiveness. The separation of these first two offices was acknowledged to be necessary from the days of Moses and Aaron, and was specially indispensable under the kings. But, on the other hand, this separation of authorities was often the occasion of jealousy and discord. Hence a third office, bound to no order, not permanent or hereditary, but only arising in time of need—the prophetic—had to play the part of mediator, to kindle new love and enthusiasm for the theocracy, and by this love not merely to establish peace between the authorities, but also to lead the developing revelation onward. . . .

Christ has the full power of the true Messianic King, as even His name affirms (i.e. of King in the Divine kingdom), although in His state of humiliation He exercises it in great measure only in veiled form. He is a King, who must first acquire His kingdom; and this cannot be done by mere demonstration of power. Still less are glory and dominion His absolute end; but He places the regal power which He possesses at the service of the spiritual redemption, the result of which will be the kingdom of glory or the consummation. . . .

Christ is the Prophet as Revealer of Divine truth. He has perfectly revealed as well as fulfilled the Divine Law, and is the consummation as well as the end of prophecy. He is all this because the Divine knowledge is His knowledge, or His Divine-human wisdom, nay, His testimony to the Divine is a testimony to and setting forth of Himself. . . .

The O. T. does not profess to be the perfected religion of atonement, but to predict it. It predicts that religion in such a way that at the same time it prepares for it by revealing on the one hand the Divine holiness and justice, and on the other the grace, which seek their interpenetration typically in sacrifice, prophetically in the Messianic idea. . . .

It is the unanimous doctrine of the New Testament, that in Christ the atonement is found, and with it the basis for perfect redemption. The means thereto described is the God-pleasing self-sacrifice, offered by Christ for the world in accordance with God's loving will, who desires to see the world reconciled with

Himself through the sacrifice. Christ's self-sacrifice is not considered as a mere attestation of His righteousness and holiness, or as an instructive indication of the fact of God's eternal reconciliation with sinners, or of His eternal readiness to forgive, but rather as the effective cause of our salvation, especially of the forgiveness of sins, so that, without prejudice to the pragmatic-historical necessity of His death, a Divine necessity of an official nature also resides in it.

34

Atonement and the Gospel

P. T. Forsyth

In regard to Christ's cross, and within the New Testament, we are to-day face to face with a new situation. We are called upon, sometimes in the tones of a religious war, to set Jesus against Paul and to choose between the historic and the biblical Christ. We are bidden to release Jesus from Paul's arrest, to raise Him from that tomb in which He was buried by the apostle of the resurrection, and to loose Him and let Him go. The issue comes to a crisis in the interpretation of the death of Christ. To treat that death as more than a martyrdom, or to allow it more than a supreme degree of the moral effect upon us of all self-sacrifice, is called a gratuitous piece of theology. To treat it as anything more than the seal of Jesus's own faith in the love of God, or in His prophetic message of reconciliation, is to sophisticate. To regard it as more than the closing incident in a life whose chief value lies in its history (which all the time criticism slowly dissolves), is a piece of perverse religious ingenuity much more like the doctrine of Transubstantiation. To regard it as having anything to do with God's judgment on man's sin, or as being the ground of forgiveness, is a piece of grim Judaism or gloomy Paulinism. The death of Jesus had no more to do with sin than the life of Jesus; and Jesus in His life made no such fuss about sin as Christianity has done. The death of Jesus had really no more to do with the conditions of forgiveness than any martyr's. Every man must make his own atonement; and Jesus did the same, only on a scale corresponding to the undeniable greatness of His personality, and impressive accordingly.

Such teaching removes Christ from the Godhead of grace and makes Him but a chief means of grace to fellow-seekers. But a Church of the Gospel is not a band of disciples or inquirers, but a community of believers, confessors, and regenerates in Christ's cross. An evangelical Church has stood, and stands, not only for the supreme value of Christ's death, but for its prime value as atonement to a holy God, and as the only atonement whereby man is just with God. The atonement which raises that death above the greatest martyrdom, or the greatest witness of God's love, is for us no piece of Paulinism.

Of course, we have all felt the reticence of the Gospels on that doctrine. But how can we avoid feeling its real presence in them except by coming to them with a dogmatic humanism, or a heckling criticism, or a conscience mainly æsthetic? Why, the most advanced New Testament criticism is now concerned to show that the main interest of the evangelists is not biographical, but dogmatic on such matters as baptism and atonement and the last things. The Gospels stand at least on the atoning deed, they were written for a Church which was created by it, and they give singular space to it. Even in John, Jesus is not a disguised God urging people to pierce His veil; He is there to do a work that only His death could do, as a corn of wheat must die to bear. And the Epistles are full of the meaning of that deed.

And where did their interpretation of its meaning come from? From Paul's rabbinism? From the Judaism of his upbringing? From the fanciful speculations of his environment? Was it an interpretation or an importation? Well, where does Paul himself say he got the atoning conception of Christ's death? He received it from the Lord? What does that mean? Was it really but some flash of insight peculiar to his own genius or his idiosyncracy? Was it a feat of ingenious interpretation? No doubt it took, in certain lights, the colour of his rabbinic mind; but was it in essence just an original and daring application of Judaic theology to the crucifixion? Was it a brilliant construction, a reorientation of his traditional theology, whose flash he mistook for a special revelation? No, in its substance it was a part of the Christian instruction which completed his conversion at Damascus. It was from his teachers that he had the atoning interpretation of Christ's death. He delivered to his Churches what he received among the fundamentals (ἐν πρώτοις) from earlier Christians (I Cor. xv. 3, xi. 23), that Christ died for our sins, that His blood was shed for their remission, that His death set up a new relation or covenant between God and man, and that all Israel's history and Bible meant this. In the year 57, that is, he states that such was the common faith of the apostolic community when he was converted, three or four years after Christ's death. It was nothing he developed or edited, but it was something which came from Jesus Himself. Paul received it from the Lord because it came to him from those who had so received it at first.

And how came the apostolic circle to have this view of Christ's death? Could they have foisted on the cross an interpretation so audacious? Must they not have been taught by Christ so as to view it in such forms as are echoed in the ransom passage and at the Last Supper? Must they not have been taught, then, by Christ either during the forty days or from within the veil? They declare they were taught many new things by Him from heaven. We have the same idea, with natural enough variants, in Peter, in John, and in Hebrews. No; the first teacher of the atonement was the Christ who made it. It is no Paulinism, except in certain side lights. Had the apostles held the humanist view that what mattered was but the life, character and teaching of Christ, would they have given the hand of fellowship to Paul when he came to them with the view that biography mattered little compared with Christ's death? Would Paul have taken their hand, with that gulf between them? And what a gulf! It is at bottom all the gulf between the genial Judaism of Hillel which let Christ go to His death as a fanatic and the Christianity which found in His death His deity. The whole history of the Church shows that there can be no standing unity of faith, spirit, or fellowship between those to whom Christ's death is but a great martyrdom and those to whom it is the one atonement of the world and God, the one final treatment of sin, the one compendious work of grace, and the one hinge of human destiny.

We have been warned against the idea that Christ taught about Himself or His work as an essential element of His own Gospel. We are told that He is detachable from His Gospel, if not in history yet in principle. We received it through Him, to be sure, but we do not necessarily have it in Him. But let us leave the question whether He taught Himself, and go back to the prior question. Does the Gospel, does Christianity consist primarily of what Jesus taught? Is that the whole Gospel? Is it the focus of it? Or the standard? Is the Gospel confined to the Galilean ministry? Are we to test every teaching of an apostle by what is left us of the teaching of the Master—either by that alone or by that in chief? Where in the New Testament do we find the authority for that limitation? Where does Jesus impose it? It is surely clear that those He taught never understood Him so. If they had, could they have done anything else than go about retailing that teaching, with a lament at its premature arrest? But is that what they did? The prime thing, and the earliest thing, we know about their teaching (I have just said) is that Christ crowned Israel by dying for the world's sins. It has not the note of regret, nor has it the note of transmitted precept. When precepts were wanted they made new ones for the occasion, on the free evangelical principle, and not on the canonist. They applied the redemption to particular junctures freely, in the spirit; they did not make a casuistic application of Christ's maxims. They did not attack Jew or Gentile even with the parables. James himself, who might have been expected to abjure the Pauline method, and take the strictly ethical line, does not draw his precepts from the armoury of synoptic injunction, or treat Christ as the Chief Rabbi of Israel. Nay, they did not even work with the mere personal impression made on them by Jesus, with the magnetism of a personality whose acts or whose words another Rabbi might criticise. They worked with His person as itself the message, and the final message. They worked with a faith which was not a piece of impressionism but the worship of their new creator, and which therefore did not fade as an impression does, but grew as a new life. Whether Christ taught Himself or not, what He gave, what He left behind, was Himself above all; and Himself as no mere impressionist but as the Saviour, the New Creator. His legacy was neither a truth nor a collection of them, nor a character and its imaginative memory, but a faith that could not stop short of giving Him the worship reserved by all the past for God alone. And what caused this? What produced this result, so amazing, so blasphemous for Jews? It was the cross, when it came home by the resurrection through the Spirit. It was then that Jesus became the matter and not merely the master of gospel preaching. It was then that He became Christ indeed, then when He became perfected! Perfected! He became the finished Saviour only in the finished salvation. And, for those who worshipped Him first, all He was to them centered in the cross and radiated from there. It was the Christ who was made sin for them in the cross that became for them God reconciling the world to Himself. He was all to them in the cross, where He died for their sin, and took away the guilt of the world, according to their Scriptures. It was then that He finished the universal task latent in their national religion, and dealt once for all before God with the sin of the world. That was the starting-point of the Gospel, that made it missionary, made the Church. It is the content of the Gospel. And it is always to there that the Church must come back, to take its bearings, and be given its course.

The very silence of Christ makes His atonement the holiest place of Christian faith. But it was not absolute silence. It was reserve. And He broke it in Paul. The exposition in the Epistles is the Saviour's own work upon His work. He becomes His own divine scholiast. If He lived in Paul submerging Paul (Gal. ii. 20) then Paul's word here was a continuation of Christ's work. It is Christ, the Lord the Spirit, giving that account of Himself which in the Gospels was restrained, partly for want of an audience that could understand or a disciple that could apprehend. His

earthly silence is not so surprising. If He showed Himself after
His resurrection only to the disciples, if He refused to make it a
miraculous appeal to the sceptical world, so, in the still holier
matter of His cross, He may well have been reserved, even to His
own. The great doers are greatly dumb. And Christ was
straitened in the doing of the mighty work. But His Church—it is
no wonder that His Church has been prompt to praise it, keen to
pierce it, and eager to construe it. For the Church is the organ
which cannot but speak and praise when the Master's silent
touch on the keys sets free its soul.

It is sometimes said that the great question of the hour for the
Church's belief is Christological; it is the question of Christ's
person. That is true. But it is the question of the cross all the
same. We know the Incarnation only as the foundation of the
cross. It is from the base of His cross that the stair descends to it.
For the question of the Christ is the question of the Saviour. It is
not a metaphysical question, but a religious. It is not philosophical, but experimental. It is theological chiefly as being
ethical—as turning on sinful man's practical relation to the ethic
of eternity, which is the conscience of a Holy God. The question
of Christ is not the question of a divine hypostasis, but of a
divine Saviour. Technically spoken, the Christology turns on a
Soterology.

But the question of a Saviour is the question of a salvation. It
turns on an experience, and not only on an experience, and the
experience of a historic person, but upon what is for us a revolutionary experience, and not a mere impression, however deep.
It turns on a new creation. The soterology turns on a soteriology.
The centre of Christ is where the centre of our salvation is. He is
Christ, He is God, to us in that He saves us. And He is God by
that in Him which saves us. He is Christ and Lord by His cross.
Christian faith is our life-experience of complete forgiveness and
final redemption in Christ. It does not include forgiveness; it is
forgiveness. Its centre is the centre of forgiveness. Only the
redeemed Church, the Church that knows the forgiveness, has
the key to the Saviour. His blessings are the key to His nature;
they do not wait till the nature is first defined. No philosopher,
as such, has the key, no theologian, no scholar, no critic; only

the believer, only the true Church. And we have it where the evangelical experience has always found its forgiveness—in the cross. Our faith begins with the historic Christ. But not with the biography of Christ (except for propædeutic purposes). We begin, in principle if not in method, with Christ the crucified. We begin with the Church's saving faith in Christ, and not with the modern man's fair verdict on Him. We do not begin with a writer's picture of Christ the prophet, but with the work of Christ the Saviour, continuous in the Church that it made, and made the mother of our own soul. Mere historic knowledge can create no salvation which is not given by certainty about a historic fact, nor by any intelligent grasp of it, but by faith in it, by faith in that within it which is super-historic. And faith finds in this fact of the cross worlds more than a prophet's martyrdom. It finds the depth of God in action, and not merely the depth of the martyr's convictions. The Christ that we trust all to is not one who died to witness for God, but one in whom God died for His own witness, and His own work on us. God was in Christ reconciling. The prime doer in Christ's cross was God. Christ was God reconciling. He was God doing the very best for man, and not man doing his very best before God. The former is evangelical Christianity, the latter is humanist Christianity. Christ's history, His person, can only be understood by His work, and by a work that we apprehend in our moral experience even when we cannot comprehend it by our intelligence. We believe with the unity of our person much that we cannot yet reduce to logical unity. And our soul, our self, finds itself in Him long before our mind does—just as, in the case of His own life, He but gradually appropriated and realised by experience the content of His own personality. The Christ we worship is Christ as forgiver, as redeemer, as new creator, and as judge of all. His relation to the God of thought is something we can wait for; it is a question of the metaphysic, or the theosophy, of Christian faith and ethic. Personal faith may overleap the centuries and go straight to the Bible Christ. But reason with any belief in evolution cannot do so. The science, the theology, of faith cannot do so. It is bound to develop the creed of the Church and not to discard it like some novelist turned theologian without capital. It is bound to correct and adjust as it develops the creed. To turn it out of doors and start on one's own account on nothing is intellectual pertness. And the Church's belief in the divinity of Christ is the result of her experience of justifying faith, of being restored and raised into the communion of God by union with His Christ in faith. To be united with Christ is, in our experience, to be united with God. Therefore, Christ is God. I am redeemed in Christ, and only God can redeem.

35

The Sacrifice of Christ

Frederick Denison Maurice

When the Scriptures speak of Christ's Sacrifice as a Redemption, you will find that they give the word its simplest and most natural force. 'Blessed be the Lord God of Israel, for He hath visited and redeemed His people,' is the burthen of all the songs of the New, and of the Old, Testament. God is assumed everywhere to be carrying out the deliverance of His people, who are, therefore, assumed, by some means, to have fallen into captivity. The sacrifice is a means to this end; the means which God uses; the power by which He ransoms the enslaved captive.

Set this thought, I beseech you, distinctly before your minds, and then compare it with what you know of the effects which heathens attributed to their sacrifices—yes, and with the notions which you have yourselves connected with sacrifices. There is, at the root of both, I am satisfied, an acute sense of some oppression, from which the suppliant wants to be set free; and of a Deliverer, who may be willing, or may be induced, to undertake his cause. But does not this thought mingle with the whole service? 'The oppression I am suffering comes from the Lord of the universe; from the highest power of all. He has laid it upon me: and, in order to shake it off, I must first secure the aid of some powerful ally; next, I must do a number of slavish acts—acts which I feel to be very burdensome and oppressive, but which it is worth while to go through, for the sake of escaping heavier penalties which may overtake me if I neglect them?' Is not this the habit of feeling which you detect in many who submit to religious duties in Christian lands? Have you not detected it in your own hearts? And is it not the very reverse of that idea of sacrifice which we should recognise, if we associated it, as the Scriptures do, with the idea of redemption?

Determine, at all events, which view of the subject, whether it agree or jars with our habits, is most consistent with that doctrine of sacrifice which we have been discovering in the Old Testament. The great truth of all which has come out before us, is that the sacrifices were God's sacrifices,—not merely in that they were offered to him, but in that He originated and prepared them. And, when they assumed the most legal and precise form, they were appointed expressly to commemorate a redemption of the Israelites,—a redemption accomplished for them with a high hand, and a stretched-out arm, by the Lord God of Israel,—a redemption from an actual tyrant.

Still the thought will present itself: 'Whatever may have been the case with the Jews, the redemption, the spiritual redemption, we, Christians, speak of, is surely from some evil inflicted or threatened by God—justly inflicted and threatened—deserved by us, no doubt,—but still proceeding from Him.' As the object I proposed to myself was to discover what the Scripture teaching is, I can only answer this question by referring you to the passages in which the word occurs. Take first, our own passage: 'Forasmuch as ye know that ye were not redeemed with corruptible things, as silver and gold, from your vain conversation received by tradition from your fathers; but with the precious blood of Christ, as of a lamb without blemish and without spot.' There is no difficulty in giving this language a definite signification. St. Peter was writing to a set of people— chiefly Israelites—who were scattered through different provinces of Asia. Their condition explained to him what he had read in the Law and Prophets, what he had experienced himself. The law speaks of the sins of the fathers as being visited upon the children. The Prophets show, how idolatrous notions respecting God,—the confusion of Him with the works of His hands, with the powers of Nature, with evil and malignant persons,— increased from generation to generation; the falsehood of the father growing falser still in the children, till the sense of truth, and with it the sense of righteousness and moral order, became nearly extinct. Such a growth of corruption in habits and notions,—such a continual alienation from the mind of God,—they led, not heathens, but their own countrymen, to expect, if they forgot that they were a chosen people, if they became mere receivers of traditions from their fathers, not believers in the Lord God of their fathers. The moral state of the Israelites, as described in the Old Testament, at various periods, is precisely that of a people sunk in a vain conversation—in a low habitual idolatry and heartlessness, which had begun in one age, and had been transmitted, with fresh accessions, to the next. The scattered Jews in the provinces of the Roman empire, whether they retained a strong sense of their separation, and held intercourse chiefly with each other, or whether they mixed with the heathens round about them, must have presented striking examples of this degeneracy. To them St. Peter came preaching of Christ the Son of David, the Son of God, who had come down from heaven, not to do His own will, but the will of Him who sent Him, who had made the one sacrifice which took away the sins of the world. The message was received by some of these degraded Jews. It became to them the message of a new life. The grovelling thoughts of God, which had been accumulating for years in their own minds, which had been the deposit of centuries, were scattered to the winds. The old words, which they had heard, that He was the Redeemer and King of His people, awakened to life in them. These words prepared them for the new, and still more astonishing, news, that this King was a Father, that He claimed them as His children, that they might arise and go to Him, in the faith that He had owned them, accepted them, delivered them.

St. Peter could turn to these people, and say boldly: You have been redeemed from your vain traditional notions, and from the degeneration that was consequent upon them; you know that you have. And recollect now, recollect always, who has redeemed you. You cannot think that I was the author of the blessing, because I declared it to you. My message must have been a lie, if it came from me; I was as much involved in these traditions, as ignorant of God, as you were. He has raised us out of that ignorance. But consider again the extent of the redemption. I did not tell you of a Father, who cared for you, the dwellers in Pontus and Galatia, above all the other people of the Earth. I told you of a Lamb of God who took away the sins of the world. It was the belief in Him which lifted you out of your miserable subjection to visible things, out of your dark and slavish notions concerning God, out of your dread and horror of Him; are you not conscious that it was? You believed that in Him God has manifested His own fatherly will; you acknowledge Him who had given up Himself, as your King. Hold fast this faith; remember, now and ever, that it is God Himself who has redeemed you out of bondage of which none can understand the bitterness and cruelty so well as yourselves. And the ransom-money, the price of your redemption, has not been corruptible silver and gold. It has been the blood of His only Son. He has made this mighty offering of that which is dearest to Him, that He might bind you to Himself, that He might vindicate His own fatherly love to you, and claim you as His adopted sons.'

There might arise a great many questions, in the hearts of St. Peter's disciples afterwards, about the meaning and operation of this sacrifice; he might reply to them in various ways, as he does in this letter. But with these questions he has no direct business in the present passage. The one thought, 'You have been delivered out of an actual bondage, not an imaginary or a technical one; and this has been the process of your deliverance,' occupies him here. He connects an experience of their minds with a fact. He treats that fact as the manifestation of an eternal law of Sacrifice; of a Person in whom that law was perfectly realised.

I have been anxious that you should dwell upon this particular instance of the use of the word, because it illustrates the practical method of the New Testament teachers, as well as the principle which is embodied in their Gospel to mankind. But I do not wish to rest upon that single instance. St. Paul's circumstances were very different from those of St. Peter: the habits of their minds were different; the people whom they taught were very different.

Let us take an example, then, of the use of the same word from him. He is writing to Titus, who settled in Crete; the overseer of a Church, in which the Gentile element was probably predominant. St. Paul is telling him, with the authority of an apostle and a father, what lessons he should impart to his flock. Here is the summary of the doctrine: 'For the grace of God that bringeth salvation hath appeared to all men, teaching us that, denying ungodliness and worldly lusts, we should live soberly, righteously, and godly, in this present world; looking for that blessed hope, and the glorious appearing of the great God and our Saviour Jesus Christ; who gave himself for us, that he might redeem us from all iniquity, and purify unto himself a peculiar people, zealous of good works.' Titus ii. 11-15. Here you have a phrase different from St. Peter's,—a more comprehensive one. Instead of 'the vain conversation received by tradition' we have 'from all iniquity.' But surely the spirit of the two passages is essentially the same. The bondage of the Cretans, as of all men, was to irregularity, disorder and lawlessness. They were slaves, because they were separated from the true spring and source of order; because they were living as if He were not, as if some other than He were, their Ruler, and the Ruler of the universe. But His grace had shone forth upon all men. It was a saving, delivering grace: one that rescued from ungodliness, and from the lusts of the world; one that produced a righteous, self-restraining, manly, devout, life; one that kindled the hope and expectation of a still brighter shining forth of the glory of God, and of Jesus Christ—who gave up Himself for the very purpose of redeeming us from evil, and making us zealous of good works. Here, as in the other case, the redemption is clearly connected with the sacrifice. God is said to manifest His own grace through that sacrifice. Christ surrenders Himself to do the will of God; and the result of that surrender is, that men may be rescued from a state which is contrary to the will of God—a state of separation from Him, and of consequent immorality, lawlessness, and moral debasement.

36

Punishment and Forgiveness

R. C. Moberly

There can be no question at all as to the exceeding prominence of the part, in the Christian religion, which belongs to forgiveness. For ourselves, as we look to Godward, it is the hope, and the faith, without which all else could be to us as nothing. The simplest form of the universal faith is incomplete without this,—"I believe in the forgiveness of sins." The primary type of the universal prayer lays exceptional emphasis upon this,—"Forgive us our trespasses, as we forgive them that trespass against us." In this form of prayer we have already passed from the thought of forgiveness as being, to Godward, our essential hope, to the thought of forgiveness as being, to manward, our indispensable duty. It is, characteristically, both. It is a duty towards men which, almost more than any other duty, stamps those who realize and fulfil it best, with the distinctive seal of the Spirit of the Christ. And it is a hope which may be said—intelligibly, at least, if not with theological exactness—to sum up all the aspiration and desire of Christians. "I acknowledge one Baptism for the remission of sins" is, in its way, a description of the Christian calling as a whole. "Thy sins be forgiven thee," spoken unerringly by the voice of Divine truth and love, comes very near to the consummation of all human yearning. In either aspect, as primary moral duty, or as primary spiritual hope, it stands plainly in the forefront of all that our Christianity means to us. In our creeds, in our prayers, in our teaching of others, in our hopes or fears for ourselves, few ideas, if any, are, or can be, more prominent than such as are represented to men's thought by that familiar and fundamental phrase, the "forgiveness of sins." Without it Christian morality would be destroyed. Without it Christian faith would be annulled. Directly or indirectly, by conscious effort or by conscious default, it is everywhere, upon our lips, in our thoughts, in our lives. And yet; is it so absolutely clear—I do not say whether forgiveness is to us, after all, an assured or familiar experience, but whether we even know what we mean by forgiveness?

What is forgiveness? Are we perfectly sure that, upon analysis, we shall be found to be attaching to that most familiar word, any defensible or adequate—or indeed any consistent or intelligible—meaning at all?

We begin with some obvious experiments, bearing not so immediately upon the grounds for the doctrine, as upon the meaning of the word. A child comes before parent or master for punishment, and the master lets him go free. The slave insults, or tries to strike, his lord; and the lord refrains from either penalty or reproach. In cases like these, if we speak (as we well may) of forgiveness, there is no doubt what we most immediately mean. We mean that a certain penalty is not inflicted. Is this, then, what forgiveness means? A remission of penalty? a forbearing to punish? This is, we may believe, quite genuinely, the first and simplest form in which forgiveness (whatever it may at last be found to mean) begins to make itself intelligible. It would be a great mistake to brush aside with contempt the idea of forgiveness as remission of penalty. It really is in this form that it first comes home to the consciousness of the child. It may fairly be presumed that it was in this form that it first came home to the child-like consciousness of the race. It may even be doubted, perhaps, whether those who have not first felt something of it in this form are likely to get much further towards the understanding of it at all.

We shall notice indeed that forgiveness cannot be apprehended even in this form, until certain earlier conceptions have been obtained. I cannot really feel myself excused from punishment, until I first feel that I have deserved to be punished; until (that is) I have some idea both of wrong as wrong, and of the distress of punishment, and of that righteousness which is expressed in punishment of wrong. But we need hardly now go further back than the conception of forgiveness as remission of punishment.

Important, however, as it is to recognize this conception as a necessary stage, and true in its degree, in the process of gradually learning what forgiveness means; it will never do to rest here. The theology which allows itself to be entangled in a theory of forgiveness of which the leading character is remission of penalty, will by and by (as not a few attempts to explain the doctrine of the atonement have shown) be landed in insoluble perplexities. Indeed we may perhaps broadly say that forgiveness cannot really mean as much as this without meaning more. The mind cannot really grasp this explanation without becoming, more or less explicitly, conscious that what it really means by the word has already transcended the limits of this explanation. If, at a certain stage, the explanation was true; yet it dimly implied, even then, a good deal beyond itself. And what was once, in its own way, really true, becomes by degrees, to a maturer consciousness, so inadequate, that if pressed now as an adequate statement of truth, it carries with it all the effect—not merely of incompleteness but of untruth.

The explanation does not say enough. Whatever place remission of penalty may have in forgiveness, we all feel that reality of forgiveness contains a great deal beyond this. "I will not punish you,—but I can never forgive," may be an immoral, but is not, on the face of it, a self-contradictory, position. I at least can hate the man whom I would not hurt. Again the explanation says too much. There may be such a thing as infliction of penalty which does not contradict—which may be even said to express—forgiveness. But in any case, the simple idea of not punishing is too negative and external to touch the real core of the matter.

But there is another reason, more directly to our purpose, why forgiveness cannot be defined as remission of penalty. Such a definition would blur all distinction of right and wrong. Remission of penalty, as such, requires an explanation and a justification: and according to the explanation which justifies it, the character of not punishing varies infinitely. Now if I speak of forgiveness as a property of God, or a duty for man, I am speaking of something essentially virtuous and good: not of something which may be either good or the extreme antithesis of goodness. I cannot admit either that forgiveness is an immoral action, or that an immoral action can be forgiveness. Remission of penalty must have a justification. If it has no justification, it is simply immoral. I cannot, for the forgiveness of the creed, or of the Lord's prayer, accept a definition which leaves the question still open, whether forgiveness is not the exact contradiction of righteousness. If this man is guilty of a heartless betrayal, and another of a dastardly murder, and a third it may be of an outrage more dastardly than murder; and I, having absolute power, use that power only to remit the punishments wholesale, without other purpose or ground except remission regarded as an end in itself: I am so far from illustrating the righteous forgiveness of God, that I do but commit a fresh outrage against righteousness, in itself as cowardly as it is immoral. Thought is only misled by a use of the word which includes at once its truth and its caricature. The so-called forgiveness which is itself an infamy,—which, in condoning sin, gives the lie to righteousness,—has nothing in common, except mere delusiveness of outward appearance, with the truth of forgiveness. It may look like it in the negative fact of not-punishing, or in the outward gesture and appearance of embracing; but its whole reality of meaning is different. There may be travesties, or imitations, more or less resembling forgiveness. But there is only one true meaning of the word: and that is the forgiveness not of ignorance or of levity, but of righteousness and truth. The only real forgiveness is the forgiveness of God,— reproduced in man just so far as man, in God's Spirit, righteously forgives; but caricatured by man, so far as man, otherwise than righteously, does the things which travesty and dishonour forgiveness, sparing penalty and foregoing displeasure—when righteousness does not. "Neither doth he abhor anything that is evil" is a terrible condemnation of the man who is ready to forgive everything alike. Forgiveness does not equally mean the truth and the travesty. Its definition cannot be found in terms merely of remission of pain or of anger, irrespective of the verdict of righteousness. When, and so far as, it is remission at all, it is remission because remission is righteous. It is the Divine reality—in God or in man.

We are hampered no doubt by words. But just as with the word "love," while we cannot altogether help verbally using it for that yearning of person towards person which hideously travesties the true spirit of love, we yet educate ourselves towards true insight of soul by protesting that this is the libel not the truth, nor part of the truth, of what love really means; so also with the word forgiveness. If we cannot wholly avoid the use of the word of those who "forgive" unrighteously, yet must we maintain that clear insight of spirit into truth can only be won by refusing to let such caricature of forgiveness colour our central conception of what real forgiveness is.

37

A Theory of Atonement

R. W. Dale

In the preceding Lectures I have endeavoured to prove that the sins of men were the cause of the Death of Christ in a sense in which they were not the cause of the death of those whose fidelity to truth and to conscience, to the highest welfare of mankind and to the authority of God, has provoked the intolerance and the vengeance of wicked men, and won for them the glories of martyrdom; and that on the ground of His Death the sins of men are forgiven.

The proof has been derived from the history and teaching of

our Lord Jesus Christ Himself, and from the testimony of His Apostles, who upon this point, if upon no other, may be supposed to have known His mind.

It being assumed that adequate evidence has been alleged of the existence of a direct relation between the Death of Christ and the Remission of sins, we have now to investigate that relation, and to discover, if we can, the principles and laws which it illustrates. The fact that Christ died to make Atonement for sin having been established, is it possible to construct a theory of the Atonement?

The inquiry upon which we are about to enter is different in kind from that which is now closed, and is of inferior importance. It is not the theory of the Death of Christ that constitutes the ground on which sins are forgiven, but the Death itself; and the faith, which is the condition on our side of receiving "redemption through His blood," is trust in Christ Himself as the Son of God and Saviour of men, not the acceptance of any doctrine which explains how it is that salvation comes to us through Him. For this Trust, it is not necessary that men should acknowledge even the fact that the Death of Christ is the propitiation for the sin of the world; much less is it necessary that they should receive from others or elaborate for themselves a theory of propitiation. It is enough that the authority and love of Christ have been so revealed to them that they rely on Him for eternal salvation.

But if it be true that there is a direct relation between the Death of Christ and the Remission of sins, the inquiry into the grounds of that relation is an inquiry of transcendent speculative importance, and may possibly issue in discoveries concerning the character and ways of God of transcendent practical interest.

On the very threshold of this investigation, we are met by a grave and startling difficulty:—Is the Remission of sins possible?

The answer to this question has been anticipated. Our Lord Himself declared that "the Son of man hath power on earth to forgive sins" (Matt. ix. 6). To a man sick of the palsy, whom He miraculously cured, He said, "Son, be of good cheer, thy sins be forgiven thee" (Matt. ix. 2); and to a woman of evil character, who, in her sorrow and shame, had crept to His feet and washed them with her tears, He said, "Thy sins are forgiven: . . . . thy faith hath saved thee: go in peace" (Luke vii. 48-50). He told His disciples before He suffered, that His blood was to be "shed for the Remission of sins" (Matt. xxvi. 28); and after His Resurrection, He "opened their understanding, that they might understand the Scriptures, and said unto them, Thus it is written, and thus it behoved Christ to suffer, and to rise from the dead the third day; and that repentance and Remission of sins should be preached in His name" (Luke xxiv. 45-47). That the Apostles, wherever they went, spoke to both Jews and heathen of the Remission of sins, as one of the chief elements of the salvation to be secured by believing in Christ; that in their letters to Christian Churches they spoke of the Remission of sins as one of the chief elements of the salvation which those who believed in Christ had already received, is a fact too familiar to every reader of the New Testament to require either proof or illustration.

But among those who do not acknowledge that the Death of Christ is a Propitiation for the sins of the world, there is a tendency either to deny that the Remission of sins is possible, or to depreciate its importance; and this tendency has very much to do with the rejection both of the Doctrine and of the Fact of the Atonement. It arises from a theory of the relation of God to the moral universe in which the idea of Atonement can find no place. . . .

Although the temper of our times makes it difficult for us to believe that the anger of God against sin, and against those that are guilty of sin, can ever become "a consuming fire," it is perhaps easier for us to believe that He is angry with the sinful and the impenitent than to believe that, in any real sense, He is hostile to them. Anger within certain limits is not inconsistent with love. Indeed, the measure of our love for others is often the measure of our anger against them when they do wrong. A comparative stranger may tell us a lie, and we may feel nothing but contempt and disgust; but if our own child, or a friend for whom we have strong affection, tells us a lie, there is often intense anger as well as intense grief. That God should be angry with us though He loves us, is perfectly intelligible; and we may even find it possible to believe that His anger may at last become so great, that if it were revealed, the revelation would utterly consume and destroy us. That He should be hostile to men on account of sin, is not so easy to believe; but unless we believe it we must suppress and reject a large part of the teaching of the New Testament. God has a great love for mankind. This is the central truth which has given light and glory to the long succession of His supernatural revelations to our race. It has received its highest proof and illustration in the Life, Death, and Resurrection of our Lord Jesus Christ, and in the blessings which God has conferred upon mankind in Him. For eighteen centuries the Church has proclaimed this truth, with unequal earnestness, but with a firm and invincible faith. The gloomiest theological systems have never been able altogether to obscure its brightness. In the coldest ages it has kindled the most fervent passion in the hearts of saints; in ages of general intellectual depression it has given inspiration to poets, and has lighted up the fires of a glorious eloquence. But to deny that He can be hostile to men on account of sin, is to emasculate and degrade our conception of Him. He is not a mere "good-natured" God. His righteousness as well as His love is infinite.

Take a case:—You have a child who is the light and joy of your home; her voice is sweeter to you than any music, and her face is fairer and brighter than a summer's morning. Her thoughts are as pure as mountain air; her life is as stainless as mountain snow. She is on the threshold of womanhood, and the very flower and perfection of her loveliness and beauty have come. And a wretch, whose crime human language has no terms black enough to describe, and human laws no punishment terrible enough to avenge—deliberately, by hypocrisy, by lying, by a deep-laid scheme, worked out with elaborate cruelty—betrays her trust, ruins her virtue, and then flings her from him on to the streets of a strange city. He has no compunction for his crime. If the opportunity comes to him again he will repeat it. Tell me now—What ought to be God's relation to such a man as that? Ought God to be at peace with him? God forbid! If He were, there would be no justice in the universe. My hope and strength and consolation in the presence of such a crime as this, come from the certainty that wherever that man goes, under whatever disguises he may live, whatever his wealth may be, whatever his rank, he is pursued by One who is the relentless enemy of his sin—and who will be his relentless enemy if he will not renounce his sin—an enemy from whose grasp he cannot escape, whose strength he cannot resist, and whose justice and wrath, if he does not repent, will inflict upon him an awful penalty. Even to the worst of men indeed God manifests patience and longsuffering. The Divine mercy clings to them while there is any hope, and endeavours to redeem them. It is better, infinitely better, that they should repent than that they should suffer. But the Divine hostility becomes more intense as the Divine grace is resisted, and if they refuse to repent they are treasuring up unto themselves "wrath against the day of wrath, and revelation of the righteous judgment of God."

An extreme case does but illustrate the real nature of the sin that is in all of us, and of God's antagonism to it. The sin may not be developed in a gross form; it may not be of a kind to startle our own conscience; it may not bring upon us the strong condemnation of other men; but God cannot endure sin in any form. In the vast and awful conflict between righteousness and sin, which gives tragic interest to the history of the universe, God is irrevocably on the side of righteousness, and on the side of those who are striving to be righteous. But for the transcendent work of mercy consummated by Christ on Calvary, God would be not only hostile to sin, but hostile to those who take sides with sin, from the first moment of their revolt against the eternal law of righteousness. For sin is a personal act; it has no existence apart from the sinner.

But it was one of the chief elements of the apostolic gospel that in and through Christ God is ready to be at peace with us. In a very true sense He is at peace with us already. His hostility to our sins has received adequate expression in the Death of Christ, and now He is ready to confer on us the Remission of sins for Christ's sake. The Remission of sins is something more than "a kind of formality." It brings to the man who has received it a sure and permanent escape from the hostility and the wrath of God.

. . . The Remission of sins is possible. Can we discover why it is that the Remission of sins is granted to men on the ground of the Death of Christ?

It may be thought that a simple and direct reply to this ques-

tion is given by the representations of the Death of Christ contained in the New Testament. Christ gave His life as a "ransom"
for us; and therefore we are emancipated from all the evils which
we had incurred by sin. Christ "bare our sins," "died for our
sins," "died for us," as an innocent man, if this were possible,
might take upon himself the guilt of a criminal, and die in his
place; and, therefore, the penalties of our sin are remitted.
Christ is the "Propitiation for our sins;" and, therefore, He has
allayed the Divine anger, so that God, for His sake, is willing to
forgive us.

But these representations of the Death of Christ as a Ransom,
as a Vicarious Death, as a Propitiation, though they illustrate the
cause of His sufferings and their effect, and contain all that is
necessary for faith do not constitute a theory. As they stand,
they are not consistent with each other. For a good citizen to bear
the punishment of a convicted criminal, is one thing; for a
generous philanthropist to pay the ransom of a slave, is a different thing; for a friend or a relative of a man who has done
wrong to propitiate the anger of a powerful superior, is a different thing again. In the first case the intervention is intended
to meet the claims of criminal law; in the second, to purchase
what can be estimated at a definite money value; in the third, to
soothe wounded feeling. The fundamental principles on which
we should have to construct our whole theory of the value and
efficacy of the Death of Christ would vary, as we adopted the
first or the second or the third of these illustrations as containing
adequate account of the Atonement.

Nor is it possible by any rough process of combination to work
these heterogeneous illustrations of the great fact into a coherent
conception of it. A slaveholder who receives a ransom as the
condition of liberating his slave is not propitiated; he may have
no resentment that needs propitiation; he is paid the commercial
value of his property. When there is righteous anger against a
base and ungrateful action, it cannot be soothed by anything
that has the nature of the money payment which purchases the
freedom of a slave; nor could righteous anger be propitiated by
the infliction of pain on the innocent instead of the wrong-doer.

There are difficulties of another kind in trying to construct a

theory on the lines of any of these illustrations. If the Death of
Christ is supposed to receive its full interpretation when described as a Ransom, to whom was the Ransom paid? Was it
paid, as some of the Fathers supposed, to the devil? That
hypothesis is revolting. Was it paid to God Himself? That
hypothesis is incoherent; God Himself provided the Ransom,
He could not pay it to Himself; and when we are redeemed, we
do not cease to be under the power of God, for we become His in
a deeper sense than we were before. Was it paid by Christ to
rescue us from the power of the Father? That hypothesis is
intolerable; there is no schism in the Godhead; "God commend-
eth His love toward us, in that while we were yet sinners Christ
died for us." Was the Ransom paid by the Divine mercy to the
Divine justice? That hypothesis is mere rhetoric. Was it paid by
God to the ideal Law of Righteousness which we had offended?
Criminal law knows nothing of ransoms, and a ransom cannot
be paid to an idea.

If, again, the nature of the Death of Christ is supposed to be
completely expressed when it is represented as a Propitiation,
new difficulties emerge, and some of the same difficulties reap-
pear in a new form. How can the incidents of propitiation, as
known among ourselves, assist us to understand a propitiation
which originates with the injured person? Or are we to conceive
of God as working down His resentment by suffering for us, and
so propitiating Himself? Or are we to think of Christ as being
filled with compassion, and subduing the wrath of the Father by
the perfection of His obedience and the urgency of His intercession?

If we adopt the remaining illustration, and attempt to construct a theory of the Death of Christ on the hypothesis that it
corresponded to what would occur in the administration of
human justice if some illustrious man, as conspicuous for his
virtue and public services as for his rank, died as a substitute for
a number of obscure persons who had been guilty of treason, we
are confronted at once by an objection which admits of no reply.
Such a substitution could not be admitted. It would be contrary
to the principle of justice, and in the highest degree injurious to
the state.

These illustrations of the nature and effect of the Death of Christ are illustrations, and nothing more. They are analogous to the transcendent fact only at single points. The fact is absolutely unique. The problem before us is to form some conception of the Death of Christ which shall naturally account for all these various representations of it; and no solution of the problem is to be found by attempting to translate these representations, derived from transient human institutions and from the mutual relations of men, into the Divine and eternal sphere to which this great Mystery belongs. The administration of human justice is at the best imperfect, and can never closely correspond to the Divine government of the moral universe; and the mutual relations of men can never be accepted as adequately illustrating the relations between God and ourselves.

The descriptions of the Death of Christ in the New Testament, as a Sacrifice, a Propitiation, a Ransom, are of infinite practical value; but we misapprehend the true principles and methods and aims of theological science if we make these descriptions the basis of a theory of the Atonement. They constitute the authoritative tests of the accuracy of a theory. A theory is false if it does not account for and explain these descriptions. But to construct a theory we must put these descriptions aside, and consider the Death of Christ itself, in its real relations to God and to man. A theory—worth calling a theory—must rest immediately on the foundation of fact. For the facts we may have to rely, partly or altogether, on testimony. Even the most distinguished scientific inquirers are constantly obliged to build their theories on observations and experiments which they have not made or verified for themselves, but which they receive on the testimony of others. But though facts may be ascertained by testimony, the relation between facts and theories must be direct. We must endeavour to arrive at our theory of the Atonement by an investigation of the Death by which it is alleged that Atonement has been effected. If our theory contains a true account of the Death of Christ, all the forms under which it is represented in the New Testament will be illustrated and explained.

Our Lord Jesus Christ Himself declared that His blood was to be "shed for the remission of sins." Can we discover anything in His Death which promises to throw light on its expiatory power?

There are three considerations which invest the Death of Christ with unique and tragic interest.

1. It was the Death of the Son of God, of God manifest in the flesh.

2. It was a voluntary Death. He came into the world to die. He declared that He laid down His life by His own free will, and that no man could take it from Him.

3. Immediately before His Death He was forsaken of God. When we remember the original glory in which He dwelt with the Father, His faultless perfection, and His unbroken communion with the Father during His life on earth, this is a great and awful mystery. That sinful men, even though they have been transformed into saints, should sometimes lose the sense of the Divine presence and the Divine love, is explicable; but how was it that He, the Son of God, was forsaken by the Father in the very crisis of His sufferings? He Himself had anticipated this desertion with a fear which sometimes became terror. It seems not only possible, but probable, and even more than probable, that the intense and immeasurable suffering which wrung from him the cry, "My God, My God, why hast Thou forsaken Me?" was the immediate cause of His Death. On any hypothesis it accelerated His Death.

In investigating the connection between this mysterious Death and the remission of the sins of men, I propose to inquire:—

1. Whether this connection can be explained by the existence of any original relation existing between the Lord Jesus Christ and the penalties of sin, or—to state the question more generally—between the Lord Jesus Christ and the eternal Law of Righteousness, of which sin is the transgression?

2. Whether this connection can be explained by any original relation existing between the Lord Jesus Christ and the race whose sins needed remission?

The first inquiry will occupy the present Lecture, the second inquiry will occupy the next.

What, then, is the relation between the Lord Jesus Christ and the penalties of sin? What is the relation between the Lord Jesus Christ and the eternal law of righteousness, of which sin is the transgression?

To these questions we have authoritative replies, both from Himself and His Apostles. In several of His discourses He declares that it belongs to Him to "reward every man according to his works" (Matt. xvi. 27). He will "send forth His angels, and they shall gather out of His kingdom all things that offend, and them which do iniquity; and shall cast them into a furnace of fire: there shall be wailing and gnashing of teeth" (Ibid. xiii. 41,42). His lips are to pronounce the sentence by which the final and irrevocable destiny of every man will be determined. He will say to the righteous, "Come, ye blessed of My Father, inherit the kingdom prepared for you from the foundation of the world" (Matt. xxv. 34); and to the wicked, "Depart from Me, ye cursed, into everlasting fire, prepared for the devil and his angels" (Ibid. xxv. 41). "The Father judgeth no man, but hath committed all judgment unto the Son" (John v. 22). The Apostles, in various forms, reassert this truth. St. Peter told Cornelius that Christ "was ordained of God to be the Judge of quick and dead" (Acts x. 42). St. Paul warned the Athenians that God had "appointed a day in the which He will judge the world in righteousness by that Man whom He hath ordained" (Ibid. xvii. 31); and the great Apostle looked forward himself to the solemn hour when "we must all be manifested before the judgment-seat of Christ; that every one may receive the things done in his body, according to that he hath done, whether it be good or bad" (2 Cor. v. 10). The penalties of sin are to be inflicted by Christ.

The final judgment of the world is, however, only part of a larger function. After our Lord's resurrection He said to His disciples, "All power is given unto Me in heaven and in earth" (Matt. xxviii. 18); and on this claim he rested the apostolic commission to "disciple all nations, baptizing them into the name of the Father, and of the Son, and of the Holy Ghost;" teaching them to observe all things that He had commanded them. St. Peter declared that Jesus had been exalted to be "Prince" as well as "Saviour" (Acts v. 31); and that He is "both Lord and Christ" (Ibid. ii. 36). St. Paul describes Him as "the

Lord both of the dead and the living" (Rom. xiv. 9), says that He has received "a name which is above every name: that at the name of Jesus every knee should bow, of things in heaven, and things in earth, and things under the earth" (Phil. ii. 9, 10); and that "He must reign till He hath put all enemies under His feet" (I Cor. xv. 25). The Lord Jesus Christ is the Moral Ruler of the human race; moral responsibility is responsibility to Him.

In the argument for the Divinity of Christ these claims have a great place. It is inconceivable that God should invest a creature with his function of judging the world, and that He should transfer to a creature the moral allegiance due to Himself. The "kingdom" was received by Christ from the Father, because Christ had voluntarily laid aside His Divine glory, and had become man. He was capable of receiving it, because in His humiliation He had not ceased to be Divine. . . .

We conclude, therefore, that the only conception of punishment which satisfies our strongest and most definite moral convictions, and which corresponds to the place it occupies both in the organisation of society and in the moral order of the universe, is that which represents it as pain and loss inflicted for the violation of a law. If the law is a righteous law, if the severity of the penalty is not out of proportion to the magnitude of the offence, the punishment is just; the offender has deserved whatever he suffers. Suffering inflicted upon a man to make him better in the future is not punishment, but discipline: to be punishment, it must be inflicted for evil deeds done in the past. Suffering endured for the sake of benefiting society is not punishment: if accepted voluntarily, it is the heroism of self-sacrifice; if inflicted by arbitrary authority, it is injustice on the one side and martyrdom on the other. What a man suffers from the resentment of another is not punishment, but mere persecution and annoyance, unless the suffering is the effect of moral indignation provoked by real or imaginary wrongs committed against the person by whom the suffering is inflicted: according as the wrongs are imaginary or real, the punishment is unjust or just.

That the suffering inflicted is deserved is a necessary element in the conception of punishment. We have now to determine

God's relation to the ill-desert of a man who has transgressed the eternal Law of Righteousness, and to the suffering which may justly come upon him for his transgression. God cannot be separated, even in idea, from the Law which has been violated, and which affirms the principle that sin deserves to be punished. Is it necessary, or is it not, that this principle should be asserted, and asserted by God Himself?

If it is not asserted, if it is ignored and suppressed, then the eternal Law of Righteousness can be no longer perfectly identified with the will of God; and if the Law is separated from the will of God, conscience will vehemently maintain that the Law is supreme; and in the case supposed will protest that while on the one hand the creature has dishonoured the Law by sin, the Creator has completed the dishonour by refusing to acknowledge the ill-desert of sin. Such a separation, however, between the ideal Law and the Divine Will is impossible. God would cease to be God if His Will were not a complete expression of all the contents of the eternal Law of Righteousness.

Is it then inevitable that God should inflict the penalties which sin has deserved? Has he no choice? Is it impossible that He should be merciful? Does He act as a blind, unconscious force? Is the moral government of the universe a vast and awful mechanism, dispensing rewards and punishments from eternity to eternity in exact proportion to righteousness and sin? Is there no difference between being under the iron rule of a Law and being under the rule, gracious as well as just, of a living God? To these questions the Christian revelation and the irrepressible instincts of our moral and spiritual nature give the same replies.

It is necessary to look a little more closely into the nature of punishment if we are to discover the solution of the difficulty in which questions like these originate.

In common, popular speech, we say that "the sinner ought to suffer;" but this is a very loose expression, loose even to inaccuracy. When so used, the word "ought" has a very different force from that which belongs to it when we say that "a man ought to be honest and to tell the truth." By being honest and truthful, a man fulfils a duty. But a man who has committed a sin fulfils no duty by merely suffering for his sin. His mere suffering is not obedience: while he suffers, his whole nature may be in fiercer revolt than ever against the Law which he has transgressed, and the penalty of which he is enduring. There may be no more righteousness in him when his suffering is keenest than there was before his suffering commenced: his mere suffering has no virtue in it.

When we use the phrase that a man who has committed a crime "ought to suffer for it," we generally mean nothing more than that he deserves to suffer; or if anything more than this is meant, we mean that some one who has the authority and power is under a moral obligation to make him suffer.

Punishment gives to the sufferer occasion for manifesting humility, patience, and a spirit of penitent submission to the pain which he has deserved by his offences; and if he does not manifest these virtues he incurs fresh guilt. But the duty of manifesting them arises from the fact that by some external force or authority he is being made to suffer the just consequences of his past offences. Whatever moral element there is in punishment itself—as punishment—is derived from the person or power that inflicts it. . . .

But if the punishment of sin is a Divine act—an act in which the identity between the Will of God and the eternal Law of Righteousness is asserted and expressed—it would appear that, if in any case the penalties of sin are remitted, some other Divine act of at least equal intensity, and in which the ill desert of sin is expressed with at least equal energy, must take its place.

The heart of the whole problem lies here. The eternal Law of Righteousness declares that sin deserves to be punished. The Will of God is identified both by the conscience and the religious intuitions of man with the eternal Law of Righteousness. To separate the ideal law—or any part of it—from the Living and Divine Person, is to bring darkness and chaos on the moral and spiritual universe. The whole Law—the authority of its precepts, the justice of its penalties—must be asserted in the Divine acts, or else the Divine Will cannot be identified with the eternal Law of Righteousness. If God does not assert the principle that sin deserves punishment by punishing it, He must assert that principle in some other way. Some Divine act is required which shall have all the moral worth and significance of the act by which the penalties of sin would have been inflicted on the sinner.

The Christian Atonement is the fulfilment of that necessity. The principle that suffering—suffering of the most terrible kind—is the just desert of sin is not suppressed. It would have been adequately asserted had God inflicted on man the penalties of transgression. It is asserted in a still grander form, and by a Divine act, which in its awful sublimity and unique glory infinitely transcends the mere infliction of suffering on those who have sinned. The penalties are not simply held back by the strong hand of infinite love. He on whom the sins of men had brought the dread necessity of asserting the principle that they deserved to suffer, and who, as it seems to us, could not decline to assert it—He through whose lips the sentence of the eternal Law of Righteousness must have come, condemning those who had sinned to exile from the light and life of God—He by whose power the sentence must have been executed—He Himself, the Lord Jesus Christ, laid aside His eternal glory, assumed our nature, was forsaken of God, died on the cross, that the sins of men might be remitted. It belonged to Him to assert, by His own act, that suffering is the just result of sin. He asserts it, not by inflicting suffering on the sinner, but by enduring suffering Himself.

Nor is this all. To affirm that, on the cross, the Moral Ruler of our race endured what He might have inflicted, is an inadequate representation of the truth. If God's love for His creatures invests the Divine act which punishes them with its highest moral value, the love of the Eternal Father for the Son invests with infinite moral sublimity the Divine act which surrendered Him to desertion and to death, that the justice of the penalties of sin might be affirmed before the penalties were remitted. The mysterious unity of the Father and the Son rendered it possible for God at once to endure and to inflict penal suffering, and to do both under conditions which constitute the infliction and the endurance the grandest moment in the moral history of God.

The question of the grounds on which the Moral Ruler of mankind could so identify Himself with our race as to assume our nature, and endure suffering instead of inflicting it on us, is the question to be discussed in the next Lecture: for the present I must assume that in this endurance of suffering the Lord Jesus Christ was acting in harmony with His original and Ideal relations to mankind. The point we have reached is this: the moral significance of the suffering by which sin is punished is derived from the fact that the suffering is inflicted by the Will of God. In the Death of Christ, He to whom it belongs to inflict suffering endures suffering instead of inflicting it. In stating the problem which arises on the hypothesis that God has resolved to remit the penalties of sin, I said that "if God does not assert the principle that sin deserves punishment, by punishing it, He must assert that principle in some other way. Some Divine act is required which shall have all the moral worth and significance of the act by which the penalties of sin would have been inflicted on the sinner;" and I repeat that "the Christian Atonement is the fulfilment of that necessity." It was a greater act to submit to such suffering as Christ endured than to inflict it.

38

Preaching the Atonement

James Denney

If the series of studies which we have now completed has reproduced with any adequacy or accuracy the mind of the New Testament writers, certain conclusions of importance may fairly be deduced from it. One is that there really is such a thing as the New Testament. There is, as we were disposed to assume, a real and substantial unity of thought in the books which we call by that name. They were not written with a view to incorporation in a canon; to repeat the paradox referred to in the introduction, New Testament theology is the theology of the Church at a time when as yet it had no New Testament. But the New Testament books have a unity, nevertheless, which is not external or imposed, nor due to the accident of their being approximately contemporary, but which is inward, essential, and spiritual, and which qualifies them to be canonical. Another conclusion to which we are led is that the death of Christ is the central thing in the New Testament, and in the Christian religion as the New Testament understands it. And when we say the death of Christ, we include, of course, the significance which the New Testament ascribes to it. Apart from that significance the death of Christ has no more right to a place in religion than the death of the penitent or the impenitent thief. The Cross and the word of the Cross—the Cross and the rationale of it in relation to the love of God and the sin of Man—are for religion one thing. This being so, it is apparent that both for the propagation and for the scientific construction for the Christian religion the death of Christ is of supreme importance. Not that I should draw too abstract a distinction. The propagation of Christianity and its interpretation by intelligence—in other words, preaching and theology—should never be divorced. At the vital point they coincide. The simplest truth of the gospel and the profoundest truth of theology must be put in the same words—He bore our sins. If our gospel does not inspire thought, and if our theology does not inspire preaching, there is no Christianity in either. Yet vitally related as they are, there is a sufficiently clear distinction between them, and in considering some consequences, for preaching and theology, of New Testament teaching on Christ's death, it will be convenient to take preaching first.

It is an immediate inference, then, from all that we have seen in the New Testament, that where there is no Atonement there is no gospel. To preach the love of God out of relation to the death of Christ—or to preach the love of God in the death of Christ, but without being able to relate it to sin—or to preach the forgiveness of sins as the free gift of God's love, while the death of Christ has no special significance assigned to it—is not, if the New Testament is the rule and standard of Christianity, to preach the gospel at all. Many ministers have suffered from the charge of not preaching the gospel, and have resented it as an injustice. In any given case it may quite well have been so. There are those who are unable to separate form from substance in thinking, and who are only too ready to believe that if the familiar form in which the truth has been expressed is varied, the substance is being injured or dissipated. But it is not saying a hard or unjust thing to say that in some cases the charge may not be groundless. It may be made not merely by the unintelligent, who fail to distinguish form from substance, but by the simple Christian spirit which has the anointing from the Holy One, and knows instinctively whether that by which it lives is present in the message it hears or not. There is such a thing as preaching in which the death of Christ has no place corresponding to that which it has in the New Testament. There is preaching in which the New Testament interpretation of Christ's death is ignored, or carped at, or exploded. We do not need to argue that no man can preach the gospel until he has absorbed into his mind and heart the whole significance of Christ's death as the New Testament reveals it; in that case, who could preach at all? But it is not unjust to say that no man will so preach as to leave the impression that he has the Word of God behind him if he is inwardly at war with the idea of atonement, constantly engaged in minimising it, maintaining an attitude of reserve, or even of self-defence, in relation to it. We may take it or leave it, but it is idle to attempt to propagate the Christian religion on the basis and with the authority of the New Testament, unless we have welcomed it with our whole heart.

It is proper to remember in this connection that very often it is the simplest expressions, and those most open to abstract criticism, in which the profoundest truth is most tellingly expressed and most really apprehended; and that when this is the case, if we are compelled to criticise, we should be careful that we do not discredit the essential truth as well as the inadequate form. It is easy, for instance, to criticise the insufficiency of any commercial figure, like that of 'debt,' to exhibit the personal and spiritual relations subsisting between man and God; yet Christ used this figure habitually, and the whole impression which it makes upon the conscience is sound. The words of the revival hymn, 'Jesus paid it all, All to Him I owe,' have the root of the matter in them; and, however inadequate they may be to the interpretation of Christ's work and of Christian experience as a whole, they are infinitely truer than the most balanced, considerate, or subtle statement which denies them. Hence, whatever the motive which prompts criticism of such forms, we should be sensitive to the meaning they bear. Even if we think they are morally inadequate, and leave the new life unprovided for, we should remember that in the New Testament the new life is the immediate response to the very truth which such forms convey. The new life springs out of the sense of debt to Christ. The regenerating power of forgiveness depends upon its cost: it is the knowledge that we have been bought with a price which makes us cease to be our own, and live for Him who so dearly bought us. And we should remember also that it is not always intellectual sensitiveness, nor care for the moral interests involved, which sets the mind to criticise statements of the Atonement. There is such a thing as pride, the last form of which is unwillingness to become debtor even to Christ for forgiveness of sins; and it is conceivable that in any given case it may be this which makes the words of the hymn stick in our throats. In any case, I do not hesitate to say that the sense of debt to Christ is the most profound and pervasive of all emotions in the New Testament, and that only a gospel which evokes this, as the gospel of Atonement does, is true to the primitive and normal Christian type.

Not only must Atonement by the death of Christ be preached if we would preach the New Testament gospel, but the characteristics of the Atonement must be clearly reflected in the preaching if justice is to be done to the gospel. As the finished work of Christ the Atonement is complete, and the perfection which belongs to it belongs also to the new relation to God into which we enter when the Atonement is appropriated by faith. There is no condemnation to them that are in Christ Jesus. Their relation to God is not determined now in the very least by sin or law, it is determined by Christ the propitiation and by faith. The position of the believer is not that of one trembling at the judgment seat, or of one for whom everything remains somehow in a condition of suspense; it is that of one who has the assurance of a Divine love which has gone deeper than all his sins, and has taken on itself the responsibility of them, and the responsibility of delivering him from them. A relation to God in which sin has nothing to say, but which is summed up in Christ and His perfect Atonement for sin—in John Wesley's words, full salvation now—is the burden of the gospel. If it is not easy to believe this or to preach it, it is because, as the heavens are higher than the earth, so are God's thoughts higher than our thoughts, and His ways than our ways. In the New Testament itself there is always something startling, something almost incredible, which breaks again and again on the soul with a sense of wonder, in the experience of reconciliation through the death of Christ. But it is this great gospel which is the gospel to win souls—this message of a sin-bearing, sin-expiating love, which pleads for acceptance, which takes the whole responsibility of the sinner unconditionally, with no preliminaries, if only he abandon himself to it. Only the preaching of full salvation now, as Wesley tells us—and who knew better from experience than he?—has any promise in it of revival.

Further, preaching which would do justice to the Atonement must hold out in the gospel an assurance corresponding to the certainty of Christ's death and to the sin-bearing love demonstrated in it. Nothing is more characteristic of churches than their attitude to assurance, and the place they give it in their preaching and in their systems of doctrine. Speaking broadly, we may say that in the Romish church it is regarded as essentially akin to presumption; in the Protestant churches it is a privilege or a duty; but in the New Testament religion it is simply a fact. This explains the joy which, side by side with the sense of infinite obligation, is the characteristic note of apostolic Christianity. The great invincible certainty of the reconciling love of God, which even when we were enemies made peace for us, this underlies all things, embraces all things, makes all things work together for good to those who love God, makes us more than conquerors in all things; take away the certainty of it, and the New Testament temper expires. Joy in this certainty is not presumption; on the contrary, it is joy in the Lord, and such joy is the Christian's strength. It is the impulse and the hope of sanctification; and to deprecate it, and the assurance from which it springs, is no true evangelical humility, but a failure to believe in the infinite goodness of God who in Christ removes our sins from us as far as the east is from the west, and plants our life in His eternal reconciling love. The New Testament spirit is not meant for our despair, but for our inspiration; that assurance of sin-bearing love, that sanctifying strength and gladness, are the type of genuine Christian life.

We can understand and appreciate the motive which, both in the Romish and in the Protestant churches, has fostered in relation to assurance a temper which is not that of the New Testament, and which does not answer to the completeness and certainty of Christ's finished work. The motive is in both cases a desire to safeguard moral interests and to put a check upon self-deception. The Romish church safeguards moral interests by making justification and the new life identical: men are justified as, and only in proportion as, they are actually and morally renewed. The objection to this method is that the security is too good. An absolute justification is needed to give the sinner a start. He must have the certainty of 'no condemnation,' of being, without reserve or drawback, right with God through God's gracious act in Christ, before he can begin to live the new life. As Chalmers put it with magnificent simplicity, 'What could I do if God did not justify the ungodly?' It is not by denying the gospel outright, from the very beginning, that we are to guard against the possible abuse of it. In the Protestant churches, on the other hand, the attempt to check presumption and to safeguard moral interests was usually made by laying stress on the proper kind of faith. The German Pietists, in opposition to a dead orthodoxy, in which faith had come to mean no more than the formal recognition of sound doctrine, spoke with emphasis of penitent faith, living faith, true faith, obedient faith, and so on. It is somewhat against qualifications like these that they are foreign to the New

Testament. What they come to in practice is this: Before the mercy of God in Christ the propitiation can be available for you, O sinful man, you must have a sufficient depth of penitence, a sufficiently earnest desire for reconciliation and holiness, and sufficient moral sincerity; otherwise grace would only minister to sin. But such qualifications do infringe upon the graciousness of the gospel—I mean on its absolute freeness—as something to be explained out of the love of God and the necessity, not the merits, of men. Christ did not die for those who were sufficiently penitent. He is the propitiation for the whole world, and He bore the sins of all that all might believe and receive through Him repentance and remission. To try to take some preliminary security for the sinner's future morality before you make the gospel available for him is not only to strike at the root of assurance, it is to pay a very poor tribute to the power of the gospel. The truth is, morality is best guaranteed by Christ, and not by any precautions we can take before Christ gets a chance, or by any virtue that is in faith except as it unites the soul to Him. Now the Christ who is the object of faith is the Christ whose death is the Atonement, and the faith which takes hold of Christ as He is held out in the gospel conducts, if we may use such a figure, the virtue of the Atonement into the heart. The mercy of God which we welcome in it, and welcome as the first and last of spiritual realities with invincible assurance, is a mercy which has deep in the heart of it God's judgment upon sin; and such a mercy, absolutely free as it is, and able to evoke in sinful men a joy unspeakable and full of glory, can never foster either immorality or presumption. But when its certainty, completeness, and freeness are so qualified or disguised that assurance becomes suspect and joy is quenched, the Christian religion has ceased to be.

There is one other characteristic of the Atonement which ought to be reflected in gospel preaching as determined by it, and which may for want of a better word be described as its finality. Christ died for sins once for all, and the man who believes in Christ and in His death has his relation to God once for all determined not by sin but by the Atonement. The sin for which a Christian has daily to seek forgiveness is not sin which annuls his acceptance with God, and casts him back into the position of one who has never had the assurance of the pardoning mercy of God in Christ; on the contrary, that assurance ought to be the permanent element in his life. The forgiveness of sins has to be received again and again as sin emerges into act; but when the soul closes with Christ the propitiation, the assurance of God's love is laid at the foundation of its being once for all. It is not to isolated acts it refers, but to the personality; not to sins, but to the sinner; not to the past only, in which wrong has been done, but to time and eternity. There will inevitably be in the Christian life experiences of sinning and being forgiven, of falling and being restored. But the grace which forgives and restores is not some new thing, nor is it conditioned in some new way. It is not dependent upon penitence, or works, or merit of ours; it is the same absolutely free grace which meets us at the Cross. From first to last, it is the blood of Jesus, God's Son, which cleanses from sin. The daily pardon, the daily cleansing, are but the daily virtue of that one all-embracing act of mercy in which, while we were yet sinners, we were reconciled to God by the death of His Son.

To say that there is no gospel without Atonement, and that the characteristics of the Atonement must be impressed upon Christian preaching and reflected in the completeness, assurance, and joy of the Christian life which is the response to it, does not mean that the preacher is always to be expressly and formally engaged with the death of Christ, nor does it determine in what way that death in its redeeming significance is to be presented to men. It is impossible to forget the example of our Lord, though we are bound to remember that what was natural and inevitable before the Passion and the Resurrection may not be either wise or natural now. But looking to the gospels, we cannot but see that our Lord allowed His disciples every opportunity to become acquainted with Him, and to grow into confidence in Him, before He began to teach them about His death. He allowed them to catch the impression of His Personality before He initiated them into the mystery of His Passion.

39

The Holy Spirit

R. W. Dale

When we pass from the Old Testament to the New we are in the presence of a great revelation of the Spirit of God as well as of the Son of God. In the earlier pages of the New Testament, indeed, we are still surrounded by the ancient forms of Jewish thought; the Spirit of God is still known as a Power—not as a Person; and, throughout the New Testament Scriptures, in such phrases as 'being filled with the Spirit,' the old idea of the Spirit of God, as a Power, survives; but in the later books the Power is known as the Power of a divine Person.

(I.) There are premonitions of the great revelation in the earlier teaching of our Lord, but its fulness was reserved for the discourse which He delivered to His disciples during the night in which He was betrayed. To those who loved our Lord best, and who had the most perfect faith in Him it was a night of despondency, of despair. The constellations of glorious hope which had been shining in the heaven of their thought were all extinguished. What a wonderful time they had had with Him for two or three years! He had raised them into a new world—a world in which they had discovered that God was nearer to them than they had ever dreamt before. And now He was about to die, and to die a most cruel and shameful death. Their Master was to leave them, and it also seemed as if the happy company of His elect friends was to be broken up for ever. Judas was a traitor; Peter had been warned that before sunrise on the next morning he would deny His Lord; if Peter's fidelity was to give way who of them was likely to stand firm?

And even if the rest remained faithful and Peter repented, to what purpose would it be? In losing Christ they lost everything. He was their light, their joy, their strength, and their defence. It was true that He had spoken mysterious words about coming to them again; but how were they to endure His absence, and how were they to make any stand against His enemies and theirs, until He returned? He had come, so they believed, to found a divine kingdom among men. He had given them the great honour of sharing His task. But they stood alone; even the elect nation was against both Him and them. Apart from Him they were powerless. The work was His; He was sent of God, so they believed, to begin and to carry it through. It depended wholly upon Him. While He was with them they could face hatred, contempt, mockery, insult, slander, outrage; but without Him they could do nothing.

It was to meet this despondency, this despair, that our Lord told them that the Father would give them 'another Advocate,' who would 'abide' with them 'for ever;' an Advocate who would maintain His cause and theirs against the whole world. This is the sense of the word which in the text of our translation is represented by the word 'Comforter.' That the Holy Spirit would console them in their sorrow for our Lord's departure, and that He still consoles us in our trouble, is true; but it was not chiefly of the consolation that the Holy Spirit would bring them that our Lord was thinking. To 'comfort,' according to the present use of the word, means to soothe distress, to quiet restless hearts and give them peace; it is the gentlest of ministries. But our Lord was thinking of a ministry of a more robust and energetic kind. Their 'Advocate' was to stand by them in the great conflict by which they were menaced. While our Lord Himself had been with them, it was to Him they looked to repel the assaults of their enemies. His presence gave them confidence and courage. How often they had listened to Him with triumph while He answered subtle questions which were meant to entangle Him; resolved difficulties which seemed to admit of no solution; brought home to the consciences of men who charged Him with unfaithfulness to the Law, their own guilt, covered them with public shame and left them without defence! What courage His miracles had given them! All things were possible to Him. Now they were to have 'another Advocate.' What our Lord Himself had been to them the Holy Spirit was to be. He was to take the place of Christ. He was not to be an 'Influence,' but what Christ was—a Person, who would lead them, protect them, support them in their struggles and sufferings for Christ and His Kingdom.

All that our Lord says of the Advocate in this discourse makes it certain that He is speaking—not of a Power but of a Person. The Advocate is to 'teach' them all things, and to 'bring to' their 'remembrance' all that Christ Himself had said to them (John xiv. 26). 'The Spirit of Truth, . . . He shall bear witness of Me: and ye also bear witness' (John xv. 26). 'He shall guide you into all the truth: for He shall not speak from Himself: but what things soever He shall hear, these shall He speak; and He shall declare unto you the things that are to come. He shall glorify Me: for He shall take of mine and shall declare it unto you' (John xvi. 13-14). To 'teach,' to 'bear witness,' to 'guide,' to 'speak,' to 'hear,' to 'declare the things that are to come,' to 'take' of the things of Christ and 'declare' them to Christ's friends,—all these are personal acts, and they are all attributed to the Spirit. And equally personal are the acts attributed to the Spirit in relation to those who are not yet the friends of Christ. He is to plead with them; to bring home to them the reality of sin and of righteousness and the awfulness of the judgment of the world (John xvi. 8-11). It is a living Person, surely, who is to do these great things, a living Person with clear thought and resolute will—a Person who is to maintain a great conflict with the moral indifference or the moral hostility of mankind.

(II.) We pass from the Four Gospels to the Acts of the Apostles and to the Epistles, and we find that this divine Person is actually present in the Church; has assumed authority there; directs and controls its action.

(a) When Ananias brought part of the money for which he had sold his land, and laid it at the Apostles' feet, Peter met him with the awful question, 'Ananias, why hath Satan filled thy heart to deceive the Holy Ghost and to keep back part of the price?' When his wife, who was confederate in the deception, came in and confirmed the falsehood of her husband, the Apostle said, 'How is it that ye have agreed together to tempt the Spirit of the Lord?' (Acts v. 3-9). The Church and its ministers were but the visible organs and representatives of an invisible and divine Person. In trying to deceive the Apostles, Ananias and Sapphira were trying to deceive and were tempting Him.

The presence and the authority of a divine Person in the Church are also illustrated in Paul's address to the Ephesian elders: 'Take heed to yourselves and to all the flock in which the Holy Ghost hath made you bishops' (Acts xx. 28). The Church at Ephesus is a supernatural society; whatever part the Apostles themselves or the commonalty of the faithful may have had in electing the ministers of the Church or consecrating them to their office—a question which it is unnecessary that I should discuss—they had been made bishops by the choice, the grace, and the authority of the Spirit of God.

(b) The free personal activity of the Spirit of God in the government of the Church appears in His distribution of spiritual gifts. 'As we have many members in one body, and all members have not the same office, so we, who are many, are one body in Christ' (Rom. xii. 4). And according to the 'office' or service which a man has to discharge, is the power that is conferred upon him. The one is given 'the word of wisdom;' to another 'the word of knowledge;' to another exceptional forms or degrees of 'faith;' to another 'gifts of healings;' to another 'workings of miracles;' to another 'prophecy;' to another 'divers kinds of tongues;' 'but all these worketh the one and the same Spirit, dividing to each one severally even as He will' (I Cor. xii. 8-11).

(c) Illustrations not less impressive of the free personal action of the Spirit of God as the leader of the Church and the representative of Christ are contained in the history of the successive movements by which the Christian Gospel passed beyond the limits of the Jewish race and reached the Gentiles.

Cornelius, a Roman soldier, who, without submitting to the Jewish rite of circumcision, had come to worship the One God, the Creator of the Heavens and the Earth, and who was generous in his compassion for the race which had borne testimony to the divine unity and greatness, was charged by an angel whom he saw in a vision to send for Peter. Peter himself saw a remarkable vision and heard a voice saying, 'What God hath cleansed, call not thou common' (Acts x. 9-16). While he was still perplexed as to what the vision might mean, the messengers from Cornelius were at the gate of the house, and were asking for him; and 'the Spirit said unto him, Behold, three men seek thee. But arise, and get thee down, and go with them, nothing doubting; for I have sent them' (Acts x. 19, 10). It was the Spirit of God who through the ministry of an angel had told Cornelius to send messengers to Peter; and now the Spirit of God sends Peter to Cornelius. Peter preached the Christian Gospel to the soldier and his house, and while the Apostle was still telling the story of Christ, those who were listening to him began to speak with tongues and to magnify God. The same Spirit that had charged him to come to Cæsarea and to tell the story of Christ to Cornelius and to his family and friends, now anticipates and sweeps away whatever hesitation Peter might have felt in baptizing persons who stood outside the sacred race which inherited the promises. 'Can any man,' asked Peter, 'forbid the water, that these should not be baptized as well as we? (Acts x. 47). 'The middle wall of partition' had been broken down. The Spirit of God had made it clear that those who 'once were far off' were 'made nigh by the blood of Christ;' that through Christ both Jew and Gentile were to have access 'in one Spirit unto the Father' (Eph. ii. 13-18).

The conversion and baptism of Cornelius marked the first great movement of the Christian Church beyond the rigid enclosure of Judaism; a few years later came a second; and the Spirit of God was the leader of the second movement as He had been the leader of the first. Some of the Jewish Christians—'men of Cyprus and Cyrene'—who had been compelled to leave Jerusalem by the persecution which followed the martyrdom of Stephen, had ventured to preach the Gospel to Greeks as well as to Jews in the city of Antioch. Large numbers 'believed and turned to the Lord' (Acts xi. 19-21); a strong church was formed, consisting chiefly of persons converted from heathenism. The Church had many 'prophets and teachers,' some of them men who afterwards became famous. The time had come to impose on this powerful Christian community great responsibilities and to confer upon it great honour. The Church had met for fasting and prayer; and 'the Holy Ghost said, Separate Me Barnabas and

Saul for the work whereunto I have called them' (Acts xiii, 1, 2). This is not the action of a 'Power' or the descent of an 'Influence;' it is the authoritative command of a Person. The command is obeyed, and Saul and Barnabas—to quote again the words of the writer of the Acts—'being sent forth by the Holy Ghost, went down to Seleucia; and from thence they sailed to Cyprus' (Acts xiii. 4). This was Paul's first missionary journey—the first great attempt to make the Christian redemption known to heathen nations; the beginning of that glorious movement by which, in the course of three or four generations, Christian churches were planted in every province of the Roman empire, and even among races which had never submitted to the Roman arms.

As Paul was 'sent forth' by the personal authority of the Spirit of God, his travels were directed by the same Spirit. He and his friends were 'forbidden of the Holy Ghost to speak the word' in the Roman province of Asia; and when they had determined to go into Bithynia, 'the Spirit of Jesus suffered them not.' He was directing them to the western coast of Asia, and there Paul learned in a vision that it was God's will that he should pass over to Europe (Acts xvi. 6-10).

Before this, the preaching of the Gospel to the Gentiles had caused a great controversy. Jewish Christians had gone down from Jerusalem to Antioch and had insisted that if the Gentile converts wished to be saved they must submit to circumcision and keep the law of Moses. These men claimed to speak in the name of James and of the other ministers and members of the church in Jerusalem, who still observed the religious and national customs of their race. It was a great crisis. If the Judaizers had been successful, the Christian Gospel would have been imprisoned within the customs and traditions of a single nation, instead of being free to make its home in the life of every race under heaven; the Christian Church would have been dwarfed to the ignoble proportions of a mere Jewish sect. Whether the Jewish zealots spoke with the authority of James and the church at Jerusalem could be easily learned; the church at Antioch sent Paul and Barnabas and some others to Jerusalem to ask the question. The Apostles and the elders and the whole Church met to receive them. James and his friends disclaimed all responsibility for the teaching of the Judaizers; but this was hardly enough to end the trouble. Jewish Christians and Gentile Christians were living together in many cities; and there were certain practices common among the heathen Gentiles—and in themselves perfectly harmless—which, if not avoided by Gentile Christians, would render friendly social relations between them and their Jewish brethren impossible. To carry the Church peaceably through a period of transition, it was desirable that the Gentile Christians should avoid these harmless practices. And there was one flagrant vice so common among heathen men, and so lightly regarded by them, that the Jews were apt to suppose that all who had been born heathen were likely to be guilty of it. And so the Jewish church and its leaders determined to send pacific counsels as well as words of brotherly affection to the Gentile churches: 'It seemed good to the Holy Ghost, and to us, to lay upon you no greater burden than these necessary things: that ye abstain from things sacrificed to idols, and from blood, and from things strangled, and from fornication' (Acts xv. 28, 29).

In this crisis—a crisis in which all the future fortunes of the Church were involved—the Spirit of God definitely intervenes, and marks out the path of safety and peace.

(III.) As the personal activity of the Spirit of God is apparent in His leadership and government of the Church, it is also apparent in His relations to individual men. Those who deny His personality are accustomed to contend that by the Spirit of God we are to understand either (a) the higher life of man, or (b) God as immanent in the higher life of man.

(a) But Paul distinguishes between the Spirit of God and our 'spirit.' For 'the Spirit Himself beareth witness with our spirit that we are children of God' (Romans viii. 16). His witness to our sonship is distinct from our personal consciousness of sonship. Again, 'we know not how to pray as we ought: but the Spirit Himself maketh intercession for us with groanings which cannot be uttered' (Romans viii. 26). What He desires for us He must know; and there are times when He is able to draw us into perfect and intelligent sympathy with His own thought and His own longing; but there are other times when the great things that He desires for us transcend our vision and our hope; and then the Spirit who dwells in us carries on His intercession for us alone; He is too near to us, too intimately one with us, for us not to be conscious of the energy and earnestness of His desires; and we ourselves, as the result of His energy and earnestness, may have a vague and even a passionate longing for some infinite good, but what it is we cannot tell.

(b) And as the Spirit cannot be identified with the higher life of man, neither can He be identified with a mere impersonal immanence of God in the life of man. Paul has said in the passage which I have just quoted that we in whom the Spirit dwells may be unable to discover what are the great things which are the subject of His intercession with God for us. But the apostle adds, 'He that searcheth the heart'—that is, God—'knoweth what is the mind of the Spirit, because He maketh intercession for the saints according to the will of God' (Romans viii. 27). He who intercedes for us with God must be personally distinguishable from God; He who makes intercession for us 'according to the will of God' must be personally distinguishable from God; He whose 'mind' God knows must be personally distinguishable from God. No such expressions as these, which occur in the Epistle to the Romans, could have been possible in Old Testament times, when the distinct Personality of the Spirit was unrevealed.

This whole passage illustrates in even a startling manner the truth and reality of the 'coming' of the Holy Ghost—the extent to which, if I may venture to say it, He has separated Himself—as Christ did at His Incarnation—from His eternal blessedness and glory, and entered into the life of man. Paul has represented the "whole creation' as sending up to God a cry of weariness and suffering and hope; the heavens and the earth and all living things were created for a perfection which, as yet, they have not reached, but towards which they have been moving through unmeasured ages,—'the whole creation groaneth and travaileth in pain together until now.' The cry of weariness and suffering and hope also rises from the whole Church of the redeemed on earth; we too are longing for a perfection as yet unattained: 'we groan within ourselves, waiting for our adoption, to wit, the redemption of the body.' And then the Apostle attributes the same cry of weariness, of suffering, of hope, to the Spirit of God Himself; He is longing to raise all that are in Christ to an unachieved power and blessedness; the sins of the Church, its infirmities, its errors, its sorrows, are a heavy burden to Him. He is 'resisted' and He is 'grieved;' His intercession for us—so intimately does He share all the evils of our condition—is a kind of agony; He 'maketh intercession for us with groanings which cannot be uttered.'

The passages which I have quoted are, I think, sufficient to show that since Christ came, there has been a wonderful revelation of the Spirit of God as a living Person; but even in the New Testament there are many passages in which the older conception of the Spirit survives. It survives among ourselves. For example, we pray to be baptized with the Spirit; we speak of the Spirit being poured out on the Church. In such phrases as these the Spirit is conceived as a Power rather than as a Person. When we use them we are thinking of the influence and grace of the Spirit as distinguished from the Spirit Himself. This form of thought is perfectly legitimate. Only we should not allow it to obtain such an ascendency as to prevent us from vividly apprehending the truth that the Power is the Power of a Divine Person.

40

Election

Charles Grandison Finney

In discussing this subject,

I. I shall notice some points in which there is a general agreement among all denominations of Christians respecting the natural and moral attributes of God.

1. It is agreed that eternity is a natural attribute of God in the sense that he grows no older. He was just as old before the world or universe was made, as he is now, or as he will be at the day of judgment.

2. It is agreed that omniscience is an attribute of God, in the sense that he knows from a necessity of his infinite nature all things that are objects of knowledge.

3. That he has necessarily and eternally possessed this knowledge, so that he never has, and never can have, any accession to his knowledge. Every possible thing that ever was, or will be, or can be an object of knowledge, has been necessarily and eternally known to God. If this were not true, God would be neither infinite nor omniscient.

4. It is agreed also that God exercises an universal providence, embracing all events that ever did or ever will occur in all worlds. Some of these events he secures by his own agency, and others occur under his providence, in the sense that he permits or suffers them to occur rather than interpose to prevent them. They may be truly said to occur under his providence, because his plan of government in some sense embraces them all. He made provision to secure those that are good, that is, the holy intentions of moral agents, and to overrule for good those that are evil, that is, the selfish intentions of moral agents. These intentions are events, and may be said to occur under Divine Providence, because all events that do, or ever will, occur, are and must be foreseen results of God's own agency, or of the work of creation.

5. It is agreed that infinite benevolence is the sum of the moral attributes of God.

6. That God is both naturally and morally immutable; that in his natural attributes he is necessarily so, and in his moral attributes is certainly so.

7. It is agreed that all who are converted, sanctified and saved, are converted, sanctified, and saved by God's own agency; that is, God saves them by securing, by his own agency, their personal and individual holiness.

II. What the Bible doctrine of election is not.

1. The Bible doctrine of election is not that any are chosen to

salvation, in such a sense, that they will or can be saved without repentance, faith, and sanctification.

2. Nor is it that some are chosen to salvation, in such a sense, that they will be saved irrespective of their being regenerated, and persevering in holiness to the end of life. The Bible most plainly teaches, that these are naturally indispensable conditions of salvation, and of course election cannot dispense with them.

3. Nor is it that any are chosen to salvation for, or on account of their own foreseen merits, or good works. 2 Tim. i. 9: "Who hath saved us, and called us with a holy calling, not according to our works, but according to his own purpose and grace, which was given us in Christ Jesus before the world began." The foreseen fact, that by the wisest governmental arrangement God could convert and sanctify and fit them for heaven, must have been a condition in the sense of a *sine quâ non*, of their election to salvation, but could not have been the fundamental reason for it, as we shall see. God did not elect them to salvation, for or on account of their foreseen good works, but upon condition of their foreseen repentance, faith and perseverance.

4. The Bible doctrine of election is not that God elected some to salvation, upon such conditions that it is really uncertain whether they will comply with those conditions, and be finally saved. The Bible does not leave the question of the final salvation of the elect as a matter of real uncertainty. This we shall see in its place. The elect were chosen to salvation, upon condition that God foresaw that he could secure their repentance, faith, and final perseverance.

III. What the Bible doctrine of election is.

It is, that all of Adam's race, who are or ever will be saved, were from eternity chosen by God to eternal salvation, through the sanctification of their hearts by faith in Christ. In other words, they are chosen to salvation by means of sanctification. Their salvation is the end—their sanctification is a means. Both the end and the means are elected, appointed, chosen; the means as really as the end, and for the sake of the end. The election of some individuals and nations to certain privileges, and to do certain things, is not the kind of election of which I treat at this time; but I am to consider the doctrine of election as it respects election unto salvation, as just explained.

IV. I am to prove the doctrine as I have stated it to be true.

It is plainly implied in the teaching of the Bible: the Bible everywhere assumes and implies the truth of this doctrine just as might be expected, since it so irresistibly follows from the known and admitted attributes of God. . . .

V. What could not have been the reasons for election.

1. It is admitted that God is infinitely benevolent and wise. It must follow that election is founded in some reason or reasons; and that these reasons are good and sufficient; reasons that rendered it obligatory upon God to choose just as he did, in election. Assuming, as we must, that God is wise and good, we are safe in affirming that he could have had none but benevolent reasons for his election of some to eternal life in preference to others. Hence we are bound to affirm, that election was not based upon, nor does it imply partiality in God, in any bad sense of that term. Partiality in any being, consists in preferring one to another without any good or sufficient reason, or in opposition to good and sufficient reasons. It being admitted that God is infinitely wise and good, it follows, that he cannot be partial; that he cannot have elected some to eternal salvation and passed others by, without some good and sufficient reason. That is, he cannot have done it arbitrarily. The great objection that is felt and urged by opposers of this doctrine is, that it implies partiality in God, and represents him as deciding the eternal destiny of moral agents by an arbitrary sovereignty. But this objection is a sheer and altogether unwarrantable assumption. It assumes, that God could have had no good and sufficient reasons for the election. It has been settled, that good is the end upon which God set his heart; that is, the highest well being of himself and the universe of creatures. This end must be accomplished by means. If God is infinitely wise and good, he must have chosen the best practicable means. But he has chosen the best means for that end, and there can be no partiality in that. . . .

2. Election was not an exercise of arbitrary sovereignty. By arbitrary sovereignty is intended the choosing and acting from mere will, without consulting moral obligation or the public

good. It is admitted that God is infinitely wise and good. It is therefore impossible that he should choose or act arbitrarily in any case whatever. He must have good and sufficient reasons for every choice and every act.

Some seem to have represented God, in the purpose or act of election, as electing some and not others, merely because he could or would, or in other words, to exhibit his own sovereignty, without any other reasons than because so he would have it. But it is impossible for God to act arbitrarily, or from any but a good and sufficient reason; that is, it is impossible for him to do so, and continue to be benevolent. We have said that God has one, and but one end in view; that is, he does, and says, and suffers all for one and the same reason, namely, to promote the highest good of being. He has but one ultimate end, and all his volitions are only efforts to secure that end. The highest well being of the universe, including his own, is the end on which his supreme and ultimate choice terminates. All his volitions are designed to secure this end.

41

Regeneration

J. M. Pendleton

It is evident that the Scriptures refer to a great change in all who become Christians—a change denoted by such forms of expression as the following: "Born again" (John iii. 3); "Born of the Spirit" (John iii. 5); "Born of God" (John i. 13); "Created in Christ Jesus" (Eph. ii. 10); "Quickened together with Christ" (Eph. ii. 5); "A new creature" (2 Cor. v. 17); "Renewed after the image of him that created him" (Col. iii. 10); "Dead unto sin, . . .

alive unto God." Rom. vi. 11. This change is, in theological writings, usually called Regeneration, and it is inseparable from "repentance toward God and faith toward our Lord Jesus Christ." Acts xx. 21. For this reason the heading of this chapter has been selected, and I purposely present in closest connection Regeneration, Repentance, and Faith. Nor is it my intention to dwell on what has been termed "the order of time." Indeed, if the view of Calvin and Jonathan Edwards is correct, regeneration and repentance are in substance the same so that the question as to the order of time is ruled out. Calvin says:

"In one word, I apprehend repentance to be regeneration, the end of which is the restoration of the divine image within us; which was defaced, and almost obliterated by the transgression of Adam." The words of Edwards are these: "If we compare one scripture with another, it will be sufficiently manifest that by regeneration, or being begotten or born again, the same change in the state of the mind is signified with that which the Scripture speaks of as effected by true repentance and conversion. I put repentance and conversion together, because the Scripture puts them together (Acts iii. 19), and because they plainly signify much the same thing."

Without fully endorsing the view of these great men, I may say that if regeneration and repentance are not identical, they are so closely connected that it is not worth while to inquire whether the one precedes or follows the other. As to regeneration and faith, a plausible argument may be made in favor of the priority of either. For example, if we turn to John i. 12, 13 it seems natural to suppose that those who believed in Christ were those who had been born of God. So also according to the correct rendering of 1 John v. 1, "Whosoever believeth that Jesus is the Christ is [has been] born of God." Some use this passage as it reads in the Common Version, "is born of God," to prove that faith is prior to regeneration, because the means of it; but the argument fails in view of the fact that not the present, but the perfect, tense is used in the original—"has been born of God." But if we turn to Galatians iii. 26, "For ye are all the children of God by faith in Christ Jesus," the obvious view is that we become God's children by faith, or, in other words, that faith is instrumental in effecting regeneration. We see, therefore, that there may be a plausible argument on either side of the question. It is, perhaps, in view of this fact, wisest and safest to consider regeneration and faith simultaneous, or so nearly so that the question of precedence should not be considered at all. The adoption of this theory will save us from perplexities which will otherwise annoy. For instance, those insisting on the precedence of regeneration are not a little perplexed when asked if there can be a regenerate unbeliever, and those taking the opposite view are equally perplexed when asked if there can be an unregenerate believer. That regeneration and faith are not separable in point of time is, all things considered, the most satisfactory position. One thing is certain—wherever we see a regenerate person, we see a believer in Christ; and wherever we see a believer in Christ, we see a regenerate person.

Regeneration

After these explanatory matters I proceed to a discussion of the subject of regeneration in the following order:

1. *The nature of regeneration.* The change which the term implies does not pertain primarily to the physical nor to the intellectual faculties. The regenerated man has the same bodily conformation after this change as before, and his mental peculiarities remain. The intellect, like the body, is affected only so far as the moral powers exert an influence over it. This leads me to say that regeneration is a spiritual change. I call it a spiritual change, not only because it is produced by the Spirit of God, as will be shown, but because it takes place in the spirit of the subject. The heart is the theatre of the operation, and the change is in the disposition of the heart. This disposition, I suppose, lies below or back of the affections and the will, controlling the exercise of the affections and the choice of the will. That is to say, the affections love as they do, and the will chooses as it does, because of the state of the heart. I will not enlarge, lest I become metaphysical. Regeneration involves the illumination of the

understanding, the consecration of the affections, and the recti-
fication of the will. To use Paul's language, "Ye were once
darkness, but now are ye light in the Lord." Eph. v. 8. The
affections of the unrenewed soul are placed on unworthy objects, and cleave to them with the greatest tenacity. There is no
relish for things spiritual and divine, no appreciation of moral
excellence, no love of holiness and of God. Regeneration recalls
the affections from unworthy objects, and places them supremely on the ever-blessed Jehovah—enshrines them in his
infinitely perfect character. It is therefore written, "Every one
that loveth is born of God." 1 John iv. 7. The will of the unregenerate man is perverse, for it conflicts with the will of God. It
chooses cursing and death rather than blessing and life. In
regeneration its obliquity is overcome and rectified, its per-
verted action is arrested and changed. "Thy people shall be
willing in the day of thy power." Ps. cx. 3. The will of the
regenerate, being conformed to the divine will, gladly chooses
the objects on which the consecrated affections are placed.

The definition to be given of regeneration must depend on the
point of moral observation we occupy. If, for example, we contemplate the sinner as the enemy of God, regeneration is the
removal of his enmity and the creation of love in its stead. If we
consider the sinner the "child of the devil," regeneration is the
change which makes him the "child of God." If we regard the
unregenerate as totally destitute of the moral image of God,
regeneration consists in stamping that image upon them. Or if
we view them as "dead in trespasses and sins" (Eph. ii. 1),
regeneration is the beginning of divine life in their souls. It is
what Paul means by being "quickened together with Christ"
(Eph. ii. 5)—that is, made spiritually alive in union with Christ.
Thus various definitions, not conflicting but harmonious, may
be given of regeneration, according to the points of moral
observation of which we avail ourselves.

2. *The necessity of regeneration.* This part of the subject has been
somewhat anticipated in what has been said of the depravity of
our nature, for it is depravity that renders regeneration necessary. Depravity has sundered man from God, so that, in the
expressive language of Scripture, he is "alienated from the life of

God." Eph. iv. 18. How is a reunion to be brought about? There must be a reunion if man is to be saved; and as the two parties, God and man, are at variance, a change must take place in one or both of the parties before there can be reconciliation. But God is unchangeable, and the change, if it takes place at all, must take place in man. We therefore clearly see the necessity of regeneration. It is as necessary as the salvation of the soul is desirable, for there can be no salvation without reconciliation with God.

The necessity of regeneration appears also in the fact that without it we cannot become the children of God. Those who are new creatures in Christ Jesus have been "born, not of blood, nor of the will of the flesh, nor of the will of man, but of God." John i. 13. Being born of God is necessary to our partaking of his nature, and this participation of his nature is implied in our being his children. "That which is born of the Spirit is spirit" (John iii. 6)—that is, partakes of the nature of its Author. If we cannot become the children of God without it, how important is regeneration! No language can adequately set forth its importance.

The necessity of regeneration is likewise apparent, because the unregenerate cannot enter heaven; and if they could, they would be miserable there. It is one of the fundamental laws of social existence that we enjoy the society of those only whose dispositions are similar to our own. On the other hand, social enjoyment results from congenial taste and feeling. We see this principle illustrated every day. We see it in the gay assemblies of the lovers of pleasure, in the vulgar carousals of the dissipated, in the associations of the educated and the intellectual, and in the companies of the saints who take "sweet counsel together." In all these there is similarity of feeling, congeniality of disposition. Now, suppose unregenerate sinners were admitted into heaven and required to join in the devotions of the sanctified. Would they be happy in the presence of a God they do not love? Would they be happy in rendering reluctant ascriptions of praise to his name? Would they be happy in mingling in society for which they feel no partiality? Surely not. Jesus labored under no mistake when he said, "Ye must be born again." John iii. 7. It has been well said, that "heaven is a prepared place for a prepared people." Regeneration furnishes the moral preparation to relish and enjoy the bliss of heaven. This of itself is sufficient to show its great necessity.

3. *The Author of regeneration.* Who accomplishes this work? It is effected by divine agency. The phrase "born of God" is of frequent occurrence in the New Testament. We have also the expression "born of the Spirit." No language could more clearly indicate the agency employed in regeneration. The Spirit of God alone can renew the soul. It is his prerogative to quicken, to give life. All is death in the moral world without his influence. What air or breath is to animal life, that his operation is to spiritual life. "It is the Spirit that quickeneth." John vi. 63. Paul says of the Corinthians, "Ye are manifestly declared to be the epistle of Christ, ministered by us, written not with ink, but with the Spirit of the living God; not in tables of stone, but in fleshly tables of the heart." 2 Cor. iii. 3. The same apostle, after telling us that those who are "in Christ are new creatures," that "old things are passed away," and "all things are become new," immediately adds, "and all things are of God." 2 Cor. v. 17, 18. Regeneration, in several passages of Scripture, is referred to under the imagery of creation. Who but God possesses creative power, the power to bring something out of nothing? To create is his inalienable prerogative, and it is also his inalienable prerogative to regenerate. He says himself, "A new heart also will I give you, and a new spirit will I put within you: and I will take away the stony heart out of your flesh and will give you a heart of flesh." Ezek. xxxvi. 26. In the provisions of the new covenant he says, "I will put my laws into their mind, and write them in their hearts." Heb. viii. 10.

4. *The means of regeneration.* The instrumentality employed is the gospel, the word of God. This is a controverted point. Some argue that God renews the soul without the intervention of means. Others suppose that the term "regeneration" may be used both in a limited and in an enlarged sense. They concede that in the latter sense the word of God is the means of regeneration. Without dwelling on these different views, I quote the following passages in proof of the instrumentality of divine truth in regeneration: "In Christ Jesus I have begotten you through the gospel" (1 Cor. iv. 15); "Of his own will begat he us with the word of truth" (James i. 18); "Being born again, not of

corruptible seed, but of incorruptible, by the word of God, which liveth and abideth for ever." 1 Pet. i. 23. There is, as we have seen, a sense in which we are born of the Spirit, and these passages teach that there is a sense in which we are begotten or born of the word of God. I know of no way of harmonizing the two views but by attributing regeneration to the agency of the Spirit and the instrumentality of the truth.

God uses means in the natural world, and why should he act on a different principle in the moral world? He does not. The gift of the Bible and the institution of Christian churches with a gospel ministry prove that he does not. I suppose that the Spirit of God, in regenerating the heart, makes use of scriptural truth previously lodged in the understanding. But if I am asked how truth can influence and instrumentally change a heart that does not love it, I answer I do not know. If asked how the Spirit operates on the heart so as to change it, either with or without the word of truth, I must still say I do not know. I can give no other answer while I remember what Jesus said to Nicodemus: "The wind bloweth where it listeth, and thou hearest the sound thereof, but canst not tell whence it cometh and whether it goeth: so is every one that is born of the Spirit." John iii. 8. Spiritual birth is a blessed reality, but the processes of this birth are among "the secret things" that "belong unto the Lord our God." Deut. xxix. 29. We must remember, however, that its importance justifies the startling words, "To be born is an everlasting calamity unless we are born again."

Repentance

No one can attentively read the New Testament without receiving the impression that great importance is attached to repentance. When John the Baptist came "preaching in the wilderness of Judea," the burden of his message was, "Repent ye: for the kingdom of heaven is at hand" Matt. iii. 1, 2. When Jesus entered on his ministry he said, "The time is fulfilled, and the kingdom of God is at hand: repent ye, and believe the gospel." Mark i. 15. The twelve disciples, in obedience to the command of the Lord Jesus, "went out, and preached that men should repent." Mark vi. 12. After the resurrection of Christ,

Peter preached repentance at Jerusalem, and Paul dwelt upon it in his one discourse at Athens and in his many discourses at Ephesus. (See Acts ii. 38; iii. 19; xvii. 30; xx. 21.)

It is, then, a question of great importance, What is repentance? The word of which it is a translation in the New Testament has as its primary meaning after-thought, and as its secondary meaning a change of mind. It is easy to see how the secondary followed the primary signification, for in all ages after-thought has discovered reasons for a change of mind. The discovery has had a close connection with the depravity of human nature and the fallibility of human opinions. Alas, how frequent have been the occasions for a change of mind! In this change of mind, so far as scriptural repentance is concerned, a great deal is involved, as we shall see; but I wish first to show that repentance is internal. I mean by this that it is a change of the mind, the heart, and not of the life, except so far as a change of life results from a change of mind or heart. Dr. George Campbell and others have not been happy in substituting "reform" and "reformation" for "repent" and "repentance." John the Baptist made a clear distinction between "repentance" and "fruits meet for repentance;" and by the fruits meet" he meant reformation of life. Repentance is the tree, and reformation the fruit it bears. Paul too, as well as John, distinguished between "repentance" and "works meet for repentance." Acts xxvi. 20. Repentance belongs to the sphere of the mind, and reformation to the sphere of the life; or, in other words, the former is inward, and the latter is outward. Let no one, therefore, suppose that the command to "repent" is obeyed by a reformation of life; and let no one think his repentance genuine, unless it leads to reformation of life. I trust I have made this important distinction plain.

There are in Greek authors many instances of the use of the words translated in the New Testament *repent* and *repentance*. Dr. Conant gives several examples in his notes on Matt. iii. 2, in his revised version. It is evident from these examples that the Greeks knew what it was to exercise after-thought, so as to change their minds and indulge sorrow of heart. There was, however, in their after-thought, change of mind, and sorrow of heart, no consciousness of the evil of sin as committed against

God. Nor is this strange, as they enjoyed not the light of divine revelation.

Of the repentance enjoined in the gospel, the following things may be said—namely, that it involves—

1. *A consciousness of personal sin.* It is a state of mind that cannot exist without conviction of sin. Of what are persons to repent if they are not sinners? The angels in heaven cannot repent, for they have never sinned. Nor could Adam and Eve repent in their state of innocence. Sin precedes repentance, and not only sin, but a consciousness of it. A sense of sin must take hold of the soul and pervade all its faculties. I have used the epithet personal, and by it I mean that the individual sinner must repent of his own sins. I mean that one man cannot repent for another, but that each man must repent for himself. I suppose, therefore, that those persons labor under a mistake who say that they have repented of Adam's sin. They may deeply regret the apostasy of Adam, and bitterly deplore the miseries in which his race is involved, but in strictness of speech they cannot be said to repent of his sin. They cannot have a personal consciousness of his sin: they can only have such a consciousness of their own, and without personal consciousness of sin there is no repentance.

2. *That sin is a great evil committed against God, for which there is no excuse.* All sin is committed against God, against his nature, his will, his authority, his law, his justice, his goodness; and the evil of sin arises chiefly from the fact that it is opposed to God, and out of harmony with his character. Truth does not require me to say, and I do not say, that the repenting sinner has no fear of the consequences of sin; but I do affirm that the evil of sin as committed against God is the thing which gives the true penitent special anxiety and trouble. He justifies God and condemns himself. He makes David's words his own: "Against thee, thee only, have I sinned, and done this evil in thy sight: that thou mightest be justified when thou speakest, and be clear when thou judgest." Ps. li. 4. David had committed atrocious sins against his fellow-creatures, but the thing which absorbed his thoughts and broke his heart was the fact that he had sinned against God. The repenting sinner does not regard his sin as a

misfortune merely, but as a crime, involving deep, personal blameworthiness. He knows that Satan has tempted him, but he does not lay his sins to the charge of Satan, so as to excuse himself. No, he feels that he has sinned without cause and deserves to die without mercy. There is a deep sense of shame, arising from a consciousness of guilt and ill-desert.

3. *Hatred of sin.* This is an essential element in repentance. The hatred is inseparable from the change of mind already referred to. The change of mind is in view of sin, and the mind undergoes the change, because sin is seen to be a great evil. Regarded in this light, it becomes an object of abhorrence. At this point, repentance and regeneration coincide. Hatred of sin is among the primary impulses of regeneration, and it cannot be abstracted from repentance without changing its character. The repenting sinner hates the sin and the sins of which he repents. I use the singular and the plural with a purpose, meaning by sin depravity, corruption of nature, and by sins actual transgressions prompted by a sinful nature. There is hatred of sin as it inheres in the nature; there is self-loathing on account of it; and there is hatred of sins committed in heart and life. The salvation of the gospel consists chiefly in deliverance from sin; nor can we conceive how God can save his creatures from their sins without saving them from the love of sin—without inspiring in them such hatred of sin as will lead them to turn from it. Penitential hatred of sin may be said to be both general and specific: it is general in the sense that it embraces all sins, and it is specific in the sense that it embraces every sin. Sin is not really hated unless it is hated in all its forms—hated in its inward workings and in its outward manifestations. Sin is the abominable thing which God hates, and it is the object of the repenting sinner's hatred.

4. *Sorrow for sin.* This accompanies the hatred. He who repents hates the sins he is sorry for, and is sorry for the sins he hates. The hatred and the sorrow are reciprocal. Indeed, each may be regarded as either the cause or the effect of the other, so close is their relation.

Those who would substitute the term "reformation" for repentance virtually exclude the element of sorrow, or at least they give it no prominent place in the change denoted by their favorite word. There is one fact which proves beyond doubt that repentance involves sorrow for sin. That fact is found in the words of Jesus: "Then began he to upbraid the cities wherein most of his mighty works were done, because they repented not! Woe unto thee, Chorazin! woe unto thee, Bethsaida! for if the mighty works, which were done in you, had been done in Tyre and Sidon, they would have repented long ago in sackcloth and ashes." Matt. xi. 20, 21.

"Sackcloth and ashes" are scriptural symbols of sorrow, and of no common sorrow. They certainly signified deep contrition and grief in the Ninevites. (See Jon. iii. 5, 6.) History, profane as well as sacred, refers to them as emblems of mourning. Now, that Jesus mentioned "sackcloth and ashes" in connection with repentance for ever settles the question that sorrow enters into it as its central element. This fact was so significant in the view of Dr. George Campbell, that he could not venture, in his *Translation of the Gospels*, to substitute in the above passage reformed for repented, but left the latter word as in the Common Version.

It is as unreasonable as it is unscriptural to suppose that there is not sorrow in the change of mind denoted by repentance. How and why does the mind change at all in regard to sin, unless there is in it something to excite sorrow? Whatever calls for a change of mind concerning sin calls for sorrow on account of sin. The heart of the true penitent is a broken and a crushed heart—broken with sorrow and crushed with grief. How can it be otherwise when sin is looked at in contrast with the purity of the divine character, and its turpitude is seen in the light which shines from the cross on Calvary?

5. *A purpose to forsake sin.* This purpose is, of course, internal, and repentance is internal. He in whom is exemplified the four preceding things is obliged to form this purpose. It is a necessity of his moral constitution. The execution of the purpose is reformation, but the purpose itself is a part of repentance. It is not necessary to elaborate a point so plain as this, for no one can feel hated and sorrow for sin without forming the resolution to abandon it.

In dismissing the subject of repentance, I may say that it is a reasonable, important, universal, and immediate duty. "God commands all men everywhere to repent," and all men should have that change of mind in regard to sin which repentance implies.

Faith

Faith, as well as repentance, accompanies regeneration. But what is faith? The term is used in the Scriptures in more senses than one. For example, an apostle says, "What doth it profit, my brethren, though a man may say he hath faith, and have not works? can faith save him?" James ii. 14. In the last clause the insertion of the definite article is required by the original Greek—"can the faith save him?" That is, the faith which is not productive of works. There is a faith, then, which is fatally defective as to the matter of salvation; for the question, "Can the faith save him?" is a strong denial of the power of such faith to save. The apostle further says, "Thou believest that there is one God; thou doest well: the demons also believe, and tremble." ver. 19. Here we see that faith in the unity of God is commended, but this faith does not save; and the proof that it does not is seen in the fact that demons, while they believe this great truth and tremble under what it implies, remain unsaved. In the last verse of the same chapter the apostle gives an impressive illustration of what he means by a "faith without works:" "For as the body without the spirit is dead, so faith without works is dead also." This illustration all can understand, for all know that when the spirit leaves the body nothing remains but a mass of inanimate clay. There is no life; the vital principle is gone. So faith which is without works is worthless, for it has in it no saving quality. Such faith is a mere intellectual assent to the truth, or rather to some parts of the truth, leaving the heart unmoved, and therefore creating no motives to action. Alas, there are many who have this faith, and who have no other faith!

Jesus, in explaining the parable of The Sower, says: "They on the rock are they which, when they hear, receive the word with joy; and these have no root, which for a while believe, and in time of temptation fall away." Luke viii. 13. Here the reference is to a temporary faith, embracing not only the assent of the intellect, but exciting superficially the feelings of the heart. Who has not seen persons fitly represented by the seed that fell on the rock thinly covered with soil? The faith of such persons has fatal defects, and therefore it is transient. They "for a while believe," but they do not believe with the whole heart. "They draw back unto perdition," and do not "believe to the saving of the soul." Heb. x. 39.

In view of the considerations now presented, it is manifest that there may be a faith that has no connection with salvation. It therefore becomes a question of the greatest importance, What is the faith of the gospel, the faith which secures the salvation of the believer? There is but one answer: It is faith in Jesus Christ. This differs very widely from a belief in the existence of God and in the historical truth of the Bible. Many believe both of these facts who do not believe in Christ, do not accept him as the Saviour. Christ is emphatically the object of faith. He so represented himself during his earthly ministry, as we may see from his words:

"And as Moses lifted up the serpent in the wilderness, even so must the Son of man be lifted up: that whosoever believeth in him should not perish, but have eternal life. For God so loved the world, that he gave his only begotten Son, that whosoever believeth in him should not perish, but have everlasting life. . . . He that believeth on him is not condemned" (John iii. 14-18); "He that cometh to me shall never hunger; and he that believeth on me shall never thirst" (vi. 35); "He that believeth in me, though he were dead, yet shall he live: and whosoever liveth and believeth in me shall never die." xi. 25, 26.

It is needless to multiply quotations from our Lord's sayings. The foregoing show him to be the object of faith in such a sense that those who believe in him are saved from perishing and put into possession of everlasting life. It is also supremely worthy of notice that unbelief, which is a rejection of Christ as the Saviour, is the great sin of which the Holy Spirit convinces men. "He will reprove the world of sin, and of righteousness, and of judgment: of sin, because they believe not on me." John xvi. 8, 9. This language of Christ teaches the greatness of the sin of unbelief. This sin is the opposite of faith, and as faith receives Christ, unbelief rejects him. As we read of "an evil heart of unbelief" (Heb. iii. 12), we know that faith has to do with the heart as well as the intellect.

I have referred to Christ as the object of faith; and as illustrative of this point there is one passage of Scripture worthy of special consideration: "Testifying both to the Jews, and also to the Greeks, repentance toward God, and faith toward our Lord Jesus Christ." Acts xx. 21. The terms "repentance" and "faith" are just where they should be. Repentance is toward God—that is, it has reference to God as a Lawgiver whose law has been broken; but faith is toward our Lord Jesus Christ—that is, it has reference to him as the Saviour. The reason is obvious: Christ by his obedience and death has satisfied the claims of the law, so that the Lawgiver can consistently pardon sinners who by faith receive Christ as the Saviour. Indeed, it is God the Lawgiver who offers his Son to guilty men as the only Saviour, and faith is the heart's response to that offer. In other words, the believer accepts the offer, accepts Christ, who is made to him "wisdom, and righteousness, and sanctification, and redemption." 1 Cor. i. 30.

In ascertaining the exact import of faith in Christ, it is well to remember that the word commonly translated "believe" in the New Testament is, in several passages, rendered "commit." (See Luke xvi. 11; John ii. 24; Rom. iii. 2; 1 Cor. ix. 17; Gal. ii. 7; 1 Tim. i. 11; Tit. i. 3.) Everybody knows the meaning of commit, and those who believe in Christ commit themselves to him to be saved by him—commit all the interests of their salvation into his hands. There is nothing kept back; the surrender to Christ is unconditional and entire. As in the gospel he is offered as the only Saviour, he is received as he is offered and relied on as the only Saviour. When Paul in 1 Thess. ii. 4 says, "But as we were allowed of God to be put in trust with the gospel," he uses the same verb, in the passive voice, which is usually translated "believe." Paul was put in trust with the gospel—that is, the gospel was entrusted to him; so Christ is put in trust with the salvation of the believer—that is, the believer trusts in him. I know of no word in our language which expresses more fully than the term "trust" the central idea of the word "faith." According to the gospel, faith is personal trust in a personal Saviour. No act can be more personal than the act of faith. It is as personal as dying. As every human being dies for himself, so every man must believe for himself—must trust in Christ for himself. I know of no better definition of gospel faith than this: It is a trustful reception of the Lord Jesus as the only Saviour.

When the trembling jailer said to Paul and Silas, "What must I do to be saved?" they said, "Believe on the Lord Jesus Christ, and thou shalt be saved." Acts xvi. 30, 31. They gave the only answer that could be given to the question. It is faith in Christ that puts the soul in possession of the benefits of redemption. "To him give all the prophets witness, that through his name whosoever believeth in him shall receive remission of sins" (Acts x. 43); "He that believeth on the Son hath everlasting life." John iii. 36.

42

Christian Faith

William Newton Clarke

The doctrine of God is an object of belief, but so, in a more important manner, is the great reality of God himself. It is much to believe the doctrine, knowing what it means, but the characteristic utterance of Christianity has always been, "I believe in God," and that is far more. There is no such thing as faith in a doctrine, but faith in God in the familiar name of the Christian act and attitude. It remains, at the end of our presentation of the Christian doctrine, to give some account of the belief that corresponds to the doctrine, and to the reality which the doctrine sets forth. It is very unfortunate that the word believe is so ambiguous; for when we summon men to believe, as in the name of the gospel we do, they may think we are calling them merely to give assent to our statements, or they may understand that we ask for an act of the whole soul rising to the acceptance of a great conviction. Belief in the doctrine of God may easily be nothing more than assent to testimony or to evidence, acceptance of reasoning, or approval of an intellectual interpretation of the world. But belief in God, of which we are speaking now, is more than assent, more than a work of intellect, more than an understanding of the world. It is greater, and at the same time simpler, than any of these. It is a dealing between the man and God himself. In its effect, it is the flight of the soul to its rest, and the rising of the soul to its strength. It cannot be described in a phrase or two, but some of its qualities may be remembered here.

The Church has always been right in regarding the Christian belief in God as a response to revelation. Naturally it would be so, if there were any God worthy to be believed in. If there is such a God, it must be his good pleasure that men should know him; and if they feel after him and find him, it is because he is not far from every one of us (Acts xvii. 27), and is seeking to be known. The God in whom Christians believe has it for his nature to be self-manifesting, and revelation is not his exceptional work but his everlasting activity. All human belief in God has risen in response to his perpetual self-expression in nature and in man. But the Christian belief is a response to his clearest self-revelation, made in humanity. In the spiritual life of men he has progressively made himself known as the God of righteousness and love, and at length in Jesus Christ he has made the self-expression that taught men more of him than they had ever known before. Those who have learned of Jesus have become acquainted with a God, in whom our deepest life can rest and be utterly satisfied: that is to say, they have found the God for whose fellowship man was evidently made. Holy, righteous, gracious, is the Being whom they have come to know; and all their acquaintance with him confirms their certainty that he is the true and living God. But such a God and Father as this was never passively discovered, or found in spite of himself by the mere groping of men. With such a character as he bears, it is absolutely certain that our knowledge of him was obtained not only with his consent, but in pursuance of his active will. God was in Christ self-revealing, and God is in our life self-revealing, and our belief in him is our response. He was beforehand with us in showing us what manner of God he was, and thus it came to pass that we knew.

Put in the more familiar terms, this is simply to say that the Christian belief in God is the child's recognition of the Father—for as Father Jesus reveals him—and it is a matter of course that the Father was there to be recognized, and was showing his face to his child that he might be recognized. The child's gaze into his face is the gaze of confidence deserved forever by his self-imparting goodness.

We do not tell the whole truth, however, when we call the Christian belief a response to the Christian revelation. We should misjudge the greatness and breadth of that belief if we were to think of it as grounded solely in experiences that we are accustomed to call religious, or in any historical revelation. This greatest of our beliefs is a response not only to that which is commonly called revelation, but also to the primary facts of life, and to the realities that encounter us in the general experience. Here, too, we may say if we choose, that we are responding to revelation, for God speaks to us in the order of our life. But it is another set of considerations that here appeals to us, and the response that we make to them when we believe in God is worthy to be mentioned by itself.

When we take for true the reality of the God of the Christian doctrine, we start from the most universal human experiences. It may seem to us that our first step is confidence in the God whom we feel to be worthy of our trust, but it is not. We could have no living confidence in God at all if it were not for certain other confidences that we all hold. Not even upon the authority of revelation could we believe in him, but for certain beliefs that enter into the warp and woof of our daily living. There is a practical substratum, a foundation, without which no belief in God could be trusted to stand fast, or even to arise. It is very true that in the experience of simple and childlike faith this underlying support of our confidence is not recognized and reasoned out: we build upon it without analysis: but none the less do we build upon it, and none the less does it lie firm beneath us.

The Christian confidence in God begins so far back as to include the confidence that we naturally have in ourselves—in our senses, our rational faculties, and our moral powers. It includes confidence in the world as an honest world and the universe as a universe of reality and truth, in which knowledge is trustworthy and religion is not in vain; confidence in the goodness of the good and the badness of the bad; confidence in the worthiness of the searchings of conscience and the inspirations of hope; confidence that the rational order is grounded in the eternal reason and the moral order in the eternal righteousness; confidence that our nature does not search in vain when it seeks divine foundations for human life; confidence, in a word, that the worthiest explanation of existence is the truest, and that that which is bears witness to an eternal interest in that which ought to be. Much of this confidence may be implicit, and as it were instinctive, but all this is included or implied in the Christian belief in God, and if we did not constantly assume these primal realities, we could not attain to that belief. It is on the wings of this comprehensive human confidence that we rise to the simple and all-unifying Christian faith. Indeed, it is in the strength of this primal confidence that we respond to the Christian revelation itself. When we put our trust in the God of Jesus Christ, that which speaks in the voice of faith is the soul claiming its birthright; for such a God is the birthright of man. The soul dares to rise in calm assertion that our nature does not fool us or the world deceive, and that therefore the God who is worthy of our confidence is the God who lives.

In a word, we trust the normal assumption of rational minds, that existence has been fairly and honestly given us, as a blessing and not as a curse. When we assume this, we are moving straight toward the recognition of the God who made us thus;

and when we behold the God whom Jesus teaches us to know, we recognize the God in whom our primal confidences have prepared us to believe. Acquaintance with our Father is our birthright, and thus we come to it.

We might make response to revelation and to the common certainties by a belief that was not more than an intellectual assent and conviction. This many do, and perhaps all sometimes do; for no faith is perfect. Such belief, though not the best, is by no means to be condemned or despised. It is a response to evidence, and is at least an honest intellectual acceptance of truth. God who knows our feebleness cannot despise it. But the full Christian belief in God is more than this. It is not merely a reasoned conviction or a free assent: it is also a faith, whose nature and privilege it is to venture out beyond sight and beyond full evidence. In rising to God it rises to the unseen and undemonstrated. It is an assurance of things hoped for, a conviction of things not seen (Heb. xi. 1).

It need not be said that our senses give us no vision of the existence and character of God. Forever is he "God whom no man hath seen or can see" (1 Tim. vi. 16). All belief in him is belief that goes out beyond the field of the senses. It should be so; for belief is a function of the invisible man, and the senses, though they may guide us toward some place of vision, cannot discern the God who is invisible. The soul's transaction of belief both begins and ends where they cannot go. But belief in God lies not only beyond the region of the senses: it lies also beyond the region of demonstration. No one can claim that the existence of God has ever been proved demonstratively. There are good reasons, and great reasons, and sufficient reasons, for believing in it, but if we ask for demonstration we ask in vain, and doubtless it will be so forever. The doctrine of God contains truth to which the method of demonstration does not correspond. The intellect must believe in him on the evidence that we possess—and it is great—and the whole man must rise to him in the direction which the evidence warrants, by an act of faith. For it is the nature of faith to go out beyond sight, and to take hold upon that which is not seen or proved. Faith is a rising of the soul to truth. It does not ascend by the mere whim of the mind, for in the best that we know there are good grounds for faith. But the eye of reason does not see the whole height of the ascent of faith: it sees the direction, but not the entire way. Faith is the daring of the soul to go farther than it can see. In it there is sound reason, and hope, and holy courage.

This is what is meant when the Christian act of believing is called, as it often is, the venture of faith. In exercising the Christian belief in God a man must go not only farther, but very much farther, than he can see. The belief to which he rises is that the Source and Lord of all is the eternal goodness loving in wisdom: it is belief in the personal Spirit, perfectly good, who in holy love creates, sustains and orders all. Here the perfect character is believed in, just as distinctly as the external existence; and as of the existence, so of the perfect character, we must own that it has never been demonstrated in our presence. Many sincere souls who might believe in a God judge it beyond their power to believe in such a God, in such a world as this. The testimony of innumerable details of dreadful fact agrees that the world in which we live, the only world we know, is an inconceivably hard world in which to believe in a God of perfect goodness. Light upon the dark problem of good and evil in our life is but dim, and it is too much to expect that any investigations of ours will solve the mystery. We are even divided against ourselves; for we feel that the best that is in us requires a different world from this at the hands of a perfect God, and yet the best that is in us feels itself to be built upon the very foundation of the perfect God as the supreme reality. It is plain that if we are to hold the Christian belief in the eternal goodness loving in wisdom, we must hold it by a venture of faith, going out beyond what we can see. We do hold it, and we hold it by such a venture. From the evidence, but beyond the evidence, that our life affords, we follow on to the assertion of God, the living God, absolutely good. From partial proof we rise to the full conclusion. There are doubts and there is darkness, but in faith the soul gathers up its most honourable energies and declares that good is the sun and evil is the cloud, and that the perfect and eternal sun is God. Contrary appearances are plentiful enough, but they are left beneath, while the soul trusts its primal certainties, follows them to their sure conclusion, and proclaims the reality of the eternal goodness loving in wisdom and ruling all.

Nor are we ashamed of the venture of faith. Some would make it a reproach against the Christian faith in God that it thus goes beyond the tangible evidence, and makes affirmations which there are no sufficient inductions to support. The reproach is a natural one coming from the outside, but it is not deserved. The venture of faith is not a wilful act, merely an assertion of something that one wishes to be true: it is the affirmation of something that we have good reason for believing to be true. Faith advances from the best convictions we possess to the only truth that could possibly make them valid, the perfect goodness of God. Such a venture is no foolish or wilful act: it simply sets things in their right order, and gives the best things the best place. Faith acts upon a reasonable judgment, and one that we cannot reject without stultifying our best selves. The venture that it makes, instead of being an unmanly thing, or an escape from untenable ground into a fool's paradise of confidence, is a consistent declaration of the supremacy of all that has a right to be supreme.

This language may sound too much as if faith were mainly a mental act based upon an argument. It is that, to a certain extent, for faith reasons, and reasons soundly; but the crowning element in faith, implied all along and now to be mentioned, shows how much more it is. The Christian faith has for its vitalizing force the element of personal self-commitment. A venture is an act, and an act of the whole man. A belief that God is worthy to be trusted becomes faith when God is trusted. Theoretical belief vanishes, and in faith the soul acts upon the being and the goodness of God. It not only beholds but casts itself upon the God who is good and doeth good, whose tender mercies are over all his works, the faithful Creator, the righteous Father, the holy Saviour. This character of faith is too secret and sacred to be minutely described: it lies in the region of mystery, for the soul itself does not understand it, and sometimes it seems verily to be a leap in the dark. It lies in the region of ecstasy, too, for here the untried is the glorious. Faith is the flight of the soul to its home in the bosom of its Father. Who shall describe it? Who can tell of the waverings and uncertainties before the flight, or of the welcome, the rest and the infinite peace that follow it? Going thus to his own place, a man trusts God for himself and for all creation: all is safe in the Father's hands, and his perfect goodness and redeeming grace are the complete satisfaction of the soul. Plainly, when this has come to pass, God and the soul have come into their right fellowship, and man has entered upon the life for which he was created. This is nature, this is right, and this is everlasting welfare. Who shall separate us from the love of God?

In speaking of the Christian doctrine of God it is only too easy to allow the divine to eclipse the human, instead of illuminating it; and from this account of faith it may seem as if its field and work were in the heavenly world, or else in that secret place of the heart where God and man meet alone in the darkness. But it would be a sad mistake thus to limit the sphere and scope of faith. The true doctrine of faith and works must not be lost sight of through the passing away of the old phraseology. Faith is an ethical force. It rules the life; or rather, it opens the life to God's ruling. It brings the life that now is, in this present world, under the moral inspiration of the heavenly Father. God knows how imperfect our response must be at present, and is more patient with us than we are with one another, or even with ourselves. But the truth is that, to accept God is to accept not only an immortal hope, but a moral standard, valid for the whole of eternity, including to-day. It is also to accept a moral power, and gladly to submit one's self to its working. Whenever an act of faith goes forth, it is a sinful being who betakes himself to God. Hatred of evil on the human side and forgiving grace on the divine are implied in the event. Now, since Father and child are together in the normal life, the Father's goodness is the accepted type of the child's being, and the Father's love is the means of holy transformation to the child. His word to his children is, "Be ye holy, for I am holy," and faith honours the call. In proportion as men believe in God with the Christian faith, there springs up an inspiration of purity, a zeal for righteousness, a fellowship with the spirit of Saviourhood. Not only do there blossom those graces of the Spirit which we are accustomed to group under the name of personal religion: all the social virtues and humane works that the world can need or goodness can inspire spring up and bring forth fruit when the Christian belief in God has free course and is glorified. Committing himself to God, man commits himself to goodness, and to the promotion of goodness, after the likeness of God.

Thus the Christian belief in God is the largest, the most exacting, the most consolatory, and the most inspiring of all the beliefs that are possible to men. No man can rise to the full height of it, nor can all the world do it justice. At the same time, it is a faith for a little child. Nothing can be simpler than to accept as a child the grace that is sufficient for the soul—and from that comes all the rest. Indeed, the Master says that, in order rightly to cherish the Christian faith, a man must become as a little child.

43

Forgiveness and New Life

George Adam Smith

In what then does the forgiveness of sin essentially consist? In the infinite riches of God's grace by Christ Jesus, it consists in many spiritual results, of which I have already, from Scripture and our experience, quoted several. But among these there is one to which we may devote the rest of this sermon for three reasons: because it is ethically the most inspiring, because it is that on which Scripture appears to lay most stress, and because, at the same time, it is one so often overlooked by ourselves.

From at least the time of the prophets up to the end of the New Testament the element in Forgiveness which the Bible most frequently emphasises is God's new trust in the soul He has pardoned: the faith that despite our frailty, our unworthiness, our guilt; despite the mistrust and despair which the memory of our sin induces, God still trusts us, God believes us capable of doing better, God confides to us the interests and responsibilities of His work on earth. That according to the Bible is the ethical meaning of forgiveness—God's belief in us, God's hope for us, God's will to work with us, God's trust to us of services and posts in His kingdom.

So long ago Isaiah found it; when immediately after his guilt had been removed by a sacrament of fire, he felt himself receive—not, mark you, to begin with, a definite commission to God's people, but—the opportunity, upon his own will and motive, to give himself to the message and work which God proclaimed as open. He had called himself *a man of unclean lips, and dwelling in the midst of an unclean people*. But when his iniquity was taken away and his sin purged; when he heard the voice of the Lord saying *Whom shall I send and who will go for us?*—he himself in the great consciousness of freedom which forgiveness brought, and in the full enjoyment of God's restored trust in him, cried out: *Here am I, send me!* And at once he received his commission.

So also long ago a Psalmist felt it—the Psalmist who, more than any other, declares to us the purely ethical motives that drive men to pray for pardon. Forgiveness came to him, too, as the instinct of a great commission from God, who trusted him.

Deliver me from blood guiltiness, O God of my salvation, And my tongue shall sing aloud of thy righteousness. O Lord open thou my lips, And my mouth shall show forth thy praise. I will teach transgressors thy ways, And sinners shall be converted unto thee (Psalm li. 13, 14).

So long ago another prophet saw it when he made God's trust of men the starting point of all salvation and providence. *For He said: Surely they are my people, children who cannot lie* or prove false. They did lie, they did fail: all the time they proved rebels to His will and traitors to the trust that He reposed in them. But He forgave them by trusting them again. He said *they are children that will not lie: so He became their Saviour. In all their affliction He was afflicted, and the Angel of His Presence saved them. In His love and in His pity He redeemed them; and He bare them and carried them all the days of old* (Isaiah lxiii. 8, 9). The whole glorious history of their salvation and their long sustenance started from their God's gracious trust in their unworthy and tainted souls.

In the New Testament it is not otherwise. Our Lord's announcements of pardon are sometimes followed by the words: *Go and sin no more.* They are in the imperative mood, but it is the fashion of the grammar of the day. What they mean is—Thou wilt sin no more: I have confidence in thee! When Peter fell by denying His Lord at the critical hour, the assurance of forgiveness came to his heartfelt penitence in the gift of a new commission in His Lord's service. *Simon, son of Jonas, lovest thou me? He saith unto him, Yea, Lord, thou knowest that I love thee. Jesus saith unto him: Feed my lambs,* and again *Tend my sheep,* and again *Feed my sheep.*

Such, then, is the Biblical doctrine of forgiveness. Amid the many blessings in which through the infinite riches of His mercy in Christ, it consists, this stands out, the most wonderful and inspiring essential of all: that God Himself should trust us when we have lost all trust of ourselves: should believe us capable of standing where we have fallen, of overcoming where we have only known defeat; and of again doing the work, in which we have been lax and unfaithful.

For it is just in all this that the tremendous moral possibilities of forgiveness consist. Let a man merely off the consequences of his sin and by that alone you do not give him much more than room and time to grow better: *though the goodness of God also leadeth to repentance,* and if men's hearts were only more open to the respites and reliefs of His ordinary Providence, they would find in them all the grace, which they are too apt to associate only with the crises of worship and religious feeling. Tell a man in addition that God so loved him that He gave His Son to die for him, and when the man believes it, though his heart was dry and obdurate, you shall indeed have wakened all over his experience—as I dare to say nothing else ever did wake in human nature—the springs of wonder, gratitude and hope. But you cannot make him feel the depths of that love, you cannot carry his gratitude or his hope to their fullest pitch, you cannot add to his affections a new conscience or fortify them past every shock, till you tell him that God's love for him includes God's trust in his loyalty, in his power to make a new start, to stand firm, and, though he should be the most fallen and stunted of men, in his power to grow at last to the full stature of his manhood. Without this trust of God forgiveness is only indulgence and the experience of it becomes a mere escape. But with the sense of being trusted forgiveness becomes a conscience, and puts into a man a new sense of honour to do his best and his bravest for the God who believes in him.

> 'The fear o' hell's the hangman's whip
> To haud the wretch in order;
> But where ye feel your honour grip,
> Let that ay be your border!'

And it is this sense of honour, which forgiveness, when it is felt as God's great trust of him, plants in a man deeper and stronger than any other motive with which religion can endow him.

Look you, there is no other view of forgiveness so lasting or so ethical as this. So ethical: for this makes it no mere absolution, no bare decree of the authority of God—whether direct by the Spirit, or mediated by His priests upon earth; no mere decree of the authority of God, but the constant influence of His grace and His will upon our hearts. In giving pardon God gives Himself.

Nor is there any other view of forgiveness so enduring or so bound to grow. For whereas the effect of forgiveness, as so often vulgarly interpreted among us, refers only to the past, and a man's sense of it is confined to a single moment or crisis of experience, however glorious that be; this other sense of forgiveness as God's gracious trust of us, though cherished at first with a faltering faith which often shrinks from the wonder of it and can scarcely believe in its reality—this sense of forgiveness, as God's trust of us, grows with the growth of the common days, finds its proof in each new morning's gift of life, and its illustrations in every fresh opportunity, however commonplace, and every additional task or trial, however dull or painful. I would not say one word against that preaching, which claims our hearts for the grace of God in a single and perfect hour of appreciation, for by such sudden conversions the lives of many have immediately been changed and shall be to the end of time; but I do know that in the sense of forgiveness, which I have put before you, you will expand the sensations of an hour to the experience of a lifetime and make God's forgiveness of you as wide and as constant as His common Providence.

I said at the outset that we would confine ourselves to the question: In what does the Forgiveness of Sins consist? and would not take up the other equally important one, How is the Forgiveness of Sin procured and assured to us? But as Christians we can never forget the answer to this other, for it is the central fact of our religion: through the love of God, who gave His own Son to die for us on the Cross. And I now conclude, with the bearing of this fact on a further application of the truth we have been studying together.

As it was Christ who brought God's pardon to us, let us remember that God's great trust, so manifest in it, is continued to us so far as we hold to Christ and abide in Him. Apart from the grace, that is so richly every man's in Christ, God cannot trust us nor could we presume on the assurance of our forgiveness nor prove ourselves worthy of it. Therefore, in this most liberating of all ethical experiences do not let a man ever feel himself independent. But as day by day the goodness of God comes upon him; as he wakens every morning into the wonder of God's patience with his unworthy soul; as the great occasions of life come upon him, work, influence, friendship, love; as knowledge and progress and a stable character become sure to him—let him remember that these are not given to him for his own sake, but for Christ's. Let him say to himself: I am trusted with them all by God, and assured of them all, only in so far as I live in Christ and by the grace which He bestows.

44

Sanctification

James Petigru Boyce

The Nature of Sanctification

What now, we may inquire, is the nature of the sanctification which is wrought out in the believer?

1. It is a personal sanctification. It is accomplished in each individual personally, and not in that of a common representative as is the righteousness which justifies.

2. It is a real sanctification, not merely one that is imputed, as is righteousness. Holiness is not merely "accounted to men," so that they are treated as though holy, but they are made holy. Holiness becomes the characteristic of their natures. It is habitually exercised in their lives. It will eventually be possessed in perfection. It is real and in no sense only virtual.

3. It is of the whole nature. The renewed nature, given in regeneration, shows that sanctification includes the whole spiritual part of man. It is not to be confined to mere outward actions. God's spiritual nature demands not only spiritual worship, but holy spiritual emotions and affections; and these belong to the heart. Hence the need of inward conformity to his will and commands is so especially set forth in the New Testament, as to mark its teachings as essentially spiritual. We are also plainly taught that between the outward fruit, and the inward condition, is such a connection that the latter is the actual producing power of the former, and is manifested by it. Matt. 12:33-35; Luke 6:43-45.

But sanctification is to be extended to the body likewise. Its appetites and passions are to be controlled, wicked actions are to cease, and unholy habits to be put away, the members of the body are to be mortified, all filthiness of the flesh to be cleansed, good works are to be exhibited to mankind, and such high moral duties to be performed as are imposed upon Christians as obligatory towards each other and the world.

The Scriptures exhort to sanctification of the whole nature, both body and soul. See 2 Cor. 7:1; Eph. 4:17-24; Col. 3:5-10; 1 Thess. 5:23. That of the body alone is urged. Rom. 6:12,13; 1 Cor. 6:20; 1 Thess. 4:3-7. The apostle tells the Ephesians about his prayers for their spiritual sanctification. Eph. 1:17-19.

4. It is not a sanctification to be completed in this life.

It is not, like justification, a single act, but is a continuous process. The work goes on throughout the lifetime of the believer, nor is it completed before death.

This is manifest from the frequent exhortations to sanctification addressed to those who are already believers in Christ, and who are actually called saints. Many of the passages containing these have been given in the preceding section.

It is also shown by the warnings, about the danger of backsliding, addressed to Christian believers. Such was that to Peter by our Lord, the reality of the danger of which was shown by his subsequent grievous fall. Luke 22:31, 32. See examples of other such warnings in 1 Cor. 10:12; Col. 1:23; Heb. 3:12,13; 12:15.

The fearful condition of actual apostasy is presented for the purpose of teaching the true people of God the extent to which knowledge of his grace may be possessed without the attainment of actual and final salvation. Heb. 6:4-6; 10:26-29; 2 Pet. 2:20. The object of this instruction is to warn against committing sins, and indulging habits to which they are still prone.

Christians are not presented in the New Testament as completely pure and holy, but, on the contrary, the very best of them acknowledge the existence of sinful tendencies, and pronounce any idea of freedom from the presence of sin to be a delusion. The faults of good men, such as Peter, James and John, and Thomas, and Paul and Barnabas (Acts 15:37-40) are especially mentioned, and John who declares that "whosoever is begotten of God sinneth not" (1 John 5:18) is the very apostle who, in a previous part of that very same epistle, teaches that "if we say that we have no sin, we deceive ourselves, and the truth is not in us." 1 John 1:8. Paul constantly speaks of himself as still struggling against the power of sin, as not counting himself to have attained, as buffeting his body and bringing it into bondage lest he should be rejected, and thus he gives us, in his descriptions of his own experience, a pattern of what has been almost universally acknowledged as that of every other Christian.

5. But sanctification will not always be incomplete. In heaven perfect purity and holiness will be the portion of the believer.

The purpose of God, in the foreordination of those whom he foreknew, is that they shall "be conformed to the image of his Son." Rom. 8:29. This conformity shall be attained in heaven, for "if he shall be manifested, we shall be like him; for we shall see him even as he is." 1 John 3:2. Such likeness involves personal sinless purity.

Paul's triumphant language as to the resurrection shows that this will be true of the body no less than of the soul. 1 Cor. 15:50-57.

The Scriptures declare as to the New Jerusalem that "there shall in no wise enter into it anything unclean, or he that maketh an abomination and a lie: but only they which are written in the Lamb's book of life." Rev. 21:27. Peter says that the inheritance reserved in heaven for the saints is incorruptible and undefiled. 1 Pet. 1:4.

6. The partial sanctification of this life is also progressive. It is not a certain degree of attainment, possessed by all alike, and remaining always in this life the same; it is a growth from the seed planted in regeneration, which is constantly bringing forth new leaves, and new fruit; it grows with increased intellectual knowledge of God's truth, with a clearer perception of human sinfulness and corruption, with stronger faith and brighter hope, and more confident assurance of personal acceptance with God, with a more heartfelt conception of the sacrificing love of Christ, and with a more realizing belief in his constant presence and knowledge of what we do. It even increases from its own acquired strength and through the suffering and doing in which it is developed. In these and many other ways do Christians grow in grace and in the knowledge of Christ, and in conformity to his image, "cleansing themselves from all defilement of flesh and spirit, perfecting holiness in the fear of God." 2 Cor. 7:1.

When, however, this sanctification is said to be progressive, it is not meant to deny the imperfections before referred to, nor to assert that there is a constant rise upward to God and toward his holy perfection. The Christian life on earth is a warfare with sin, and the believer is not always without failure. He often yields to temptation, sometimes falls even into most grievous sin. The personal experience, presented by Paul, in the seventh chapter of Romans, is so strong a statement of such struggles that some have been inclined to confine its application to a time prior to acceptance of the gospel. But there can be no question of the applicability to Christians of the declaration made to the Galatians, "The flesh lusteth against the spirit, and the spirit against the flesh; for these are contrary the one to the other, that ye may not do the things that ye would." Gal. 5:17.

But the progress of sanctification is nevertheless continuous. These temptations and struggles enter into that progress, and not only they, but even the sins and falls which mar the Christian life. The process of sanctification is like the ascent of a mountain. One is always going forward, though not always upward, yet the final end of the progressive movement of every kind is the attainment of the summit. Sometimes, because of difficulties, the road itself descends, only more easily to ascend again. Sometimes certain attractions by the way cause a deviation from the route most suitable for ascent. Often it is feared that there has been no higher attainment, often that it has been but a continual descent, until, perchance, some point of view is gained from which to look down upon the plain whence the journey was begun and behold the height which has already been overcome. Often, with wearied feet, and desponding heart, the traveller is ready to despair, because of his own feebleness, and the difficulties which surround. But he earnestly presses forward and the journey is completed, the ascent is made, the end is attained.

The Author of Sanctification

1. From what we have learned of the persons who are sanctified, and of the nature of the work performed, it is evident that

the author of it must be more than man. The Scriptures teach that it is God.

The work is attributed to God without reference to any distinction of persons. 1 Thess. 4:3; 5:23. It is also ascribed to the Father, John 17:17; Heb. 13:21; and to Christ, Eph. 5:26; Tit. 2:14.

But it is the especial work of the Holy Spirit, who is the author of the process of Sanctification, as he is also of the act of Regeneration. 1 Cor. 6:11; 2 Cor. 3:18; 2 Thess. 2:13; 1 Pet. 1:2.

He enlightens the mind. John 14:26; 1 Cor. 2:9-16; Eph. 1:18; 3:18, 19; 1 John 2:20, 27. On this account he is called "the Spirit of truth," John 14:17; 15:26; 16:13; and the "Spirit of wisdom." Eph. 1:17.

He gives spiritual strength (Eph. 3:16), lusting against the flesh (Gal. 5:17), enabling the believer to mortify the deeds of the body (Rom. 8:13), leading the sons of God (Rom. 8:14), and enabling them to purify their souls in obeying the truth. 1 Pet. 1:22.

Inasmuch as he dwells within them (Rom. 8:9), so that they are his temple (1 Cor. 3:16), with whom they are sealed as the earnest of their inheritance (Eph. 1:13, 14), so, also, does he bear witness with their spirits that they are the children of God, and, removing the spirit of bondage to fear, bestows on them the spirit of adoption, whereby they cry Abba, Father. Rom. 8:15, 16.

The fruit of this indwelling Spirit is declared to be "in all goodness and righteousness and truth." Eph. 5:9. It is specifially stated to be "love, joy, peace, long-suffering, kindness, goodness, faith, meekness, temperance." Gal. 5:22.

2. But, while there is such need of a divine author of sanctification, it is not a work in which the believer is passively a recipient, but one in which he actively co-operates. This is exhibited in various ways in the word of God.

Christians are called upon to recognize this presence of the Spirit. 1 Cor. 3:16, 17. They are exhorted to "walk by the Spirit," and assured that, in so doing, they "shall not fulfill the lust of the flesh." Gal. 5:16. They are taught that "they that are after the flesh do mind the things of the flesh, but they that are after the

Spirit the things of the Spirit." Rom. 8:5. They are told that, because of the indwelling Spirit, "we are debtors, not to the flesh to live after the flesh," and thus, by implication, that we are debtors to live after the Spirit. Rom. 8:12. They are charged to "grieve not the Holy Spirit of God, in whom ye were sealed unto the day of redemption." Eph. 4:30. In these, and in other ways, their co-operation with the Spirit in the work is implied quite plainly.

They are exhorted to engage in the work of self-purification. The apostle exhorts the Ephesians not to "walk as the Gentiles also walk, in the vanity of their mind, . . . to put away . . . the old man, which waxeth corrupt after the lusts of deceit; and be renewed in the spirit of their mind, . . . and to put on the new man, which after God, hath been created in righteousness and holiness of truth." Eph. 4:17-24.

This self-purification is declared to be the work of every one that has the hope of likeness to Christ. 1 John 3:3.

Direct promises and commands, and exhortations to perfection and holiness, imply co-operative action in those who are in process of attaining sanctification. Matt. 5:48; 2 Cor. 7:1.

All warnings against the power of temptation, the lust of the flesh, the subtlety of Satan, the influence of the world, the grievous character of sin; all exhortations to lead a virtuous and godly life, to set the affections on heavenly and divine things, to consecrate soul and body to God; all motives to these ends drawn from the work of Christ, as an exhibition of divine love and mercy, as an example of purity of life, and of patient suffering, or as personally connected with the believer because of his union with the Lord,—in short, all that the Scriptures contain fitted to lead the Christian to a higher spiritual life, is evidence of his co-operation with the Holy Spirit in the work of sanctification.

The author of sanctification is indeed the Divine Spirit, but the Christian actively unites with that Spirit, "working out his own salvation with fear and trembling," being exhorted and encouraged to do so, because "it is God which worketh in him, both to will, and to do, for his good pleasure." Phil. 2:12,13.

The Means of Sanctification

The manner in which the Spirit operates in sanctification is beyond our knowledge. In none of the acts of God can we tell how he exerts his power, not even in creation. "As thou knowest not," says the preacher, "what is the way of the wind, nor how the bones do grow in the womb of her that is with child; even so thou knowest not the work of God who doeth all." Ecc. 11:5. In sanctification the Spirit moves as mysteriously as we are taught that he does in regeneration. John 3:8. In general, undoubtedly, it is in accordance with the laws of mind and of spiritual life. Yet we know no reason why there is not a place for supernatural action in sanctification, as well as in regeneration. We can only know the effects produced, and the means which are revealed in the word of God, and in Christian experience.

1. The primary means which the Spirit uses for our sanctification, as both of these sources of information teach, is the truth of God. "Sanctify them in the truth; thy word is truth" (John 17:17), was the prayer of the Lord, in which the whole work, both of consecration and cleansing, is set forth as thus to be accomplished. (See also John 17:19). "Growth in the grace" is inseparably connected with growth "in the knowledge of our Lord and Saviour Jesus Christ." 2 Pet. 3:18.

This is further taught in Scripture by

Such passages as connect spiritual life with truth; as John 6:63; 8:32.

Such as ascribe quickening power to the word of God; as Ps. 119:50, 93.

Such as teach that truth is promotive of obedience; as Ps. 119:34, 43, 44.

Such as declare its usefulness in preventing sin; as Ps. 119:11.

Such as associate it with cleansing from sin; as Ps. 119:9; 1 Pet. 1:22.

Such as state that produces hatred of sin; as Ps. 119:104.

Such as assert its power to lead to salvation; 2 Tim. 3:15-17.

Such as say that "all things that pertain unto life and godliness" have been given through the knowledge of God, and Christ; as 2 Pet. 1:2, 3.

Such as imply that growth in grace is due to greater knowledge; as Heb. 5:12-14.

Such as account for inability to accept higher doctrinal truth, by such weakness as should be characteristic only of those who are babes in Christ; as 1 Cor. 3:1-3.

Such as set forth the word of God as "the sword of the Spirit;" as Eph. 6:17.

Such as announce that all the ministerial gifts bestowed by Christ are "for the perfecting of the saints, unto the work of ministering, unto the building up of the body of Christ; till we all attain unto the unity of the faith, and of the knowledge of the Son of God, unto a full grown man, unto the measure of the stature of the fulness of Christ." Eph. 4:11-16.

2. In connection with this primary means of divine truth others are presented. But they are not only secondary, but actually subordinate means to the word of God. They rather furnish occasions for the exercise of the means of sanctification contained in the truth of God than are proper means in themselves to that end. In themselves they have no efficacy, and only accomplish the end of sanctification by bringing the believer into connection with the truth of God.

Such are the providences of God, which tend in various ways to arouse and move his children, and avail unto sanctification so far only as they recall, and lead to the apprehension of divine instructions. They are frequent, and effective means of such apprehension, and, through this, of the believer's growth in holiness. Such especially are the afflictions, sent as chastisements by the Heavenly Father upon his children. Such, also, are the temptations and trials to which they are subjected. Such, likewise, are infirmities of the flesh, and perplexities of the spirit which God permits to remain, or causes to arise in his own elect. In these, and in numerous other ways, as well of what is called good, as of what is called evil, does God surround his people with the acts of his providence. But these acts themselves avail not unto their sanctification but are only made effective through the truth of God apprehended amid such events, and received as spiritual food for the growth of the believer.

The good works of the Christian, furnish another secondary

means for his sanctification. By these are not meant works that are good in a legal sense, for such goodness would require a perfection and freedom from taint which no work of fallen man can possess; but it is the privilege of the Christian to live unto the Lord, and the name of good works is given in Scripture to such outward actions as are the results of his life through the Spirit.

These good works are the result of sanctification; but, in their performance, they naturally become the means of further sanctification. John 14:23; Eph. 3:16-20. Yet, is this accomplished, not apart from, but in connection with, the truth of God. The new development will always be in the direction of the particular truths, contemplated in their performance. These will furnish the motives to further action, the strength for additional duty, the earnest purpose of deeper consecration, or, whatever else the Spirit may graciously use for a more complete sanctification of the believer.

Prayer is a still further means to the same end; which, from its nature, can be effective only through the believer's apprehension of divine truth.

Hence the worthlessness of mere lip service (Isa. 29:13; Ezek. 33:31; Matt. 15:8), or vain repetitions, Matt. 6:7. Not only are they offensive to God, but without value to the soul. Hence also the necessary spirituality of divine worship, because that only is true worship which is the service of the soul. John 4:23,24. Prayer, which is a mere formal or mechanical utterance of words, can have no value; because the one that offers it, does so in ignorance, or forgetfulness of the truth of God appropriate to accompany it.

The Lord's day is another secondary means of sanctification, which manifestly becomes such only in the Christian's use of divine truth; either such as is suggested by God's appointment of such a day, or such as is attained through the opportunity for such purpose which it affords.

The association of believers in church relations, is another of the means ordained by God for the increase of individual spiritual life and consequently of sanctification. This is attained not only through social prayer, and the preaching of the word, but also by Christian watchcare and discipline, and by the mutual sympathy and aid of believers in matters both temporal and spiritual. Whatever in these pertains to sanctification, must be connected with the recognition of divine truth in the moving influences which bestow, or the accepting thankfulness which receives.

The ministry given by Christ, is also a means for the sanctification of his people, in the preaching of his truth, in the spiritual guidance and rule of the flock, and in the sympathizing bestowment of the consolations of his grace. But, even these, though officially appointed, cannot either of themselves, or by virtue of their office, confer or increase spiritual grace. Their ministry is one only of the word of God, and it is only through his inspired truth "that the man of God may be complete, furnished completely unto every good work." 2 Tim. 3:17. What these works are, is shown by verse 16, viz: "for teaching, for reproof, for correction, for instruction which is in righteousness." Ministers are in no other sense vehicles of grace. They are not appointed as personal channels of access to God, or of the bestowment of blessings by him, except so far as he has made it their duty to make known his truth. In connection with that truth they are means of sanctification to his people, and only thus are to be regarded as occupying relations between their fellow-men and God.

The ordinances of baptism and the Lord's Supper are also means of sanctification. It is especially important to understand in what respects they are so. . . .

The true statement of the sanctifying power of these ordinances seems the rather to be,—

1. A denial of all inherent power in them as means of grace.

2. Recognition of them as conveying truth by symbolical instruction.

3. The fact that they are partaken of because of the command of Christ also makes the act of obedience to him a means of grace to the recipient.

4. Only as truth is, in some way or other, brought by them to the acceptance of the heart and mind, can they have sanctifying power.

It is thus seen that all the means of sanctification are connected with the truth, and are secondary to it. They only become such, as they convey truth, or as they suggest truth, or as they are employed in the recognition of some truth.

45

Christian Prayer

Horace Bushnell

I will only bring to your notice the single fact of a remarkable agreement between the historic life of Christ and the institution of prayer, a fact not commonly observed. What God is and will be to man is accurately shown, of course, by the incarnate life and ministry of Jesus. And here first of all we are deeply touched by the feeling of brotherhood in which he comes. His descent to the lowly, his perfect attention to all that seek him, his full compassions open to all sickness and sorrow, his patience with wrong, his outgoing sympathy and help, even down to the hem of his garment, all to recover a world in sin—here we love to say is the true greatness of Jesus, a most worthy and sublime expression of the greatness of God. We think of God thus revealed, not as an abstraction or some cold, far-off, theoretic immensity of absolute power, but as a living person in the sweetest, dearest terms of charity and friendship, faithful, attentive, tender and nigh. And this exactly is the doctrine of prayer. In this tender of the right of prayer we have the same attention to each want and sorrow, the same personal care and consideration, the same uplifting help, the same outgoing love to weakness and wrong. Given the fact of Christ, the doctrine of prayer follows of course, and the honors we pay to one ought to certify us also of the other. Either Christ is no true manifestation of God, or else God is the God of prayer. And therefore it is that Christ affirms, many times over, a fixed relation between himself and prayer, such that prayer is forever certified by him.

And then, to give you a clear confidence of approach, he gives his Holy Spirit to help you and draw your mind into the best things. He wants your prayer so much and bows to it in such tenderness that he will even fashion it himself; even as some qualified counsellor might help you frame a petition for the state according to the laws of the state. "Likewise also the Spirit helpeth our infirmities; for we know not what we should pray for as we ought, but the Spirit maketh intercession for us with groanings that cannot be uttered"—literally, "groanings inaudible," that is, back of the prayer we make. All great and strong prayer is prayer therefore in the Spirit. It mounts into faith because the Spirit certifies it by his sanction and lifts it by his impulse. All doubts therefore about our petitions will be more and more completely surmounted, and we shall get a kind of divine skill, more and more perfect, in asking only for things according to the will of God.

The prayer is wanted to put us in a fit condition for receiving the thing prayed for. Our state without the prayer might even be such as to forbid the gift and make it hurtful. Besides, it is not so much the gifts that we want, after all, as an open relation to God himself; to get acquainted with him in a way of reciprocal action, finding him and being found of him, in a dialogue with him, so to speak, of petition and answer. In the persistent strain of earnest prayer, too, we get our motives purified and are drawn to a more affectionate trust. And then as we are drawn closer to God ourselves, we are also drawn closer to one another, when uniting two or three or many in the same struggle of petition; and so the intensest, broadest, holiest kind of brotherhood is established. And yet again, as we pray for others who never pray for themselves, our love to them is drawn out as it otherwise never could be, kindled as it were by God's love, and they in turn are impressed by the love that is so fervently revealed in prayers in their behalf, and are drawn to pray for themselves. The whole institute and economy of prayer is in this manner sure to have a practical working. Were God to give the gifts prayed for of his own motion, without prayer, there would scarcely be any practical working left. We should be forgiven without asking for it, receive our gifts when our backs are turned, and use them without thanks. They would come when, having no fitness to our state, they would only do us harm. We should plough along under them just as we do under causes, without faith or feeling, learning no approach to God and trained to no practical acquaintance with him. Everything, in short, by which Christ in his gospel now works for the renovation of souls and a general kingship and brotherhood in them, would be wanting. So deep and solid and profoundly beneficent is God's counsel in his institute of prayer. We want the condition of prayer just as much as we do God himself and for the same reason.

Again, it is a great point as regards successful prayer that we truly want and fixedly mean the things prayed for. "Ye shall seek me and shall find me if ye search for me with all your heart." How often do men pray by their lives directly against what they supplicate in words, desiring, it is proved, what actually hinders their petitions more than they want what their petitions ask—the conversion for example of a child or a friend, when their own chosen mode of life is the chief obstacle in fact to such conversion; or, perhaps, that God will correct their consciously increasing greediness of gain, when to do it he would even have to turn back all their successes and strip them of all the gains they have made. Do they in such cases really want the things they dare in pious words to ask? A son, it may be, is going fatally astray, and nothing will save him but to revolutionize the whole life of his praying father and take him quite away from his most cherished pleasures. Do we really want the things we ask? If we mean to [do] more than play with words we must come to this. No prayer takes hold of God until it first takes hold of the man. He must mean it. And if it is for some blessing or another, he must be so deep in the meaning of what he prays for as to be bowed in heavy burden before God. His oppressed feeling, his almost agony in the prayer, may even be the necessary argument with God and a good part of the reason for which his prayer is heard.

It is another important condition of successful prayer that we pray much; for in that manner only do we get skill in prayer. An old, thoroughly practised Christian learns how to approach unto God. God's handling of him has taught him many things: what to ask, when to persist, and when to desist. The holy skill he has gotten is like all other kinds of skill, experimentally obtained. And here is one of the chief reasons why there is so little success in prayer; we do not pray enough to get the manner. We only bungle in it, and therefore fail.

Once more it requires a very high kind of life, a practised way of purity, a close and tender walk with God, to be at all successful in the highest offices of prayer. The motives must be purified and become habitually unselfish, ambition must be taken away, humility must be graded down to a level of meekness, the love must be sweetened by a Christly walk, the vehemence of will and passion must be chastened, and, above all, the faith must be so brought up into God's secret as to abide there. Let us not wonder, my brethren, if our prayers are weak and fruitless; how can they be otherwise, without living a holier life and abiding more closely with God?

Probably there are among you such as never pray. God has given you for so many years this wonderful right of petition, but you have never accepted or even thought of it as your privilege. Often are you conscious that you want mercy and grace to help, but you have not been willing as yet to ask it. What a fact is this, that the wise good God and Father of our Lord Jesus Christ offers you converse, free approach, close acquaintance, powerful help, and you are not drawn to so much as speak with him! O the loss!—loss of dignity, greatness of feeling, help out of evil up into God, society with the highest, enduement of peace and power!

Here is the true spring of life and fertility for us, and the waters of this spring are free. Wanting grace to help, we can have it always, grace upon grace, for the throne is a throne of grace. To be in the Spirit, high in the Spirit, filled with the Spirit, endued in that manner with power, is God's absolute gift, never withheld from those who seek it. And then all sorts of fruit will follow. There will be no barren prayers or barren years, no pinings, condolings, objurgations, decays, or desertions. Our courage will be equal to our duties, our brotherhood will grow like a tree that is planted by living waters, and our peace itself will be like a river.

46

The Church and the Divine Purpose

Horace Bushnell

"But ye are come unto Mount Zion, and unto the city of the living God, the heavenly Jerusalem, and to an innumerable company of angels, to the general assembly and church of the first-born, which are written in heaven, and to God the Judge of all, and to the spirits of just men made perfect."—Heb. 12:22, 3.

When we read this passage of Scripture, we seem to scarcely know what world it is in or about, and not much better what world we are in ourselves. "But ye are come," says the apostle,—are come, in the present tense—that is, come already. And yet a great part of the terms that follow,—city of the living God,—heavenly Jerusalem,—innumerable company of angels,—general assembly and church of the first-born whose names are written in heaven,—appear to be upper-world terms, proper only to the kingdom of God above. Which blending, again, of celestial sceneries, in terms of the present tense, with sceneries partly terrestrial, is permitted the apostle, it may be, on the ground of a large analogy and comprehensive unity, including both spheres of life together. All the more competent and commensurate is the grasp of idea in the specification given; all the more fit, too, we shall see, is the double compass of the language, to the purpose I have now in hand; viz., to magnify

the church of God, and freshen up, if possible, some due conception of its universality and of our responsibility for it.

It is one of the remarkable, and, it seems to me, gloomy signs
of our time, that we are so evidently losing interest in the church
and respect for it. It is not a thing so very new, that a great many
persons outside of the church take up a prejudice against it, and
begin to prophecy, with airs of exultation, its shortly going by, to
be among the things that were; but it is a matter of far more
appalling significance that so many of its own members appear
to be somehow losing out even their confidence in it. They do
not really care much for it, and for this reason probably, appeals
of duty made for it get as little fixed hold of impression, or
practical conviction, as in such a case they must. Even if they
pray for it, and occasionally speak in a way to magnify the duties
we owe it, there is yet a certain slackness in their manner, which
indicates rather a wish to have some concern for it, than a real
concern. I sometimes hear the question raised by such, what,
after all, is the use of the church? Would it not be just as well if it
were given up, or disbanded? Is it not in fact gone by already?

No, it is not, I am sure,—and never can be. Do we not know
that Christ gave himself for it, that he purchased it with his own
blood, and set it on a rock, and declared that not even the gates
of hell should prevail against it? It is then going down just now?
Is it coming to be an outgrown fact? Not unless Jesus Christ is
outgrown and his kingdom antiquated, which I do not think will
very soon appear. Until then, be the look just now as it may,—
until then, the church will stay, and we may as well be sure of it.
Besides, I think we shall finally discover, after we have fairly
worn out our extempore and shallow strictures, that there is
interest and meaning enough in it, to make it the grand, everlasting fact of the creation of God—all which I now proceed to
show.

The church is bottomed, for its final end or cause, in society.
Man, as we are all the while saying in the tritest manner possible, is a social being; only we conceive but very partially and
dimly what we are to mean by it. We ought to mean, as regarding both him and all other like moral natures in other like
worlds, that they are items only or atoms—incomplete beings,

and scarcely more than candidates for being—till they become organically set and morally joined in society. Existing simply as units, in their natural individualities, they are not of much consequence either to themselves or to each other. In that kind of merely sole existence they have nothing to raise the pitch of their consciousness, no moral dues of brotherhood or sentiments of justice and charity, no religious affinities that put them reaching after God and things above the world, and no high sense of being approved by God and other kindred beings. They make, in short, no part of a divine whole or society, sweetened by the possession they take of it, and in being taken possession of by it. As being merely creatures made, they are scarcely better than nobodies waiting to get some consequence, when society arrives at them, and they at society. Calling them men, they are not so much whole natures related to society outside, but they own, as we may say, scarcely a one-tenth part of their personality, and society the other nine-tenths. Or if we conceive that they own their complete whole constitutionally, that whole, existing chiefly for society, is chiefly owned by society. They are made for society as a moral affair, and have their property in it as being owned by it, and morally configured to it. In their natural instincts and family affections and such like fellow-fondnesses, they begin a faint preluding of society on the footing of mere nature; but this is only the sign, so to speak, or type, of that vaster, nobler society, which is to be fulfilled, under and through the great love-principle that claims their moral and socially religious nature. In this love principle they are kindled as by a kind of infinite aspiration, wanting in fact the whole universe—all there is in it, or can be, of righteous mind—each to possess it, and in the possession be himself complete. And it would even pain them to know that there is or can be any living nature which they can not touch, or be touched by, any society that must be unrelated to them, in any out-most world, or kingdom of God, known or unknown. The principles that are to organize the society are of course identical in all worlds, and the love by which it is organized is an all-worlds' love. Hence, the society organized must be an all-worlds' society.

Inasmuch now as the great society is to be, and to have any

real significance can only be, a moral affair, it will be seen at once that it could not be organized by mere natural constitution. The animals could have a certain rudimental show of society prepared in their natural instincts. But when we speak of moral society as appointed for men, the most that could be done for its organization was to make them capable of it—capable that is of acting themselves into it, in all the qualities, and tempers, and divine principles, that compose it. They must be capable, that is, of law, truth, love, and sacrifice; and then the whole body of the society will be fitly joined together and compacted by that which every joint supplieth. Creation first, then society—this much we say preparatory to any right and living conception of the church, such as we are now after.

And here we strike into the text we began with, proposing henceforward to keep the vein of it. It is, we have noted already, a kind of both-worlds' Scripture, bearing, as it were, a church celestial and a church terrestrial on the face of its terms. And the distinction of the two is, that heaven, the upper-world church, is Society Organized; and the church below, Society Organizing—both in fact one, as regards their their final end or object, and the properties and principles in which they are consummated. Of course the incomplete society below comprehends aberrations, misconjunctions, half-conjunctions, and a great many mere scaffoldings which the other does not. Let us look now at the two in their order.

I. The Society Organized. It is called a city, the city of the living God; because it is the most condensed, completest form of society. It also includes or takes in "angels an innumerable company," some of them, we are to believe, from worlds more ancient than ours and from empires afar off, quite unknown to us. It gathers in also "the first-born" of the church, and puts their names in register on the roll of the grand all-worlds' society. And "the spirits of just men made perfect," are either there or on the way up, to be joined in the general city life and order, for which they are now made ready. All the indications are that a complete organization is so far made, and all its distributions and relations adjusted; as when men of all grades and races are gathered into and unified in, the state of city organization.

In this organized society it is one of the first points to be noted that there is no distribution by sect or sectarian names. Not even the peoples of different worlds, and of old-time, gone-by creations come in as sub-societies, under names to be maintained against other names, though it will not be strange if matters so grandly historical are somehow kept in memory, as by calling these Uranians, these Saturnians, these Orionites, these the Earth-born people; for in being so represented, they are not antagonized, but are only made to show the variety of their populations. Meantime the myriads that arrive, new-comers from the church below, drop off the names of their sects, having left them in their graves not raised—for there is no resurrection promised of these names. They are not Romish any more, not Anglican, not Calvinistic, not Arminian, or Wesleyan, their general assembly is not the Presbyterian, their crowns are not brimmed as being Friends, and since baptism is no more wanted, there are no Baptists. But they are all earth's people and Christian to a man, all other names being sunk and forgot in their now complete society.

Again, the organization is not bodied under official magistracies. There are no pontiffs, patriarchs, or prelates; no bishops, priests, deacons. Probably it was so bodied, in what was called the church order below, and the magistracies too were in a large variety. But the organization was never in any respect from them, but from God and the headship of his Son; in being joined to whom—every man by his faith—the whole body was fitly joined together and became the fullness of him that filleth all in all. Still the magistracies had their day and their uses, not equally well appointed, perhaps, but sufficiently authorized in all cases when doing a good work. They were not mere straws on the flood, and yet the flood has moved directly on, leaving them we know not where. In the completed society they are all gone by and forgot, and not even ministers, in the cleric sense, any longer remain—only all are made priests unto God in their ransomed state of exaltation, and all do service work, as ministers for the common good of all. I do not by this intend to say that there are no precedences in stature, and personal weight, and consequent dignity and power. They move in great quaternions doubtless, and holy satrapies—thrones, dominions, principalities, powers—but we are only to see, in this, that they are all regnant alike in their order, which is what these figures signify. Some of them are as much above all priestly and pontifical orders, and carry a sway as much more advanced as they are more transcendently advanced in thought, and weight, and character. And yet they fall into their places, unenvied, undecried, there to be admired and loved, and had in reverence gladly, because they are wanted for the perfect society by the humbler natures themselves. In one view these more advanced ones are lifted into virtual leadership, because they have such weight of being and true counsel as makes them leaders gladly accepted.

It is another point to be observed, that there is no theologic base in the society thus organized. Because the new faith now is alive all through in the society finished; which is itself a confession unwritten, only more full and perfect than there could be in any most rugged articulations of doctrine. They require of course to be fastened by no bonds of catechism or creed, in order to keep their liberty safe; for being the truth themselves they can bear to be free. Some of us here below are much concerned for these matters, much concerned for theology; and perhaps with reason, considering how much of trammel is wanted to keep organization safe among creatures that are unsafe. But there is no such concern above. Theology is there even quite gone by, and nothing but truth remains. And there is more truth alive in a single one of the now free saints, than there ever was in all the fathers, and councils, and schools of the world. These are grown up now into Christ the head, from whom the whole body is fitly joined together.

But these are negatives mainly. Passing over then to what is more positive, we begin to look after the crystallizing power in which the grand celestial society is organized. And—

First of all and at the base of all we find the righteousness and love of God. The righteousness of God is God in everlasting, absolute right, and all created beings who are with him in it, standing fast in sinless integrity, will be organized by it, as their common inspiration. For not even they will be self-righteous in their integrity, but will have the righteousness of God by faith upon them—an everlasting inbreathing, or influx, an eternal radiation from the central sun—and be organized by it, as the common bliss of their conduct and character. But as far as the great all-worlds' society is made up of spirits that were fallen, these could not be organized till the righteousness gone by is somehow restored, and become a new inspiration. And here comes in the love of God as the quickening grace of the cross, for it is at once the wonder of God's love, and the organizing power of it, that he loves against all unloveliness, loves what offends him, what disgusts his feeling, the wrong, the cruel, the abhorrent, descending to any bitterest sacrifice that he may gather even such into his family and friendship. Could he only love the lovable it would not signify much; and not any more, as respects organization, if we should do the same. The society organized would only be a society of mutual admiration—a picture gallery in perfect good taste and nothing more. No, there is a grandly tragic side of God's glory which is not here. That can only be seen when his love takes hold of the bad, the wrong, the shameful, and defiled, able to suffer cost and be redeeming love. Only blood can show these tragic depths in God. Of course we can not congratulate ourselves that we have sinned, but if there be vast orders of being, as many think, who have not, one can not but regret the very little knowledge they must have of what is in the love of God. All that is deepest, grandest in God's character must be to them, so far, a hidden book. And if they have not learned themselves to love, and suffer cost for the bad, even their noble integrity will leave them something to regret, though perhaps they will make up in chastity what they lack in experience, and obtain also by their questions what they have not learned by defilement and sorrow.

Again the great all-worlds' society is still farther advanced in organization by worship. It coalesces in worship; and worship, as it is the grandest felicity, so it is the most effective spell of organization. Of course we do not take the impression that singing hymns about the throne of God and the Lamb, is the total occupation of the everlasting society. We only take such representations of concord in song as figures that completely express the glorious harmonies of feeling, and the common felicities and homages by which it is swayed. Worship is the highest joy of mind, because it is the looking up to behold and feel what is highest and most adorably great. Thus we take long journeys, to just behold and feel what of physical grandeur there may be in a cataract; which feeling of physical grandeur is a kind of natural worship, a feebly effective symbol of what takes place in the worship of the adoring, all-worlds' society. And in that common joy of worship—oftener silent probably than expressed—they are forever coalescent in closer and more powerful bonds, because they feel themselves together everlastingly in it.

Again they have also common works, no doubt, in which they are yet more practically organized, even as a team is brought into line by the stress of a common draught. What their works are we do not know, save as we catch brief glimpses here and there; sometimes sent forth as for guard and watch, also as couriers, also as convoys home of spirits departed, also to be escort trains for the Almighty—chariots of God counting twenty thousand, even thousands of angels. One of them, great Michael, is sent forth to head a war against the dragon-power of persecution, though exactly what that means we may not know. Perhaps they go forth on excursions among distant worlds and peoples, reporting, for new study, what of God may be discovered among them. Doubtless they have all enough to do forever, and that which is good enough and high enough for their powers.

They are united and consolidated also in the society life by their victories; for whether they have vanquished all sin, or all temptation, or great forces of hate and cruelty banded against them, they come in all as victors bearing palms, to be organized by the common all-hail, and the *te deum* that celebrates their story. Indeed they come in like an army in register, "the church of the first-born whose names are written in heaven;" and no organization is so completely made up as one that shows a complete register. As God's register also is true, there are no hangers on, no pretenders, or doubtful members. Their enrollment is by inside knowledge, and allows them to know even as they are known.

And now it only remains to note, in this connection, the very remarkable fact, coincident with what I said at the beginning, that when the Revelator John shows the grand society emerging full organized, in his last two chapters, you hardly know what world it is in, whether in the upper descending upon this, or this borne upward to the other. No matter; enough that now the eternal city-life is come, a state of exact society, represented by the figure of an exactly cubal city, as many hundreds of miles high as it is broad and long. An image that is hard and violent, and yet on the second view, wondrously significant; as if society, that loosely-shapen factor of the creation, were become the perfect cube of order, in exactest and most solid measurement.

Thus we sketch, as in stammering words, our conception of the church above, the society organized; and from this we descend to a relative conception—

II. Of the church below, the Society Organizing. It is, in fact, the same as the other, and is pouring on its trains continually to be merged in that other, and become a part of it. It is even called a family—"of whom the whole family in heaven and earth is named." Just as we sing in our sublimest of all hymns—

> One family we dwell in him,
> One church above, beneath,
> Though now divided by the stream,
> The narrow stream of death.
>
> One army of the living God,
> To his command we bow,
> Part of the host have crossed the flood,
> And part are crossing now.

The supposition here is, that in what we call the church on earth, the peoples composing it are being organized in, or into, the state of everlasting society just now described.

And here the first thing we have to settle is, that the church is not properly what we recognize under this and that formula, meeting in this and that place, presided over, taught, confessed, or kept in discipline, by one or another kind of church magistracy. The church, as we are now speaking, is what is called "the communion of saints," and the saints themselves, in their union to Christ, are the staple matter of it—all in training here for the complete society. I am not questioning, observe, the right of their covenants and cures, and forms, and ministries, or even of their parishes and bishoprics and councils. I only say that these are at best only scaffoldings all, and that the real import of what they are, and what they are for, is in the souls who are training under their husbandry. And they undoubtedly have great uses often in this way. As to there being intendancies divinely authorized and the only ones to be allowed, composing, as it were, the whole church institute in their own official right and sanction—of all this I know nothing. I suppose that it would be competent for any brotherhood, meeting in the Spirit, if not already organized, to organize in what form, under what offices and rules they please, and that in this manner any known form of organization is allowable, even that of the Quakers; if only they can find how to grow in it, and make an ever-spreading society in the communion of saints. These regimental machineries are none of them the church, they are only the scaffolding of the church, and are all alike to be done away, when that which is perfect is come.

47

The Marks of the Church

H. Martensen

Apostolicity

The epoch of inspiration and of extraordinary gifts came to an end; but the Spirit abides permanently in the Church. Inspiration had to do with the establishment of the Church, but not with its subsequent growth. By it the true foundation was laid, the perfect principle of development was bestowed. But what has once for all been given by inspiration still needs to be confirmed, to be expanded, and to be made fruitful throughout a long historical probation. The progressive development of the Church advances in close connection with the life of the world, which is to be renovated and regenerated by the Church. And inasmuch as the Church becomes a power in the history of the world, and developes herself in a free and reciprocal action upon all other agencies in human life and history,—on various nationalities and periods, on various stages of natural enlightenment and cultivation;—she must subject herself in turn to the laws of worldly development. As the Church has travelled on from that paradisaical state which inspiration had described and secured, it cannot be denied that the due relation between the divine and the human in her constitution has been in many respects very inadequately maintained; but this arose from the fact that she had necessarily to submit to the general laws of historical development, and was beset with every form of worldly influence, limiting, from without and from within, her normal growth. But in all vicissitudes of her history, in all changes of her forms of rule and modes of work, the Church has remained essentially the same; after each season of corruption and adulteration she has been renewed again to the purity of her ideal; and thus she furnishes abundant proof that she has never been forsaken by her Founder, that the spirit of her Founder has never left her.

We here stand at the very point where Catholicism and Protestantism begin to diverge. Placing ourselves in imagination at the point of time when the last of the Apostles died, we ask the question, "Where is the Apostolate now?" Catholicism answers—"It is in the living successors of the Apostles to whom the true tradition is intrusted, in Bishops, Councils, and Pope, who are to be recognised as the representatives and possessors of continual Apostolic inspiration." The Evangelical Church, on the other hand, replies—That the only full and valid embodiment and expression of the Apostolate is to be found in Holy Scripture, which is the abiding voice of the Apostles in the Church. While Catholicism assumes a progressive inspiration continued through all times, Protestantism traces inspiration back to, and derives it from the Church's foundation. Historical criticism has now sufficiently proved, that progressive inspiration, such as the Catholic Church lays claim to, is the very opposite of what it gives itself out to be. Ideally, the divergence between the two Churches arises from their entertaining a widely different conception of what the historical development of the Church really is. Protestantism views the history of the Church as a free development, because with the Apostolic ideal before it, the Church ever aims at and endeavours after the perfect union of its divine and human elements—"Not that I have already attained, either were already perfect, but I follow after, that I may attain it." Catholicism looks upon Church development as a mechanical and self-progressive development of tradition, in which the divine is rendered so prominent that the human element becomes a mere name. Protestantism, on the other hand, makes the essence of development to consist in their free reproduction on the part of the Church, by active labour, and continual efforts of historic reflection, of what has once for all been given her by inspiration. Catholicism considers development to be a quantitative prolongation of the beginning; forgetting that the various forms lying dormant in that pregnant beginning must become manifest in analysis, in free reciprocal relation, and even in alternate strivings with one another. . . .

Unity

As there are not Lords many, but one Lord; as there are not many Spirits, but one Holy Ghost; as there are not many humanities, but one Humanity; which is to be united with Christ the Head; so certainly there is but ONE Church (Eph. iv. 6). But this true unity reveals itself in variety and manifoldness. We see, even in the first and apostolic church, how the One Spirit revealed Himself in many gifts, and how the One Christ is represented in various aspects by the Apostles. In its relation with the world, with various nationalities, and at different stages of human development, the one Church has been divided by a variety of confessions, and by different formulae, or church symbols. The differences and separations involved in these different confessions must be viewed as arising from our sinful nature, in so far as they maintain points of truth exclusively relative and partial, or even errors, to be absolute truth. These various confessions are in reality individual embodiments of Christianity, the germs of which lay hid as possibilities in the apostolic church, but which did not become active until the fulness of the times, and which, as they appear, are to be looked upon as so many progressive stages in the education of Christendom and its advance toward perfection. In so far as these differences of Creed are the result of sin, they must be looked upon as perishable fragments, which must be cast away; but so far as they have their foundation in the necessary varieties of human life, they will be established and purified, and they should be viewed as gifts of grace, and types of apostolic doctrine. These various confessions must be looked upon as various chambers, various dwellings in the house of the one Lord. "In my Father's house are many mansions," (John xiv. 2). To distinguish what is erroneous and sinful in these confessions, from what has its foundation only in the actual varieties of human life, is among the most difficult tasks of ecclesiastical history; and constitutes the main difficulty in all questions of church union.

Universality

The one Church is at the same time the UNIVERSAL Church; universality or catholicity is the outward and historical expression of its unity. The unity of the Church must thus become manifest in historical activity. If there were not a common, universal bond of ecclesiastical union, historically uniting the various particular churches, the unity of the Church would be merely an ideal thing, a mere invisibility. The ecclesiastical universality, which stands high above all individual differences, whether confessional or national, is the APOSTOLIC. The only really Catholic Church is therefore the Apostolic, because it is founded upon Apostolic tradition, and preserves the connection with the Apostolic mother Church as that tradition advances from generation to generation,—holding fast the primitive and apostolic doctrine as of continual value and universal authority. The authentic statement of this apostolic tradition is furnished in the New Testament; and hence it follows that the really Catholic Church must also be the Church which is conformable to Scripture. But the present Church has its connection with the apostolic community in virtue also of that fundamental confession, the apostolic symbol, in which the early church expresses the doctrine received from the Apostles, and hands it down as a pattern and type to the present day. This apostolic confession of faith was afterwards more accurately defined and developed,— in opposition to individual and heretical notions,—in the Nicene and Athanasian creeds. Throughout church history these œcumenical symbols have ever been esteemed the fundamental types of all church confessions; not only on account of their traditional authority, but on account of their Scripturalness and eternal verity; and all the various confessions are tested as forms of the Catholic Church by their recognition of these œcumenical fundamental creeds; which exist anterior to and independently of the separations of Greek Catholic and Roman Catholic, of the Lutheran Church and the Reformed. . . .

Holiness

The Church, one and universal, is also HOLY. True unity and universality have their basis in what is holy, and apart from holiness all is partial and perishable. The holy church stands out distinctly from the world: it does not take its rise from a merely natural development, like the kingdoms of the world, nor from the self-development of the spirit of man. God, the Holy Ghost, is the author and principle of its growth, and its aim is not merely the culture of the human race, but the redemption and sanctification of every man. But inasmuch as the church necessarily has the world within its pale as well as without—the divine spirit being united in her with sinful humanity—her development is not absolutely but only relatively perfect. The church is absolutely faultless as regards her principle and her beginning; absolutely faultless also as to her final aim; but in the interval between these extremes, in her historical and free development, her relative fallibility lies. The historical development of the church is not, as Catholicism asserts, normal; it is subject, like a ship upon the billows, to the undulations of the times; and there are seasons when she fulfils her mission as "the steward of the mysteries of God," only in a most imperfect way. *Ecclesia potest deficere.* But the Holy Ghost, who abides within her, is her invisible preserver and Reformer, withstanding the encroachments of worldliness; and though particular churches may lose their spiritual life in the world, the church herself can never become secularized. Notwithstanding corruptions, notwithstanding relative pauses and backslidings, the church holds on her course, and cannot miss her final goal. *Ecclesia non potest deficere.*

The ideal holiness of the Church affects alike the whole community and each individual member, and its healthy development depends upon the reciprocal influences of both these upon each other. The growth of the individual Christian towards Christ-like perfection is conditioned by the degree of perfection attained by the entire fellowship; and on the other hand, the perfection of the fellowship is influenced by the state of each individual member;—being advanced by those in whom the ideal of a free personal vitality is realized, in whom the idea of a universal priesthood of Christians (1 Peter ii. 9), has become a truth, and whose piety and spirituality leaven the entire lump. . . .

Militancy

For as much as the Church has the world without as well as within her pale, she is the holy church MILITANT. Whereas the Roman Catholic Church carries on its contest, chiefly with the outward world, and is content to rid itself by external means of the hostile elements which she finds within her, (by excommunication for example, and the burning of heretics); the Evangelical Church strives, on the other hand, by spiritual means to solve the inward contradictions which exist in relation both to doctrine and to practice, to realize her holy ideal, and to obtain the victory over her spiritual foes by the power of the Spirit and the Word. The true Church, seeing that we have to wage war, "not against flesh and blood, but against principalities, against powers, against spiritual wickedness" (Eph. vi. 12), acknowledges her own sinfulness and her infinite distance from the ideal. "Not as though I had already attained, either were already perfect" (Phil. iii. 12). The true Church is ever putting forth new endeavours to reform and purify herself according to the reforming patterns. We can trace this criticizing and reforming movement in the Church's history from the first century downwards; it never dies; even in the darkness of the middle ages, there have not been wanting witnesses of evangelical truth (*testes veritatis*) who have criticized the corruptions of the Church;—a line of witnesses which cannot fail, because the Holy Ghost has never wholly forsaken His Church. Even in the darkest days the word spoken to the despairing prophet Elijah has been true, "Yet have I left me seven thousand in Israel, who have not bowed the knee before Baal" (1 Kings xix. 18.) A reforming activity appears within the Church in every age; but the chief era of reformation, the greatest reforming catastrophe, took place in the sixteenth century; and this is pre-eminently styled the Reformation.

Triumph

The Church militant is also the Church TRIUMPHANT; the gates of hell shall not prevail against her. The Church's victory is not only a final one at the end of time; it is a progressive victory in every age. After the pattern of her Lord, she is herself developed, not only by a progressive course of sufferings, but also in an ever-advancing course of joyous resurrection. "Destroy this temple," said our Lord, "and in three days will I raise it up!" This saying holds good in reference to the Church, as well as to our Lord. Herein consists the triumph of the Church in history;—in virtue of the indwelling spirit, she continually renews herself; after every interval of corruption and dissolution, when she lay in ruins, when faith seemed to be vanquished by the world, she has risen anew, like life from the dead. That vision of the prophet Ezekiel—wherein he saw the valley of dry bones, and, behold, they were very dry, and the Spirit of the Lord came from the four winds, and breathed upon the slain, and they lived again, and the breath came into them;—that vision is a parable of the spiritual resurrection of the Church, repeated in her history from age to age. This fact that the Church has never wholly died out, but ever rises anew from the dead, is a pledge, a certain surety, of her future glory.

48

The Importance of Local Congregations

J. M. Pendleton

The term *church* frequently occurs in the New Testament. It may be found there more than a hundred times. The word thus translated means congregation or assembly, but it does not indicate the purpose for which the congregation or assembly meets. Hence it is used Acts xix. 32, 39, 41, and rendered *assembly*. In every other place in the New Testament it is translated *church*. In its application to the followers of Christ it is usually, if not always, employed to designate a particular congregation of saints or the redeemed in the aggregate. It is used in the latter sense in several passages, as, for example, when Paul says, "Christ also loved the church, and gave himself for it; . . . that he might present it to himself a glorious church, not having spot or wrinkle, or any such thing." Eph. v. 25-27. In these places and in several others it would be absurd to define the term "church" as meaning a particular congregation of Christians meeting in one place for the worship of God.

The other signification of the word claims special attention. In a large majority of instances it is used in the Scriptures to denote a local assembly convened for religious purposes. Thus we read of "the church at Jerusalem," "the church of the Thessalonians," "the church of Ephesus," "the church in Smyrna." Nor are we to suppose that it required a large number of persons to constitute a church. Paul refers to Aquila and Priscilla, and "the church that is in their house;" to "Nymphas, and the church which is in his house." 1 Cor. xvi. 19; Col. iv. 15. A congregation of saints, organized according to the New Testament, whether that congregation is large or small, is a church. The inspired writers, as if to preclude the idea of a church commensurate with a province, a kingdom, or an empire, make use of the following forms of expression: "the churches of Galatia," "the churches of Macedonia," "the churches of Galatia," "the churches of Macedonia," "the churches of Asia," "the churches of Judea." But they never say "the church of Galatia," "the church of Macedonia." Wherever Christianity prevailed in apostolic times there was a plurality of churches.

In answer to the question, What is a church? it may be said, A church is a congregation of Christ's baptized disciples, acknowledging him as their Head, relying on his atoning sacrifice for justification before God, depending on the Holy Spirit for sanctification, united in the belief of the gospel, agreeing to maintain its ordinances and obey its precepts, meeting together for worship, and co-operating for the extension of Christ's kingdom in the world. If any prefer an abridgment of this definition, it may be given thus: A church is a congregation of Christ's baptized disciples, united in the belief of what he has said, and covenanting to do what he has commanded.

If this definition of the term "church" is correct, it is manifest that membership is preceded by important qualifications. These qualifications may be considered as moral and ceremonial. All moral qualifications are embraced in Regeneration, with its attendants, Repentance and Faith, already discussed.

It is obvious that the purposes of church organization can be carried into effect by regenerate persons alone. Those who become members of a church must first have exercised "repentance toward God and faith toward our Lord Jesus Christ." They are "called to be saints," and must "walk worthy of the vocation wherewith [they] are called."

Baptism is the ceremonial qualification for church membership. There can, according to the Scriptures, be no visible church without baptism. An observance of this ordinance is the believer's first public act of obedience to Christ. Regeneration, repentance, and faith are private matters between God and the soul. They involve internal piety, but of this piety there must be an external manifestation. This manifestation is made in baptism. The penitent, regenerate believer is baptized into the name of the Father, and of the Son, and of the Holy Spirit. There is a visible, symbolic expression of a new relationship to the three persons of the Godhead—a relationship entered into in repentance, faith, and regeneration. As Baptism will be the topic of a distinct chapter, it is briefly referred to here.

Officers of a Church

It cannot be said that officers are essential to the existence of a church, for a church must exist before it can appoint its officers. After this appointment, if, in the providence of God, they should be removed by death, it might affect the interests, but not the being, of a church. It has been well said that "although officers are not necessary to the being of a church, they are necessary to its well-being." Paul, referring to Christ's ascension gifts, says: "And he gave some, apostles; and some, prophets; and some, evangelists; and some, pastors and teachers; for the perfecting of the saints, for the work of the ministry, for the edifying of the body of Christ." Eph. iv. 11, 12. Apostles, prophets, and evangelists filled extraordinary and temporary offices. There are no such offices now. Pastors and teachers, the same men, are the ordinary and permanent spiritual officers of the churches, while the office of deacon has special reference to the secular interests of the churches. Of these two offices, the following things may be said:

1. Pastors.—This term was first applied to ministers having oversight of churches. The reason, no doubt, was in the resemblance between the work of a pastor and that of a literal shepherd. A shepherd has under his charge a flock, for which he must care and for whose wants he must provide. The sheep and the lambs must be looked after. The Lord Jesus, "that great Shepherd of the sheep" (Heb. xiii. 20), virtually says to all his undershepherds, as he did to Peter, "Feed my lambs," "Feed my sheep." John xxi. 15, 16. It is worthy of remark that this

language was not addressed to Peter until the Saviour had obtained from him an affirmative answer to the question, "Lovest thou me?" As if he had said, "I love my spiritual flock so well that I cannot entrust the sheep and lambs composing it to any man who does not love me." Love to Christ must be regarded in all ages and in all places as the pastor's supreme qualification. All other qualifications are worthless if this is absent. Talent and learning are not to be undervalued, but they must be kept under the control of piety and receive its sanctifying impress.

The work of pastors is referred to by Paul when he says, "If a man desire the office of a bishop, he desireth a good work." 1 Tim. iii. 1. It is indeed a good work—the best work on earth—but a work. The term *bishop* must not be suffered to suggest any such idea as its modern acceptation implies. In apostolic times there were no bishops having charge of the churches in a district of country, in a province, or a kingdom. A bishop was the pastor of a church, and the New Testament, so far from encouraging a plurality of churches under one pastor, refers in two instances at least to a plurality of pastors in one church. (See Acts xx. 28; Phil. i. 1.) In the former passage the elders of the church of Ephesus are called *overseers*, and the word thus translated is the same rendered *bishop* in Phil. i. 1; 1 Tim. iii. 2; Tit. i. 7; 1 Pet. ii. 25. Thus does it appear that pastor, bishop, and elder are three terms designating the same office. This view is further confirmed by a reference to 1 Pet. v. 1, 2, where elders are exhorted to "feed the flock of God"—that is, to perform the office of pastor—"taking the oversight thereof;" that is, acting the part of bishops, or overseers. For the word translated "taking the oversight" belongs to the same family of words as the term rendered "bishop" in the passages cited. It is plain, therefore, that a pastor's work is the spiritual oversight of the flock, the church he serves. Like a good literal shepherd, he must care for the feeble and the sick as well as for the healthy and the vigorous. Some he can feed with "strong meat," while others can digest nothing but "milk." He must exercise a sanctified discretion, and "study to show" himself "approved unto God, a workman that needeth not to be ashamed, rightly dividing the word of truth." 2 Tim. ii. 15. Much depends on dividing the word of truth rightly; hence the necessity of study, prayerful study, imbued with the Spirit of the Master.

The administration of the ordinances—which are two, baptism and the Lord's Supper—as well as the preaching of the word, is the proper business of the pastor. As it does not accord with the plan of this volume to elaborate any topic, the work of the pastor cannot be enlarged on, nor is there room to present the many motives to pastoral fidelity. The mention of two must suffice: The church over whose interests the pastor watches has been bought with "the precious blood of Christ," and the faithful pastor will, when "the chief Shepherd" comes, "receive a crown of glory that fadeth not away." 1 Pet. v. 4. What motives to diligence and faithfulness could possess more exhaustless power?

2. Deacons.—The office of deacon originated in a state of things referred to in the sixth chapter of the Acts of the Apostles. It is said, that "when the number of the disciples was multiplied, there arose a murmuring of the Grecians against the Hebrews, because their widows were neglected in the daily ministration." The "Grecians" were Jews as well as the Hebrews, but they spoke the Greek language, and were probably not natives of Palestine. The members of the church at Jerusalem "had all things in common," and a distribution was made out of the common stock "as every man had need." Acts iv. 35. This seems to have been done at first under the immediate direction of the apostles; and the intimation is that the large increase of the church interfered with an impartial distribution of supplies. The apostles saw that if they made it their business to "serve tables," it would greatly hinder their work in its spiritual aspects. They said, "It is not reason that we should leave the word of God, and serve tables. Wherefore, brethren, look ye out among you seven men of honest report, full of the Holy Ghost and wisdom, whom we may appoint over this business. But we will give ourselves continually to prayer, and to the ministry of the word." Acts vi. 3, 4.

Thus the creation of the office of deacon recognizes the fact that the duties of pastors are pre-eminently spiritual, and that they should not be burdened with the secular interests of the churches.

The words "men of honest report, full of the Holy Ghost and wisdom," applied to the first deacons, indicate that they were men of unblemished reputation, ardent piety, and good common sense. The phrase "full of the Holy Ghost" is an admirable definition of fervent, elevated piety; and in the selection of deacons their spirituality must be regarded, for their duties are not exclusively secular. Their secular duties, however, should be performed in a spiritual frame of mind, and in this way they "purchase to themselves a good degree, and great boldness in the faith which is in Christ Jesus." 1 Tim. iii. 13. In visiting the poor to distribute the charities of the church, deacons must not perform the duty in a formal manner, but must inquire into the spiritual as well as the worldly circumstances of the recipients of the church's bounty. They will often witness such an exhibition of faith, patience, gratitude, and resignation as will richly repay them for their labor of love. As occasion may require, they should report to the pastor such cases as need his special attention, and thus they will become a connecting link between the pastor and the needy ones of the church.

As deacons were first appointed "to serve tables," it may be well to say that there are three tables for them to serve:

1. The table of the poor; 2. The table of the Lord; 3. The table of the pastor. The pecuniary supplies to enable them to serve these tables must be furnished by the church. The custom of taking a "collection" for the poor after the celebration of the Lord's Supper is a good one. It is suitable at the close of the solemn service to think of the pious poor whom sickness or some other misfortune may have kept from the sacred feast.

As some pecuniary expenditure is necessary in furnishing the table of the Lord, this should be made through the deacons; and it is eminently proper, though not indispensable, for them to wait on the communicants in the distribution of the elements.

Deacons should serve the pastor's table. It is not for them to decide how liberally or scantily it shall be supplied. The church must make the decision, and enlarged views should be taken when it is made, for the energies of hundreds of pastors are greatly impaired by an incompetent support. The pastor's compensation having been agreed on by the church, the deacons must see that it is raised and paid over. They may appoint one of their number acting treasurer, who shall receive and pay out funds; but it should never be forgotten that deacons were originally, by virtue of their office, the treasurers of the church.

As all pecuniary expenditures are to be made through deacons, they should at the end of every year make a report to the church of what moneys they have received during the year, and how they have been expended. This will keep everything straight and plain, while it will do very much for the promotion of a church's influence and efficiency.

Deacons as well as pastors should be ordained to office by prayer and the laying on of hands.

Church Government

In the language of theology, and in popular language too, there are three forms of church government, known by the terms Episcopacy, Presbyterianism, and Independency.

Episcopacy recognizes the right of bishops to preside over districts of country, and one of its fundamental doctrines is that a bishop is officially superior to other ministers. Of course, a modern bishop has under his charge the "inferior clergy," for it is insisted that the "ordaining power" and "the right to rule" belong to the episcopal office. The modern application of the term "bishop" to a man who has under his charge a district of country is very objectionable. It has almost banished from Christendom the idea originally attached to the word. In apostolic times, as we have seen, "bishop," "pastor," and "elder" were terms of equivalent import.

Presbyterianism recognizes two classes of elders—preaching and ruling elders. The pastor and ruling elders of a congregation constitute what is called "the session of the church." The "session" transacts the business of the church, receives, dismisses, and excludes members. From the decisions of a session there is an appeal to the Presbytery, from the action of the Presbytery an appeal to the Synod, and from the action of the Synod an appeal to the General Assembly, whose adjudications are final and irresistible.

Independency is in irreconcilable conflict with Episcopacy and Presbyterianism, and distinctly affirms these three truths:

1. *That the governmental power is in the hands of the members of a church.* It resides with the members in contradistinction from bishops or elders; that is to say, bishops, or elders, can do nothing strictly and properly ecclesiastical without the concurrence of the members.

2. *The right of a majority of the members of a church to rule in accordance with the law of Christ.* The will of the majority having been expressed, it becomes the minority to submit.

3. *That the power of a church cannot be transferred or alienated, and that church action is final.* The power of a church cannot be delegated. There may be messengers of a church, but there cannot be, in the proper use of the term, delegates.

These are highly important principles; and while the existence of the independent form of church government depends on their recognition and application, it is an inquiry of vital moment, Does the New Testament inculcate these principles? For if it does not, whatever may be said in commendation of them, they possess no obligatory force. Does the New Testament, then, inculcate the foundation-principle of Independency— namely, that the governmental power of a church is, under Christ, with the members? Let us see.

It was the province of the apostolic churches to admit members into their communion. In Rom. xiv. 1, it is written: "Him that is weak in the faith receive ye." The import of this language is, "Receive into your fellowship and treat as a Christian him who is weak in faith." There is a command: "receive ye." To whom is this command addressed? Not to bishops, not to the pastor and "ruling elders," but to the church, for the Epistle was written "to all that be in Rome, beloved of God, called to be saints.". . .

A second principle of Independency, already announced, is

the right of a majority of the members of a church to rule in accordance with the law of Christ. I refer again to 2 Cor. ii. 6: "Sufficient to such a man is this punishment, which was inflicted of many." A literal translation of the words rendered "of many" would be "by the more"—that is, by the majority. Dr. MacKnight's translation is, "by the greater number." If, as has been shown, the governmental power of a church is with the members, it follows that a majority must rule. This is so plain a principle of Independency and of common sense, that it is needless to dwell upon it.

A third truth involved in the independent form of church government is, that the power of a church cannot be transferred or alienated, and that church action is final. The church at Corinth could not transfer her power to the church at Philippi, nor could the church at Antioch convey her authority to the church of Ephesus. Neither could all the apostolic churches combined delegate their power to an association or synod or convention. That church power is inalienable results from the foundation-principle of Independency—namely, that this power is in the hands of the people, the membership. If the power of a church cannot be transferred, church action is final. That there is no tribunal higher than a church is evident from Matt. xviii. 15-17. The Saviour lays down a rule for the adjustment of private differences among brethren: "If thy brother shall trespass against thee, go and tell him his fault." If the offender, when told of his fault, does not give satisfaction, the offended brother is to take with him "one or two more, that in the mouth of two or three witnesses every word may be established." But if the offender "shall neglect to hear them," what is to be done? Tell it to the church. What church? Evidently the particular congregation to which the parties belong. If the offender does not hear the church, what then? "Let him be unto thee as a heathen man and a publican." But can there be no appeal to an association or presbytery or conference or convention? No; there is no appeal. Shall any kind of organization put the offender back in church fellowship when the church by its action classed him with heathen men and publicans? This is too absurd. What sort of fellowship would it be?

49

Christian Baptism

J. M. Pendleton

If, as has been stated in the preceding chapter, a church is a congregation of Christ's baptized disciples, then we must consider two important questions, What is baptism? and Who are to be baptized? In other words, What is the act of baptism? and who are subjects of the ordinance? These two points now claim consideration.

I. The Act of Baptism

Baptism is the immersion in water, by a proper administrator, of a believer in Christ, into the name of the Father, and of the Son, and of the Holy Spirit. Immersion is so exclusively the baptismal act that without it there is no baptism; and a believer in Christ is so exclusively the subject of baptism that without such a subject there is no baptism. That immersion alone is the baptismal act may be shown by the following considerations:

1. *Greek lexicons give immerse, dip, or plunge, as the primary and ordinary meaning of baptizo.* Here it is proper to say that *baptizo* and *baptisma*, being Greek words, are, in the Common Version of the Scriptures, anglicized, but not translated. By this it is meant that their termination is made to correspond with the termination of English words. In *baptizo*, the final letter is changed into e; and in *baptisma*, the last letter is dropped altogether. To make this matter of anglicism plain, it is only necessary to say that if the Greek verb *rantizo* had been anglicized, we should have *rantize* in the New Testament where we now have *sprinkle*. King James I. of England, by whose order the Common Version was made in the year 1611, virtually forbade the translation of *baptize* and *baptism*. This has been sometimes denied, but it is susceptible of

conclusive proof. The king's third instruction to his translators reads thus: "The old *ecclesiastical words* to be kept, as the word *church* not to be translated 'congregation.' " It is absurd to say that this rule had exclusive reference to the word "church," for this term is plainly given as a specimen of "old ecclesiastical words." Why should plurality of idea be conveyed by the phrase "ecclesiastical words," if the rule had respect to but one word? The question, then, is, Are *baptism* and *baptize* "old ecclesiastical words"? They were words when the Bible was translated or they would not be found in it. They had been used by church historians and by writers on ecclesiastical law, and were therefore ecclesiastical. They had been in use a long time, and were consequently old. They were "old ecclesiastical words." Such words the king commanded "to be kept," "not translated." It is worthy of remark, too, that the Bishop of London at the king's instance, wrote to the translators, reminding them that His Majesty "wished his *third* and *fourth* rule to be specially observed." This circumstance must have called special attention to the rule under consideration. In view of these facts, it may, surely, be said that the translators knew what were "old ecclesiastical words." Let their testimony, then, be adduced: In their "Preface to the Reader" they say that they had, "on the one side, avoided the scrupulosity of the Puritans, who left the old ecclesiastical words and betook them to other, as when they put washing for baptism, and congregation for church; and, on the other hand, had shunned the obscurity of the Papists." Is not this enough? Here there is not only an admission that baptism was an old ecclesiastical word, but this admission is made by the translators themselves—made most cheerfully—for it was made in condemnation of the Puritans and in commendation of themselves. . . .

2. *Distinguished Pedobaptist theologians concede that baptizo means to immerse.* John Calvin, in his *Institutes*, says: "But whether the person who is baptized be wholly immersed, and whether thrice or once, or whether water be only poured or sprinkled upon him, is of no importance; churches ought to be left at liberty, in this respect, to act according to the difference of countries. The very word baptize, however, signifies to im-

merse; and it is certain that immersion was the practice of the ancient church."

We have here some of Calvin's opinions, but what concerns us is his positive testimony as to the meaning of baptize. . . .

3. *The classical usage of baptizo establishes the position that immersion is the baptismal act.* It has been already stated that lexicons are not the ultimate authority in settling the meaning of words. Lexicographers are dependent on the sense in which words are used to ascertain their meaning. But it is not impossible for them to mistake that sense. If they do, there is an appeal from their definitions to usage, which is the ultimate authority. It is well to go back to the ultimate authority. Want of room forbids the insertion of extracts from classical Greek authors, but it will be sufficient to refer to the treatise of Professor Stuart on the *Mode of Baptism.* The reader will see that the learned professor, in proving that *baptizo* means immerse, gives the word as used by various Greek authors—namely, Pindar, Heraclides Ponticus, Plutarch, Lucian, Hippocrates, Strabo, Josephus, etc. . . .

It is said by some that, though *baptizo* in classic Greek means *immerse,* it has a different meaning in the New Testament. Let them prove it. On them is the burden of proof, and they will find it a burden indeed. Let every man who takes this view answer this question: Could the New Testament writers, as honest men, use *baptizo* in a new sense without notifying their readers of the fact? It is certain that they could not, and equally certain that no such notification was ever given.

4. *The symbolic import of baptism furnishes a conclusive argument in favor of immersion.* There is in baptism a representation of the burial and resurrection of Jesus Christ. Paul says, "Know ye not that so many of us as were baptized into Jesus Christ were baptized into his death? Therefore we were buried with him by baptism into death; that like as Christ was raised up from the dead by the glory of the Father, even so we also should walk in newness of life. For if we have been planted together in the likeness of his death, we shall be also in the likeness of his resurrection" (Rom. vi. 3-5); "Buried with him in baptism, wherein also ye are risen with him, through the faith of the operation of God who raised him from the dead." Col. ii. 12.

Peter says, "The like figure whereunto even baptism doth also now save us (not the putting away of the filth of the flesh, but the answer of a good conscience toward God), by the resurrection of Jesus Christ." 1 Pet. iii. 21.

It is clear from these passages that baptism has a commemorative reference to the burial and resurrection of Christ. The two ordinances of the gospel symbolically proclaim the three great facts of the gospel. These facts, as Paul teaches (1 Cor. xv. 3, 4), are that Christ died, was buried, and rose again. The Lord's Supper commemorates the first fact. At his table the disciples of Jesus are solemnly reminded that he, for their sakes, submitted to the agonies of death. They weep over him as crucified, dead. In baptism they see him buried and raised again, just as they see him dead in the sacred Supper. Baptism is therefore a symbolic proclamation of two of the three prominent facts of the gospel—the burial and resurrection of Christ. . . .

II. The Subjects of Baptism

While the import of the word "baptize" indicates what is the baptismal act, it does not determine who are to be baptized. We must therefore look elsewhere than to the meaning of the word to ascertain who are scriptural subjects of baptism. Where shall we look? Evidently to the commission given by Christ to his apostles, for this commission is the supreme authority for the administration of baptism. Apart from it there is no authority to baptize. The circumstances connected with the giving of this commission were replete with interest. The Saviour had finished the work which he came down from heaven to accomplish. He had offered himself a sacrifice for sin. He had exhausted the cup of atoning sorrow. He had lain in the dark mansions of the grave. He had risen in triumph from the dead, and was about to ascend to the right hand of the Majesty on high. Invested with perfect mediatorial authority, he said to his apostles:

"All power is given unto me in heaven and in earth. Go ye, therefore, and teach all nations, baptizing them in the name of the Father, and of the Son, and of the Holy Ghost; teaching them to observe all things whatsoever I have commanded you" (Matt. xxviii. 18-20); "Go ye into all the world, and preach the gospel to every creature. He that believeth and is baptized shall be saved; but he that believeth not shall be damned" (Mark xvi. 15, 16); "Thus it is written, and thus it behoved Christ to suffer, and to rise from the dead the third day; and that repentance and remission of sins should be preached in his name among all nations, beginning at Jerusalem." Luke xxiv. 46, 47.

Surely the language of this commission is plain. Matthew informs us that making disciples (for the word translated "teach" means to make disciples) is to precede baptism; Mark establishes the priority of faith to baptism; and Luke connects repentance and remission of sins with the execution of the commission. No man can, in obedience to this commission, baptize an unbeliever or an unconscious infant. The unbeliever is not a penitent disciple, and it is clearly impossible for the infant to repent and believe the gospel. . . .

It will be said by those who oppose the views of Baptists—for it has been said a thousand times—that if infants are not to be baptized because they cannot believe, they will not be saved because they cannot believe. If the salvation of infants depends on their faith, they cannot be saved. They are incapable of faith. They are, doubtless, saved through the mediation of Christ, but it is not by faith. Our opponents fail to accomplish their object in urging this objection to our views. They must intend to make us admit the propriety of infant baptism or force us to deny infant salvation. But we make neither the admission nor the denial. When we say that infants are saved, not by faith, but without faith, their objection is demolished.

In considering the commission of Christ it is well to observe how it was understood and carried into effect in apostolic times. The first practical interpretation of it was given on the day of Pentecost. Acts ii. The gospel was preached, the people were pierced to the heart, and cried out, "Men and brethren, what shall we do?" Peter replied, "Repent and be baptized, every one of you." No man will say that the command "repent" is applicable to infants, and it is certain that the same persons were called on to repent and be baptized. The result of Peter's sermon is given in the following words: "Then they that gladly received his word were baptized: and the same day there were added unto them about three thousand souls." ver. 41. The baptism was limited to those who gladly received Peter's words; and as infants were not of that number, to infer that they were baptized is utterly gratuitous. The Pentecostal administration of baptism shows that penitent believers were considered the only subjects of the ordinance. . . .

Without enlarging on these topics, what is the conclusion of the whole matter? Clearly this: The commission of Christ, as understood and exemplified in the apostolic age, requires the baptism of believers, disciples; and the baptism of all others, whether unbelievers or unconscious infants, is utterly unwarranted. There is, as Paul has written in the Epistle to the Ephesians, "one Lord, one faith, one baptism." ch. iv. 5. The one Lord is the object of the one faith, the one faith embraces the one Lord, and the one baptism is a profession of the one faith in the one Lord.

The baptism is one in the action involved, and one in the subjects of the action. I can see it in no other light.

50

The Lord's Supper

H. Martensen

Baptism is the setting-up of the new covenant; the Lord's Supper is its renewal. By baptism man is incorporated into the new kingdom, and the possibility of, the necessary requirements for, the new personality are given therein: by means of the Lord's Supper this new personality is brought to perfection.

Differences of creed gather round the Lord's Supper especially, as round a central point, because it is the sacrament of those of full age, and it has, therefore, specially to do with the reciprocal relations between divine grace and the free will of man.

The Lord's Supper, as a church ordinance, must be looked upon as an act of confession, appointed by the Lord to refresh our remembrance of Him. As the Passover in Israel was to be a means of renewing the recollection of the covenant of the Lord with Israel, and as an act of thanksgiving for the deliverance from Egyptian bondage, the Lord's Supper is in like manner a commemoration and a giving of thanks—a Eucharist—on account of the propitiation and redemption provided in Christ; a sacred feast in which the partakers "show forth the Lord's death." In partaking of the bread, they must think with gratitude of Him, whose body was broken in death; in partaking of the cup they must think of Him whose blood was shed for the remission of sins; they must recognize themselves as permanent sharers in the new covenant, desiring to grow and increase in the fellowship of their Lord. But the Lord's Supper is not only an act of confession on the part of the Church, it also involves a present act of Christ himself. He who said, "This do in remembrance of Me," also declared, "Lo! I am with you always." It is His will that His Church think of Him, not as the absent but as the present Lord, not as the dead Christ, but as risen from the dead, as the Redeemer living in their midst. With the recognition of this truth, the recognition of the mystery begins. In the Lord's Supper the believer must not only look back to the death of the Lord and His crucifixion, he must also look up to the risen Redeemer, now ascended up into heaven, who fills His Church with the fulness of His power, and allows those words to be realized in their full import in the sacrament, when it is performed in harmony with His command.

If it be understood that the mystery of the Lord's Supper consists in this: that it is not only a human act of commemoration and thanksgiving, but an act of the heaven-ascended Redeemer,—a living bond between heaven and earth,—it will also be recognized as the holy pledge of the renewal of the Covenant. As often as thou eatest this bread, and drinkest this cup, the

Lord renews the covenant of grace with thee which was established in thy baptism, assures thee anew of the forgiveness of thy sins, vouchsafes to thee anew the comfort of His atonement! Graciously true as all this is, it does not constitute the mystery of the sacrament. The Lord has associated with His Supper not only the promise of forgiveness of sins, and a display and explanation of grace, but under the sacred pledges of grace He gives to His own people a new aliment of life. "This is my body," "This is my blood" (Matt. xxvi. 26-28; Mark xiv. 22-24; Luke xxii. 19, 20; 1 Cor. xi. 24, 25). However variously these words may be explained, they clearly indicate an actual participation of Life with the Lord. "Except ye eat the flesh of the Son of man, and drink His blood, ye have no life in you," John vi. 53: Unless ye so appropriate Me, that not only my word and my promise, but I Myself—my whole undivided personality, become the aliment of your life, you have not life. Though these words are not spoken in immediate connection with the Lord's Supper, it is nevertheless plain, that they must find their full and complete realization in this ordinance. If, however, there is this union with Jesus in an especial manner in the Lord's Supper; if, again, this special union is, by the express words of the Lord, associated with and conditional upon the partaking of bread and wine, the question arises, In what way is this union to be explained? how is it to be defined? How are we to understand this relation between the heavenly aliment, between the invisible gift of grace and the visible gifts of nature, represented in the bread and wine? It is upon this point that creeds and confessions disagree. Some consider this controversy useless and unpractical, because these things cannot be the subject of human comprehension. But our business here is not to comprehend what in its nature is and must be above our comprehension, but to arrive at a true conception of what the mystery is. Our province is not to endeavour to solve the mystery by means of human sophistry. The Christian confessions, with the exception of the Zwinglian, unanimously teach, that in the Lord's Supper we have to bow before a most sacred mystery. The question is, What is that mystery before which we have to bow?

The common view is that of the real presence . . . and real communication of the Lord himself. The Roman Catholic Church takes this to be so immediate, as to annihilate all that is symbolical and natural in the ordinance; according to her, the visible signs are changed into the body and blood of the Lord; the substance of the bread and wine is literally transformed into the substance of the body and blood of Christ; and earthly bread and wine only seem to be present to the senses. Against this doctrine of Transubstantiation,—which volatilizes the natural elements into mere appearances, and detracts from the kingdom of nature in order to magnify the kingdom of grace,—the whole Evangelical Church protests, and gives to the visible signs their due place in their natural and independent state. "Bread is bread, and wine is wine," and these are only symbols of the body and blood of Christ. In this sense, as the rejection and denial of Transubstantiation, the entire Evangelical Church adopts Zwingli's exclamation, . . . "This is what it means." Zwingli's intelligent view obtains in this historical connection greater weight than one would otherwise feel disposed to accord to it. Zwingli himself indeed was content to abide for the most part by this protest merely; Luther, on the other hand, maintained the real presence of the Lord, but a presence which is veiled or hidden beneath the outward and natural signs, and which communicates its heavenly gifts of grace in, with, and beneath these. Calvin endeavoured to take a middle course between Zwingli and Luther, but his theory of the real presence presents only the one-sidedness of opposition to the doctrine of Transubstantiation.

Calvin's doctrine is biassed by opposition to the extreme doctrine of transubstantiation, inasmuch as it somewhat unfairly separates what, according to Catholicism, is one and indissoluble. Calvin's doctrine rests upon a dualism, distinguishing between the kingdom of grace and that of nature, between heaven and earth, Spirit and body. The glorified Saviour cannot be present upon earth, for upon the laws of corporeity and individuality He must be in a definite place in heaven. In the celebration of the Lord's Supper upon earth, therefore, there is nothing more than the distribution and partaking of bread and wine; but when these are partaken of in faith, something occurs simultaneously in heaven, for the believing soul is as if transported into heaven, by the mystical working of the Spirit, and in a supernatural manner is united to the Saviour, and made partaker of His glorified body, as the true aliment of the Spirit. . . . The Lord's Supper, according to the Calvinistic view, thus divides itself into two parts, or consists of two acts, one in heaven, the other on earth; one in spirit, the other in body. It is only the faithful who take part in the heavenly act; the unbelieving may go through the outward celebration—partaking of the bread and wine, and nothing more; and could we imagine a communion in which all the guests were unbelievers, there would be no real sacrament, but only the outward semblance of one. Whereas, according to the view taken by the Catholic Church, the heavenly part is present as an immediate object, appearing with the entire impress of the external reality,—according to the Calvinistic view the presence of Christ is purely spiritual, a presence only in the devotion and in the inwardness of the believing heart.

The Lutheran doctrine is opposed not only to the doctrine of transubstantiation, but to the Calvinistic separation of heaven and earth likewise. Christ is not in a literal manner separate from His believing people, so as that they must go to heaven in order to find Him. Christ is on the right hand of God; but the right hand of God is everywhere. . . . And therefore He is present wholly and entirely . . . in His Supper, wherein He in an especial manner wills to be. There are not in the ordinance two acts, one heavenly and one earthly, distinct from each other, but the heavenly is comprehended in the earthly and visible act, and is organically united therewith, thus constituting one sacramental act. The heavenly substance is communicated in, with, and under the earthly substances. And as the sacramental communion is not a partaking of the corporeal nature of Christ apart from His spiritual nature, no more is it a mere partaking of the spiritual nature of Christ apart from His corporeity. It is one and undivided, a spiritual and corporeal communion.

51

The Coming of Christ

Charles Hodge

This is a very comprehensive and very difficult subject. It is intimately allied with all the other great doctrines which fall under the head of eschatology. It has excited so much interest in all ages of the Church, that the books written upon it would of themselves make a library. The subject cannot be adequately discussed without taking a survey of all the prophetic teachings of the Scriptures both of the Old Testament and of the New. This task cannot be satisfactorily accomplished by any one who has not made the study of the prophecies a specialty. The author, knowing that he has no such qualifications for the work, purposes to confine himself in a great measure to a historical survey of the different schemes of interpreting the Scriptural prophecies relating to this subject.

The first point to be considered is the true design of prophecy, and how that design is to be ascertained. Prophecy is very different from history. It is not intended to give us a knowledge of the future, analogous to that which history gives us of the past. The truth is often overlooked. We see interpreters undertaking to give detailed expositions of the prophecies of Isaiah, of Ezekiel, of Daniel, and of the Apocalypse, relating to the future, with the same confidence with which they would record the history of the recent past. Such interpretations have always been falsified by the event. But this does not discourage a certain class of minds, for whom the future has a fascination and who delight in the solution of enigmas, from renewing the attempt. In prophecy, instruction is subordinate to moral impression. The occurrence of important events is so predicted as to produce in the minds of the people of God faith that they will certainly come to pass. Enough is made known of their nature, and of the time

355

and mode of their occurrence, to awaken attention, desire, or apprehension, as the case may be; and to secure proper effort on the part of those concerned to be prepared for what is to come to pass. Although such predictions may be variously misinterpreted before their fulfilment; yet when fulfilled, the agreement between the prophecy and the event is seen to be such as to render the divine origin of the prophecy a matter of certainty. Thus with regard to the first advent of Christ, the Old Testament prophecies rendered it certain that a great Redeemer was to appear; that He was to be a Prophet, Priest, and King; that He would deliver his people from their sins, and from the evils under which they groaned; that He was to establish a kingdom which should ultimately absorb all the kingdoms on earth; and that He would render all his people supremely happy and blessed. These predictions had the effect of turning the minds of the whole Jewish nation to the future, in confident expectation that the Deliverer would come; of exciting earnest desire for his advent; and of leading the pious portion of the people to prayerful preparation for that event. Nevertheless, of all the hundreds of thousands to whom these predictions of the Hebrew Scriptures were made known, not a single person, so far as appears, interpreted them aright; yet, when fulfilled, we can almost construct a history of the events from these misunderstood predictions concerning them. Christ was indeed a king, but no such king as the world had ever seen, and such as no man expected; He was a priest, but the only priest that ever lived of whose priesthood he was Himself the victim; He did establish a kingdom, but it was not of this world. It was foretold that Elias should first come and prepare the way of the Lord. He did come; but in a way in which no man did or could have anticipated.

It follows, from what has been said, that prophecy makes a general impression with regard to future events, which is reliable and salutary, while the details remain in obscurity. The Jews were not disappointed in the general impression made on their minds by the predictions relating to the Messiah. It was only in the explanation of details that they failed. The Messiah was a king; He did sit upon the throne of David, but not in the way in which they expected; He is to subdue all nations, not by the sword, as they supposed, but by truth and love; He was to make his people priests and kings, but not worldly princes and satraps. The utter failure of the Old Testament Church in interpreting the prophecies relating to the first advent of Christ, should teach us to be modest and diffident in explaining those which relate to his second coming. We should be satisfied with the great truths which those prophecies unfold, and leave the details to be explained by the event. This the Church, as a Church, has generally done.

The Common Church Doctrine.

The common Church doctrine is, first, that there is to be a second personal, visible, and glorious advent of the Son of God. Secondly, that the events which are to precede that advent, are

1. The universal diffusion of the Gospel; or, as our Lord expresses it, the ingathering of the elect; this is the vocation of the Christian Church.

2. The conversion of the Jews, which is to be national. As their casting away was national, although a remnant was saved; so their conversion may be national, although some may remain obdurate.

3. The coming of Antichrist.

Thirdly, that the events which are to attend the second advent are:—

1. The resurrection of the dead, of the just and of the unjust.
2. The general judgment.
3. The end of the world. And,
4. The consummation of Christ's kingdom.

The Personal Advent of Christ

It is admitted that the words "coming of the Lord" are often used in Scripture for any signal manifestation of his presence either for judgment or for mercy. When Jesus promised to manifest Himself to his disciples, "Judas saith unto Him, not Iscariot, Lord, how is it that thou wilt manifest thyself unto us, and not unto the world? Jesus answered and said unto him, If a man love me he will keep my words: and my Father will love him, and we will come unto him, and make our abode with him." (John xiv. 22, 23.) There is a coming of Christ, true and real, which is not outward and visible. Thus also in the epistle to the Church in Pergamos it is said: "Repent; or else I will come unto thee quickly." (Rev. ii. 16.) This form of expression is used frequently in the Bible. There are, therefore, many commentators who explain everything said in the New Testament of the second coming of Christ, of the spiritual manifestation of his power. Thus Mr. Alger, to cite a single example of this school, says: "The Hebrews called any signal manifestation of power—especially any dreadful calamity—a coming of the Lord. It was a coming of Jehovah when his vengeance strewed the ground with the corpses of Sennacherib's host; when its storm swept Jerusalem as with fire, and bore Israel into bondage; when its sword came down upon Idumea and was bathed in blood upon Edom. 'The day of the Lord' is another term of precisely similar import. It occurs in the Old Testament about fifteen times. In every instance it means some mighty manifestation of God's power in calamity. These occasions are pictured forth with the most astounding figures of speech." On the following page he says he fully believes that the evangelists and early Christians understood the language of Christ in reference to his second coming, as predictions of a personal and visible advent, connected with a resurrection and a general judgment, but he more than doubts whether such was the meaning of Christ Himself. (1.) Because he says nothing of a resurrection of the dead. (2.) The figures which He uses are precisely those which the Jewish prophets employed in predicting "great and signal events on the earth." (3.) Because He "fixed the date of the events He referred to within that generation." Christ he thinks, meant to teach that his "truths shall prevail and shall be owned as the criteria of Divine judgment. According to them," he understands Christ to say, "all the righteous shall be distinguished as my subjects, and all the iniquitous shall be separated from my kingdom. Some of those standing here shall not taste death till all these things be fulfilled. Then it will be seen that I am the Messiah, and that through the eternal principles of truth which I have proclaimed I shall sit upon a throne of glory,—not literally, in person, as you thought, blessing the Jews and cursing the Gentiles, but spiritually, in the truth, dispensing joy to good men and woe to bad men, according to their deserts." It is something to have it admitted that the Apostles and early Christians believed in the personal advent of Christ. What the Apostles believed we are bound to believe; for St. John said "He that knoweth God, heareth us." That the New Testament does teach a second, visible, and glorious appearing of the Son of God, is plain.

52

The Christian Hope for Heaven

J. L. Dagg

The Righteous Will Be Taken to Heaven, and Made Perfectly Happy for Ever in the Presence and Enjoyment of God (Matt. xxv. 34; Luke xii. 32; John xiv. 2; Col. iii. 4; 1 Thess. iv. 17; Luke xxii. 29,30; Acts xiv. 22; Rev. iii. 21; vii. 15-17; xiv. 4; 1 Pet. i. 3, 4; Matt. xxv. 21; John xvii. 24; Rev. xxi. 4; xxii. 3).

Godliness has the promise of the life that now is, and of that which is to come. It often happens that the believer in Christ has an afflicted lot in the present world; but, in the midst of tribulations, he is enabled, through grace, to rejoice in hope of the glory of God. So much does the happiness of his present life depend on the hope of a better portion hereafter, that he is said to be "saved by hope" (Rom. viii. 24). This hope has for its object an inheritance that is incorruptible, undefiled, and that fadeth not away (1 Pet. i. 3, 4). He is taught by the doctrine of Christ, to look for this portion, not in this world of sin, not in the pursuits and enjoyments of carnal men, but in another and better world, to which his faith and hope are ever directed.

The believer's portion is laid up in heaven (Col. i. 5). That heaven is a place, and not a mere state of being, we are taught by the words of Christ, who said, "I go to prepare a place for you" (John xiv. 2); but in what part of universal space this happy place is situated, the Bible does not inform us. It is sometimes called the third heavens (2 Cor. xii. 2), to distinguish it from the atmospheric heaven, in which the fowls of heaven have their habitation, and from the starry heavens, which visibly declare the glory of God. The glory of the third heavens is invisible to mortal eyes; and the place may be far beyond the bounds within which suns and stars shine, and planets revolve. Some have imagined that it is a vast central globe, around which the stars of heaven are making their slow revolutions, carrying with them their systems of attendant planets. There is something pleasing in this conjecture, which connects astronomical science with the hopes of the Christian: but it must be remembered that it is mere conjecture. No telescope can bring this glorious place within the reach of human view. "Eye hath not seen, nor ear heard, neither have entered into the heart of man, the things which God hath prepared for them that love him" (1 Cor. ii. 9). Yet, though science cannot give us a knowledge of this happy world, divine revelation has made us to some extent acquainted with it. Paul adds to the words just cited, "but God hath revealed them to us by his Spirit." By faith, which is the evidence of things not seen, we look at things unseen and eternal. The light of revelation brings the glories of the distant land before the eyes of our faith; and in the spiritual enjoyment which we are made to experience, even in this land of exile, we have an earnest (Eph. i. 14) and foretaste of heavenly joy. These drops of heaven sent down to worms below, unite with the descriptions found in God's holy word, to give such ideas of heaven as it is possible for us to form; but at best, we know only in part. "It doth not yet appear, what we shall be," or where we shall be, or in what our bliss will consist. But though in looking forward to the inheritance in prospect, we are compelled to see through a glass darkly, we may yet discover that the future happiness of the saints will include the following elements:

1. *An intimate knowledge of God*. Now we know in part, but then we shall know even as we are known (I Cor. xiii. 12). Heaven is "the high and holy place, where God resides, the court of the great King." He says, "heaven is my throne" (Isaiah lxvi. 1). Though present everywhere throughout his dominions, he manifests himself in a peculiar manner in this bright abode, of which the glory of God and the Lamb are the light. Here the blessed are permitted to see God. To see God, as human eyes now see material objects, by means of reflected light, will be as impossible then as it is now, for God is a spirit: but we shall have such a discovery of God, as is most appropriately expressed by the word see; otherwise, the promise of Christ would not be fulfilled. "Blessed are the pure in heart; for they shall see God" (Matt. v. 8). The knowledge of God will be communicated through the Mediator. "No man hath seen God at any time; the only begotten Son, who is in the bosom of the Father, he hath declared him" (John i. 18). Though God dwells in light which no man can approach unto, and is a Being whom no man hath seen, or can see (1 Tim. vi. 16); yet the light of the knowledge of the glory of God, in the face of Jesus Christ, the same that shines into the hearts of God's people on earth, fills the world of bliss. There no sun or moon shines; but "the glory of God did lighten it, and the Lamb is the light thereof." The glory of God is the illumination, and the Lamb is the luminary from which it emanates. Jesus will still be our teacher there, and through him we shall acquire our knowledge of the perfections and counsels of God.

Our knowledge of God will be for ever increasing. On earth, believers "grow in the knowledge of God and our Saviour Jesus Christ," and the advantages for attaining to higher knowledge, instead of ceasing at death, will be far greater in heaven. The perfections and counsels of the infinite God, will be an exhaustless source of knowledge, a boundless subject of investigation; and the Mediator, the equal of the Father, and his bosom-counsellor, will be our all-sufficient instructor; and our glorified spirits will be fitted to prosecute the study through eternal ages. It follows, that we shall continue to grow in the knowledge of God, while immortality endures. . . .

2. *Perfect conformity to God*. The first man was made in the image of God; and the subjects of regeneration are renewed,

after the image of God. But the likeness given in creation has been lost; and that which is reproduced in regeneration is incomplete. God's people are striving and praying for a higher degree of conformity; and they are looking to the future world for the consummation of their wishes: "Then shall I be satisfied, when I awake in thy likeness" (Ps. xvii. 15). They are predestinated to be conformed to the image of God's Son (Rom. viii. 29), who is the image of the invisible God (Col. i. 15). As they study the divine character here, they grow in conformity to it: "We, beholding as in a glass, the glory of the Lord, are changed into the same image, from glory to glory, even as by the Spirit of the Lord" (2 Cor. iii. 18). The same transforming influence which the knowledge of God exerts in this life, will continue in the future world. As we make progress in the knowledge of God, we advance from glory to glory, in the likeness of God; and this progress will be interminable, through all our immortal existence. We shall be like him; for we shall see him as he is" (1 John iii. 2).

In being conformed to God, who is love, we shall love the display of divine perfection, of which we shall obtain increasing discoveries, in our study of the character, works, and government of God. As our knowledge enlarges, our love to the things learned will become more intense, and the new developments which will be made at every stage of our endless advancement will be increasingly ravishing. What would be subjects of barren speculation to merely intellectual beings, will be to us as moral beings, having a moral likeness to God, sources of ineffable bliss, ever rising higher and higher in its approach towards the perfect and infinite blessedness of God.

3. *A full assurance of divine approbation.* In this world we groan, being burdened. A sense of sin, and God's displeasure on account of it, often fills the mind with gloom. We see, in the gospel of Christ, how God can be just, and the justifier of the believer in Jesus: but our faith is often weak. We are conscious of daily offences against infinite love; and the bitterness of grief possesses the soul. Oh! to see our Father's face, without a cloud between, and to feel that perfect love occupies the full capacity of our hearts, and governs every emotion! We pant after God,

the living God. We long for heaven; because there we shall dwell for ever in the light of his countenance. The sentence of the last judgment, "Come, ye blessed of my Father," will give an eternal assurance of divine acceptance, and perfect love in the heart will for ever exclude all fear.

4. *The best possible society.* Paul thus describes this society: "Ye are come unto Mount Zion, and unto the city of the living God, the heavenly Jerusalem, and to an innumerable company of angels, to the general assembly and church of the first born, which are written in heaven, and to God, the Judge of all, and to the spirits of just men made perfect, and to Jesus the Mediator of the new covenant" (Heb. xii. 22-24). Our brethren who have gone before us, with some of whom we took sweet counsel here, and went to the house of God in company, are there waiting to welcome our arrival. The angels that attend on us as ministering spirits, during our pilgrimage here, will convey us, when we leave the world, to the glorious abode, in which they ever behold the face of our Father in heaven, and will form part of the happy society into which we shall be introduced. There we shall be with Jesus, the Mediator, who loved us, and gave himself for us, in whose blood we shall have washed our robes, and made them white; there we shall approach to God, the Judge of all, who is our Father, the object of our love, and the source of our joy. In such society we shall spend eternity. We are travelling to our final home, through a desert land, a waste howling wilderness, but we seek a city; and God is not ashamed to be called our God, for he hath prepared for us a city (Heb. xi. 16). A city is a place where society abounds. The rich and noble resort to cities, that they may enjoy life. Here they display their wealth, erect magnificent palaces for their residence, and multiply the means of enjoyment to the utmost possible extent. In our eternal home, we shall not be lonely pilgrims; but we shall dwell in the city of our God; where the noblest society will be enjoyed, where the inhabitants will be all rich, made rich through the poverty of Jesus, and all kings and priests to God; and where the King of kings holds his court, and admits all into his glorious presence.

5. *The most delightful employment.* The future happiness of the saints is called a rest: but it is not a rest of inactivity; which,

however desired it may sometimes be, by those who inhabit sluggish bodies, is not suited to spiritual beings. The rest resembles the Sabbath, the holy day, in which the people of God now lay aside their worldly cares and toils, and devote the sacred hours to the worship of God. Such a sabbatism remains for the people of God, when the cares and toils of this life shall have ceased for ever. To the glorified saints, inaction would be torture, rather than bliss. Their happiness will not consist of mere passive enjoyment. They will serve God day and night; and, in this service, will find their highest enjoyment. They pray now, that his will may be done on earth, as it is done in heaven; and when they are themselves taken to heaven, they will delight to do his will, as it is done by all the heavenly host. The worship of God, and the study of his holy word, form a part of the delightful employment of the saints on the earthly Sabbath. So, to worship God with joyful songs of praise and suitable ascriptions of glory, constitutes, according to the Scripture representation, a part of the saints' employment in glory. The subjects of their transporting songs, and rapturous ascriptions of praise and glory, will be supplied by their continually fresh discoveries of the divine perfections, the study of which will also form an important part of their blissful employment.

6. *The absence of everything which could mar their happiness.* Sin, which here pollutes all our joys, will never enter there; for nothing entereth that defileth (Rev. xxi. 27). Devils and wicked men will be confined in their eternal prison, and will be able to molest no more. The sorrows and afflictions of this world will have passed away. There will be no more sickness, no more curse; and death, the last enemy, will have been destroyed.

7. *A free use of all the means of enjoyment.* Future happiness is promised as a kingdom: "Fear not, little flock, it is your Father's good pleasure to give you the kingdom" (Luke xii. 32). "Come, ye blessed of my Father, inherit the kingdom" (Matt. xxv. 34). A king is superior to all the nobles of his realm, and holds the highest place of dignity in his dominions. Christ, as king, is crowned with glory and honor; and believers also will be exalted to glory, honor, and immortality. The subjects of earthly despots are often deprived of their possessions by the injustice of those

who have power over them; but the king is above the reach of such injustice. He commands the resources of his dominions, and makes them contribute to his pleasure. Hence, to minds accustomed to regal government, royalty conveys the idea of the most abundant resources, and the highest measure of undisturbed enjoyment; hence the language of Paul: "Now ye are full; now ye are rich; ye have reigned as kings." (1 Cor. iv. 8). In this view, the children of God will be made kings. Besides the honor to which they will be exalted, their enjoyments will be boundless. All the resources of creation will be made tributary to them, and no one will dispute their claim, or hinder their enjoyment. Earthly crowns are often tarnished by the iniquity of those who wear them, but the crown bestowed on the children of God is a crown of righteousness, not only because it is righteously conferred, but because, without any unrighteous violence, the wearers will have all the honors and enjoyments of royalty secured to them for ever.

53

The City of God

A. M. Fairbairn

"Glorious things are spoken of thee, O city of God."
—Psalm lxxxvii. 3.

I

1. Augustine, the greatest and the noblest of the Western Fathers, lived when the Empire of Rome was far gone in decay. The growth of luxury, the deterioration of morals, the decline of

the old Roman virtues before an almost oriental licence, wasted her energies within, while the barbarian hosts assailed her in quick succession from without. Those inner and outer forces of decay were stronger than the strength of the Cæsars. Though the religion of Christ had poured new blood into the state, yet it could only prolong the days, could not restore the exhausted energies of the immense body politic. The Cross had indeed given the crown to Constantine, but it could not secure their authority and dominions to his successors. And so the Romans, enfeebled throughout, were forced to look on in almost utter helplessness while the barbarians spoiled their cities, made their most fertile plains desolate, seized and held their splendid colonies, ravished their hearths, and defiled their altars. Amid the universal misery and impotence, so sternly and terribly brought home to every mind by the storm and sack of the Eternal City herself, many a noble heart recalled for comfort the ancient valour and fame, the days of Roman heroism, when the old gods reigned and made the state they loved victor and queen of the world. They thought of the strong patriotism that had driven the Tarquins forth and held the Tarquins out, of the spirit that could face unconquered the swift victories of Hannibal; of the Scipio who saved Rome by assailing her enemy in his home; of the Cato, so stern in spirit and mighty in arms, who had destroyed more towns than he had spent days in Spain, and then they said:—

"If we had the old faith we should have the old days. If Rome had her ancient gods she would regain her ancient majesty. This Christian faith has many mysteries; one God who is yet conceived to be Three, springs from a Man, yet speaks of Him as God. But these mysteries are small things, might be believed were it not that this new Faith has been so fatal to our city. Ever since the Cross floated from the Capitol disaster and defeat have come to Rome. We hate this new religion, not for its doctrines, but for its action on our state; its life has worked our death. We will not believe that what has caused so many calamities is Divine. Our divinities are those of our fathers, the men of our heroic and glorious past."

Augustine stood forward to defend the Faith so gravely

assailed. His apology was twofold—concerned at once—fact and idea. As to the matter of fact, Rome, he pleaded, was dying of her pagan vices. They had weakened her, stolen away her courage, dimmed her ancient honour, poisoned all the springs of liberty and action. But the new Faith had created new virtues, which were working like a healing and beneficent spirit in the heart of Society. When the barbarians besieged and sacked a city, what happened? The Church of Christ awed them and stayed the ruin. The pagans, selfish while rich, fled from danger, famine and pestilence; but the Christians remained, opened to the perishing their sanctuaries and their churches. And those they sheltered were saved alike from the sword and the lust of the barbarians. And so mighty for good was the new Faith, that it made weak woman strong, so pure that the rampant evil of the world could not defile her, so good that as matron, gentle yet deft of hand, or as maiden, soft of voice and swift of foot, she loved to feed the famishing and nurse the diseased. The Rome that had died of paganism Christ was doing His best to save.

But it was the matter of ideal principle that moved Augustine to grandest eloquence and argument. He said, in effect: "Ye were proud, O Romans, of your city. Ye called her eternal, imperial, divine. But her history has rebuked your pride and proved her deities false. There is another city, so glorious in ideal and achievement that yours may not be named beside her. Two cities began to be with man, founded by two loves. The one by the love of self, even to the despising of God; the other by the love of God, even to the despising of self. The first is the city of earth, whose grandest creation was Rome, which glories in self and seeks glory from men; but the second is the heavenly city, whose greatest glory is God, whose witness is conscience. In the one city its princes and people are ruled by the love of ruling; in the other city the princes and subjects serve one another in love. This city is coextensive with the good, comprehends all the saints of earth, has created all its virtues and graces, all its truth and righteousness and love. It is the true divine city, for it is built by the only true God; it is the alone eternal, for it shares the eternity of its Builder. The city of Rome ruled the bodies and died through the vices of its people; but this city rules the spirits and lives through the virtues of its citizens, the saints of God." And so he answered the lament of the Romans by setting over against their ideal of the state a state which incorporated an infinitely loftier ideal, stretching not from Romulus till then, but from creation to eternity, and the words which began his splendid apology were but a paraphrase of these: "Glorious things are spoken of thee, O city of God!"

2. Abraham lived in an age very unlike Augustine's. The world was yet young, the mighty empires were still in the distant future, though the foundations of the earliest were being laid. From his home in Ur of the Chaldees he could see the builders at work, the men of Babylon and Nineveh. But he saw that they were building their cities on idolatry, and he knew that a multitude of gods meant a divided sovereignty, man the master of the gods rather than God the master of man. He knew, too, that to abide in his ancestral home would be to be absorbed into its idolatries; but to his open spirit the Divine voice came calling him to go forth and build a city on a simpler and purer faith, to become the father of a people who should be the people of God. So in his early manhood, with all its boundless promise unrealized, he and his beautiful Sarah turned their backs on the valley which the rivers of Paradise watered, and on the mighty builders who were at work on the foundations of empires vaster than they dreamed of; and, hand in hand, they moved westward in search of the land God was to give that they might found a people and a city for Him. They wandered long, saw the wealth of Egypt, fed their flocks on the broad plains of Mamre, looked wistfully on the fertile fields and valleys of Canaan, felt age and feebleness steal on apace, and yet no land or child was theirs. And when at length the promised son came, the gentle Isaac, they loved him with so large a love that the old man feared lest he were dearer to them than even their God. But the sacrifice which at once took and restored the son assured the father, and he waited in eager hope the word that was yet to be fulfilled. But he waited in vain, no land, no field even, became his, and when the beautiful Sarah of his youth, the lovelier, for the more loved, Sarah of his age, died at his side, the old man, bearing the common human sorrow that does not grow lighter for all the

centuries of our collective experience and life, had to stand up before the sons of Heth and say: "I am a stranger and a sojourner with you: give me a possession of a burying place with you, that I may bury my dead out of my sight" (Gen. xxiii. 4). Yet his faith did not fail; he did not think that God had made a promise to the ear only to break it to the hope. He thought rather, "The word of God is larger and diviner than I had believed; the city is to be His, not mine, built in man's time, but for His own eternity. The cities of earth, they perish, but the city of God remaineth." And so from his disappointment a sublimer hope was born, and "he looked for the city which hath the foundations, whose Builder and Maker is God" (Heb. xi. 10).

3. John lived in an age unlike Augustine's, still more unlike Abraham's. The men of Egypt and Mesopotamia, Persia and Greece, had successively made their endeavours at empire, had each seemed for a few centuries to succeed, but only the more disastrously to fail. The multitude of deities could not keep their cities, the watchmen waked in vain. But an immenser, mightier state filled their vacant places. Rome from her hills beside the Tiber ruled the world. She seemed at the moment to merit her proud name of "the Eternal." The change Cæsar had worked in the empire was thought to have its type in the change Augustus had worked in the city. He found it brick, he left it marble, all graceful, strong, durable. Who could resist her will? Did not all peoples bow down before her? Feeblest of all the hostile forces, if hostile this could be called, was the society of men who were known as Christians. The empire had but to say, "Let them perish," and its will would be done. And so who cared,—who, indeed, was there to care, but a community so poor as to awaken concern in no one?—when John was banished from the Church and city he loved to a solitude he hated? In Patmos; as the image of his scattered flock rose before him, the sunny Ægean, with all its laughter and music, could not woo him to happy thoughts; but visions at once darker and brighter came both to awe and to cheer his spirit. He saw Rome seated on her seven hills, drunk with the blood of saints, drawing upon herself the judgment of Heaven; but as he turned from the wicked present to the righteous future, from Cæsar to God, a grander image met his sight.

He saw, as only the seer can see, what centuries were to be needed to make visible, "the Holy City," the substitute and supplanter of Rome, "New Jerusalem coming down from God out of heaven, made ready as a bride adorned for her husband" (Rev. xxi. 2).

II

In these so dissimilar and distant men a similar faith stands expressed. There is a city of God invisible, spiritual, which knows no place or time, which embodies God's ideal of society, the ordered and obedient life of man.

1. As so understood and interpreted, they supply the point of view from which the city is to be here regarded. It does not mean to us either a material heaven or a visible church. There are men who feel as if heaven could have no being unless placed in a city which stands square and strong to every wind that blows, whose walls are of precious stones, whose streets are of fine gold, paced perpetually by pilgrims who sing and carry palms, while in the midst, visible to all, is the throne of God and the Lamb. And there are men who think that the city of God must be a kind of political corporation, an articulated and organized system, which can boast a continuous life, an immense body of tradition, and can speak with the authority which belongs to its inherited experience, its collective wisdom, and its supernatural gifts and powers. But these ideas are alike sensuous, stand on the same level as regards spiritual culture and significance. A heaven which were but a city of marble palaces and streets resonant with song, would grow so wearisome to spirits that loved contemplation, or to spirits devoted to beneficent service, that they would soon become unable to distinguish its pleasures from pains,—might even come to think annihilation better than such bliss. And were the city of God identical with any church, or even with all the churches, then so much of human craft and error would enter into it,—so many things not noble or gentle would have been done in its name, it would so often have condemned as false what God has proved most surely true, that it would have to descend from its ideal perfection and stand

among the imperfect and not rarely unjust states or societies of men. But the city of God may not be so construed; it is spiritual throughout. He is a spirit, and it is to be realized in and through the spirits He has formed. But it is on this account only the more real. The region of the spirit is the region of the eternal, therefore of the sublimest realities. In this region the city of God has its seat, that it may the more absolutely mould man in the days of his mortal being into the very image and form of his immortality.

What is a city? As men now understand it, it is but a place where men have most congregated and built to themselves houses and workshops; where the exchange and the cathedral stand together, the one for admiration, the other for business; where warerooms run into long unlovely streets; where narrow and unfragrant closes are crowded with the poor, and spacious yet hard and monotonous squares are occupied by the rich. But city was not always so conceived. The Latin *civitas*, the Greek πόλις, had nobler meanings. Their cardinal and honourable sense was not the place, but the living community,—the men of kindred blood and spirit, who claimed the same parentage, heired the same past, lived under the same laws, possessed the same privileges, liberties, and rights, followed the same customs, observed the same worship, believed the same religion. They were terms that expressed all that was ideal in the state and fatherland,—all in them that appealed to the heart and conscience, evoked patriotism, and made freedom better and dearer than life. Over the men of Thermopylæ the words were written,

> "To those of Lacedæmon, stranger, tell,
> That as their laws commanded, here we fell."

They fell not for the Spartan earth, but for the ideals embodied in the community and its liberties, for Sparta as she lived to faith and love. A Greek tragic poet speaks of his fatherland as his mother, nurse, sister, the anchor and home of his soul. It made his manhood, and he loved it for what it made. So these words πόλις and *civitas* were to the Greek and Roman respectively the parents of the terms that expressed their noblest ideas as to the collective and corporate life of their peoples, the qualities which gave them distinction, made them freeborn and privileged men. Outside the πόλις men were but slaves or barbarians; within the *civitas* men were civilized, lived ordered, kindly, courtly lives.

And the city we here speak of bears this high ideal sense, only enlarged, exalted, and transfigured by the relation in which it stands to God. It is the society He has created, the community of men who know that they are His sons, regenerated and inspired by His truth, possessed of His Spirit, obedient to His will, working for His ends. What the Jew meant by the kingdom, the Greek meant by the city of God; but they viewed the truth they so expressed under different aspects and from different standpoints. The kingdom accentuated the idea of the reign of God realized in the righteousness or obedience of man; but the city accentuated the idea of the Divine law or will realized in his free and ordered and richly beautiful social life. Spirits were needful to the realization of this ideal, but still more the creative and constitutive truths which made the spirits and organized the society. It was too immense to be limited to earth: the sainted dead and the saintly living were alike citizens. It was too imperishable to be bounded by time; the possibilities of obedience were inexhaustible. The realization of the ideal—though not the ideal itself, that was as eternal as God—had its beginning in time, but it would proceed throughout eternity. The more perfect a spirit becomes the greater its conformity to the Divine will. But above the highest degree reached, higher degrees rise in endless progression. The city of God is the society of godlike spirits with all their godlike capabilities and affinities in exercise and development, moving, as it were, out of their imperfection as creatures to the perfection loved and desired of the Creator.

2. The city of God, then, is an eternal, unrealized, yet realized ideal,—an ideal that is to be for ever in the process of realization. This everlasting process is its very glory and last excellence, the secret of its endless attraction, the spell that awakens the activities that constitute heaven. God's is the only absolute perfection; man's is relative, contained in the high destiny which bids him ever struggle towards the Infinite which he yet can never reach. There is no perfection so incomplete as the one which admits of no increase; that is the imperfection of death, not of life. God

thinks too highly of man to be ever satisfied with what he is. The best possible for one moment is only the condition of a better possible for the next. But it is not enough that the city be a progressive ideal; it must possess the means and agencies necessary to the realization. And these exist. The eternal truths as to God and His Christ, the Divine energies and influences active in man, working in and through the churches, the benevolent and beneficient forces which act in society, in politics, in commerce, in art, in civilization as a whole, are of the city and work for it. Without these it could never be. They are the builders of the city, the agencies God uses to prepare and lay the living stones of the temple He designed, and inhabits and glorifies. By His truth He makes true men, conformed to the image of His Son. By His Spirit which dwelleth in them He brings them into a unity which expresses and exercises their life divine. Through the truths of God the ideals of God are realized, and the eternal way which leadeth to perfection opened to the energies, endeavours, and hopes of man.

Now, it is at this point that we see the relation of all our past discussions to the idea and ideal of the city of God. They have been concerned with the truths that make it at once possible and real,—that are, as it were, the factors of its reality, the conditions and agencies that work its realization. The eternal God builds the city, creation happens that He may build it. Man was made to be a citizen, and all his religions witness to his yearning after his end, his passion for the fulfilment of his being. God calls, disciplines, and guides Israel, that He may the better bring to man the truths that at once create and qualify for citizenship. Jesus Christ comes as the Way to the city, the Truth from God which gives the Life of God, so creating the new or filial humanity, whose units are as He is, sons of God. To this end Christ was born and died and rose; to this end He reigns as King, He saves as Priest, He speaks as Prophet the things of God to men. Creation stands rooted in Him, and He completes it. Redemption, though later in history, was not later in the Divine purposes. God being God, the home of all rectitude, truth and graciousness, would never have made a world He did not mean to redeem; and Jesus Christ, the chief Corner-Stone of the city designed from eternity, its creative and normative personality, appeared in the fulness of time to bring in the everlasting righteousness. Through Him man becomes a "fellow-citizen with the saints," reaches and realizes his chief good, finds the way to that complete harmony with the Eternal Will which is purest beatitude and highest perfection.

III

But these discussions must have a practical end. What function has the faith in the eternal city, with the hopes it creates, to fulfil in the common and often commonplace life of man? It were too large a matter to attempt to look at and answer this question on all its sides. The action of the ideal in humanity has been most beneficient; it is at this moment a centre of mighty moral energies. What forbids hope paralyses effort. Men speak of the strength of despair, but despair has no strength; it is only impassioned weakness struggling with a might that mocks it. There is strength in hope, and the energy of the present works for good when it believes in a better and happier future. But to believe in a better future a man must believe in God. The energies of the universe must work for righteousness if righteousness is ever to prevail. And so the Pessimism that denies the beneficence of Deity, and the Pantheism that can allow Him no power of moral initiative, are unable to create the hopes that call into action those moral and ameliorative energies that are the great progressive forces in history. From this point of view we can certainly say that man's belief in the city of God, with all it involves, has created ideals, awakened enthusiasms, inspired hopes, developed energies and agencies that have lessened the miseries, increased the happiness, enlarged the liberties, augmented the righteousness and quickened the progress of mankind. But these are matters we may not touch; our concern must be with the worth of the ideal to the individual man, its action and function in our every-day and commonplace lives.

1. The belief in the city creates hopes that exalt, ennoble, and transform our ordinary lives. These are in good sooth tame and mean enough. Angels have always been rare guests, more

through man's fault than their own. To see God face to face is the joy of eternity. The most that time knows is the season of quiet communion which rises now and then like a beautiful sunlit island out of the troubled ocean of life. All men feel more or less the monotony, the satiety, the sickness born of the weary labour with which we toil over the immeasurable levels of common-place. Work in these days becomes ever more strenuous, approaches nearer and nearer to drudgery, and drudgery more than anything not immoral bemeans man, takes out of him all incipient nobleness. The man who works in a dismal mine, or digs in a ditch, or drives a laden cart, with eating and sleeping or drunken play as the only relieving conditions of his life, does not rise very far above the level of the toiling animal. The man who stands behind the counter retailing day by day slander or senti-ment as the humour of the customer may demand, speaking truth or untruth, with small conscience of the distinction be-tween, as the interest of the seller may require, may well feel now and then as if in his calling as he lives it there was little to exalt or honour his manhood. The woman whose spirit is bur-dened with a multitude of minutest cares, distracted besides by the need of solving the rather intractable problem, how to recon-cile an increasing expenditure with a stationary or diminishing income; or her still unhappier sister whose soul kindles to no-thing higher than the now vacant, now spiteful, gossip of soci-ety,—must surely in their serener or better moments come to know how little the water drawn from the common springs of life can satisfy or cheer. Our age boasts its men of action and invention, praises them according to the amount of work they can do and their skill in doing it; but physical endurance and mechanical ingenuity are poor characteristics for man, especi-ally in presence of the forces that work in nature or the instincts that act in the brute. We hear now and then the quantity and quality of a man's brains determined by his ability to make money—brains good at that, good for anything; poor at that, good for nothing—but if the power to accumulate and distribute constitutes man's best title to manhood, what do the arts, the sciences, the literatures and religions that have enriched the world signify and mean? Reduce man to the categories of the political economist, make him a mere producer, distributor, and consumer, and where is his manhood? If man could be defined as a creature who makes, sells, carries, eats, would he be man—made of God for God—any more?

Man, then, needs more than this prosaic and narrow life, with its material comforts, its toils that harden, its rewards that punish the spirit, its worship of secular success and unpitying blame of secular failure. He needs the hope of a nobler future, the vision of the city of God. Without this vision, earth, even where most full of material wealth, can be but a galley and the man a galley slave, or, with its hard limitations, its rules that cramp most where they most exercise, like a menagerie with its herd of bond animals, shadows of the free born, soured by the well-fed bondage that frets though it may not break the spirit. Man the worker is changed by the hope of a diviner hereafter into man the immortal; by it man the artificer becomes a spirit conscious of a Divine descent and destiny. When out of the future the light of the eternal city gleams it glorifies the meanest moments of the present. The dignity it brings to man affects all he touches, dignifies through him toil, the commonest everyday mechanical labour. The citizen of heaven feels no work drudgery, for he can never be a drudge; in the hour of humblest endeavour he stands in the midst of the immensities, in the centre of the eternities which God inhabits. Dusty and wayworn, he may have long, bare, burning roads to travel, but he will find here and there hills he can ascend, whence he can see the light of the Celestial City afar, hear its angel-music, feel its fragrant and grateful breezes on his heated brow. He may with little strength of arm or skill of weapon have to fight a hard battle for life; but if the nights he spends in the tented field be nights of Bethel-visions, when, with sense asleep and imagination awake, earth and heaven melt into the common home of God and man, then the rest that comes will be rest that brings a nobler and more regal manhood to the life of the morrow. The royalties of earth grow dim in the light of immortality, but its obscurities grow lustrous. It is a splendid hope that quenches fictitious dignity, but touches with radiant glory the common nature of man. . . .

2. These high hopes look for realization to the city of God; it is the sphere of their fulfilment. City is the synonyme for Society in its richest and most varied forms; there the privileges, rights, liberties, and honours of citizenship are combined with the grandest opportunities of mutual service, the ministries of love and devotion, the fellowship of living minds. In the first aspect the city is the realm of law and order, where man, knowing and obeying the will of God, lives to realize the ideals of His eternity; in the second aspect the city is the arena where spirits know and serve each other, where the joy of each contributes to the common beatitude, and the beatitude of the whole to the perfection of each. . . .

The city of God, then, as the realm of love and obedience, ministry and fellowship, is the sphere for the development and realization of all the Divine ideals in man, individual and collective. It is a society of spirits on their way through obedience and service to perfection. All spirits are akin; we are human not by virtue of our bodies, but by virtue of our souls, and man stands related to man through all time and over all the world as brother to brother because all have been made in the same image and bear the same nature. And the city of God but means that the ideal of each man and of all his relationships is being realized. Variety is not thus destroyed, but rather created. In this city there will be father and mother, sister and brother spirits, spirits married in the wedlock of mutual affinities, and spirits whose paths shall lie as far apart as the poles of God's intellectual universe. But variety only deepens joy and enlarges duty. Uniformity is the death of happiness. Men must differ if they are to rejoice in each other, to serve and be served. . . .

3. The city, in order to fulfil the hopes of its citizens, must have throughout two qualities, it must be of God and eternal as God. These two are one. What is of God, spirit as He is, must partake of His eternity. Yet the two are distinct. To be of God is the source and spring of the city's perfection; to be eternal, the condition of its realization. The ideal is God's, the perfect mirror of His perfect mind, but it can be translated into reality only through obedience. And an obedience which answers to the

idea in the Eternal Mind must be eternal. The relation of the city to God has its counterpart in man's relation to Him. The city is a city of sons, the will of the Sovereign expresses the love of the Father, the obedience of the citizen is the realized affection of the child. This affinity to God is the secret of our immortality; it is ours because we are akin to Him, of His kind. Give to a godlike spirit an immortality with God; and what height may it not win? What ministry of light, what service of love and beneficence may it not perform? As hope looks down into a future rich in such infinite possibilities, man is now awed and humbled, now uplifted and ennobled, and whether he be the one or the other, he alike feels as if his time were eternity, and work among men service of God.

"Thus saith Jehovah, The heavens are My throne, and the earth is My footstool: what manner of house would ye build for Me? and what manner of place for My rest? For all these things did My hand make, and all these things came into being, saith Jehovah: but this is the man upon whom I look, even he who is afflicted and of a contrite spirit, and trembleth at My word" (Isa. lxvi. 1-2).

"He shall feed His flock like a shepherd: He shall gather the lambs with His arm, and carry them in His bosom, and shall gently lead those that are with young" (Isa. xl. 11).

"Ye are come unto Mount Zion, and unto the city of the living God, the heavenly Jerusalem, and to innumerable hosts of angels, to the general assembly and church of the firstborn, who are enrolled in heaven, and to God the Judge of all, and to the spirits of just men made perfect, and to Jesus the Mediator of a new covenant, and to the blood of sprinkling, that speaketh better than that of Abel" (Heb. xii. 22-24).

"And thus, Glaucon, the tale has been saved and has not perished, and may be our salvation if we are obedient to the word spoken; and we shall pass safely over the river of Forgetfulness, and our soul will not be defiled. Wherefore my counsel is, that we hold fast to the heavenly way, and follow after justice and virtue always, considering that the soul is immortal and able to endure every sort of good and every sort of evil. Thus shall we live dear to one another and the gods, both while remaining here and when, like conquerors in the games who go round to gather gifts, we receive our reward, and it shall be well with us both in this life and in the pilgrimage of a thousand years which we have been reciting" (Plato: Repub. Bk. x. 11, 621. Jowett's translation).

54

The Revelation of the Holy Trinity

R. W. Dale

'Through Him (the Lord Jesus Christ) we both have our access in one Spirit unto the Father.'—EPH. ii. 8.

In previous discourses I have endeavoured to show that the Christian Gospel reveals that the Lord Jesus Christ is the Eternal Son of the Eternal Father, and that the Holy Spirit is not merely a divine Influence or a divine Power, but a divine Person; I have also endeavoured to show that these great truths do not rest merely on authority, but have been confirmed in the experience of Christian men in all countries and all ages.

I

The doctrine of the Trinity affirms that Father, Son, and Spirit are one God. In its substance it is not a merely speculative doctrine; it is a brief summary of those great facts which through eighteen hundred years have revealed their power and glory in the moral and spiritual life of the Christian Church. It is a declaration that in the Lord Jesus Christ, heaven and earth have been brought together; that in Him a divine Person became man; that having found Christ, we have found God; that 'He is the same yesterday, and to-day, yea, and for ever,' Son of God, Son of man, the Lord, the Saviour, the Brother of our race. It is a declaration that the great 'Advocate,' who now sustains the life of the Church, leads it into all the truth, directs its activity, and consoles its sorrows, is a divine Person whose 'coming' has brought with it such transcendent grace as more than to compensate for the withdrawal from the world of our Lord's visible presence and His return to the Father.

It may, indeed, be contended that one and the same Person

has manifested Himself as Father, Son, and Spirit; and that, therefore, it is possible to believe in the divine glory of our Lord and in the personal solicitude of the divine Spirit for the life and perfection of the Church without believing in the Trinity. I rejoice to acknowledge that the substance of some great truths is received by many who find insuperable difficulties in the traditional definitions of them. If you love and obey and trust and worship the Lord Jesus Christ as a divine Person; if you shrink from sin lest you should 'grieve' the Holy Spirit, if His care for you and His patience with you fill your heart with courage and gratitude; and if you believe, at the same time, that the Son and the Spirit are one with the Eternal Father, your life is rooted in the facts which the doctrine of the Trinity is intended to express, although you may be unable to accept the Trinitarian creed.

But the theory that Father, Son, and Spirit are but three forms in which one and the same Person is manifested—as one and the same person may be the father of a family, sovereign of a kingdom, and commander of an army—appears to give no adequate account of the facts of our Lord's history, or of some of the most memorable parts of His teaching. Our Lord prayed to the Father; He said that the Father loved Him; and He gave as the reason for the love, 'for I do always the things that are pleasing to Him' (John viii. 29). It is clear that He Himself was not the Father but Another. His whole relation to the Father was that of a Person to a Person. Nor can the Lord Jesus Christ be personally identified with the Holy Spirit. The Spirit was not Christ; for Christ was to 'send' Him and He was to 'bear witness of Christ' (John xvi. 14). He was not Christ; for He was to 'glorify' Christ: 'He shall take of mine and shall declare it unto you' (John xv. 26). The relations between Father, Son, and Spirit are analogous to those which exist between different persons; they are not analogous to the relations which exist between different forms of the activity of the same person.

II

That the Lord Jesus Christ, as known to us, is a divine Person, and that the Spirit of God, as known to us, is also a divine Person, has been shown in previous discourses. The immediate question with which we have to deal this morning is whether in the Incarnation of our Lord and in the 'coming' of the Spirit and His permanent activity in the Church and in the world there is a revelation of the inner and eternal life of God. Have we the right to assume that the historic manifestation of God to our race discloses anything of God's own eternal being? But this is really to ask whether the revelation of God really reveals God—shows us what God is—manifests His 'eternal life.' It is to ask whether when we have seen Christ, and seen Him in His relations to the Father, we have seen the 'Truth.' To those who have been filled with wonder by the glory of Christ, and have known the power of His redemption, the answer to this question cannot be uncertain. Wherever else we may be surrounded by illusions, we are in contact with eternal realities when we are in the presence of Christ. We are sure that in Him God is really revealed, and that the relations between Him and the Father have their ground in the life of the Eternal. The mystery of that life remains impenetrable; but the Incarnation reveals the truth that the eternal life of God has not been an awful loneliness; that in some wonderful sense the Father has always been the Father, and the Son the Son. And the revealed relations of the Spirit to both Father and Son have also their eternal ground in the Godhead; they did not originate in order that God's mercy might achieve our redemption; they are revealed in the great acts by which redemption is achieved; that they are revealed implies that they already existed.

From Eternity to Eternity—this is the Trinitarian doctrine— God is Father, Son, and Holy Spirit. The Father is God—but not apart from the Son and the Spirit. The Son is God—but not apart from the Father and the Spirit. The Spirit is God—but not apart from the Father and the Son. There is one God, but in the Godhead there are, according to the technical language of theology and the creeds, three Persons. There are not three Gods, but, in the life and being of the One God, there are three Centres of consciousness, volition, and activity; and these are known to us as the Father, the Son, and the Holy Spirit.

III

There have been philosophical attempts to demonstrate that by an eternal necessity there must be a Trinity in the divine life. These attempts do not seem to me to have been successful. When the discovery has been made, whether through authority or experience, or both, that the Father is divine, the Son divine, and the Spirit divine, a philosophical scheme may, perhaps, be constructed to show that the idea of a divine Trinity in unity is not unreasonable; but I doubt the possibility of demonstrating the doctrine of the Trinity by any processes of philosophical reasoning.

There have also been attempts to alleviate the difficulties which surround the doctrine by suggesting that there are some familiar analogies to the mystery; that, for instance, in our own nature there is a trinity of body, soul, and spirit, and that this trinity is consistent with the unity of human life. I should be unwilling to deprive any one of the aid to faith that he may find in analogies of this kind; but I must acknowledge that, for me, they are wholly worthless. Nor am I surprised that no real analogy can be discovered in created life to the life of the Eternal. God is God. There can be none like Him. He stands apart.

It was not by any process of philosophical speculation on the nature of God that the Church finally reached the doctrine of the Trinity, but by the path of faith and Christian experience. The Church was sure that Christ is a divine Person; this belief was implicated in its very life; to surrender it would have been to surrender all its hopes and the characteristic power of the Christian Gospel. It was sure that the Spirit is a divine Person; this belief was also implicated in its very life; to surrender it would have been to surrender some of the great promises of Christ, and to lose all the courage and strength that come from the belief that a divine Person has His home in the Church and in the individual life of Christian men. Holding fast these two truths, that the Son is a divine Person, and the Spirit a divine Person, the Church, in order to maintain the unity of God, affirmed the doctrine of the Trinity. The doctrine is an attempt to assert the divine unity, while asserting the divinity of the Son and of the Spirit.

The doctrine is no doubt infinitely mysterious. But God must always be an infinite mystery to us, whatever may be our conception of Him. His eternal life must be a mystery whether we conceive of it as an awful and loveless solitude, or whether we conceive of it as an eternal and blessed fellowship of love. His relations to the universe must also be a mystery; the understanding is as powerless to conceive how the Infinite can be related to the finite, the Eternal to creatures that have their existence in time, as it is to determine how Father, Son, and Spirit can be one God. We are no nearer to an intellectual apprehension of the life and nature of God when we deny the doctrine of the Trinity, than when we accept it. The cloud of mystery which conceals from us the Eternal mystery has shifted its place, but it is not dissipated. It is as impenetrable as it was before.

IV

But I go further. Though infinitely mysterious, the revelation of the One God as Father, Son, and Holy Spirit, fulfils—and it alone fulfils—the profoundest, the richest, the noblest conception of the divine life.

'Nothing is easier,' as Dr. Newman said, 'than to use the word God and mean nothing by it.' What do we really mean when we speak of God? For what kind of a Being does the word stand? The very terms in which I have stated the question show how ineffectual are all the common instruments of human thought in this high inquiry; for God can belong to no 'kind;' He is not one of a class; He is alone; He is not part of the universe; He is above it; we learn what God is, not so much from what the world is, as from what it is not. Let me then change the form of the question, and ask, For whom does the word 'God' stand?

(I.) It stands for One of whose greatness it seems presumptuous to speak, and in whose presence silence seems the truest worship. He lives from Eternity to Eternity. He is here; He is everywhere; there is no remotest region where He is not. To say that He created all things, and that, after sustaining all things through countless ages, He fainteth not, neither is He weary, is to say nothing concerning His infinite strength: He Himself is infinitely greater than the universe, and he lives, has ever lived, and will live for ever, in the power of His own life. We say—and yet we know not what we are saying—that all things in this world and in all worlds, are present to His mind. . . .

(II.) We need, I say, a God who is 'afar off,' infinitely greater than ourselves—belonging to other realms of life.

But we also need a God who is 'nigh at hand.' The legendary incarnations of divine persons, which have so great a place in some Oriental religions, are rude and coarse witnesses to this craving. A remote God reigning in inaccessible heights of majesty and glory does not satisfy us. He is too far away for us to be sure of His sympathy, compassion, and grace. We think that He can have no real knowledge of our troubles, our perplexities, our moral and spiritual conflicts. To Him on those heights of peace, human life must present an altogether different aspect from that which it presents to us, who are weary under its burdens, vexed by its cares, disheartened by its disappointments, incessantly harassed by its temptations. There are times, I suppose, in the history of many of us when, though we hardly acknowledge it to ourselves, there is a latent discontent that He who created the world should, as we imagine, have no share in its troubles.

The Christian doctrine of the Trinity meets these cravings, and more than meets them. Christ not only reveals the Infinite and the Eternal God who in His Infinitude and Eternity transcends the universe and remains for ever above and apart from it. He accepts human limitations, knows, by actual experience, human joys and the sharpest of human pains; He hungers and thirsts; He has not where to lay His head; He has friends who love Him and whom He loves; He has bitter enemies; He is tempted; He dies a cruel death. We sometimes resent the shame and the suffering which by the divine order of the world come upon us from the sins of other men, and are almost ready to ask—not, Has God forgotten to be gracious?—but, Has He forgotten to be just?—and Christ dies for the sins of the race.

This is a most wonderful and glorious revelation of God. It is true that God transcends the universe and that the distance between Him and our race is infinite: but it is also true that in the Eternal life of the Godhead there is a divine 'Person' so near akin to us that it was possible for Him to take our life into His own, to 'become Flesh,' to make His home in the world, to share the happiness and the misery of the race. Now we know that God is a God 'nigh at hand' as well as a God 'afar off.'. . .

(III.) Let us now turn to the Holy Spirit. The springs of our righteousness are in Christ; it is in the power of His Sonship that we are sons of God, and in the power of His life that we live the life of the sons of God—a life of obedience, submission, trust, and love. But how is the life that dwells in Christ to become ours? It is the gift of God's grace; but this is a kind of gift which must be received, or it remains ineffectual. God's free approach to man must be met by man's free approach to God. To consider the great subject in another form—in Christ, God who transcends the universe is revealed to our race—and, as I believe, to all races of spiritual beings in all worlds; but how are we to receive the revelation? Our eyes are too dim to perceive the divine glory, our ears too dull to catch the divine voice and to discover in its the accent of the Eternal. The Christian doctrine of the Trinity answers these questions. The Divine Spirit enables us to see God in Christ and to recognise the voice of the Good Shepherd. 'No man,' said our Lord, 'can come to Me, except the Father which sent Me draw him' (John vi. 44); and the Father 'draws' men to Christ by the power of the Spirit. The grace which draws men to Christ may be resisted and defeated; but apart from it no man believes in Him, follows Him, and receives eternal salvation. . . .

The Hebrews, while maintaining firmly the unity of God and His transcendent greatness, escaped the desolation of philosophical Deism by finding the activity of the 'Spirit of God' in the visible creation and in the life of man. They approached, as I have said in an earlier discourse, the conception of the divine immanence. But the truth is affirmed, in its noblest form and in relation to the highest regions of human life, in the Christian doctrine of the Trinity. In the Father, God personally transcends the life and thought of man; in the Son, God is personally revealed to man; in the Spirit, God is immanent in the higher life of man. Transcendence, immanence, the power of self-revelation—these are all included in the Christian conception of God in relation to man; and this conception may be the solid ground of a philosophical conception of God's relation to the whole universe.

V

There are large numbers of persons to whom these inquiries into the mysteries of the life of God seem alien from the true and original genius of the Christian Gospel. A contrast, as to both form and content, has been drawn between the Sermon on the Mount and the Nicene Creed; 'an ethical sermon,' it has been said, 'stood in the forefront of the teaching of Jesus Christ, and a metaphysical creed in the forefront of the Christianity of the fourth century.' And, according to the late Dr. Hatch, whose premature death was an irreparable loss to more than one branch of theological learning, the contrast indicates 'a change in the centre of gravity from conduct to belief.'

Dr. Hatch was a distinguished scholar, and his contention, with all that it implies, requires grave and elaborate discussion. But many of those who speak with the greatest scorn of Christian theology seem never to have read, or to have wholly forgotten, a large part of that very Sermon on the Mount for whose ethical teaching they express so much enthusiasm. In that sermon our Lord said, 'Blessed are they that have been persecuted for righteousness' sake: for theirs is the kingdom of heaven. Blessed are ye when men shall reproach you, and persecute you, and say all manner of evil against you falsely, for my sake. Rejoice and be exceeding glad: for great is your reward in heaven' (Matt. v. 10-12). Who is this that places persecution for His sake side by side with persecution for 'righteousness' sake,' and declares that whether men suffer for loyalty to Him or for loyalty to righteousness they are to receive their reward in the divine kingdom? Who is it that in that sermon places His own authority side by side with the authority of God, and gives to the Jewish people and to all mankind new laws which require a deeper and more inward righteousness than was required by the ten commandments? (Matt. v. 21-28). Who is it that in that sermon assumes the awful authority of pronouncing final judgment on men? 'Not every one that saith unto Me, Lord, Lord, shall enter into the Kingdom of Heaven; but he that doeth the will of My Father which is in Heaven. Many will say to Me in that day'—to Me—'Lord, Lord, did we not prophesy in Thy name, and by Thy name cast out devils, and by Thy name do many wonderful works? And then will I profess unto them, I never knew you: depart from Me, ye that work iniquity' (Matt. vii. 21-23). These are not words that we ever heard before, or have ever heard since, from teacher or prophet. Who is He? That question cannot be silenced when words like these have once been spoken.

And the ethical teaching of the Sermon on the Mount derives its unique power from the profound faith of Christian men in all ages that it comes from the lips of One who is infinitely greater than man,—from the lips of One who, among all the prophets that have spoken to us of duty and of God, stands alone and supreme—of One in whom the Eternal Son of God, at the impulse of an infinite love for our race, became man that He might give us not only the law but the example of the perfect life, and by a stupendous act of self-sacrifice deliver us from sin and from eternal destruction. The Nicene Creed was only a definite protest against forms of thought which, by denying to the Lord Jesus Christ His divine glory, would have paralysed the characteristic power of His ethical teaching.

Nor is it true that 'a metaphysical creed' stood 'in the forefront of the Christianity of the fourth century,' or that a metaphysical creed has stood in the forefront of Christianity in any century. To a theological scholar the great creeds of the Church have naturally a dominant interest; in the chosen province of his investigation they hold the most conspicuous place. But when he says that they stand 'in the forefront' of the Christianity of the fourth century, or of any other century, the theological scholar commits an error of the same kind as that which is committed by secular historians who have placed 'in the forefront' of the history of nations, the accession and the death of kings, dynastic changes, the rise and fall of great statesmen, the battles which have been lost and won. All these are to the historian immensely interesting, and they are really important; but their importance is derived from their effect on the life and condition of the forgotten millions who had no immediate concern in them. To the common people the great events in the national life have been the years of plenty, in which they have had abundant food, and the years of famine when they have died of starvation; the new inventions and the changes in agricultural and manufacturing industry which have brought wealth or poverty to hundreds of thousands of obscure homes; the discoveries by which great epidemics which once inflicted desolation on whole continents have been averted or lessened in virulence; the growth in the community of a spirit of compassion which has led to the creation of agencies for the relief of human misery; the awakening of intellectual activity among masses of the people to whom intellectual activity had been unknown; the improvement or the deterioration of private morals; the revival or the decline of religious faith.

Ecclesiastical historians have naturally placed the creeds of great councils 'in the forefront' of the history of the Church; and the creeds have their importance—an importance I should be the last to disparage. The struggle of Athanasius was a struggle for the very substance of the Gospel of Christ; and the creed of Nicæa is the symbol of his victory. But to the common millions of Christian men in all ages, the anxieties of poverty, the exhaustion of care, physical pain, the guilt of sin, the incessant struggle with temptation, the agonies of bereavement, the mystery of death, the dread of judgment to come, have been infinitely more urgent and more absorbing than the controversies of theologians; and the Gospel, with its revelation of an infinite mercy and an eternal redemption, with its divine consolations and its immortal hopes, has had a far larger place in their life and thoughts than the greatest of the creeds.

The warning of Thomas à Kempis may be less necessary in our own age than it has been in some past ages; but it is still necessary: 'What will it profit thee to be able to discourse profoundly on the Trinity if thou art wanting in humility and so art displeasing to the Trinity. But a clear knowledge of eternal things—so far as they can be clearly known—has also its value in relation to life and practice. And while giving heed to the warning of the saintly mystic we should also follow the example of the great apostle, who said, 'I will pray with the Spirit, and I will pray with the understanding also: I will sing with the Spirit, and I will sing with the understanding also' (1 Cor. xiv. 15).

55

The Glory of the Holy Trinity

Brooke Foss Westcott

It is obvious, I think, how these general reflections which fill our minds today, apply to the Christian conception of the Triune God. The conception was not given to us first in an abstract form. The abstract statement is an interpretation of facts, a human interpretation of vital facts, an interpretation wrought out gradually in the first years of the Church and still mastered gradually in our individual growth. We are required each in some sense to win for ourselves the inheritance which is given to us, if the inheritance is to be a blessing. We learn through the experience of history, and through the experience of life, how God acts, the Father, the Son, and the Holy Spirit, and by the very necessity of thought we are constrained to gather up these lessons into the simplest possible formula. So we come to recognise a Divine Unity, which is not sterile, monotonous simplicity; we come to recognise a Divine Trinity, which is not the transitory manifestation of separate aspects of One Person or a combination of Three distinct Beings. We come to recognise One in whom is the fulness of all conceivable existence in the richest energy, One absolutely self-sufficient and perfect, One in whom love finds internally absolute consummation, One who is in Himself a Living God, the fountain and the end of all life.

Thus we rise almost unconsciously from earth to Heaven,

from the confession of what God does for us as Creator, Redeemer, Sanctifier, to the contemplation of His own Infinite Majesty, that is, from the action of God to the being of God, from the Trinity of the Christian dispensation to the Trinity of essence. And I will venture to say that the conception of God which we thus gain and which we could not have anticipated, does meet in a marvellous way the needs of men, so that it is not, as the boldness of rationalistic speculation has made it, a burden imposed upon the submission of faith, but indeed an implicit Gospel.

Our powers of thought and language are indeed very feeble, but we can both see and to some extent point out how this idea of the Father revealed through the Son, of the Son revealed through the Spirit, One God, involves no contradiction, but offers in the simplest completeness of life the union of the "one" and the "many" which thought has always striven to gain: how it preserves what we speak of as "personality" from all associations of finiteness; how it guards us from the opposite errors which are generally summed up under the terms Pantheism and Deism, the last issues of Gentile and Jewish philosophy; how it indicates the sovereignty of the Creator and gives support to the trust of the creature. We linger reverently over the conception, and we feel that the whole world is indeed a manifestation of the Triune God, yet so that He is not included in that which reflects the active energy of His love. We feel that the Triune God is Lord over the works of His will, yet so that His Presence is not excluded from any part of His Universe. We ponder that which is made known to us, that when time began *the Word was with God* in the completeness of personal communion; that the life which *was* manifested to men was already *in the beginning with the Father* realised absolutely in the Divine Essence. We contemplate this archetypal life, self-contained and self-fulfilled in the Divine Being, and we are led to believe with deep thankfulness that the finite life which flows from it by a free act of grace corresponds with the source from which it flows.

In this way it will at once appear how the conception of the Triune God illuminates the central religious ideas of the Creation and the Incarnation. It illuminates the idea of Creation. It enables us to gain firm hold of the Truth that the "becoming" which we observe under the condition of time answers to "a being" beyond time; that history is the writing out at length of that which we may speak of as a divine thought. It enables us to take up on our part the words of the four-and-twenty elders, the representatives of the whole Church, when they cast their crowns before the throne and worshipped Him that sits thereon, saying, *Worthy art Thou, our Lord, and our God, to receive the glory and the honour and the power; for Thou didst create all things, and because of Thy will they were and were created; they were,* absolutely in the ineffable depths of the mind of God, they *were created* under the limitations of earthly existence.

The same conception illuminates also the idea of the Incarnation. It enables us to see that the Incarnation in its essence is the crown of the Creation, and that man being originally made capable of fellowship with God, has in his very constitution a promise of the fulfilment of his highest destiny. It enables us to feel that the childly relation in which we stand to God has its ground in the Divine Being; and to understand that not even sin has been able to destroy the sure hope of its consummation, however sadly it may have modified in time the course by which the end is to be reached.

Following, as we have the power, such lines of thought as these, we can, I think, acknowledge thankfully that the Christian conception of the Triune God is, as I said, an implicit Gospel; that it inspires us with the sustaining conviction of a vital unity in all created things; that it brings before us the noblest, the most comprehensive, view of nature and history, as essentially the working out of a Father's will in the Son through the Spirit; that it covers, if only we will dare to trust it, all the facts of existence most completely, and welcomes the interpretation of them most gladly; that it enters into the life of the individual, the life of the nation, the life of the Church, and by entering into each carries them all forward to the eternal; that it gains efficacy and fulness through every development of human power; that it contains the promise of moral progress which the material world cannot itself justify: that it rises ever before us with transcendent glory, guiding us to new effort; that it hallows the simplest and commonest duties, giving personal reality to prayer and transfiguring every relationship of life.

For, as I said before, the Truth is not speculative but practical. The Christian conception of God is the translation into the language of thought of the facts of Christmas, and Easter, and Whit Sunday. By our faith in these facts we confess that the Divine Life has been united with human life; we confess, even if we do not distinctly realise the force of the confession, that the Divine Life in its absolute, inherent, ineffable perfection, is the foundation and the end of the human life. And we live, so far as life deserves the name, by this faith through which, consciously or unconsciously, we are stirred to toil and sustained in sacrifice.

Take away the facts, take away the conception which the facts quicken and shape, and what remains? Nothing, if I may speak my own mind, but a blind necessity, a movement, which even in a measurable term of years issues in the universal stillness of death. The inexorable sequence, which we call law, remains; but it is no longer the voice of One in whom we move. The darkness remains, but it is no longer as the shadow of a passing cloud, behind which the sun shines in its splendour. Every difficulty, every riddle of being remains, without the promise of relief and without the knowledge in which patience can rest unshaken.

It is, I know, most difficult to gain any real notion of life; difficult to feel what the broad sheet which tells us every morning of the past day's intrigues and strifes, joys and sorrows, sins and heroisms, births and deaths, really means; difficult to trace back the present to the past; difficult to foresee the harvest of our sowing. It is most difficult, and not often well, even to seek seriously for this vision of awful solemnity. We are children, always children; yet children who look wistfully upon a world which is for those whose eyes are opened a manifestation of our Father; and a festival like this bids us, as we can, for a brief space take in the widest view of things, that we may with clearer sight and fuller hearts *discern Him that is true*, the Living God, in whom we live, who satisfies the last wants of the soul, and thus learn a little more plainly that the "mystery," the revelation, of faith, answers to the "mystery," the revelation, of life. The vision of God is always, as it was in old time, the inspiration of the prophet; and even when the vision fades away the power which it has quickened remains, a power able, alone able, to realise a new world amidst the chaos of ruins which seems to encompass us.

Yes; the Christian conception of the Triune God is, I repeat, a message of glad tidings. And do we not too often do dishonour to the truth by accepting the position of apologists? We dwell upon the difficulties which the conception involves, difficulties which belong to the imperfection of our own powers, and not upon the Majesty which belongs to God. We are in danger of making Him dependent on the world for the satisfaction of His love. When we read that He is love we have found the truth; and the Truth will justify itself to him who knows what man is and what life is. Meanwhile it is given to us that we may use it as a help in striving towards the Divine likeness. That it can do this is its verification within us and without us.

And surely I need not pause to shew that it has the power. Anyone who believes, however imperfectly, that the universe with all it offers in a slow succession to his gaze is in its very nature the expression of that love which is the Divine Being and the Divine Life; who believes that the whole sum of life defaced and disfigured on the surface to our sight 'means intensely and means 'good'; who believes that the laws which he patiently traces are the expressions of a Father's will, that the manhood which he shares has been taken into God by the Son, that at every moment, in every trial, a Spirit is with him waiting to sanctify thought, and word, and deed; must in his own character receive something from the Divine glory on which he looks.

What calm reserve he will keep in face of the perilous boldness with which controversialists deal in human reasonings with the things infinite and eternal. What tender reverence he will cherish towards those who have seen something of the King in His beauty. With what enthusiasm he will be kindled while he remembers that, in spite of every failure and every disappointment, his cause is won already. After what holiness he will strain while he sees the light fall about his path, that light which is fire, and knows the inexorable doom of everything which defiles.

So we are brought back to the beginning. The revelation of God is given to us that we may be fashioned after His likeness.

The Son of God is come and hath given us an understanding that we may know Him that is true. God first loved us that knowing His love we might love Him in our fellow men. Without spiritual sympathy there can be no knowledge. But where sympathy exists there is the transforming power of a divine affection. So far, therefore, as we are conscious of a deeper life when we behold the depths of the life—the love—of God we learn even here to raise the strain of heaven: *Holy, holy, holy, is the Lord God, the Almighty, which was, and which is, and which is to come. Holy, holy, holy, is the Lord of hosts.* Our eyes are dim and our faith is weak; we behold thick clouds of misery and sin hanging over nature and men. We find no escape from their blinding, chilling, numbing vapours. But yet hope pierces though them, and ever entering afresh within the veil gains, as on this day, a vision of great joy; and then, while we regard that Will which is love, that Wisdom which is sacrifice, that Power which is holiness, we dare to look through the seen to the unseen, through the temporal to the eternal, and to complete the prophet's confession with trembling lips, casting ourselves wholly upon the revelation which interprets the longings of our soul: *Holy, holy, holy, is the Lord of Hosts: the whole earth is full of His glory.*

The fulness of the earth is His glory. May He in His great mercy grant us to see it, and seeing it to make it known.

56

A Theological Pilgrimage

Augustus Hopkins Strong

Words fail me, Doctor Burton, to express my sense of the graciousness of your introduction, and of the kindness of the alumni whom you represent. Who am I, and what is my father's house, that I should receive such honor as this? The eight hundred pupils who have been under my instruction, and who are now scattered to the end of the earth, are doing great and blessed work for Christ and his truth, and I am profoundly thankful that I have been able to teach them. But they are full of their own cares and burdens; it is a wonder that they remember me, and that they contribute to this memorial. This is my reward here and now, though I had not expected any part of my reward on earth.

It is said of Crœsus, king of Lydia and reputed the richest man on earth in ancient times, that he showed his treasures to Solon, the lawgiver of Greece, and declared himself a happy man. But Solon replied, "Account no man happy before he dies." I am not yet dead; or, if I am, as the native of Erin said, "I am not conscious of it." But I cannot refrain from calling myself happy. In spite of many labors and some trials, I have had a happy life. I have had friends and daily bread and honest work to do. Above all, I have lived my regenerate life under the shadow of Christ's cross, and I have had Christ himself for my Counselor.

I hope to spend what remains of life under the shadow of that same cross, "until the day dawn and the shadows flee away." And if, when I have departed, the portrait in bronze which you have presented to the Seminary will incite any who knew me to greater faithfulness in proclaiming the unsearchable riches of Christ, it will be the best of all rewards for me. I beg you, Doctor Burton, to give my most humble and hearty thanks to the dear brethren who have subscribed for this memorial, and to assure them that I shall hold them in everlasting remembrance.

And yet, on this occasion that can never come again, I am expected to say something more. I ought, indeed, to say something significant, and to bring you some special message. I come with hesitation, because I have no message except the message of my personal religious experience. My subject therefore will be, "Theology and Experience." Example speaks louder than precept, and if I can show you how my views of evangelical doctrine have been necessarily determined by the circumstances of my individual history, I shall render you the best service of which I am capable. And yet there are difficulties attending such a narration. My religious history is so interwoven with my secular history, that it will be impossible to relate the one without also relating the other. I run the risk of both garrulity and egotism. If I inflict either one of these upon you, I beg you to remember that I do it for your good, and that I do it with the intent, at least, not to exploit myself, but to honor Christ, our Lord. Before we go further, let us ask his special blessing:

> O Lord Jesus, who art with us alway according to thy promise, who hast bidden all who labor and are heavy laden to come to thee with the assurance that thou wilt not cast them out, and who hast said that thou wilt give thy greatest and best gift, the Holy Spirit, to those who simply ask, we pray that thou wilt fulfil thy promise to us to-night, both to him who speaks and to those who hear, that the words of our lips and the meditations of our hearts may be acceptable in thy sight, O Lord, our Strength and our Redeemer, for thy name's sake. Amen.

I was born and bred in a Christian household. The very first religious impression that I received was on a certain Saturday afternoon, at the age of six years, when my dear mother, after her work was done, took me into a large and dimly lighted closet, where we knelt together by an old oaken chest, and where she taught me, or tried to teach me, to pray. When words failed me, she put the words into my mouth, and I never shall forget how her hot tears came down upon my upturned face when I succeeded in offering the first prayer of my own to God. I have always made it my illustration of the work of the Holy Spirit, who "when we know not what to pray for as we ought, helps our infirmities and makes intercession for us" and in us.

At the age of ten I waked on a Sabbath morning amid a howling snow-storm. I looked out of the window and saw that the drifts were like Alps in the street. I came down in great glee to my father, and I said, "Father, there will be no church to-day." He said, "My son, why not?" and I said, "Why, there'll be nobody there." "Well," said he, "if there is nobody else there, it will be very important that we should be there." So he trotted me all the way through the snow-drifts, and there were only seven persons present. We had a prayer meeting, . . . and never since that time have I been able to be quite comfortable away from church on a Sunday morning.

On the thirty-first of December, when I was twelve years of age, the panorama of my sins seemed to roll before me. I felt that the record of all my past, sealed up forever, to be brought against me in the Judgment, was more than I could bear; and I made resolutions to begin the very next morning a Christian life. But the festivities of New Year's Day banished the resolutions from my mind, and I had no conviction of sin for quite a number of years afterward.

My intellectual awakening occurred when I was fourteen years of age. I had begun the study of Latin. I had read through the exercises of the Latin Reader, and had mastered, as I supposed, the declensions and conjugations. Just then the spring vacation occurred, and an older student, who made his living by sweeping the floors and ringing the bell of the academy, proposed to me and to my cousin that we should spend the three weeks of the spring vacation in reading Latin by ourselves. My cousin declined the invitation. He proposed to spend his time in quite a different way and to make it a play-spell, but I concluded that I would yield; and during those three weeks I rose at five in the morning, and with some intervals I studied Latin until ten o'clock at night. At the end of those three weeks I and this older student had gone over the whole Latin Reader, fables and history and whatever else was there, and on presenting the record of what we had done to the principal of the school, he said at once: "Why, you can skip a year, and go into the Cicero class." That was the first time in my life when I came to the conclusion that, if I tried, I could do something in the world. The principal was a man who was guiltless of grammar—that is, comparatively speaking—but he was a great lover of the Latin and Greek classics, and he infected me with his own strong interest. Under his tutelage, or apart from him, before I was sixteen years of age, I had read the whole of Virgil's Æneid, together with the Georgics and Bucolics, and a very large portion of the Odes of Horace; three books of Herodotus, the Prometheus of Æschylus; and I had written out a translation, which I still possess, of the Clouds of Aristophanes.

My father thought that I was too young to go to college, and so he took me into his counting-room. He was the proprietor of the *Rochester Daily Democrat;* and in that counting-room, in a year and a half, I learned to keep all the books of the establishment by double entry; I learned to set type; I learned to read proof; I learned to take telegraph reports from the dictation of the telegraph operator. In the counting room, which was a place of exchange for all the news of Western New York, my father probably having the largest acquaintance with men of any single man in Rochester, there were all kinds of discussions, sometimes hot discussions, with regard to the candidacy of Henry Clay for the presidency, the laying of the Atlantic Cable, the prospects of the wheat crop in the Genesee Valley, and, strange to say, the differences between the Old School and the New School Presbyterians.

My father thought it very desirable that I should have a large amount of reading. The booksellers used to send in to us the books which they desired to have reviewed, and I had the privilege of taking home whichever of those books suited my fancy. The result was that I took home the complete works of Lord Bacon, the Essays of Macaulay and of De Quincey, Milton's "Paradise Lost," and the Poems of Henry Wadsworth Longfellow.

I might say that up to that time all my literary attainments had been built upon a foundation of dime novels. The "Phantom Ship," the "Pirate's Bride," and literature of that stamp had engaged my attention. Even in that there was an occasional quotation from a poet, or an allusion to history; and I have made up my mind, since that time, that it does not make so much difference what a man reads, so long as he has in him the love for reading. Before I went to college I had read through the six volumes of Gibbon's "Decline and Fall of the Roman Empire," and works of like character, such as Robertson's "History of Charles the Fifth." Then I joined a debating society, and whatever ability I have ever had of thinking and speaking on my feet is due, I think, to the practice that I gained in that society of older men.

My father thought it necessary that I should have a knowledge of the world. So he sent me to the Albany State Fair, and to Niagara Falls to take a journey across the river in the little car that was suspended between heaven and earth on a single cable in preparation for the building of the Suspension Bridge. He also sent me to the Courts. I heard a whole murder trial from beginning to end; heard the sentence passed upon the convicted criminal; and then, I regret to say, my father sent me to the jail to see the man hanged.

I mention all of these exploits, not for the purpose of showing to you how much I myself did, but because of what followed. I went to Yale convinced that I was going to stand first in every respect. I was full of pride and full of ambition, but my pride and my ambition collapsed like a bubble at the first recitation in Homer's Iliad. Prof. James Hadley, the father of President Hadley, gave out, as a lesson for the first recitation of the term, four lines of Homer's Iliad. I smiled; but I wept afterward, for Professor Hadley called up an Andover man to recite. I think he put fifty questions on those first four lines, and the very meaning of those questions I did not know. The "analysis of the verb"? I never knew there was any analysis of the verb. My instructor had never given me information with regard to such matters. All my expectations of scholarship were dashed in a moment, and I made up my mind that I must devote my college course to something else.

My dear friends, I have a Phi Beta Kappa key, and I got through the course fairly well as to scholarship. But I did not put upon the studies of the course the main strength of my mind and my heart. I devoted myself to reading, writing, and speaking. I took pretty much everything in the way of prizes that there were to take, from the prize compositions in the freshman year to the De Forest gold medal in the senior year; so that, after all, with the investigation that I gave to the subjects for prize debates, my time was by no means thrown away. Yet I now regret that I did not put my heart and mind more fully into the studies of the curriculum.

All that I have said with regard to these studies is only preliminary to my showing you what the effect was upon my religious life. Concluding that devotion to scholarship was not the thing for me, I fell into irregular habits and associations; and, if I had religious thoughts and ideas at all at the beginning of my college course, I lost them very speedily after that course began. In my ungodly and half-dissipated course I was a model of merely selfish and worldly ambition. I was never intoxicated in my life, but I was on the verge of evil; I knew that if I went very much farther I would be damned; and yet, until just before the spring vacation in my junior year, no single man in my class and no single man in college ever said one word to me about the subject of religion. But one afternoon I was standing, when the south wind was blowing in the month of March, in front of the college chapel, and the college bell was ringing for evening prayers. A hand was laid upon my shoulder. I looked around, and saw a man who for two years and a half had sat next to me in the recitation-room. It was Wilder Smith. Evidently something was agitating him, for the muscles of his face were twitching, and as I looked into his face, he said, "O Strong, I wish you were a Christian!" And then the bell stopped ringing, and we both had to rush in to evening prayers. But that one word never left me until I gave my heart to God. I have often thought how little a thing will sometimes turn the whole current of a man's life. For me that was the parting of the ways; that one word was my salvation.

I must anticipate in my story, and tell you the result. Both Wilder Smith and I studied for the ministry, and we both became pastors of churches. After I had settled in the eastern part of Massachusetts, I heard that he was to make a visit within a short distance of my home, and I invited him to come and spend Sunday with me. I told him that he could preach in the morning and I in the afternoon. All the while I had it in my mind to tell Wilder Smith what he had done for me, for I had never mentioned the matter to him, and we had never had any conversation on the subject.

So, after the afternoon service, I took Wilder Smith home with me. We sat down in the parlor, and I said: "Wilder, do you know that you did me the greatest service that ever was done for me by any mortal man?" "Why, no," said he; "what do you mean?" I said: "Don't you remember how, one afternoon in March, in front of the college chapel, you put your hand on my shoulder and said, 'Strong, I wish that you were a Christian'?" "Why, no," said he; "did I?" He had forgotten all about it. I suppose he had said the same thing to others, and that this was only one of a great many good words that he had spoken during his college course. It had utterly gone from him. He will be like the righteous going up before the judgment-seat of Christ and saying: "Lord, when saw we thee an hungered? when did we do anything that was worthy of this great reward?" He had forgotten; but God had not forgotten; nor had I.

When the spring vacation began I went home. I reached my father's house late in the afternoon. I had just time to sit down to the supper-table with my parents and with a young lady cousin who was visiting with us at the time. Curiously enough, this cousin said: "Won't you go with us to the meeting to-night to hear Charles G. Finney, the great evangelist? He is going to preach." Well, I knew that Charles G. Finney had come to Rochester twenty-six years before, and that my father had been converted under his preaching, and I had myself heard him preach in Oberlin, Ohio. I had no particular thought with regard to my own duty, but I went to that Presbyterian church, and I sat in the middle of the great congregation, the aisles being packed with seats. I do not remember what the sermon was, but I do remember that great, stalwart man standing up at the close of the service, with his eyes fixed apparently upon me, and saying: "If there is any one in this congregation who thinks he ought to begin to serve God, let him rise out of his place and go down the aisle into the basement. There will be some ministers there who will talk with him on the subject of religion." It was like a thunderbolt to me. I did not expect anything like that. But I somehow felt that my hour had come. I turned to my cousin and said, "Can you get home alone?" She was glad enough to say, "Yes." I got up from my place and started down the aisle. There were about fifty others that had come in, and the pastor of that Presbyterian church, Doctor Ellinwood, to whom I shall always be grateful, came and sat down by my side. He said: "I see you have some feeling on the subject of religion." "No," said I, "I have none at all." "What?" said he, "how does it happen that you are here?" I said: "I have no feeling at all; I simply know that I ought to begin a Christian life; but I do not know how to begin." "Well," he said, "will you begin a Christian life now; will you begin to serve God now?" "Oh!" said I, "that is a very large contract to take; I don't know what it means to be a Christian; and I don't know how to begin."

"Well," said he, "you will never have a better opportunity to make a decision than now; sometime you will have to decide the great question whether you will, or will not, serve God. Now," he said, "I will leave you for five or ten minutes, and you can settle that in your mind. I will go and talk to some one else, and I will come back and learn your decision." He went away, and I think I had the most uncomfortable ten minutes I ever had in my life. But the more I thought, the more I knew that I could not safely let that occasion pass. So, when Doctor Ellinwood returned, he said: "Will you now begin to serve God, just as well as you know how, looking to God for light, and looking to him to show you what to do?" I said, "Yes, I will." He shook hands with me; he did not pray with me. I went out into the dark; and all the way home I said to myself: "What a confounded fool you have made of yourself to-night! You have made a promise that you do not know the meaning of; you do not know how you are ever going to keep it." I went to my room; my parents had retired to rest; but, strangely enough, my mother had put a little Bible upon the table. I said to myself: "Well, there is one thing that I ought to do; I haven't read my Bible of late; I ought to begin reading it." So I read a chapter in the Bible; it did not mean anything to me at all. Then it occurred to me that I had not prayed for a long time. "Now, you ought to form the habit of prayer." So I knelt down to pray, and tried to pray. But all was words uttered into the air, without sense or meaning. I could not think of any other duty that I had to perform except to go to bed, and I went to bed.

The next morning, as soon as I awoke, it occurred to me, "Well, you should tell your parents"; so I told them. Then it occurred to me, "You ought to tell your cousin"; so I told her. Then it occurred to me that I ought to go to the morning prayer meeting; so I went to the morning prayer meeting; there those who wanted to serve God were asked to rise, and I rose. My dear friends, I suppose I rose for prayer twenty times in those meetings before I went back to college, and every time I rose I had the same old feeling that "this is a perfectly vain struggle; I am not making anything by it; I am not getting ahead at all; there is no peace for my soul. What shall I do?" and I learned during those three weeks my first lesson in theology—the depth and enormity of sin. I learned that my sinful nature was like an iceberg, seven-eighths beneath the surface of the water; seven-eighths of my being was below consciousness. It was my first lesson in theology, and it prepared me to accept from my own experience, as I afterward did, Doctor Shedd's statement that "sin is a nature and that nature is guilt." I discovered within me a coldness of heart, a lack of love, an inability to believe, that I had never suspected before. Why, I had thought I could be a Christian any time I chose. I found out that I was in the hands of God, that unless he had mercy upon me I was lost. I tried to do every duty that appeared, but the end of those three weeks came; my father and my mother went down to the train with me to see me off. When the conductor said, "All aboard," and I got up into the car, I said to myself: "The harvest is past, the summer is ended, and my soul is not saved. This train is taking me to hell." Then, as I sat alone in the seat, I began to ask myself: "What is the matter? Why is it that I have no rest or peace for my soul?" It occurred to me that the trouble possibly was that I had been making an experiment of this thing; I had been saying secretly to myself that, if my effort did not succeed, I could go back again where I was before; that was not what God wanted of me. What God wanted of me was an entire and absolute consecration of my heart and life for time and eternity. Then I put my head forward on the seat before me, and I said to God: "Lord, from this time I am thine; I will live for thee, if I never have a moment of peace in my life; I will serve thee, whatever may come; I leave all the results in thy hands." I sat up again in my seat, but I was no better off than I was before.

I went down to college; I took the key out of my pocket, opened the door of my room, and when I opened that door the first thing I saw on the mantel was a box of cigars. I stood there for a few moments riveted to the floor. Said I: "What about that? What about smoking? What about drinking?" I knew all those things; knew the associations that I had been engaged in, and I said to myself: "There is just one thing for me to do—I will cut that dog's tail off right behind the ears;" and I never smoked after that for forty years. I gave that box of cigars to my chum. That reminds me of the young woman who had a necklace that was dragging her down to hell; so she gave it to her sister. But the humor of it did not occur to me then. It was solemn business to me. But I gave up my wrong associations and wrong habits; still I was no better off than before. It occurred to me that it was my business to give my witness for God before the college and before my class. I had never been to a class prayer meeting. On a Sunday morning I appeared there. Those fellows looked askance at me, but in the middle of the meeting I arose and said: "My friends, I am not a Christian; I do not pretend anything of the sort, but I want to be; can you do anything to help me?" And they came around me and did help me from that time, and I made some of the best friends that I have had in all my life.

I declined various positions that were open to me because I thought they would interfere with my walk with God. I tried to do my duty to my classmates, though often it was a grievous thing to do. I remember one man whom I tried to influence. I walked all the way down to the post-office with him and all the way back, thinking I would say a word to him about his soul. But I couldn't muster up courage to do it until we got back again in the shadow of the college walls, and then I said, "O Buckland, come with me, and be a Christian." Buckland broke down. All the while he had been waiting for that word. I went to Sandys' room after the Fast-day services were over and I said: "Sandys, I have come to you to talk to you about religion." Sandys said, "Do you think that I can be a Christian?" I said: "Why, yes, you can. Let us kneel down here," and within three minutes he had given his heart to God.

I went to the room right above, and the same thing was repeated with another man. And yet I was not conscious that I was myself a Christian. I had begun to read my Bible, and one afternoon, several weeks after I went back to college, I was reading by lamplight a chapter in Corinthians, where were these words: "Wherefore come ye out from among them, and be ye separate, and touch not the unclean thing, and I will be a Father unto you, and ye shall be my sons and daughters, saith the Lord Almighty." "Oh," said I, "I never read that before; I have tried to be separate; I will not touch the unclean thing. Now, I have the word and promise of God that he will be a Father to me." Then for the first time in all my life I felt there was a tie between me and God. I looked out through the branches of the elm trees and saw the stars shining in the sky, and I said to myself: "When those stars grow old and die, God will be my Father and my Friend."

O dear friends, do you wonder that every time I go back to Yale I go up to the north entry of old South Middle, and, knocking gently at the door of some freshman there, I say: "Let me come in; let me see the place where I first saw the light and the burden of my heart rolled away?" The only sacred places in this world are those places where God has revealed himself to our souls, and that place will be forever sacred to me.

I had a lovely time that summer.

> The earth and every common sight
> To me did seem
> Appareled in celestial light.

I walked out and saw the apple trees in blossom; and curiously enough, an old Scotch Presbyterian appeared upon the scene, and said to me, without knowing who I was, nor what my condition was: "Oh, see the beauty of those blossoms! how like a Christian, adorned with the Christian graces!"

Please notice that my experience was thus far a purely Arminian experience. I had yet to learn the truth in Calvinism. In my conversion, so far as I can remember, I had no thought of the Holy Spirit or of Christ. I had no idea that God was working in me to will and to do; I was only bent on working out my own salvation. There was no reliance on Christ's atonement; I was trusting in my own power to begin and to continue the service of God. When I think how infantile was my early faith and how far I was from understanding the workings of my own mind, I wonder at the mercy of God in accepting the offering that I made. He leads the blind by a way that they know not, and so he led me. As he had taught me the greatness of my sin, so he next taught me that salvation is of the Lord.

In the midst of the joy and peace of my new religious life, I found that I could not keep myself in the Christian way. Old habits and inclinations sprang up little by little, and I could not repress them or keep them out of my soul by any power or wisdom of my own. Then I learned my second great lesson in doctrine, namely, Man's need of God's regenerating grace. If I could not keep myself from falling, after I had gotten into the Christian way, how could I ever have entered that way without God's help at the beginning? Man must be born again, as well as kept by God's mighty power. Without God's regenerating and sanctifying grace, we should be forever lost.

So far I had gotten, when I began the study of theology—I had to be a preacher. I knew, from the very moment of my conversion, that I must serve God in the ministry. So I went to Rochester, and in the Theological Seminary there I gained whatever scholastic preparation I had for the work before me. But I had another source of instruction in the work I began to do as preacher in a little mission congregation in the neighborhood of Rochester. We had a canal there, and the canal-boats were laid up in winter. The men who operated them spent their time mainly in card-playing, drinking, and fighting, so that the police of Rochester had more to keep their attention in that little quarter of the city than in all the rest of the town together. There was no church at all, and only a little broken-down schoolhouse. But there was one good woman, a woman who had the love of Christ in her heart; and who went around, like an angel of mercy, visiting the sick and making clothes for the children. She had begun a little Sunday-school on Sunday afternoon, and had instituted a preaching service on Sunday evening. She did me the honor of inviting me to help her. After teaching a Bible class in our home school on Sunday morning, I went out and superintended this little Sunday-school in the afternoon. Then in the evening I preached a sermon. I have always thanked God that I preached to so small a congregation. There were only seventy-five people, men and women on whom rhetoric would have been thrown away, and I was compelled to use the simplest language, to preach about sin, about Christ and salvation, about heaven and hell; and, if I have ever succeeded in my after ministry, it is because I have, from the very beginning, said: "I will not preach about the odds and ends of religion; I will preach about sin and about Christ," and around those two all my preaching has revolved.

We had a little evening meeting, at which I read the fifty-third chapter of Isaiah to a dozen young women, and then proposed that they should all kneel down and give themselves to the service of the Lord. Almost all of them made that decision, and that was the first instance I had of real effect following any preaching of mine. But there was one young woman, of considerable mind, who could not see her way clear to accept the promise of God, and after making all manner of effort, as I had made in my own experience, she remained just where she was. It occurred to me to speak to her of Candlish's idea of a deferred atonement. Candlish, you know, says: "Suppose Christ should come now for the first time into the world, and he came to you, a sinner, and said: 'I am going to suffer for all who will put their case into my hands. I will take all your sins and responsibilities upon my own shoulders. Are you willing that I should do this? If you are willing to take me for your substitute, I will pay your debts and I will save you.' " I asked this young woman if she would take Christ for her Saviour. I saw the light of heaven shine suddenly upon her face. She looked up to me and said, "Oh! I see it; yes, I will." And from that moment she was an earnest Christian woman. From that experience I learned a third lesson in Christian doctrine, viz., that only the objective atonement of Jesus Christ, only Christ's sufferings upon the cross, can furnish the ground of our acceptance with God.

But, curiously enough, at the end of my senior year in the theological seminary, I had what seemed to be a hemorrhage of the lungs, and the doctors told me I must spend a whole year in the open air. So I went to Europe, and pedestrianized, and studied German. I went to Switzerland, and to the East; I saw the Holy Land, and I learned many things of value. But I found that falling in with the current of pleasure-lovers weakened my Christian resolutions. I had ended my seminary course with the desire of going to the heathen as a missionary, if God would permit me. My health was such that I could not go, and that plan had to be given up. In my European experience the edge of my Christian feeling became dull. I lost the desire and the love for Christian service, although I learned a great deal of German, and got together a library of German books, which was very useful to me afterward. I have always felt that the loss to a man, by a residence in Europe before he has actually begun the work of his ministry, is too great a loss to make up for any mere gain in his knowledge. I would rather have a son of mine go to Europe after he has had some experience in the ministry.

After returning to this country, I became pastor of a church, and working as I did, with much weakness of body, and not only that but also with weakness of Christian feeling, I found that the chariot wheels dragged heavily; that work was hard; and that, although I spent all my afternoons in pastoral calling and working, up to the very limit of my ability, yet, at the same time, I had no joy in my work. In spite of the fact that revival services were held and there were quite a number of conversions, I felt deserted by God. I was set there to stand for him, and stand for him I would, till I died; but I felt that I was standing alone, with a whole universe of evil influences fighting against me: What was I, that I should be able to overcome the world, the flesh, and the devil, all combined?

I had learned about Christ for us, on the cross, as an external Saviour; I had yet to learn about Christ in us, by his Spirit, as a Saviour within. Fortunately my summer vacation came, and I went home for rest. I went determined that I would read nothing but the Bible, until I found out where I stood before God. I read the Acts of the Apostles, and learned that they served God with gladness and singleness of heart. I looked back to the Gospel according to John, to find the cause of that joy. It was their faith that Christ was still alive, and was in them as the power of an endless life. I read about the Vine and the Branches. I had thought of union with Christ as a union of sympathy and moral likeness; now I saw that it was a union of life; a union in which the Spirit of Christ interpenetrates and energizes ours; a union in which he joins himself so indissolubly to us that neither life nor death, nor height nor depth, nor any other creature shall be able to separate us from himself.

So I learned my fourth great lesson in doctrine: the union of the believer with Christ. It is the inmost mystery of the gospel— "Christ in you, the hope of glory." The Christian is not simply in touch with Christ, but he has Christ in his heart; and he can say with Paul, "Not I live, but Christ liveth in me." At the very beginning of my Christian experience Christ had taken up his abode within me. I had in ignorance and unbelief banished him to some remote corner of my soul. Now that I opened all the doors, he filled the whole house with his light and love.

I went back to my church with an entirely new spirit. I do not like the phrase "a new conversion," but the change in me, two years after my ministry began, was more wonderful than the change that took place when I was first converted. Instead of feeling that I was fighting single-handed against a whole universe of evil influences, I felt that, with Christ in my heart, all the wheels of the universe were made to revolve to help me in every effort to improve my own spiritual life or to bring others to the feet of Christ. It was like life from the dead. I have never lost from that time that essential experience, and I believe, with Doctor Alexander—the older Alexander—that the doctrine of union with Christ is the central truth of all theology and of all religion. That doctrine of union with Christ had a reflex influence upon my doctrine of sin. I saw that not only was sin a nature and that nature guilt, but that my connection with the first father of the race was analogous to my connection with Christ. By union with Christ I derived the benefit of his work, and by my union with the first father of the race I was involved in his loss and condemnation. The vital union comes first; the forensic and legal union comes second, as a natural and necessary consequence.

I wish I could tell you some of the experiences that followed my discovery of this great truth of union with Christ. I preached in an entirely new way; the sermons that had taken me a whole week to prepare, I could prepare in an hour. People came to me with tears in their eyes, and said, "O Brother Strong, we never heard this before!" The truth is, my predecessor had never told them about this vital, spiritual union with Jesus Christ.

I would go out from my study in the afternoon with the desire to be led by the Spirit of the Lord in my ministry, and I would find that many doors were open to me, and that my words had wonderful effect. There was one man in my congregation, one of the most prominent men in the community, a large-hearted and large-minded man, philanthropic and wealthy, one of the largest manufacturers in the place. His wife was a Christian, but he himself was far from it. I met him on the corner of the street, and I said: "Mr. Swett, I have wanted to speak to you for a long time; I want you to be a Christian." He said: "I think I am pretty well off; I think I am as well off as most of the members of your church are." I said, "You have never done your duty to Jesus, your Saviour." That was the end of the conversation. He excused himself, and I went away. Next morning I went down to my church, and the first deacon of the church came to me and said: "A great thing has happened. Mr. Jackson Swett is converted, and he wants to come before the whole congregation and tell the story of it." I could only reply, "We will let him." That great man came forward at the close of the service, and said with trembling voice: "My friends, I thought I was a good man, but I have found that I am one of the wickedest of all God's creatures. How I have treated my Saviour!" It appeared that, on the preceding Saturday evening, he had left his wife in the entry of his house and gone down to his office to post his books. He went up the stairs to his office; went to his safe; took his ledger out; and right then and there it occurred to him that there was an account with God which he needed to settle first; he was so overwhelmed by his conviction of sin that he let the ledger fall, and he absolutely groveled on the floor. But right then and there the Saviour manifested himself to him in his grace and love, and he rose a Christian and went home. When his wife heard the door open, she said, "Jackson, I thought you had gone to your office." He had been gone so short a time that it almost seemed to her that he could not have left the house. That man became a faithful Christian and a deacon in the church, and he died in the Christian faith.

I used to feel it my duty to go to all the workmen in that large manufacturing town and at least give them the opportunity of recognizing their duty to Christ. So I went around among these gangs of men and invited them to come to the meetings of the church. I am not sure that I should do so again. There was one man whose wife was a member of the church, but he was not only irreligious, but bitterly hostile to religion. I talked with him, but he would not listen to anything I said. He went on hammering, to drown my voice. At last I said: "Mr. Long, I will have to let you go, but I have wanted you to come to Christ."

The next morning I was going down from my house to the church, and I met his wife. She said: "O Mr. Strong, come and see my husband. He came home yesterday in the afternoon, and he hasn't been able to rest since then. He has not eaten, and he has not slept, and he has been walking the streets all night long in distress. He wants to see you at the church." I went and found him there. I asked him to kneel down and give his heart to the Lord, and he rose from his knees with the consciousness that his sins were forgiven. My friends, I believe that we can have just as marvelous conversions in our day as the conversion of the apostle Paul. What we want is faith in a living Christ; with Christ in our hearts we can speak the things that will save men's souls.

What have I said thus far? I have said that my first lesson in theology was the depth and enormity of sin; the second, absolute dependence on God's regenerating power; the third, the objective work of Christ upon his cross, the only ground of peace and reconciliation with God; the fourth, the union of the believer with Christ. A Christ within is just as important as a Christ without. The gospel presents to us Christ in us, as well as Christ for us. We may preach the external atonement of Christ without preaching Christ in the heart. But this last truth is the secret of pardon, peace, purity, and power.

After four years of service in an eastern pastorate I went west, to a larger parish. There I began to study science. I took up in succession mineralogy, geology, botany, microscopy, chemistry, biology, astronomy, meteorology, economics, and finally, psychology and metaphysics. To each of these I devoted the spare time of six months, beginning with some elementary treatise and following it with some more thorough text-book. At the same time I preached a series of doctrinal sermons, taking up on the second Sunday morning of each month some one of the articles of faith. This combination of scientific study and doctrinal preaching had great influence upon my theological development. My life had been largely subjective; now it became more objective. I had been introspective; now I began to look out upon the world. I had learned my entire dependence upon Christ as an atoning and also as an indwelling Saviour. I now learned that Christ is the life of the universe, as well as the life of the believer; that in him all things consist, or hold together; that he is the one and only medium through whom God creates, upholds, and governs the world. This discovery of Christ's creatorship was my fifth great lesson in doctrine. My studies in science gave me inspiring views of the wisdom and power of God, and I drew from science a multitude of illustrations for my preaching. My preaching took a wider range than before. It dealt more with universal interests. I began to apply Christianity to all the relations of life. History, art, literature, society, as well as science and philosophy, might have place in my teaching. But the center must be Christ; all treasures must be laid at his feet; he must be Lord of all.

My course of doctrinal sermons, made interesting and broadened by the study of science, prepared me for the teaching of theology, and when an invitation came to exchange the pastorate for a professorship in the theological seminary, I felt it to be the call of God. For forty years I have tried to be a teacher of the teachers, and to help those who are to be leaders of the churches. But the making plain of Christian doctrine to successive classes of students for the ministry has not been without its effect upon my own theological development. There was still a step forward which I was compelled to take. I had learned that the same Christ who recreated and dwelt in believers was also the Creator and Life of nature, and that all science was only the shining of his light. The person of Christ was the clue I had followed; his deity and atonement were the two foci of the great ellipse. How to reconcile these two, how to make deity and atonement comprehensible, *hoc opus, hic labor est.*

I had adopted the realistic explanation of justification by virtue of the believer's vital union with Christ. I had adopted the realistic explanation of the race's condemnation by virtue of its vital union with Adam and the derivation of its life from him. How now was to be explained the imputation of the sin of the race to Christ? The only possible answer seemed to be that our sin was laid upon him because of his vital union with humanity. Christ's creatorship was now invested with new meaning. His union with the race in his incarnation is only the outward and visible expression of a prior union with the race which began when he created the race. It follows that he who is the life of humanity must, though personally pure, be involved in responsibility for all human sin, and it must needs be that Christ should suffer. And so I learned my sixth great lesson in theology; namely, that Christ, who is the life of the universe, must also bear the sins of the world. Thus suffering was a reaction of the divine holiness against sin, and so was a bearing of penalty, but it was also the voluntary execution of a plan that antedated creation. Christ's sacrifice in time showed what had been in the heart of God from eternity. The atonement then is not only possible but necessary, because Christ is from the beginning the life of humanity.

I regard this explanation of the method of the atonement as my specific contribution to theological science. Imputation of Christ's righteousness to us, because of our vital union with Christ, had been explained before. Imputation of Adam's sin to us, because of our vital union with Adam, had been explained before. But, so far as I know, imputation of the sins of the race to Christ, because of the vital union of the race with Christ, had not been explained before. I have tried to show how this truth is an outgrowth of my personal religious experience. I trust it may lead others to see the rational foundation of the atonement. If nature is the continual manifestation of Christ, then he is the omnipresent and immanent God. The hand that was nailed to the cross sustains the fabric of the worlds and guides the stars in their courses. His historical atonement is but a manifestation to sense of what, as preincarnate Logos, he has been doing and suffering ever since man's first sin. Christ must suffer because, as the Creator, Upholder, and Life of the universe, he is identified with humanity, and cannot escape its liabilities and penalties. But he bears them in love, and he has redeemed us from the curse of the law by being made a curse for us. To the elucidation and defense of this doctrine I have devoted a large part of my time and strength for the past forty years. A full statement of my views can be found in my book entitled "Christ in Creation," and in my "Systematic Theology."

Time fails me to tell of my still later progress. I can only mention two recent developments. I have come to a seventh stage of theological knowledge by applying the principle of

Christ's immanence to the Scriptures. Inspiration is Christ's gradual enlightenment from within. It can make use of all the ordinary methods of literary composition. Truth can be communicated in germ at first, and by means of parable, apologue, and even drama. The Christ who is behind and in the process guarantees the unity, the sufficiency, and the authority of Scripture. The truth dwells, not in the outward form, but in the inspiring Spirit; for Christ is himself the Truth. So the ever-living Christ makes rational our faith in the Bible, while he encourages the most rigorous inquiry into the methods of its growth. Taken together, the written word commends itself as a revelation of the eternal Word, and as able to make us wise unto salvation.

The eighth and last of my doctrinal discoveries has been an ethical one, this namely, that, while regeneration is the indispensable inward beginning, Christ's Spirit works outwardly, to the reform of human society. The Christian cannot fold his hands and content himself with his individual salvation. Christ is "the Saviour of all men," and his religion requires the proclamation of his gospel to every human creature. As the Creator and Upholder of the universe, Christ has a natural connection with every human heart, and service done to any human being is service done to him. But he is also the Creator of a new society; and to follow him is to enlist in all manner of effort for the reform of industrial and business and governmental relations, until these are pervaded by his Spirit. Not the church as an organization, however, but rather the individual members of the church, are to engage in trade and politics, with a view to the bringing of society under dominion of Christ. The church is Christ's organ for individual regeneration, and Christians are Christ's organs for the regeneration of the social order. My personal experience teaches me that both politics and business can be Christianized only by individual Christians, who carry into them the Spirit of Christ.

You have perceived, I trust, that this experience of mine is centered in Christ; and that it is simply a growing manifestation of Christ to my mind and heart. I believe in Christ; I believe in his veritable deity; I believe in prayer to Christ. If Christ is really divine, then he is the object of prayer. Let us recognize Christ in his omniscience, omnipotence, omnipresence; for he is with us alway, even unto the end of the world; able to save to the uttermost; the same yesterday and to-day and forever. He is himself the greatest gift which he can bestow upon his ministers; and the one gift above all others that I desire for the alumni and students of this seminary is, that for you to live may be Christ, that you may know Christ for you and Christ in you, the power of God unto salvation. If I have even slightly contributed to such a result as this, I will appropriate to myself the words of the Latin poet, and say:

> I have erected a monument more lasting than bronze,
> More lofty than the regal structure of the pyramids;
> Which gnawing storm and impotent north-wind cannot destroy,
> Neither the innumerable succession of the years,
> Nor the flight of time, I shall not wholly die;
> The larger part of me will escape the tomb.

Better words than these of Horace are the words of Paul: "Be ye stedfast, unmoveable, always abounding in the work of the Lord, forasmuch as ye know that your labor is not in vain in the Lord"; and better still are the words of Christ, "Because I live, ye shall live also."

About the Editor

Fisher Humphreys is professor of theology at New Orleans Baptist Theological Seminary, a position he has held since 1970. Since 1975 he has been editor of *The Theological Educator*, a journal published by the faculty of the seminary. Dr. Humphreys is an honors graduate of Mississippi College (B.A.). He continued his formal education at New Orleans Baptist Theological Seminary (B.D.; Th.D.) and studied theology at Oxford University (B.L.). Dr. Humphreys has pastored churches in Alabama, Illinois, and Mississippi. He is the author of six books, including *The Death of Christ* and *The Heart of Prayer*.